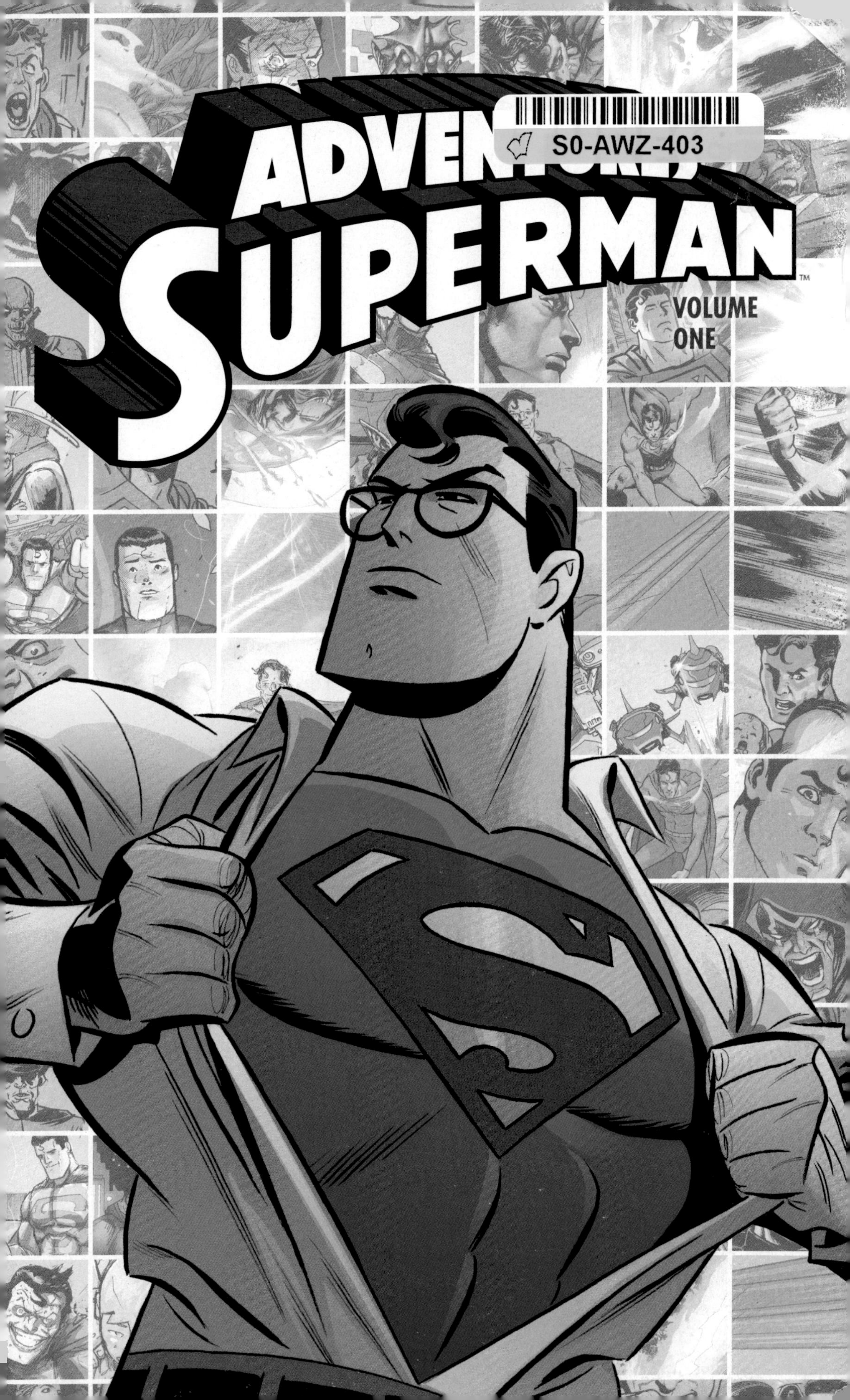
ADVEN
SUPERMAN
VOLUME
ONE

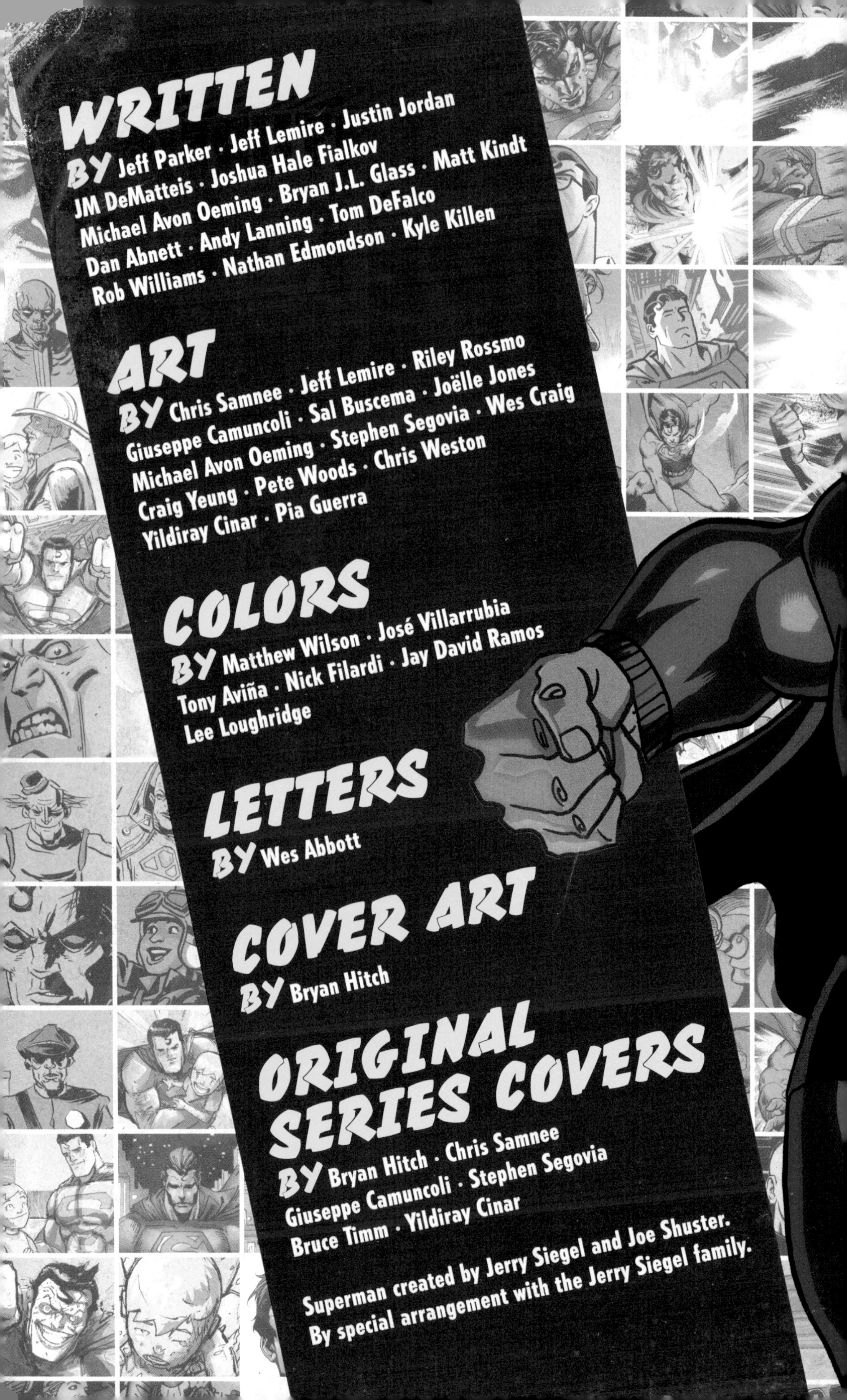

WRITTEN

BY Jeff Parker · Jeff Lemire · Justin Jordan
JM DeMatteis · Joshua Hale Fialkov
Michael Avon Oeming · Bryan J.L. Glass · Matt Kindt
Dan Abnett · Andy Lanning · Tom DeFalco
Rob Williams · Nathan Edmondson · Kyle Killen

ART

BY Chris Samnee · Jeff Lemire · Riley Rossmo
Giuseppe Camuncoli · Sal Buscema · Joëlle Jones
Michael Avon Oeming · Stephen Segovia · Wes Craig
Craig Yeung · Pete Woods · Chris Weston
Yildiray Cinar · Pia Guerra

COLORS

BY Matthew Wilson · José Villarrubia
Tony Aviña · Nick Filardi · Jay David Ramos
Lee Loughridge

LETTERS

BY Wes Abbott

COVER ART

BY Bryan Hitch

ORIGINAL SERIES COVERS

BY Bryan Hitch · Chris Samnee
Giuseppe Camuncoli · Stephen Segovia
Bruce Timm · Yildiray Cinar

Superman created by Jerry Siegel and Joe Shuster.
By special arrangement with the Jerry Siegel family.

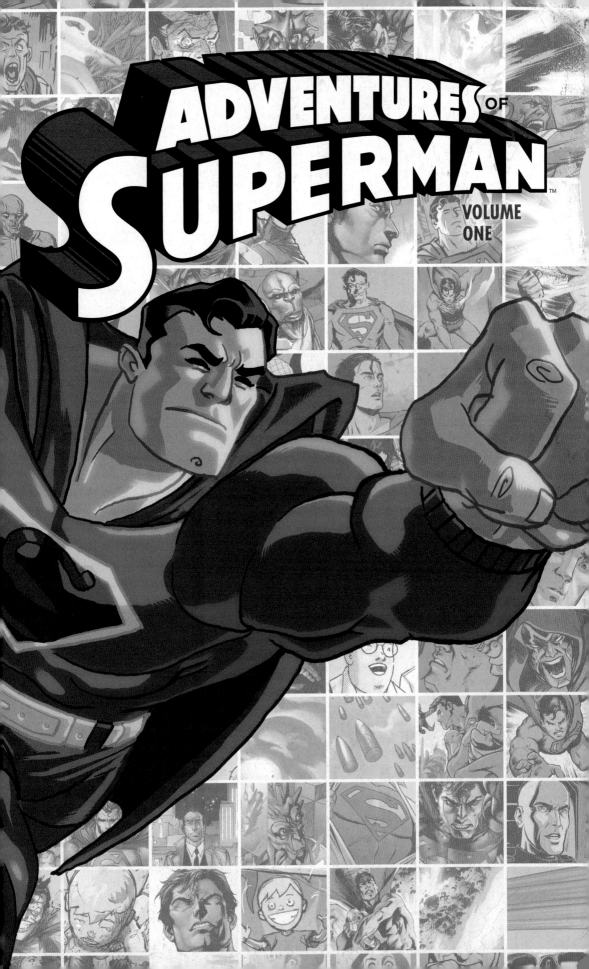

ADVENTURES OF SUPERMAN

VOLUME ONE

ALEX ANTONE EDITOR - ORIGINAL SERIES SCOTT NYBAKKEN EDITOR
ROBBIN BROSTERMAN DESIGN DIRECTOR - BOOKS DAMIAN RYLAND PUBLICATION DESIGN

HANK KANALZ SENIOR VP - VERTIGO & INTEGRATED PUBLISHING

DIANE NELSON PRESIDENT DAN DIDIO AND JIM LEE CO-PUBLISHERS GEOFF JOHNS CHIEF CREATIVE OFFICER
JOHN ROOD EXECUTIVE VP - SALES, MARKETING & BUSINESS DEVELOPMENT
AMY GENKINS SENIOR VP - BUSINESS & LEGAL AFFAIRS NAIRI GARDINER SENIOR VP - FINANCE
JEFF BOISON VP - PUBLISHING PLANNING MARK CHIARELLO VP - ART DIRECTION & DESIGN
JOHN CUNNINGHAM VP - MARKETING TERRI CUNNINGHAM VP - EDITORIAL ADMINISTRATION
ALISON GILL SENIOR VP - MANUFACTURING & OPERATIONS JAY KOGAN VP - BUSINESS & LEGAL AFFAIRS, PUBLISHING
JACK MAHAN VP - BUSINESS AFFAIRS, TALENT NICK NAPOLITANO VP - MANUFACTURING ADMINISTRATION
SUE POHJA VP - BOOK SALES COURTNEY SIMMONS SENIOR VP - PUBLICITY BOB WAYNE SENIOR VP - SALES

ADVENTURES OF SUPERMAN VOL. 1

DC COMICS
1700 BROADWAY, NEW YORK, NY 10019
A WARNER BROS. ENTERTAINMENT COMPANY.
PRINTED BY RR DONNELLEY, SALEM, VA, USA. 3/14/14. FIRST PRINTING.
ISBN: 978-1-4012-4688-4

LIBRARY OF CONGRESS CATALOGING-IN-PUBLICATION DATA

ADVENTURES OF SUPERMAN VOL. 1 / JEFF LEMIRE, PIA GUERRA, JEFF PARKER.
    PAGES CM
ISBN 978-1-4012-4688-4 (PAPERBACK)
1. GRAPHIC NOVELS. I. LEMIRE, JEFF. II. GUERRA, PIA. III. PARKER, JEFF, 1966-
PN6728.S9A34 2014
741.5'973—DC23
                    2013049637

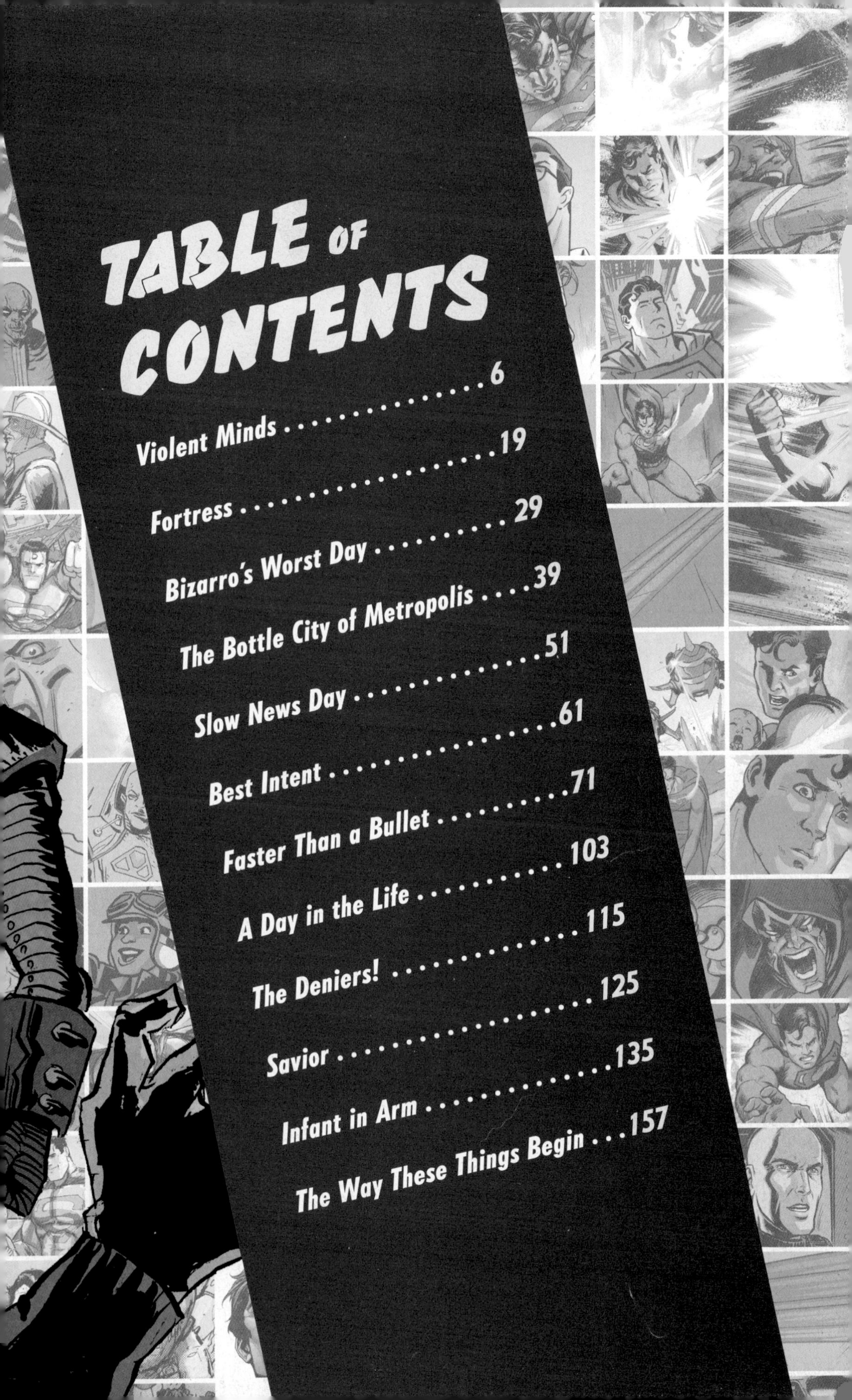

TABLE OF CONTENTS

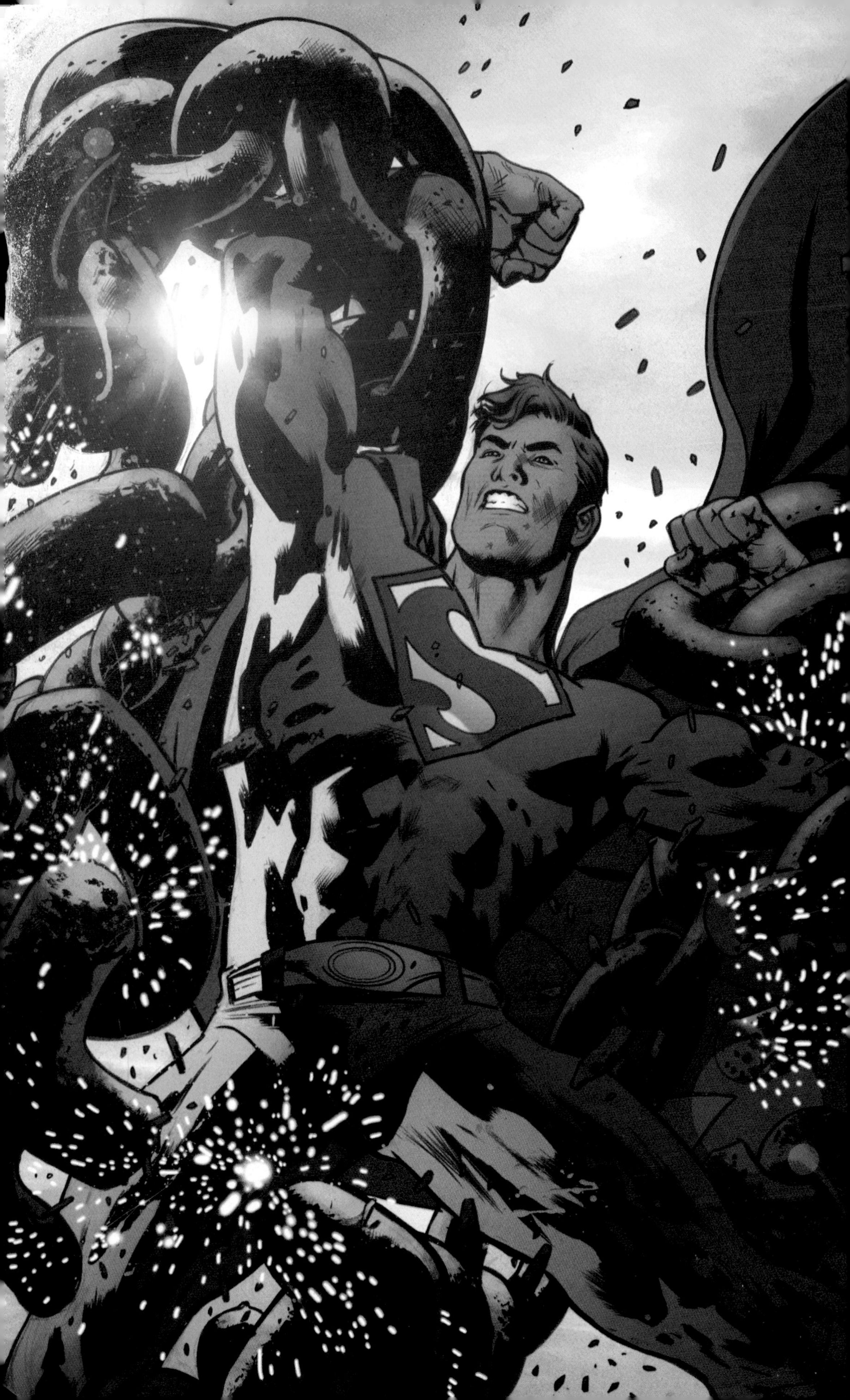

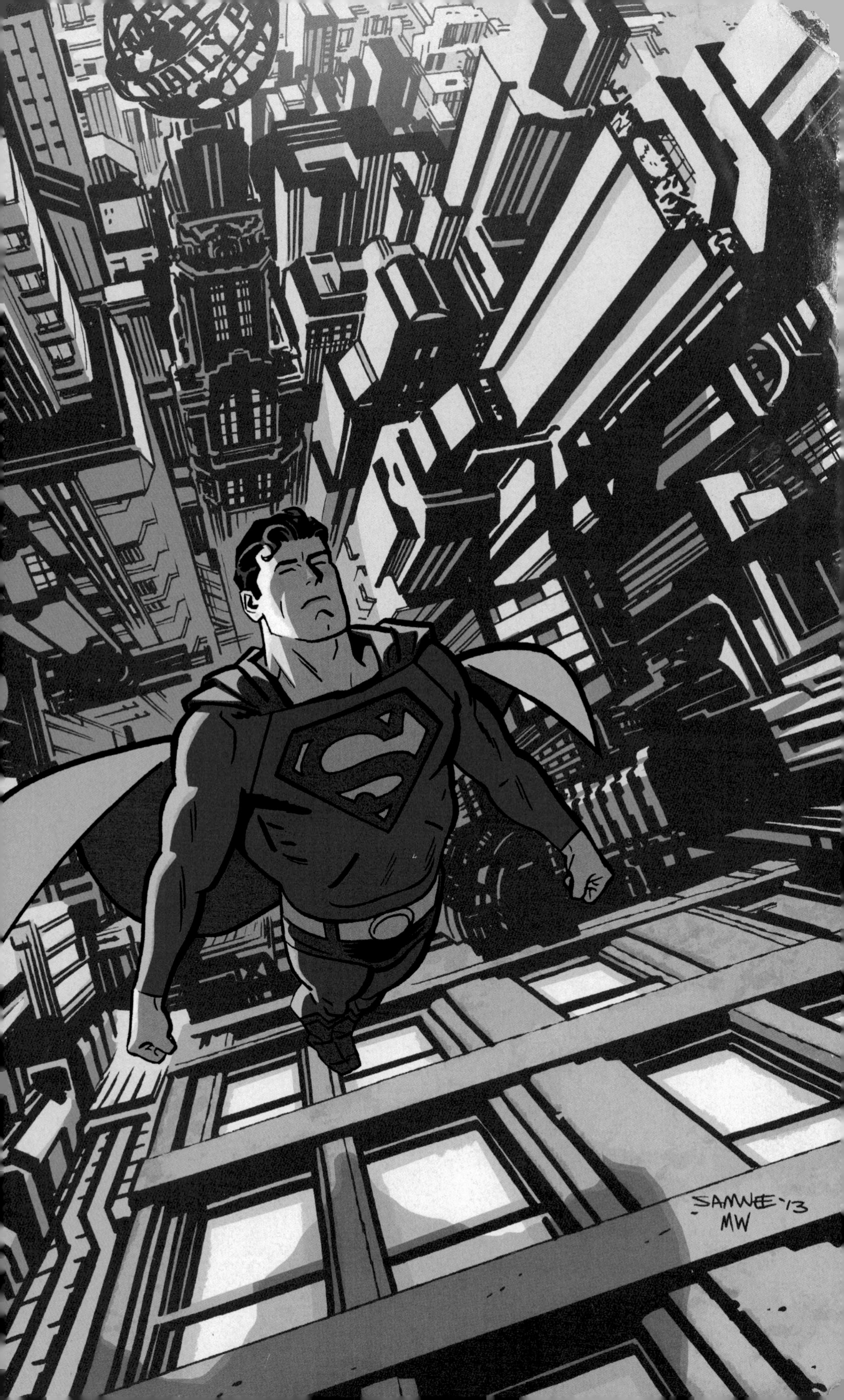
SAMNEE-'13
MW

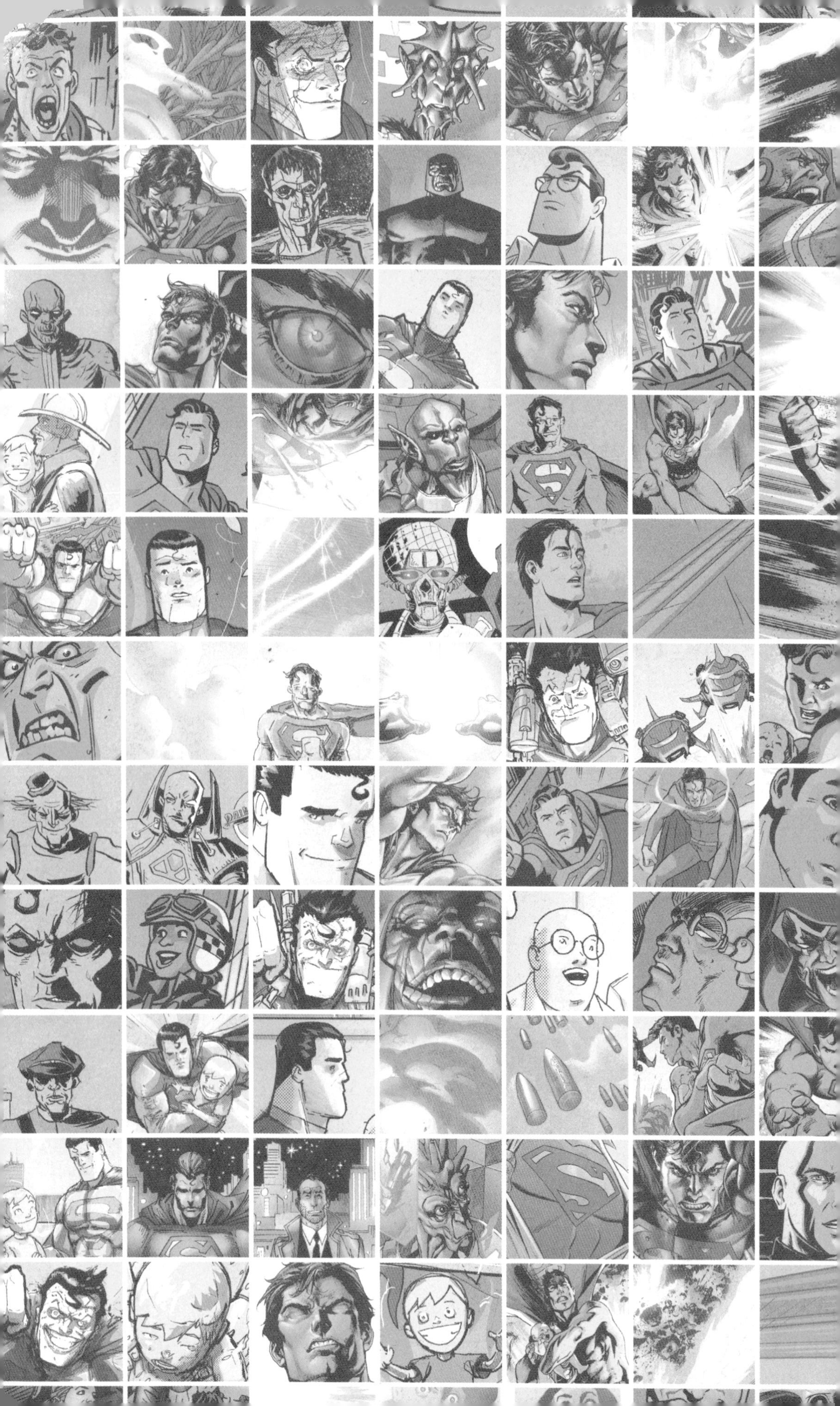

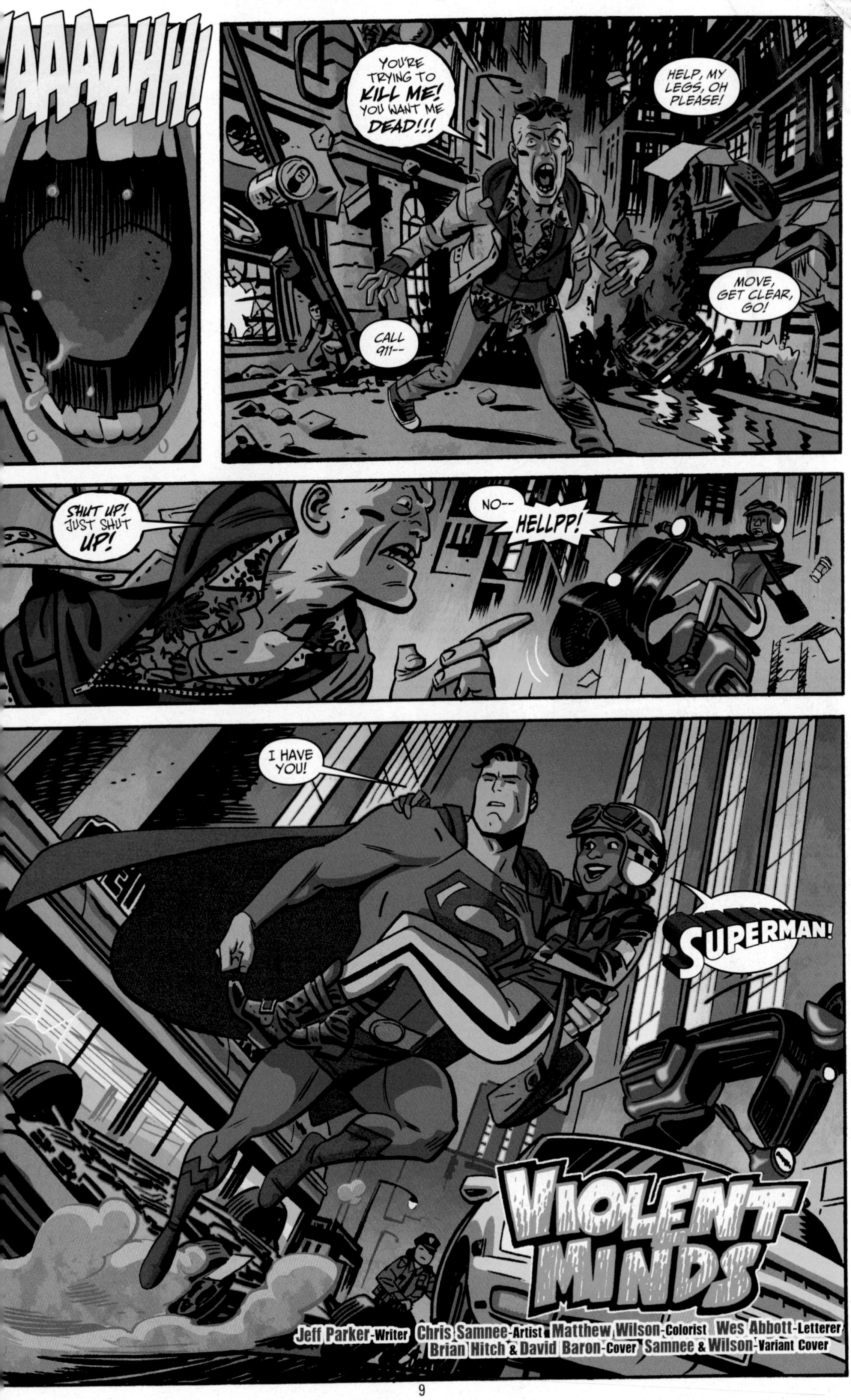
AAAAAHH!
YOU'RE TRYING TO KILL ME! YOU WANT ME DEAD!!!
HELP, MY LEGS, OH PLEASE!
MOVE, GET CLEAR, GO!
CALL 911--
SHUT UP! JUST SHUT UP!
NO--
HELLPP!
I HAVE YOU!
SUPERMAN!
VIOLENT MINDS
Jeff Parker-Writer Chris Samnee-Artist Matthew Wilson-Colorist Wes Abbott-Letterer
Brian Hitch & David Baron-Cover Samnee & Wilson-Variant Cover

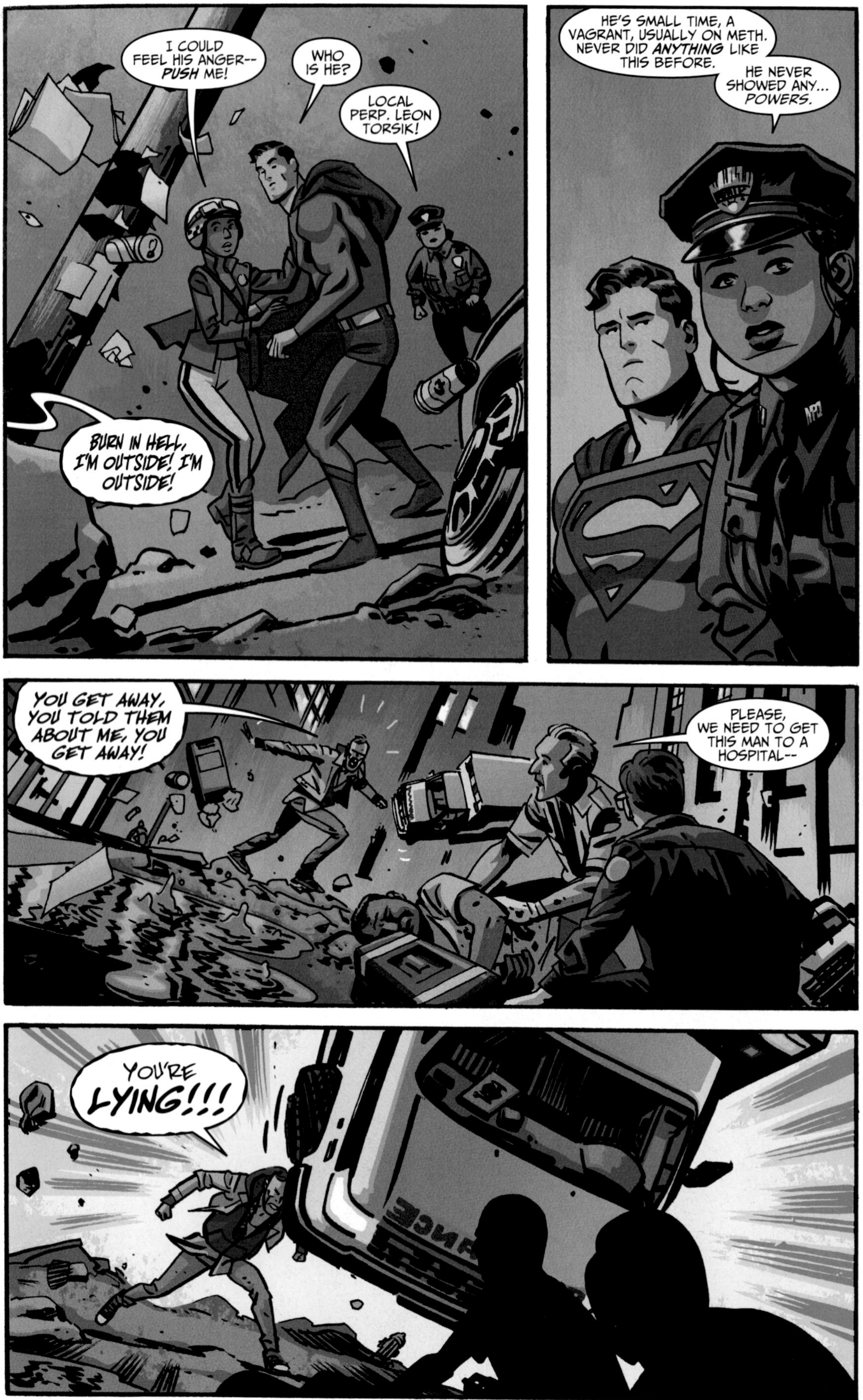
I COULD FEEL HIS ANGER-- PUSH ME!
WHO IS HE?
LOCAL PERP. LEON TORSIK!
BURN IN HELL, I'M OUTSIDE! I'M OUTSIDE!
HE'S SMALL TIME, A VAGRANT, USUALLY ON METH. NEVER DID ANYTHING LIKE THIS BEFORE.
HE NEVER SHOWED ANY... POWERS.
YOU GET AWAY, YOU TOLD THEM ABOUT ME, YOU GET AWAY!
PLEASE, WE NEED TO GET THIS MAN TO A HOSPITAL--
YOU'RE LYING!!!

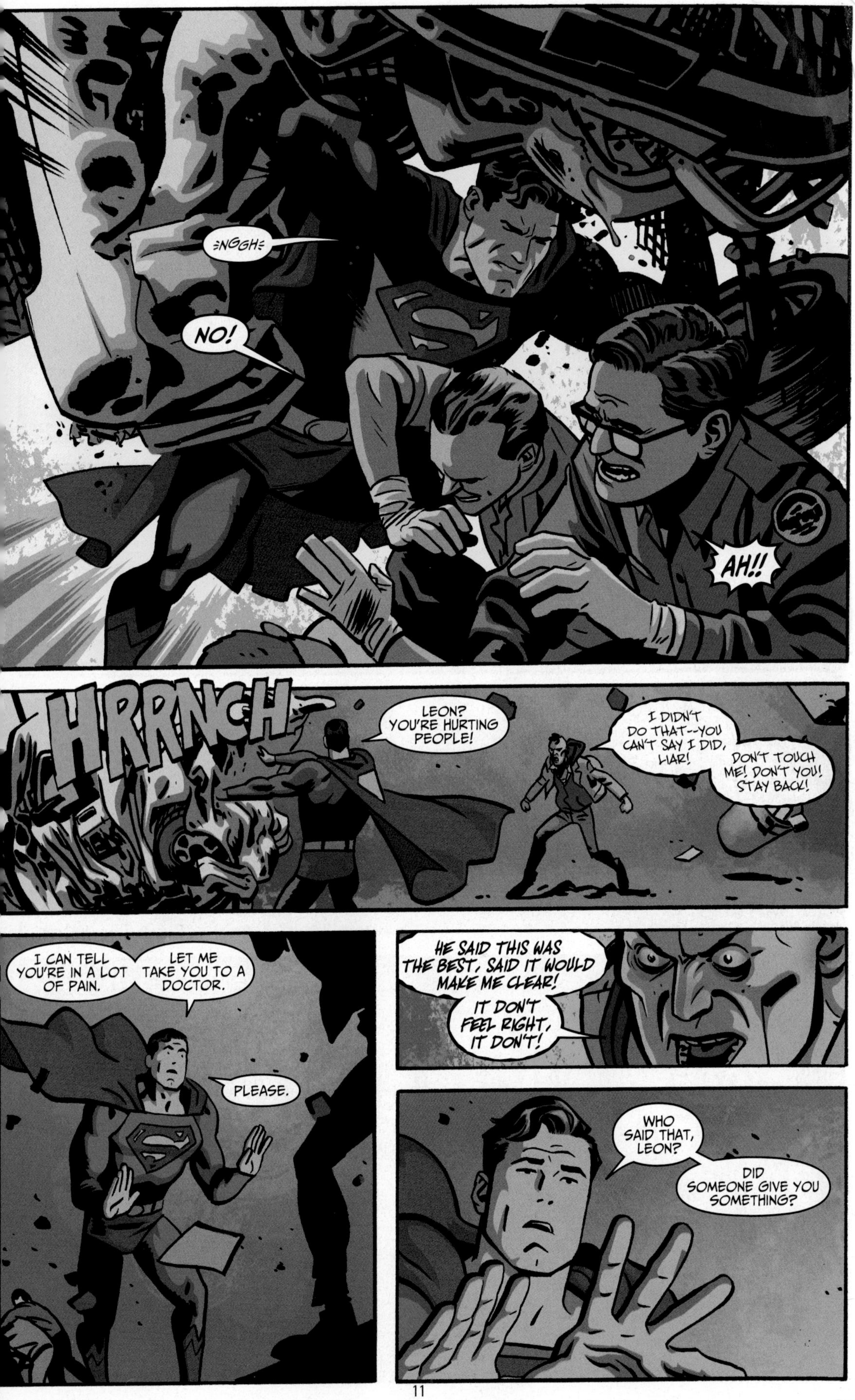
NGGH
NO!
AH!!
HRRNCH
LEON? YOU'RE HURTING PEOPLE!
I DIDN'T DO THAT--YOU CAN'T SAY I DID, LIAR!
DON'T TOUCH ME! DON'T YOU! STAY BACK!
I CAN TELL YOU'RE IN A LOT OF PAIN.
LET ME TAKE YOU TO A DOCTOR.
PLEASE.
HE SAID THIS WAS THE BEST, SAID IT WOULD MAKE ME CLEAR!
IT DON'T FEEL RIGHT, IT DON'T!
WHO SAID THAT, LEON?
DID SOMEONE GIVE YOU SOMETHING?

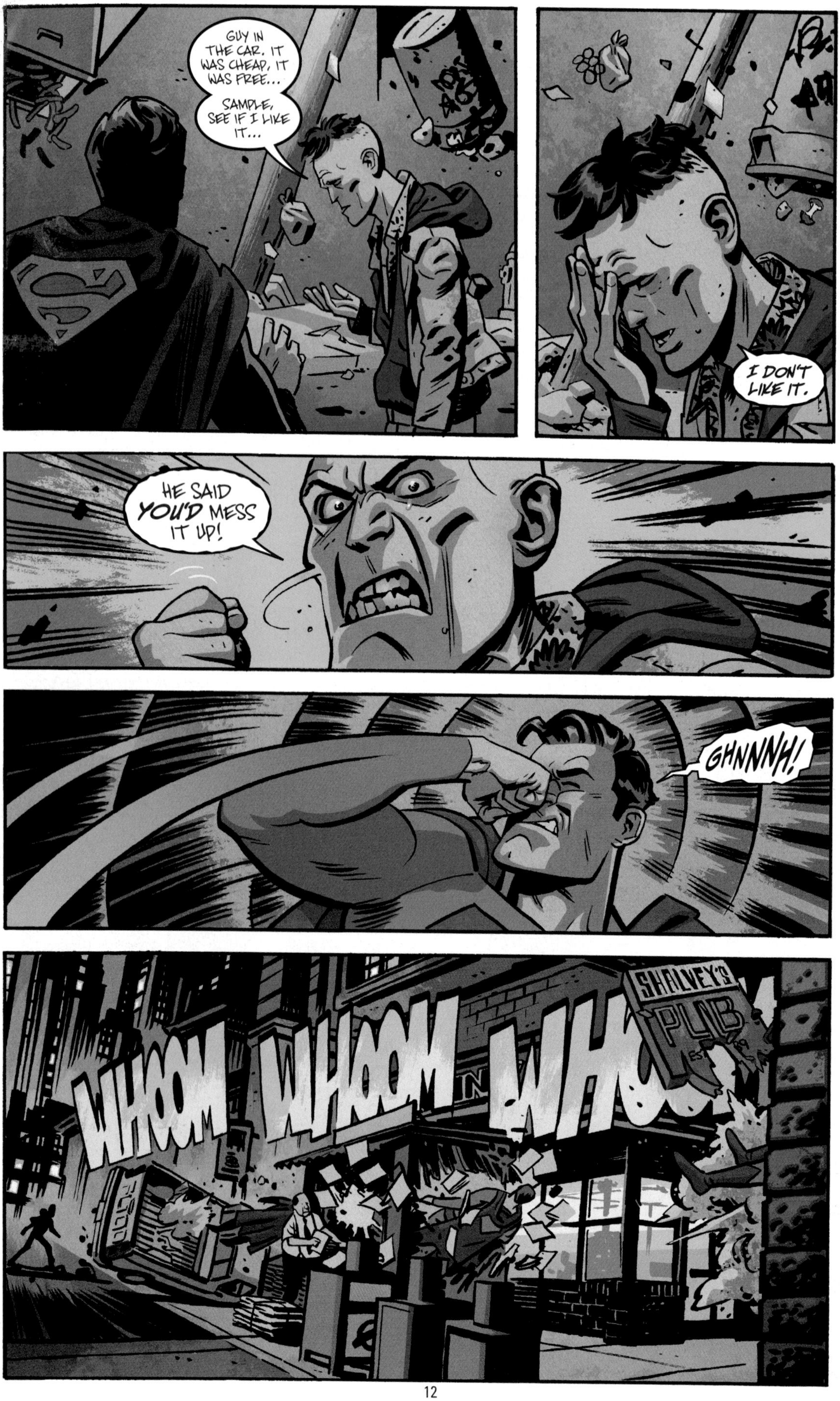
GUY IN THE CAR. IT WAS CHEAP, IT WAS FREE...
SAMPLE, SEE IF I LIKE IT...
I DON'T LIKE IT.
HE SAID YOU'D MESS IT UP!
GHNNNH!
WHOOM WHOOM WHO
SHALVEY'S PUB

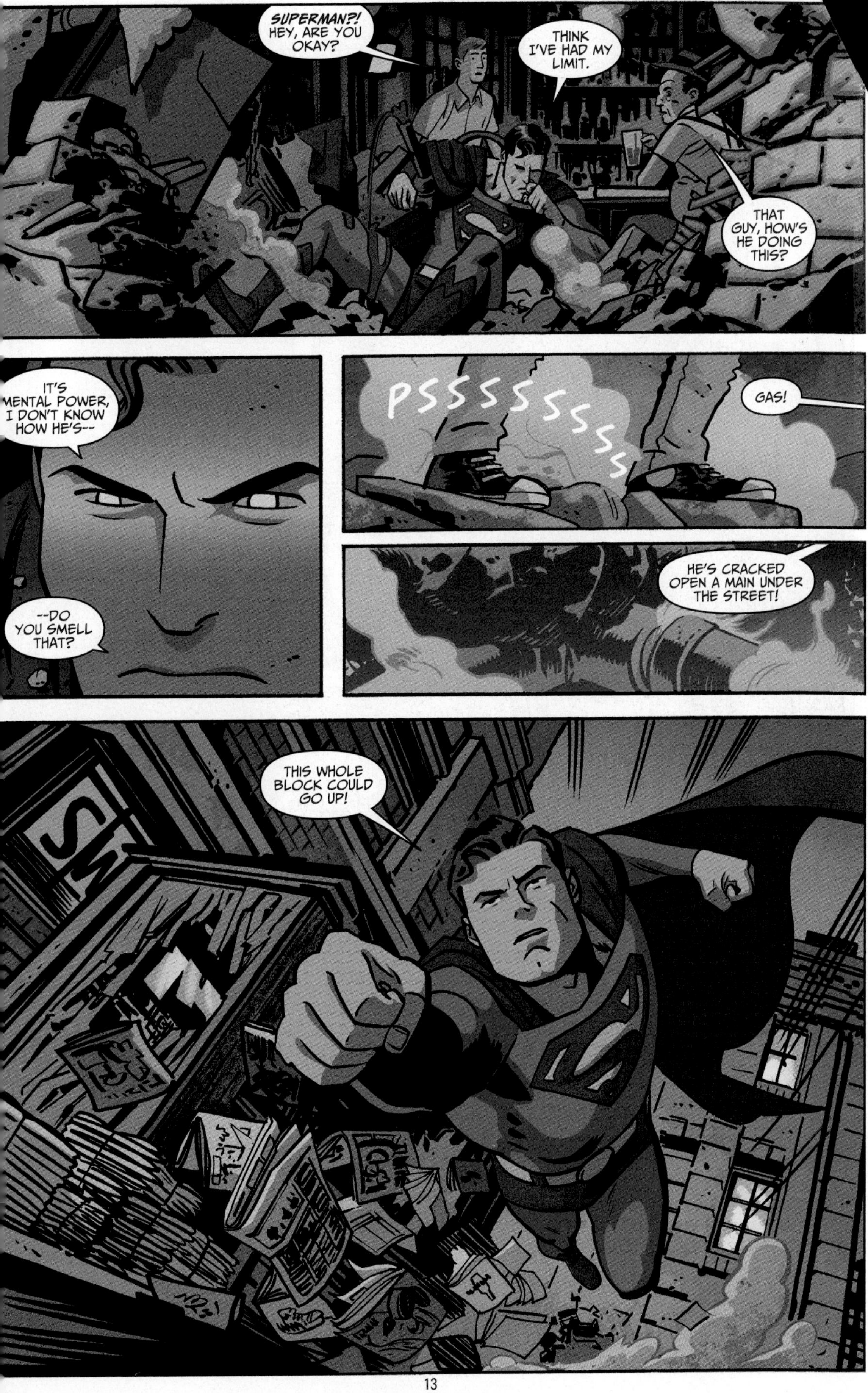
SUPERMAN?! HEY, ARE YOU OKAY?
THINK I'VE HAD MY LIMIT.
THAT GUY, HOW'S HE DOING THIS?
IT'S MENTAL POWER, I DON'T KNOW HOW HE'S--
--DO YOU SMELL THAT?
PSSSSSSSSS
GAS!
HE'S CRACKED OPEN A MAIN UNDER THE STREET!
THIS WHOLE BLOCK COULD GO UP!

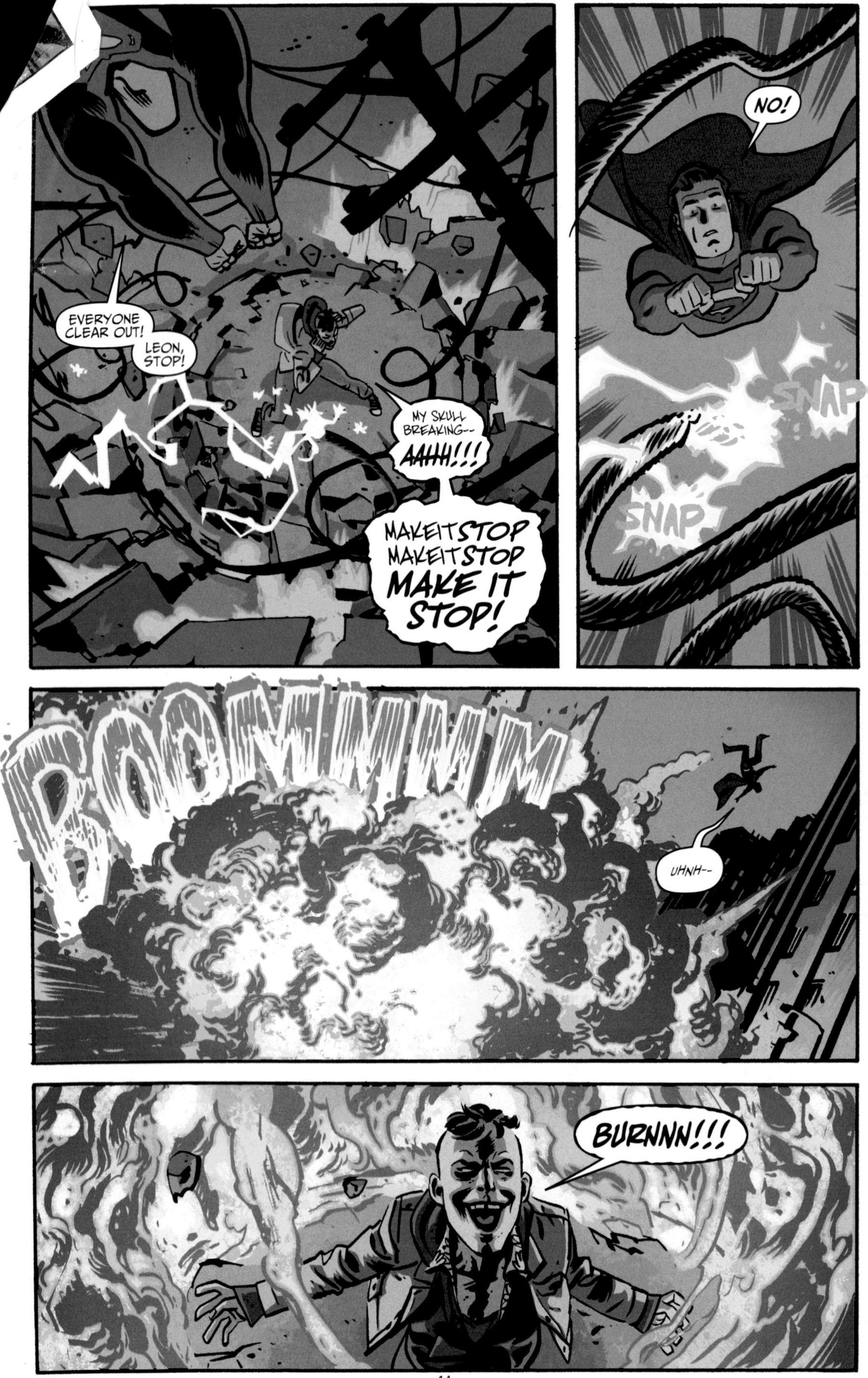
EVERYONE CLEAR OUT!
LEON, STOP!
MY SKULL BREAKING-- AAHH!!!
MAKEITSTOP MAKEITSTOP MAKE IT STOP!
NO!
SNAP
SNAP
BOOMMMMM
UHNH--
BURNNN!!!

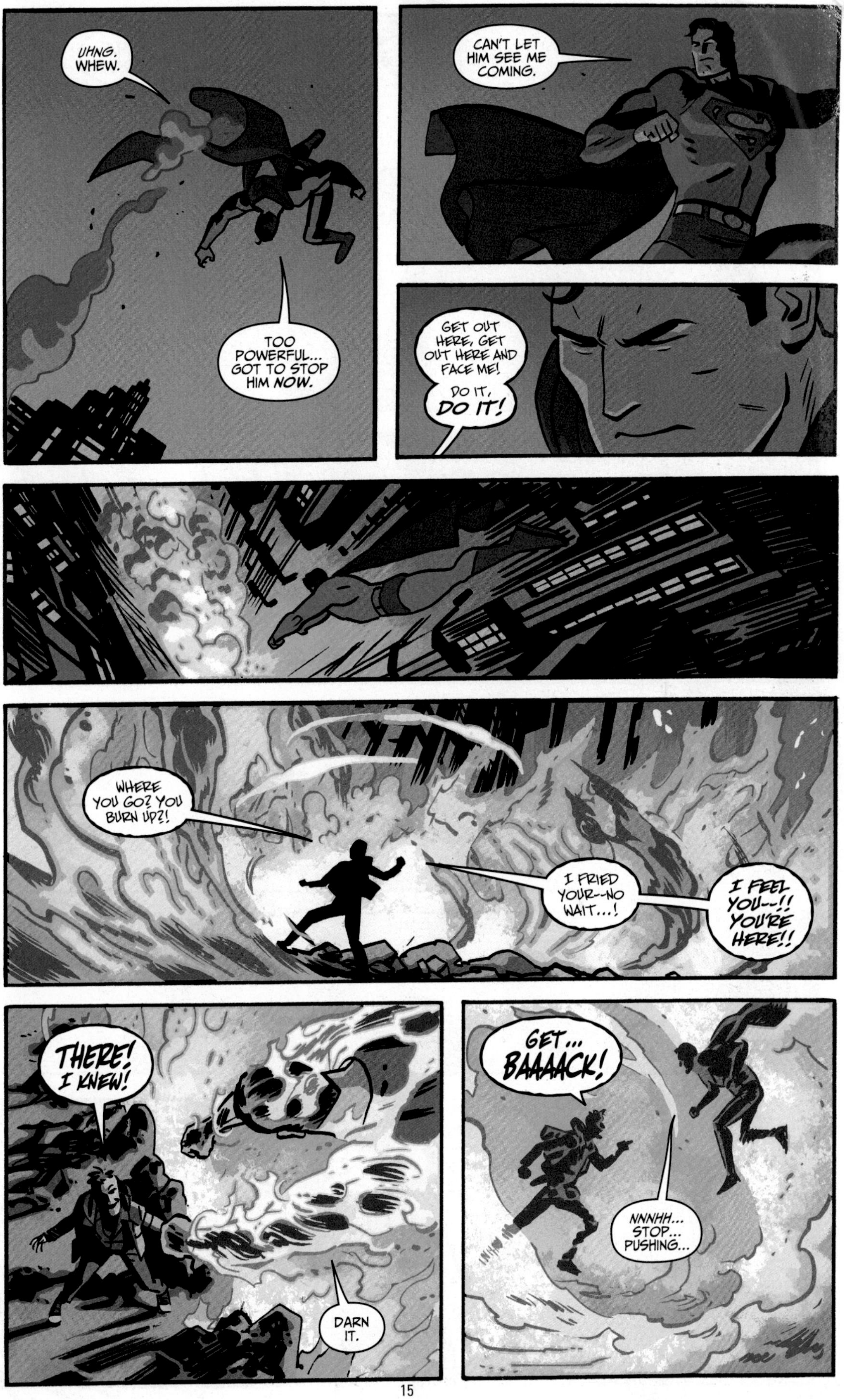
UHNG. WHEW.
TOO POWERFUL... GOT TO STOP HIM NOW.
CAN'T LET HIM SEE ME COMING.
GET OUT HERE, GET OUT HERE AND FACE ME!
DO IT, DO IT!
WHERE YOU GO? YOU BURN UP?!
I FRIED YOUR--NO WAIT...!
I FEEL YOU--!! YOU'RE HERE!!
THERE! I KNEW!
DARN IT.
GET... BAAAACK!
NNNHH... STOP... PUSHING...

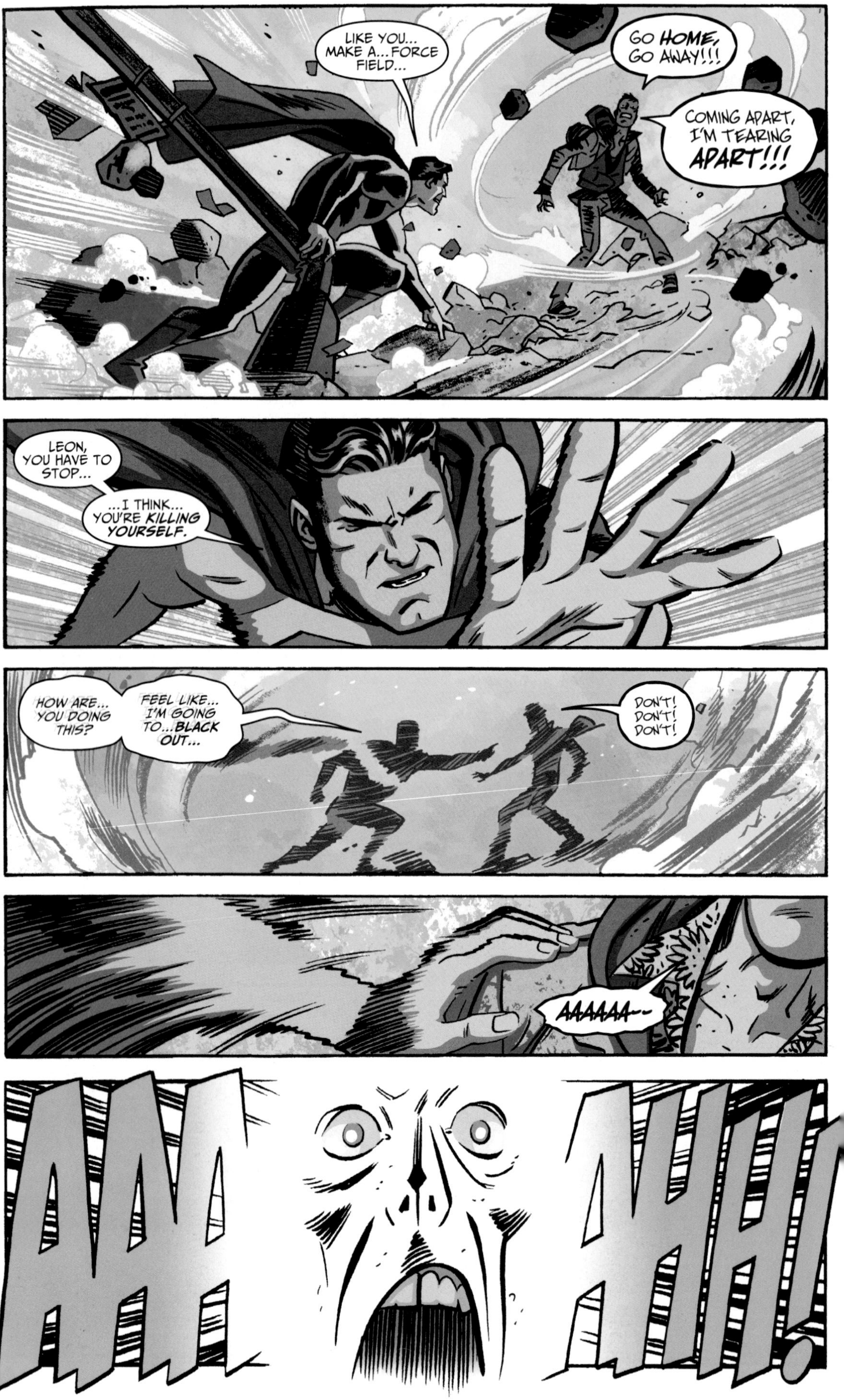
LIKE YOU... MAKE A...FORCE FIELD...
GO HOME, GO AWAY!!!
COMING APART, I'M TEARING APART!!!
LEON, YOU HAVE TO STOP...
...I THINK... YOU'RE KILLING YOURSELF.
HOW ARE... YOU DOING THIS?
FEEL LIKE... I'M GOING TO...BLACK OUT...
DON'T! DON'T! DON'T!
AAAAAA--
AAAHH!

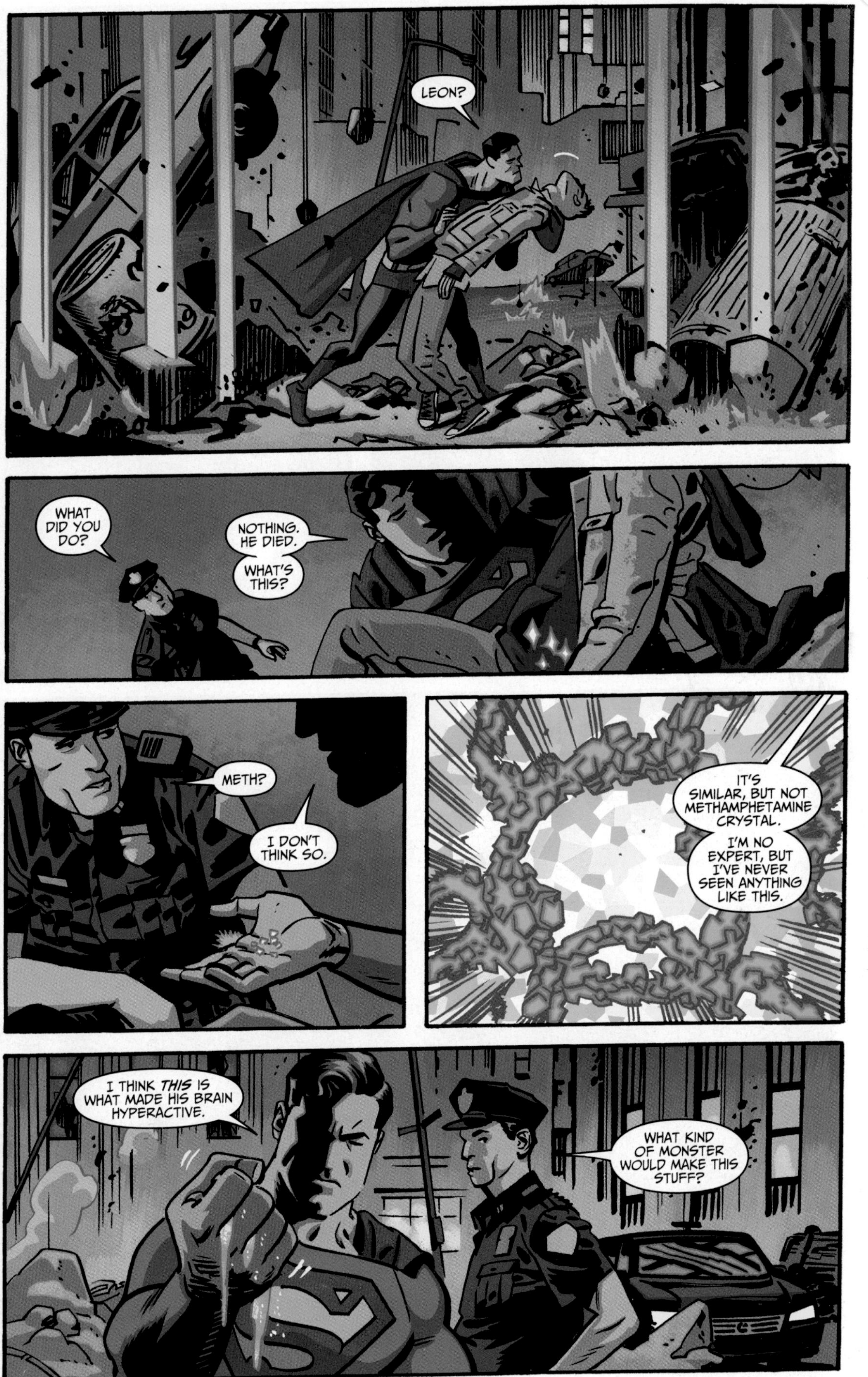
LEON?
WHAT DID YOU DO?
NOTHING. HE DIED.
WHAT'S THIS?
METH?
I DON'T THINK SO.
IT'S SIMILAR, BUT NOT METHAMPHETAMINE CRYSTAL.
I'M NO EXPERT, BUT I'VE NEVER SEEN ANYTHING LIKE THIS.
I THINK *THIS* IS WHAT MADE HIS BRAIN HYPERACTIVE.
WHAT KIND OF MONSTER WOULD MAKE THIS STUFF?

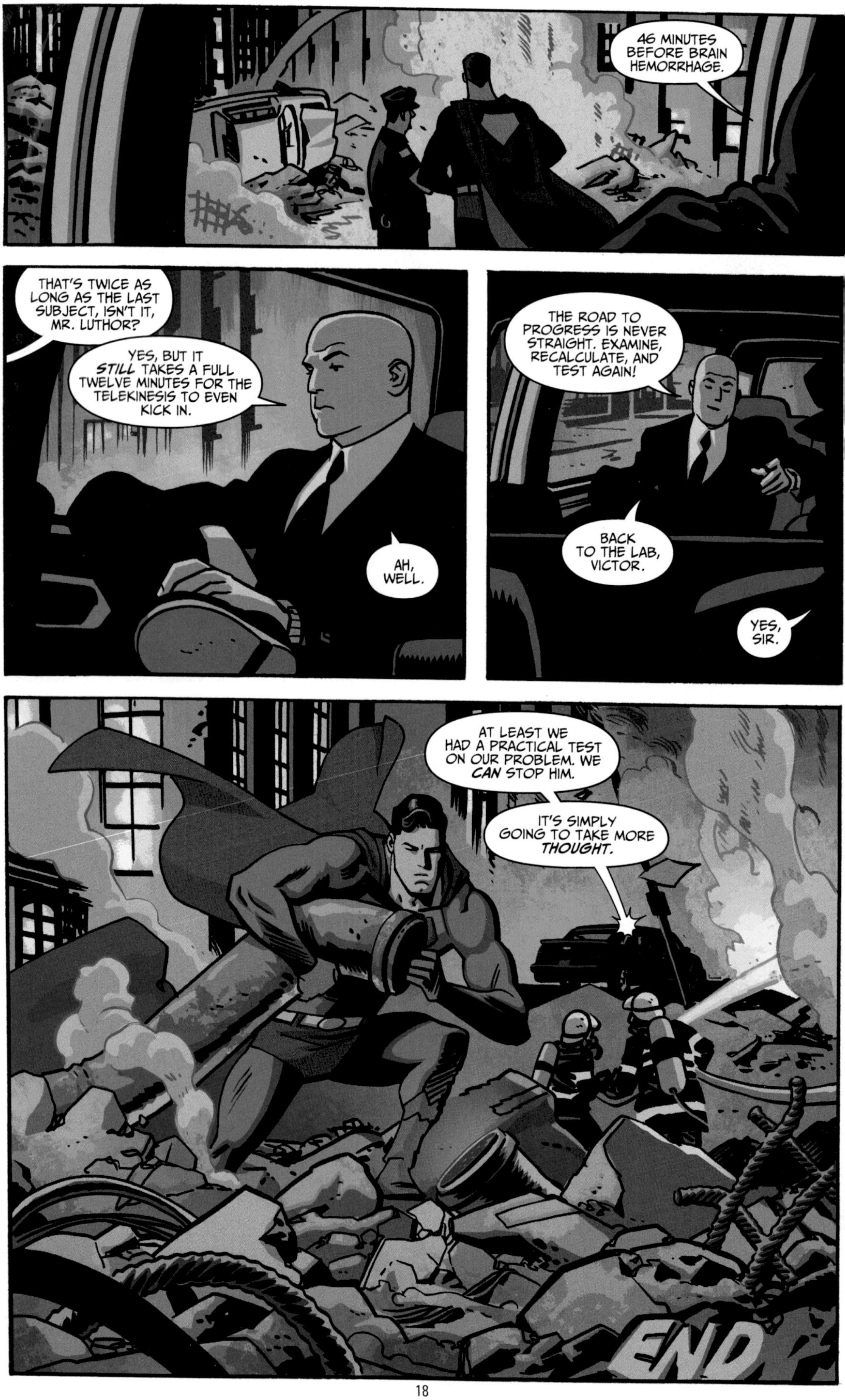
46 MINUTES BEFORE BRAIN HEMORRHAGE.
THAT'S TWICE AS LONG AS THE LAST SUBJECT, ISN'T IT, MR. LUTHOR?
YES, BUT IT *STILL* TAKES A FULL TWELVE MINUTES FOR THE TELEKINESIS TO EVEN KICK IN.
AH, WELL.
THE ROAD TO PROGRESS IS NEVER STRAIGHT. EXAMINE, RECALCULATE, AND TEST AGAIN!
BACK TO THE LAB, VICTOR.
YES, SIR.
AT LEAST WE HAD A PRACTICAL TEST ON OUR PROBLEM. WE *CAN* STOP HIM.
IT'S SIMPLY GOING TO TAKE MORE *THOUGHT.*
END

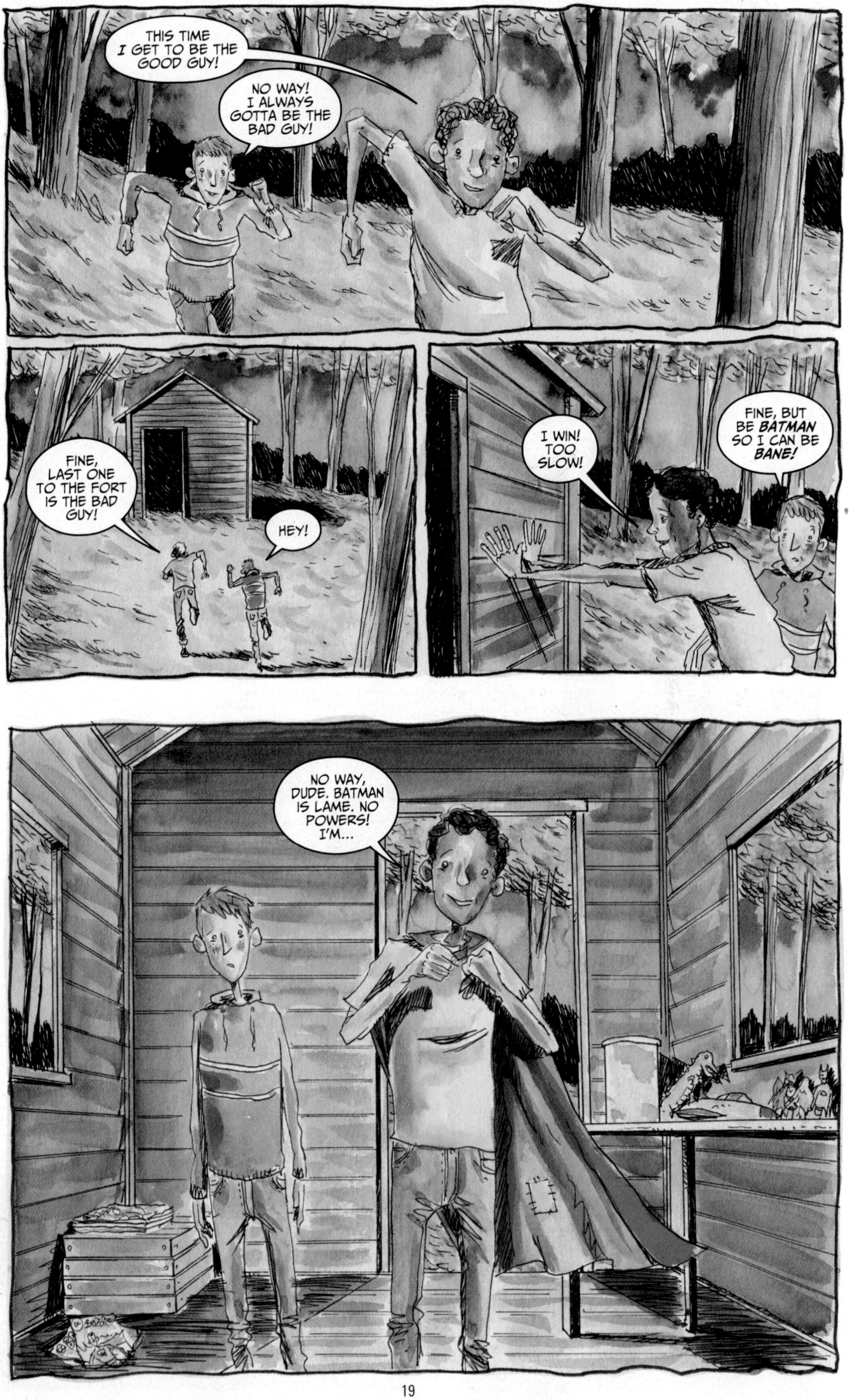
THIS TIME I GET TO BE THE GOOD GUY!
NO WAY! I ALWAYS GOTTA BE THE BAD GUY!
FINE, LAST ONE TO THE FORT IS THE BAD GUY!
HEY!
I WIN! TOO SLOW!
FINE, BUT BE BATMAN SO I CAN BE BANE!
NO WAY, DUDE. BATMAN IS LAME. NO POWERS! I'M...

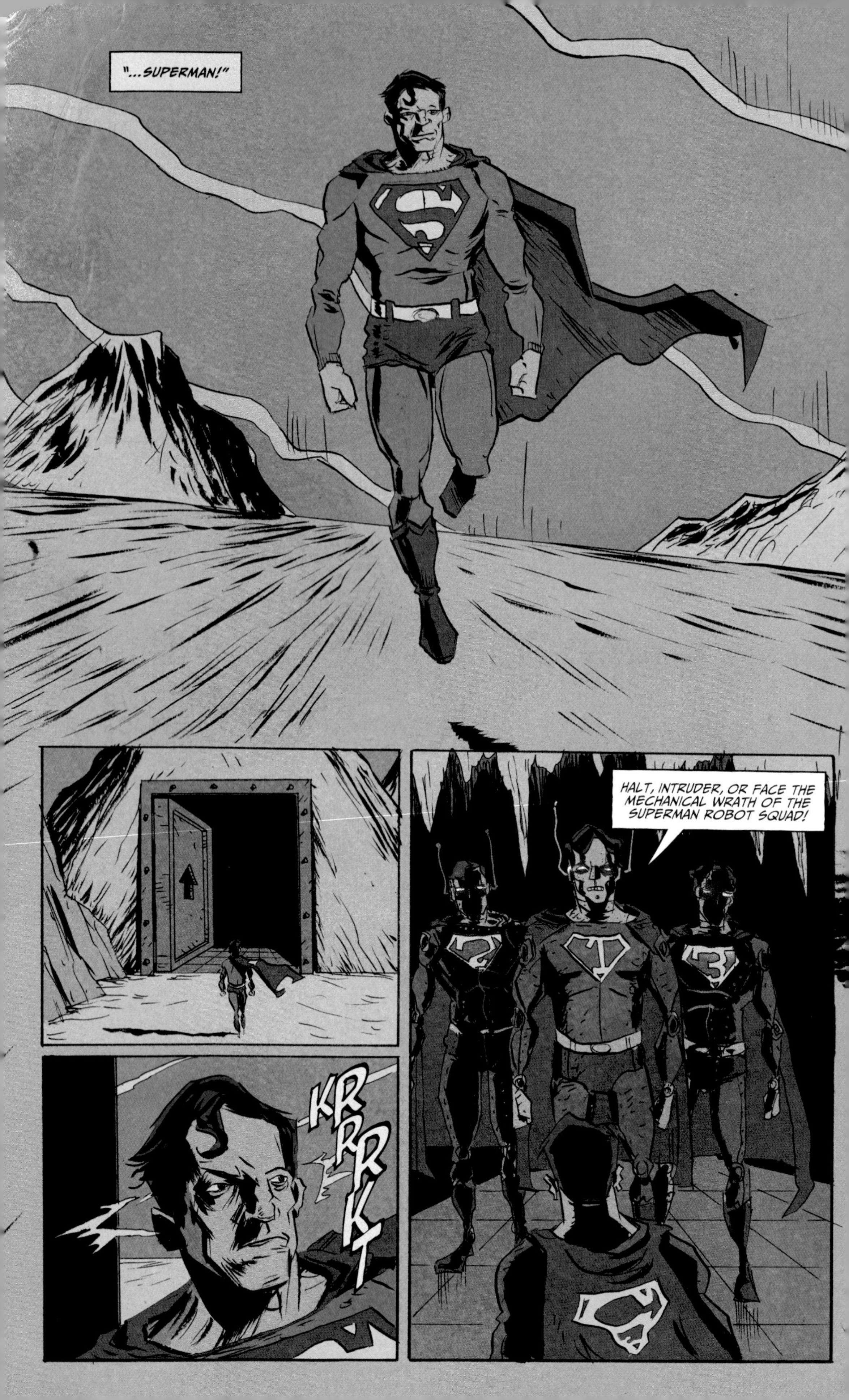
"...SUPERMAN!"
KRRRKT
HALT, INTRUDER, OR FACE THE MECHANICAL WRATH OF THE SUPERMAN ROBOT SQUAD!

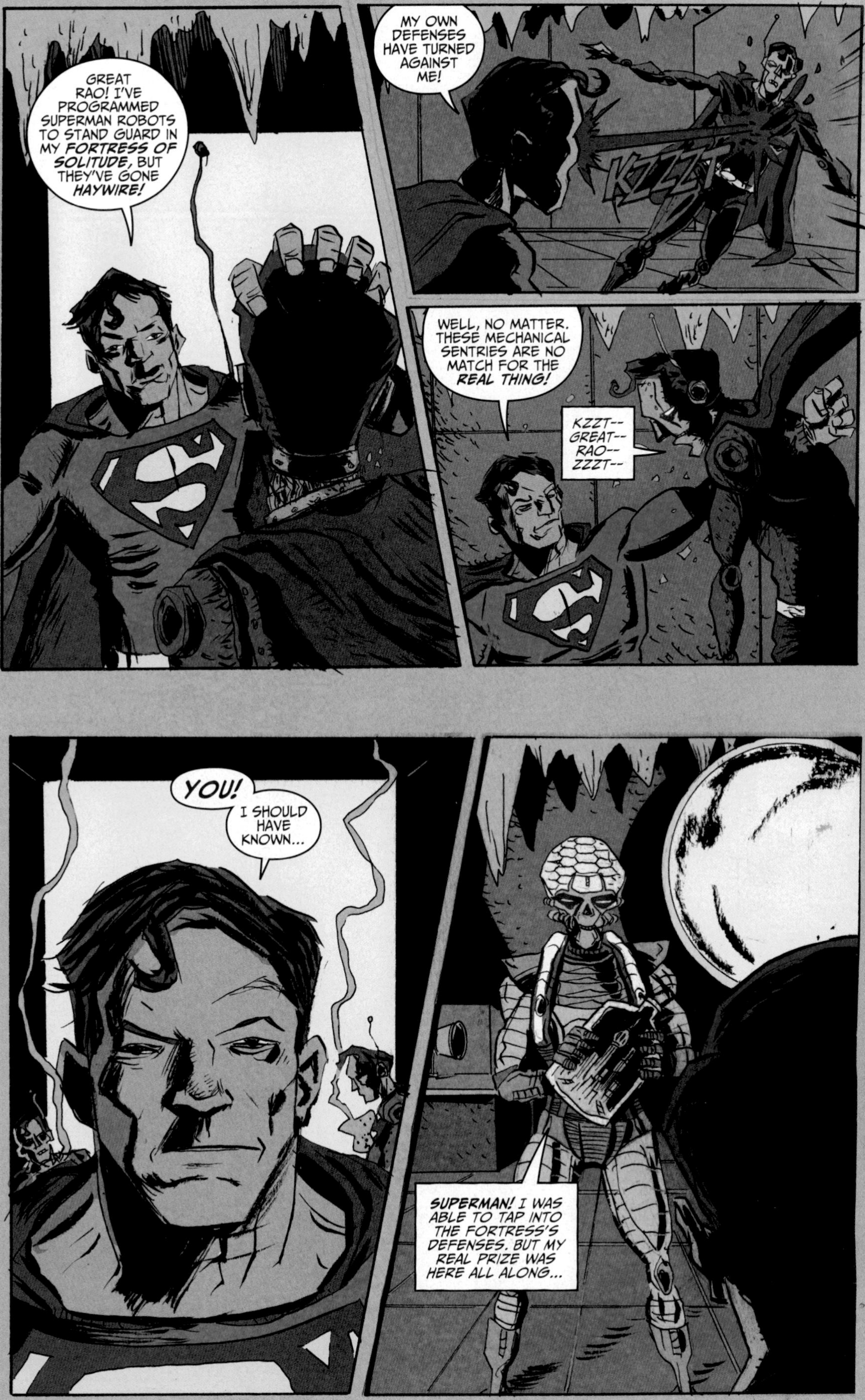

GREAT RAO! I'VE PROGRAMMED SUPERMAN ROBOTS TO STAND GUARD IN MY FORTRESS OF SOLITUDE, BUT THEY'VE GONE HAYWIRE!
MY OWN DEFENSES HAVE TURNED AGAINST ME!
KZZZT
WELL, NO MATTER. THESE MECHANICAL SENTRIES ARE NO MATCH FOR THE REAL THING!
KZZT-- GREAT-- RAO-- ZZZT--
YOU!
I SHOULD HAVE KNOWN...
SUPERMAN! I WAS ABLE TO TAP INTO THE FORTRESS'S DEFENSES. BUT MY REAL PRIZE WAS HERE ALL ALONG...

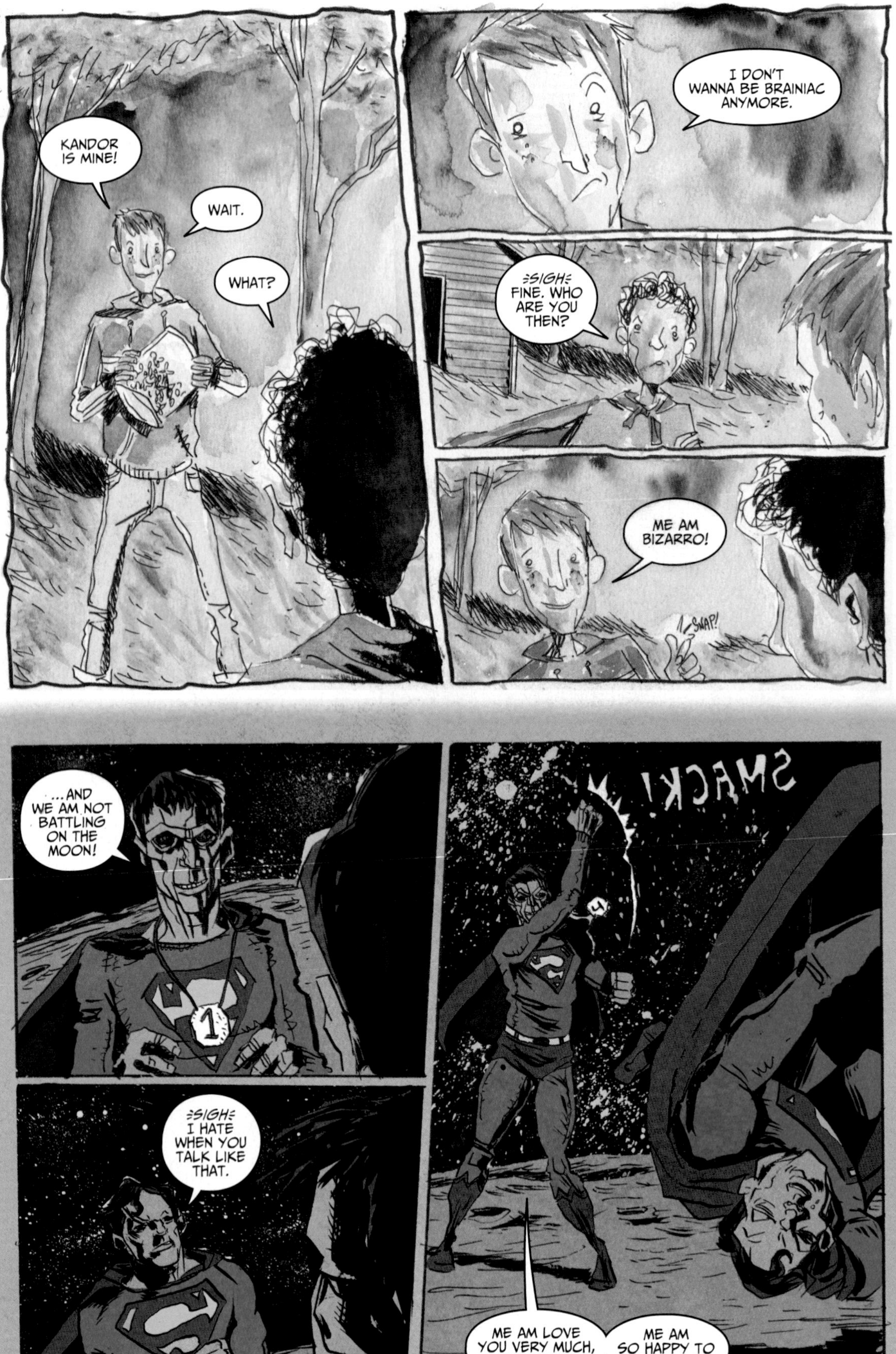
KANDOR IS MINE!
WAIT.
WHAT?
I DON'T WANNA BE BRAINIAC ANYMORE.
SIGH FINE. WHO ARE YOU THEN?
ME AM BIZARRO!
SNAP!
...AND WE AM NOT BATTLING ON THE MOON!
SIGH I HATE WHEN YOU TALK LIKE THAT.
SMACK!
ME AM LOVE YOU VERY MUCH, SUPERMAN!
ME AM SO HAPPY TO SEE YOU!

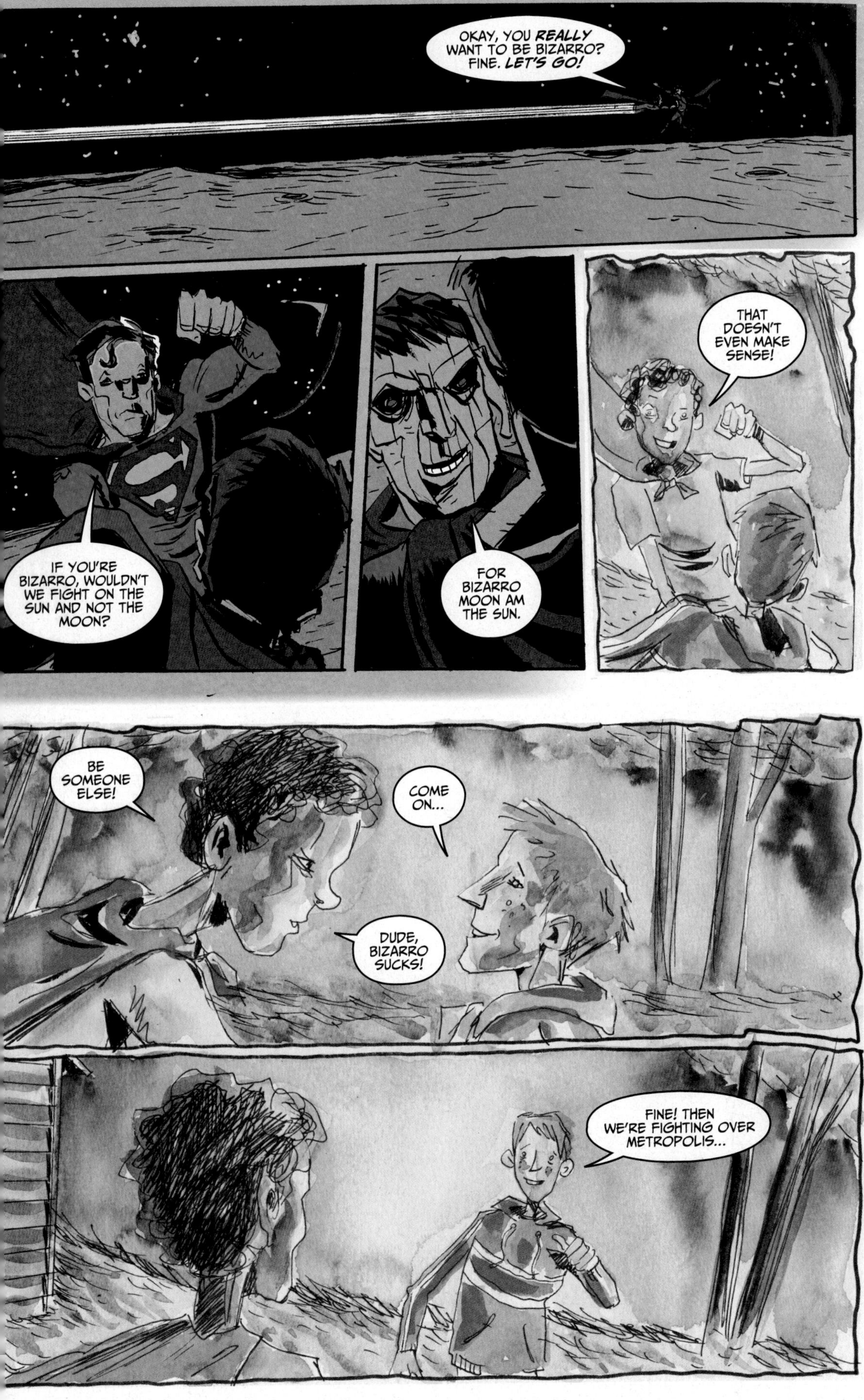
OKAY, YOU REALLY WANT TO BE BIZARRO? FINE. LET'S GO!
IF YOU'RE BIZARRO, WOULDN'T WE FIGHT ON THE SUN AND NOT THE MOON?
FOR BIZARRO MOON AM THE SUN.
THAT DOESN'T EVEN MAKE SENSE!
BE SOMEONE ELSE!
COME ON...
DUDE, BIZARRO SUCKS!
FINE! THEN WE'RE FIGHTING OVER METROPOLIS...

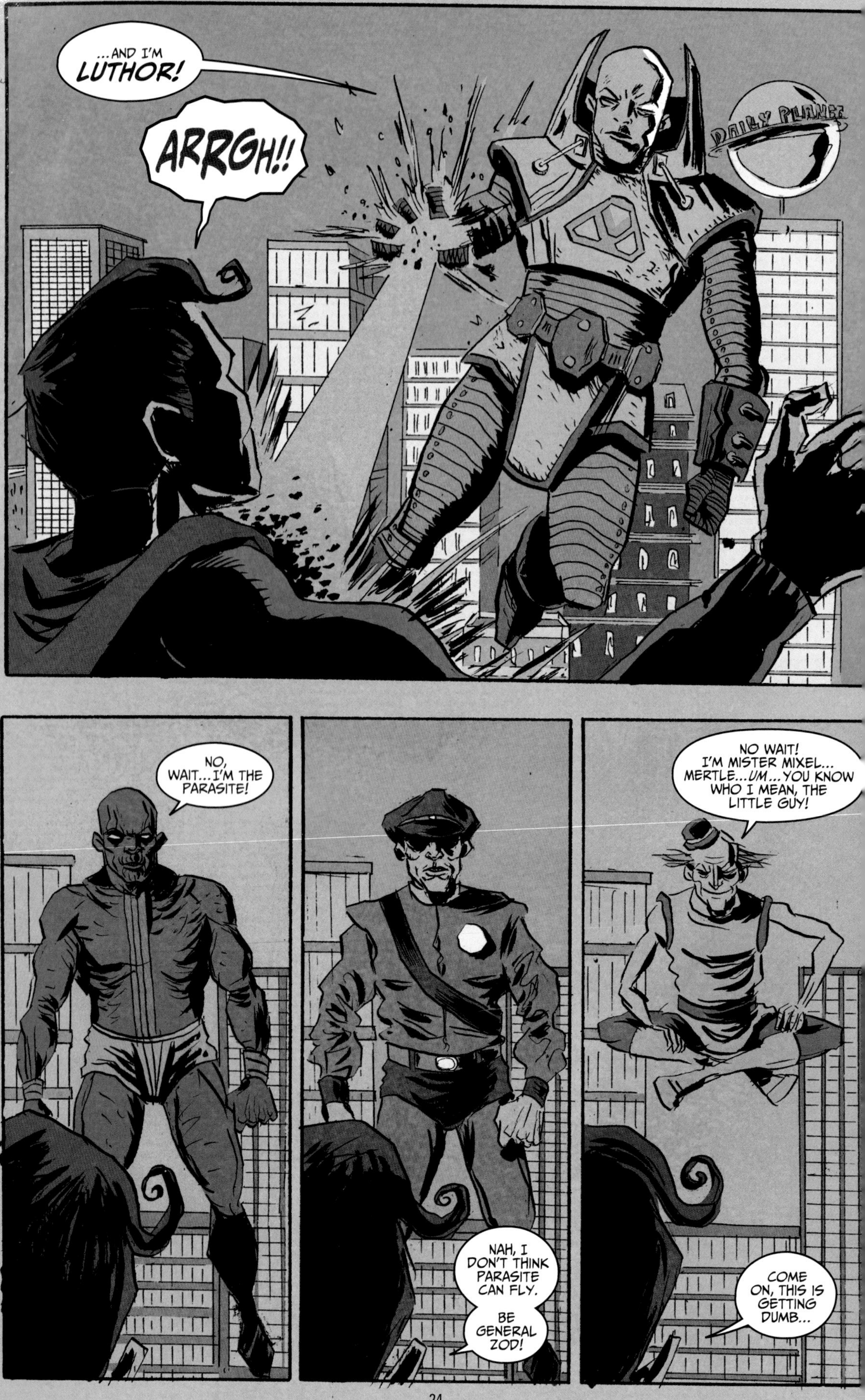
...AND I'M LUTHOR!
ARRGH!!
NO, WAIT...I'M THE PARASITE!
NAH, I DON'T THINK PARASITE CAN FLY.
BE GENERAL ZOD!
NO WAIT! I'M MISTER MIXEL... MERTLE...UM...YOU KNOW WHO I MEAN, THE LITTLE GUY!
COME ON, THIS IS GETTING DUMB...

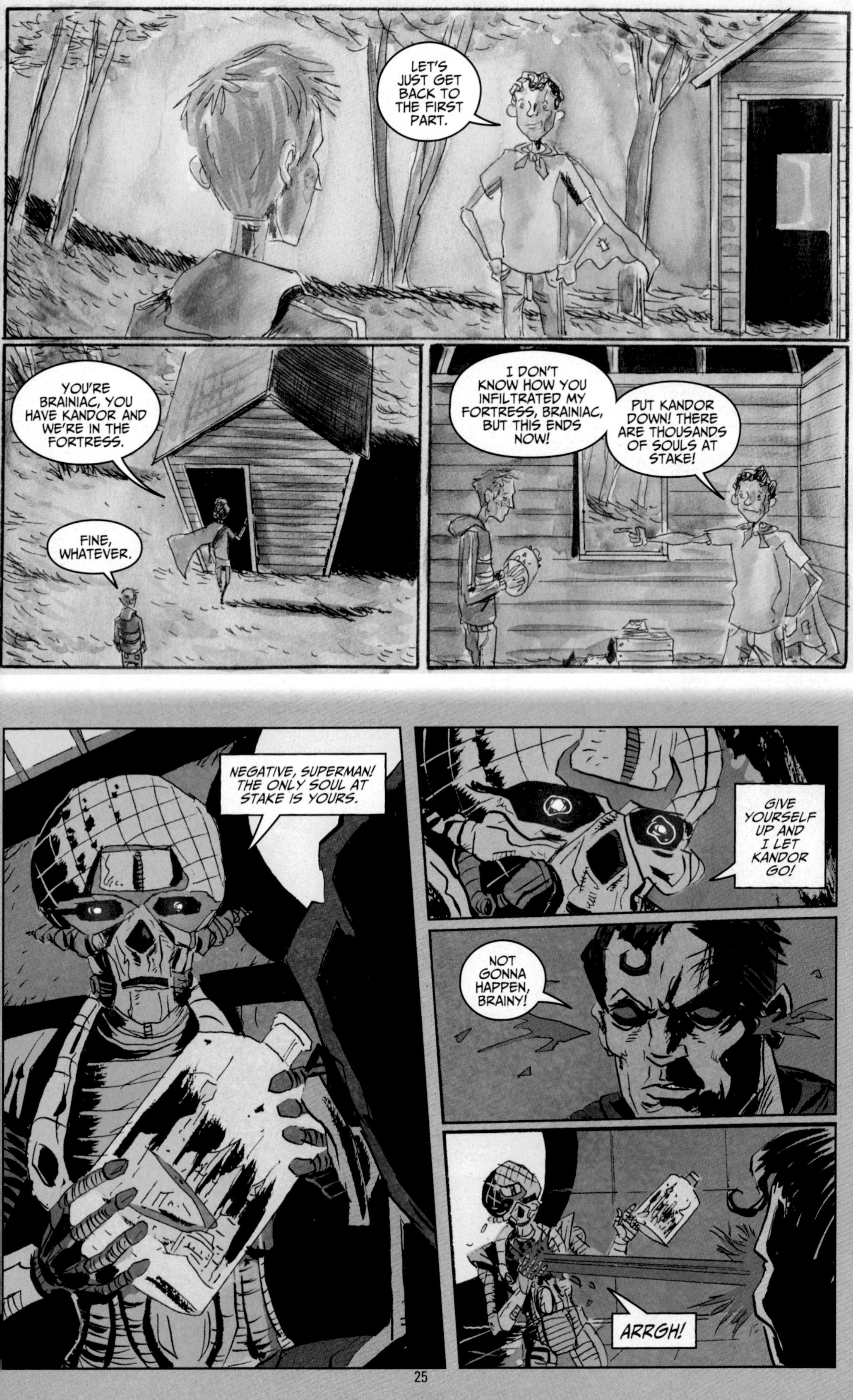
LET'S JUST GET BACK TO THE FIRST PART.
YOU'RE BRAINIAC, YOU HAVE KANDOR AND WE'RE IN THE FORTRESS.
FINE, WHATEVER.
I DON'T KNOW HOW YOU INFILTRATED MY FORTRESS, BRAINIAC, BUT THIS ENDS NOW!
PUT KANDOR DOWN! THERE ARE THOUSANDS OF SOULS AT STAKE!
NEGATIVE, SUPERMAN! THE ONLY SOUL AT STAKE IS YOURS.
GIVE YOURSELF UP AND I LET KANDOR GO!
NOT GONNA HAPPEN, BRAINY!
ARRGH!

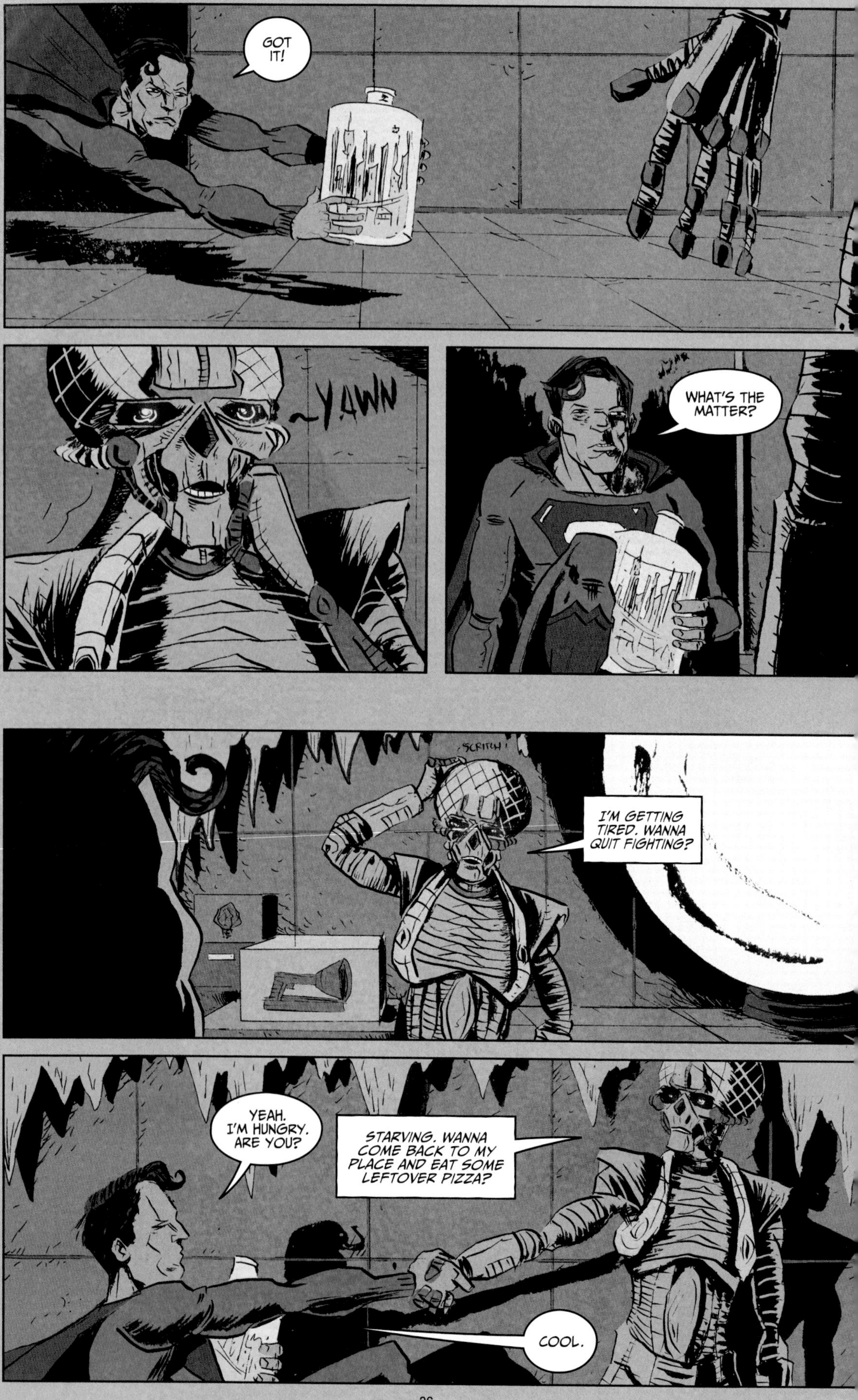
GOT IT!
~YAWN
WHAT'S THE MATTER?
SCRITCH
I'M GETTING TIRED. WANNA QUIT FIGHTING?
YEAH. I'M HUNGRY. ARE YOU?
STARVING. WANNA COME BACK TO MY PLACE AND EAT SOME LEFTOVER PIZZA?
COOL.

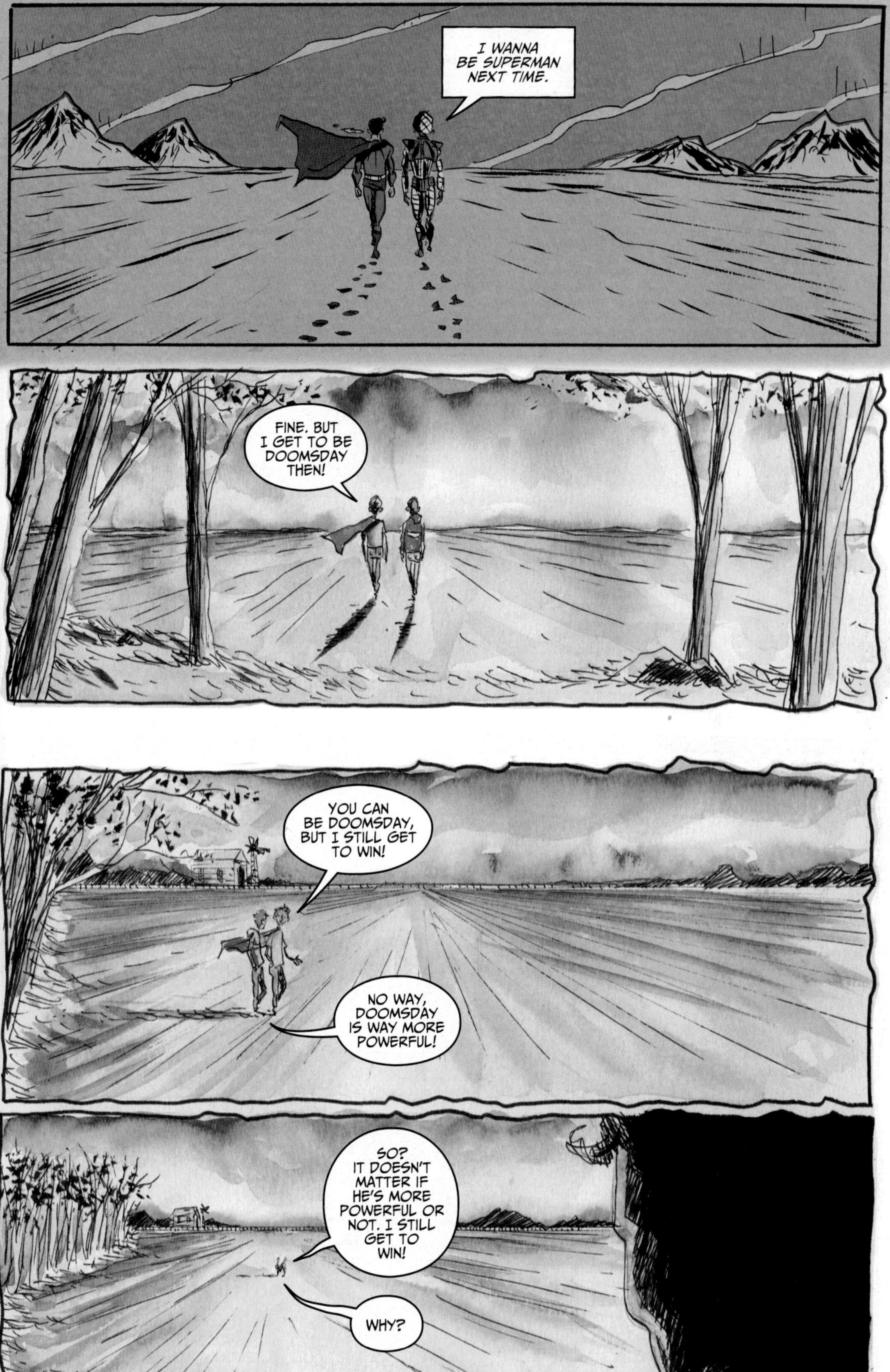
I WANNA BE SUPERMAN NEXT TIME.
FINE. BUT I GET TO BE DOOMSDAY THEN!
YOU CAN BE DOOMSDAY, BUT I STILL GET TO WIN!
NO WAY, DOOMSDAY IS WAY MORE POWERFUL!
SO? IT DOESN'T MATTER IF HE'S MORE POWERFUL OR NOT. I STILL GET TO WIN!
WHY?

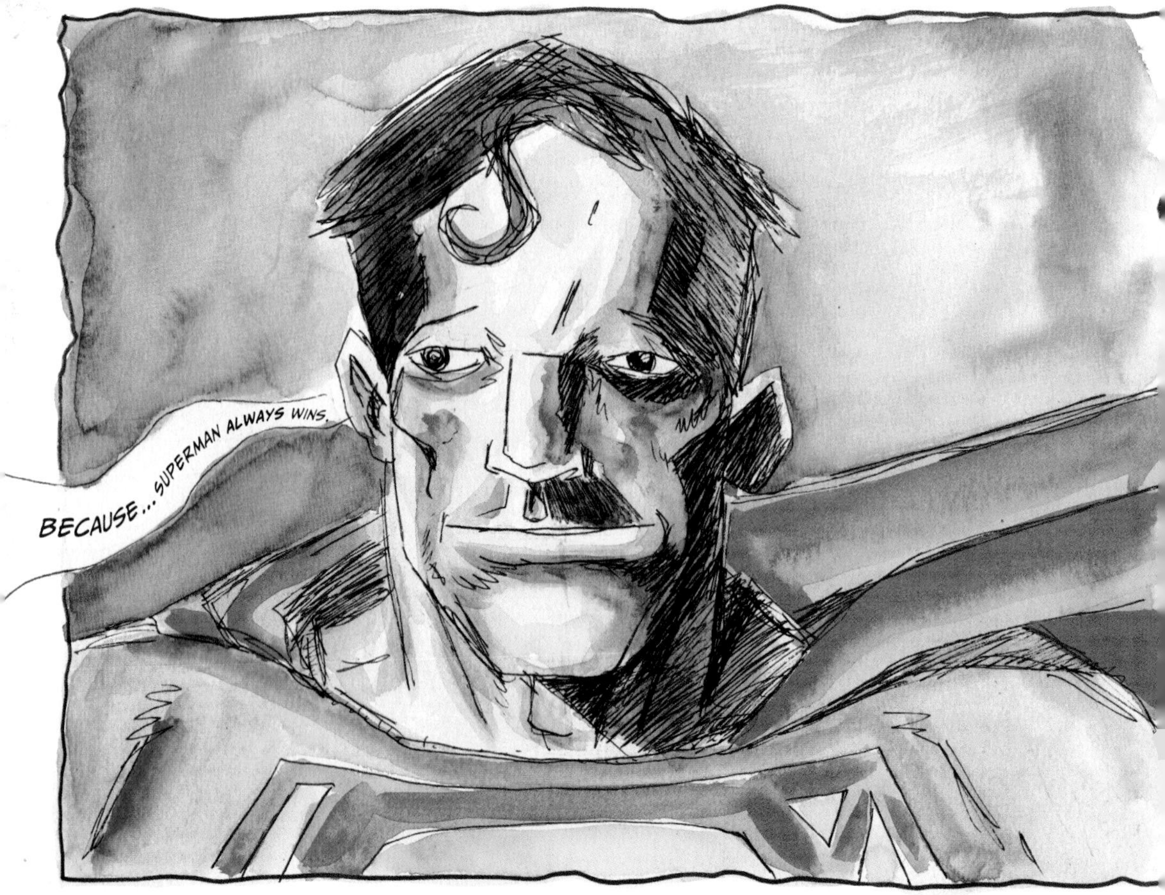
BECAUSE... SUPERMAN ALWAYS WINS.

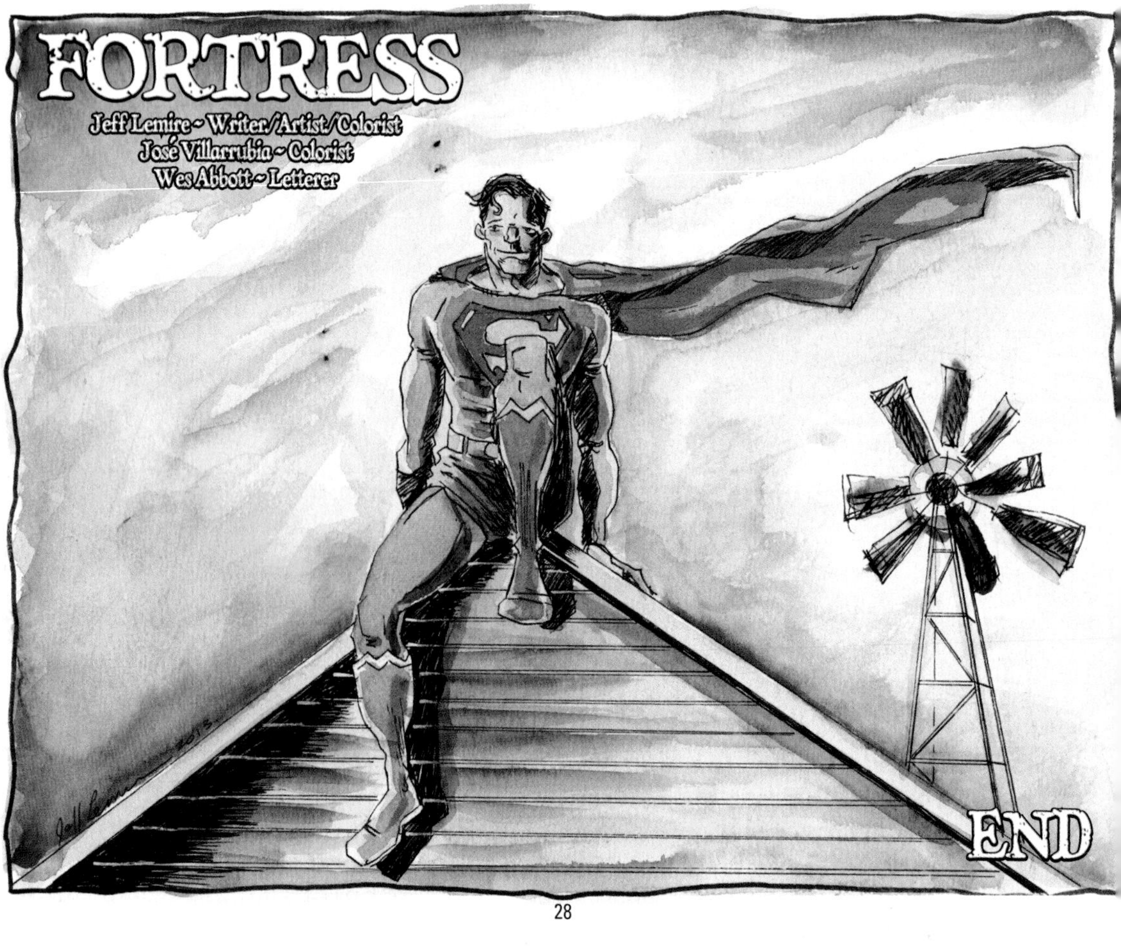
FORTRESS
Jeff Lemire ~ Writer/Artist/Colorist
José Villarrubia ~ Colorist
Wes Abbott ~ Letterer
END

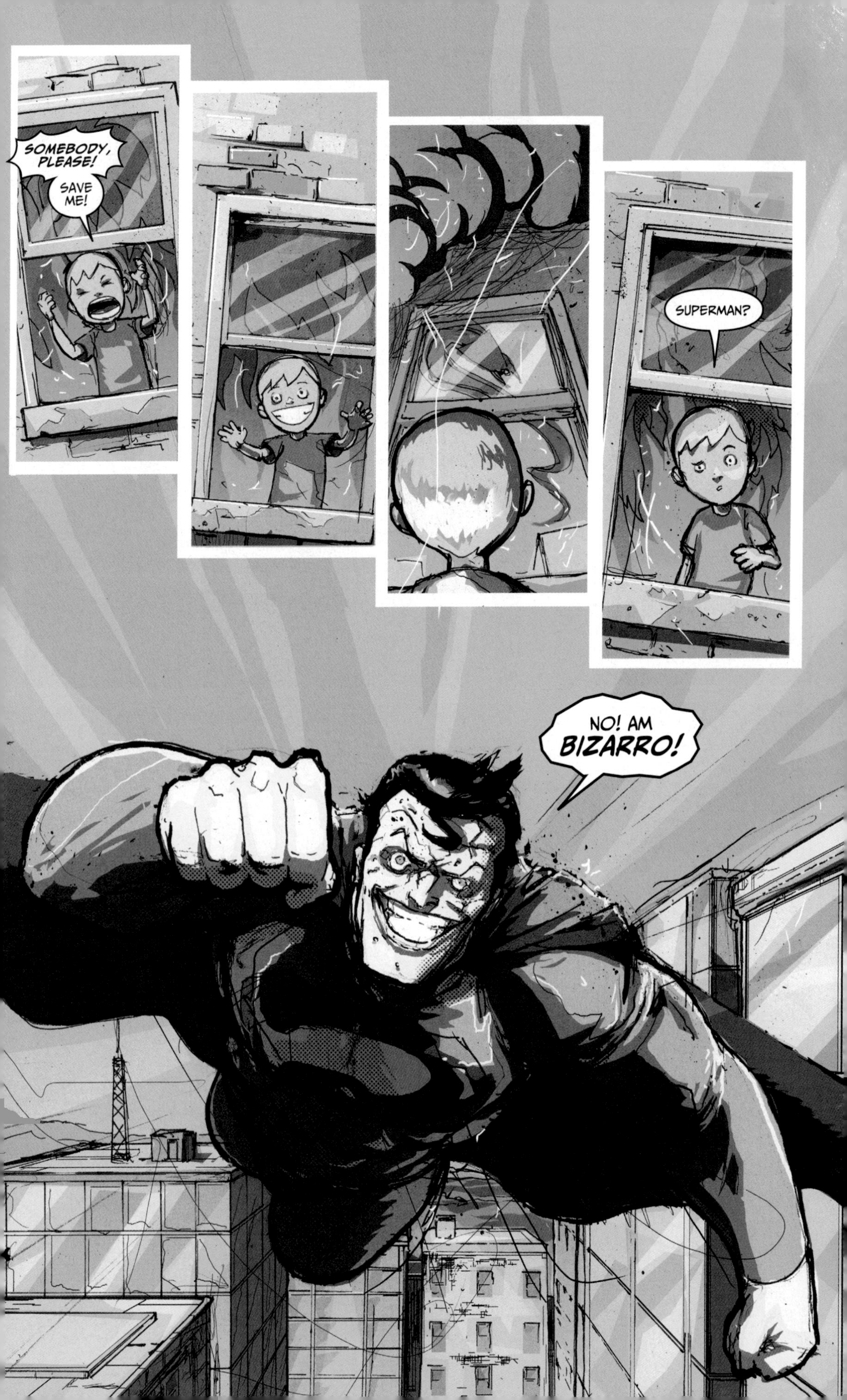
SOMEBODY, PLEASE!
SAVE ME!
SUPERMAN?
NO! AM BIZARRO!

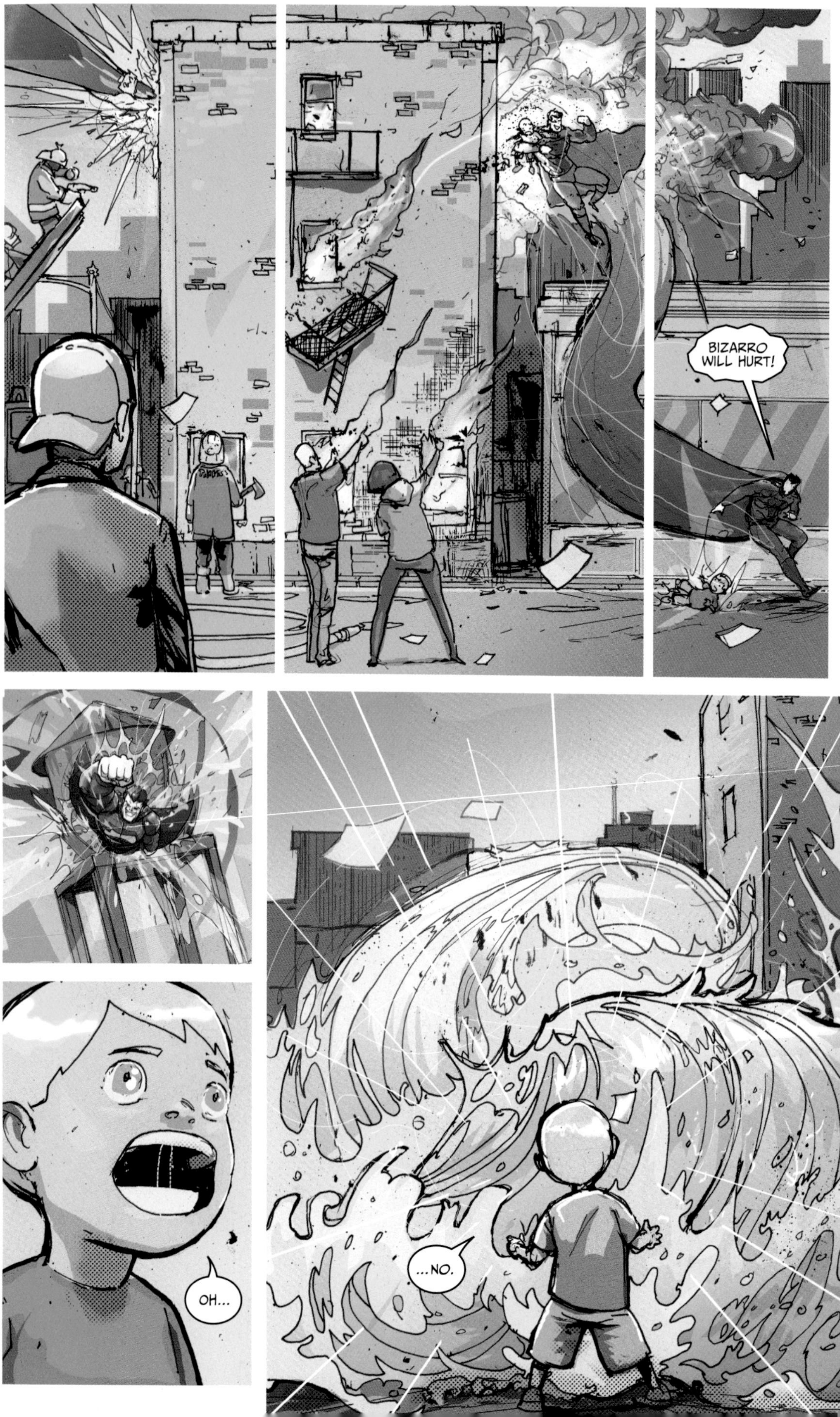
BIZARRO WILL HURT!
OH...
...NO.

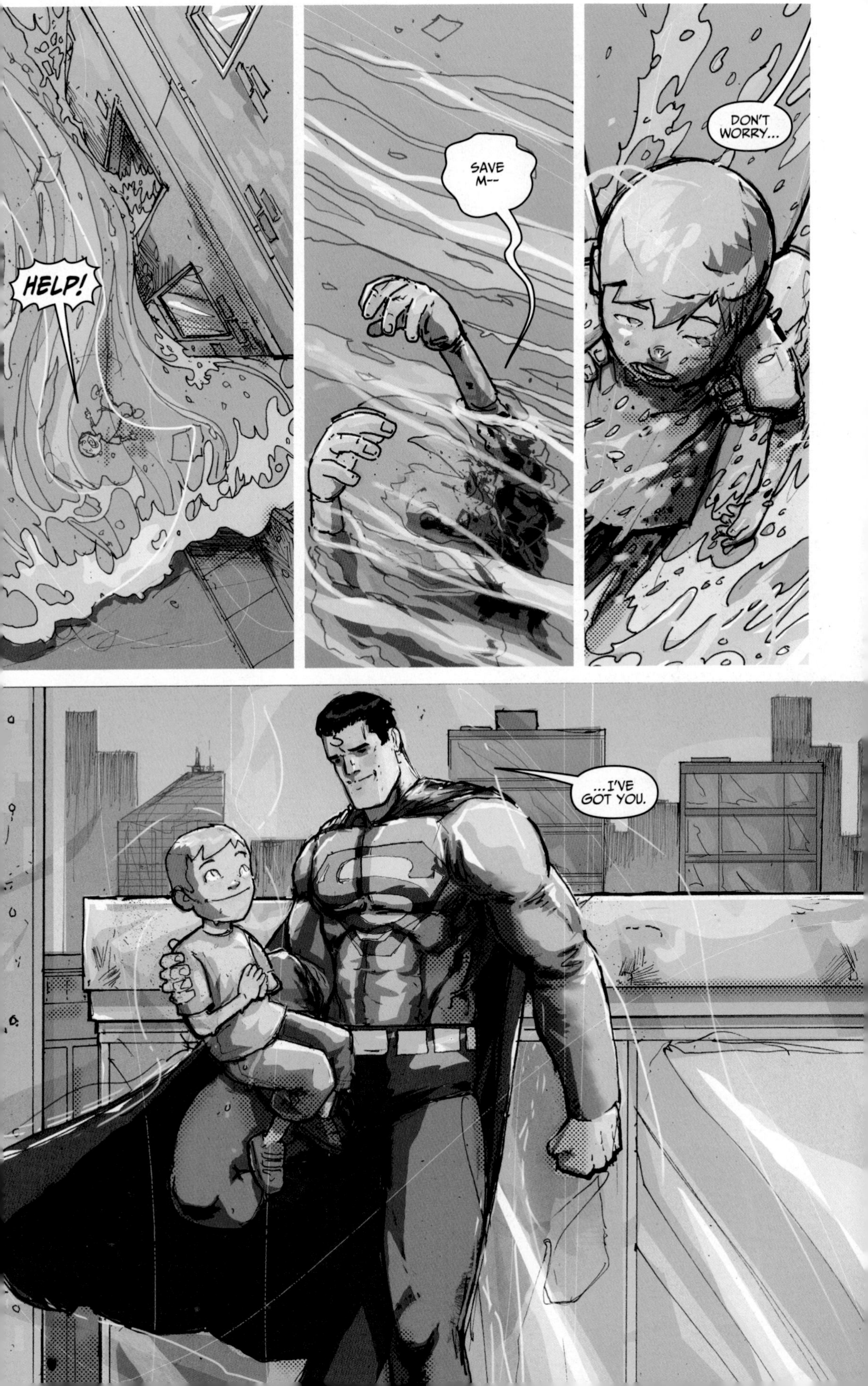
HELP!
SAVE M--
DON'T WORRY...
...I'VE GOT YOU.

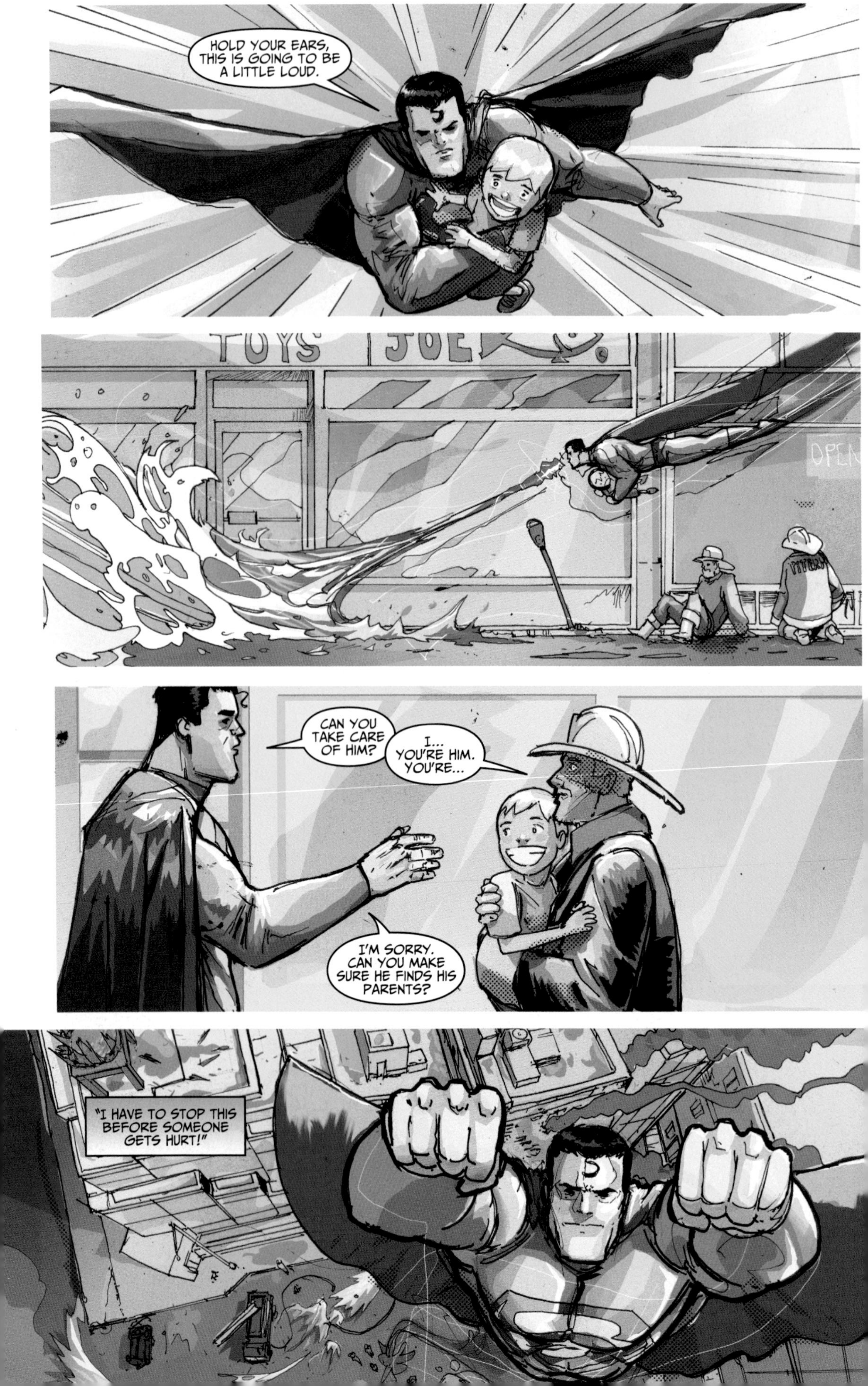
HOLD YOUR EARS, THIS IS GOING TO BE A LITTLE LOUD.
TOYS
CAN YOU TAKE CARE OF HIM?
I... YOU'RE HIM. YOU'RE...
I'M SORRY. CAN YOU MAKE SURE HE FINDS HIS PARENTS?
"I HAVE TO STOP THIS BEFORE SOMEONE GETS HURT!"

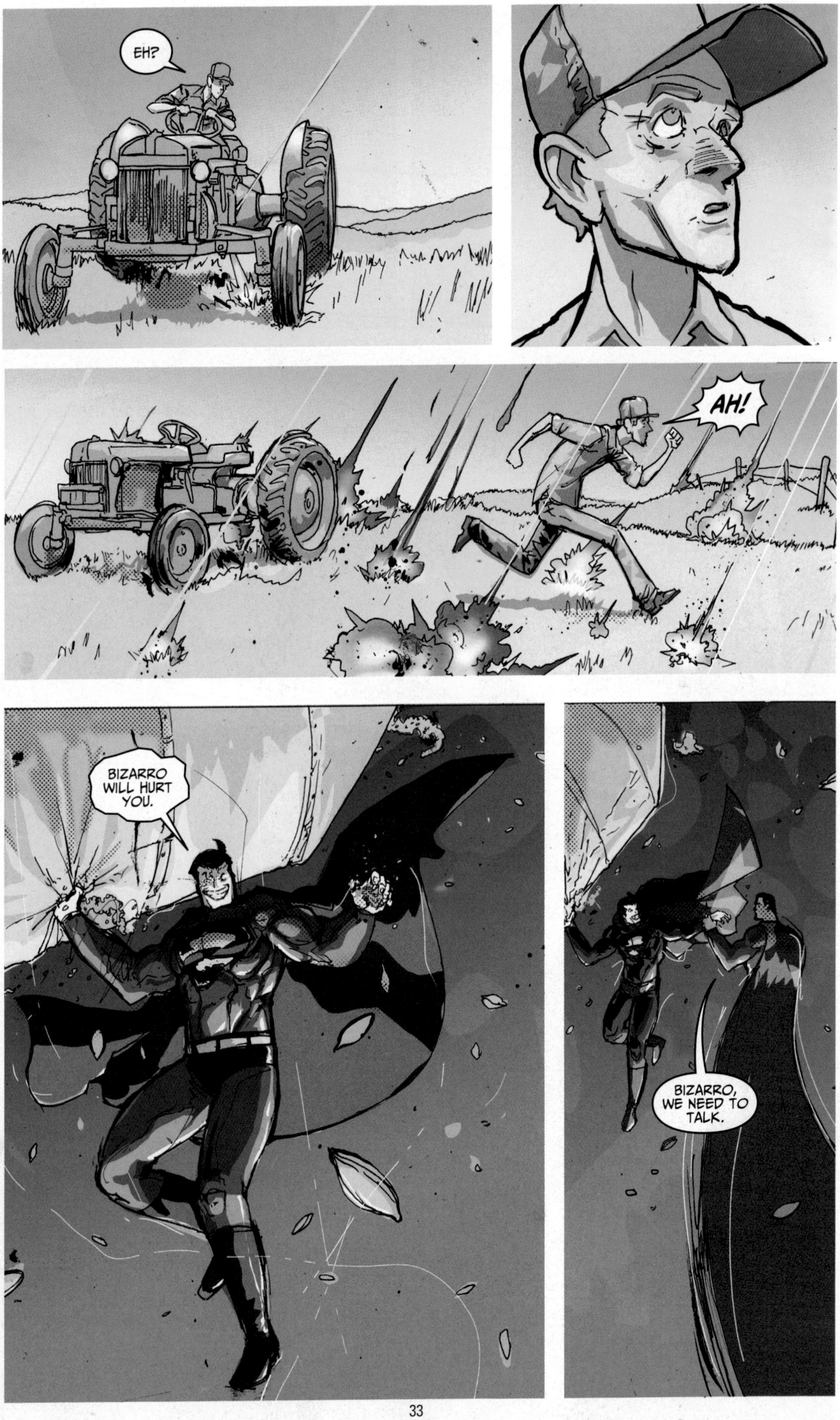
EH?
AH!
BIZARRO WILL HURT YOU.
BIZARRO, WE NEED TO TALK.

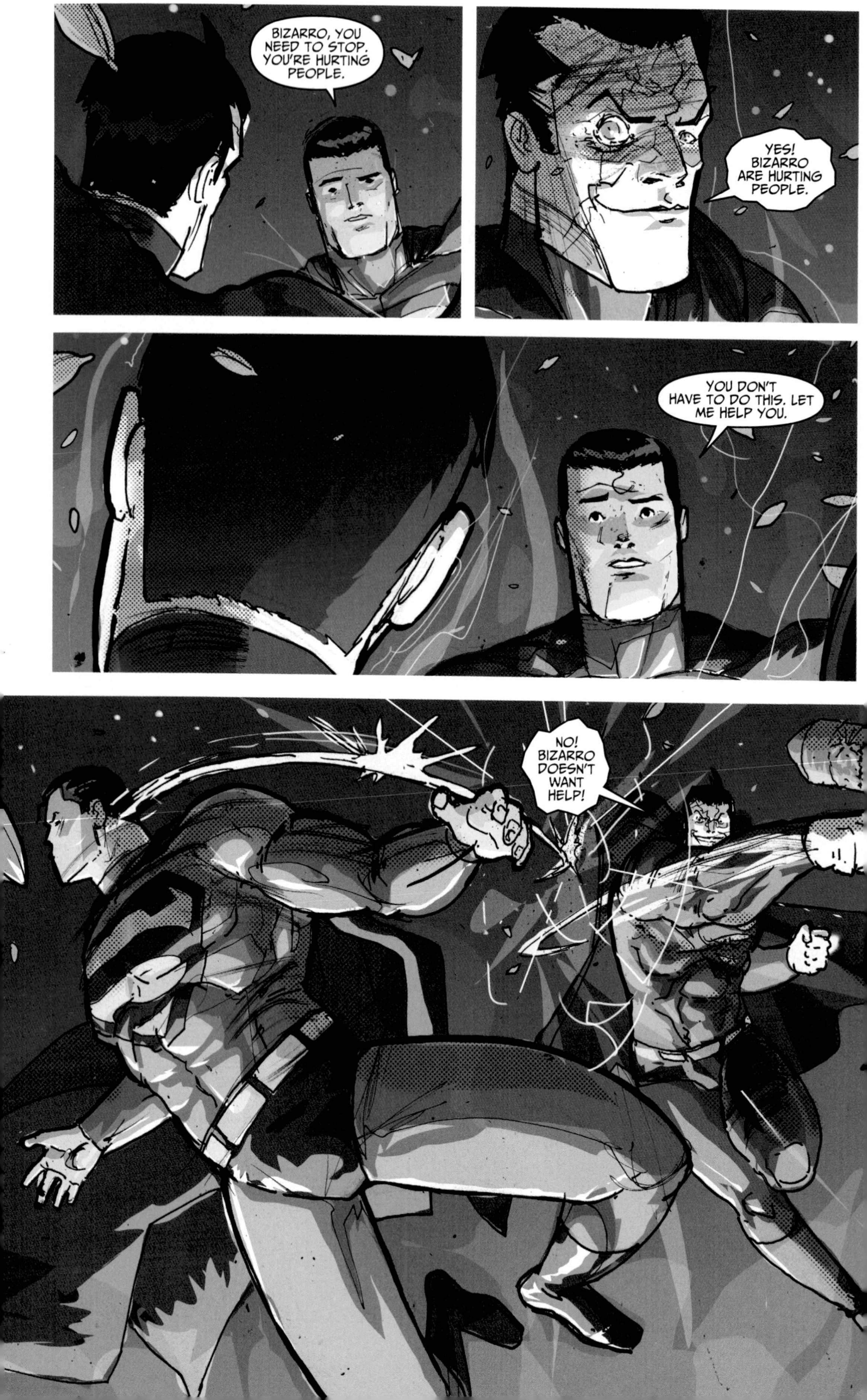

BIZARRO, YOU NEED TO STOP. YOU'RE HURTING PEOPLE.
YES! BIZARRO ARE HURTING PEOPLE.
YOU DON'T HAVE TO DO THIS. LET ME HELP YOU.
NO! BIZARRO DOESN'T WANT HELP!

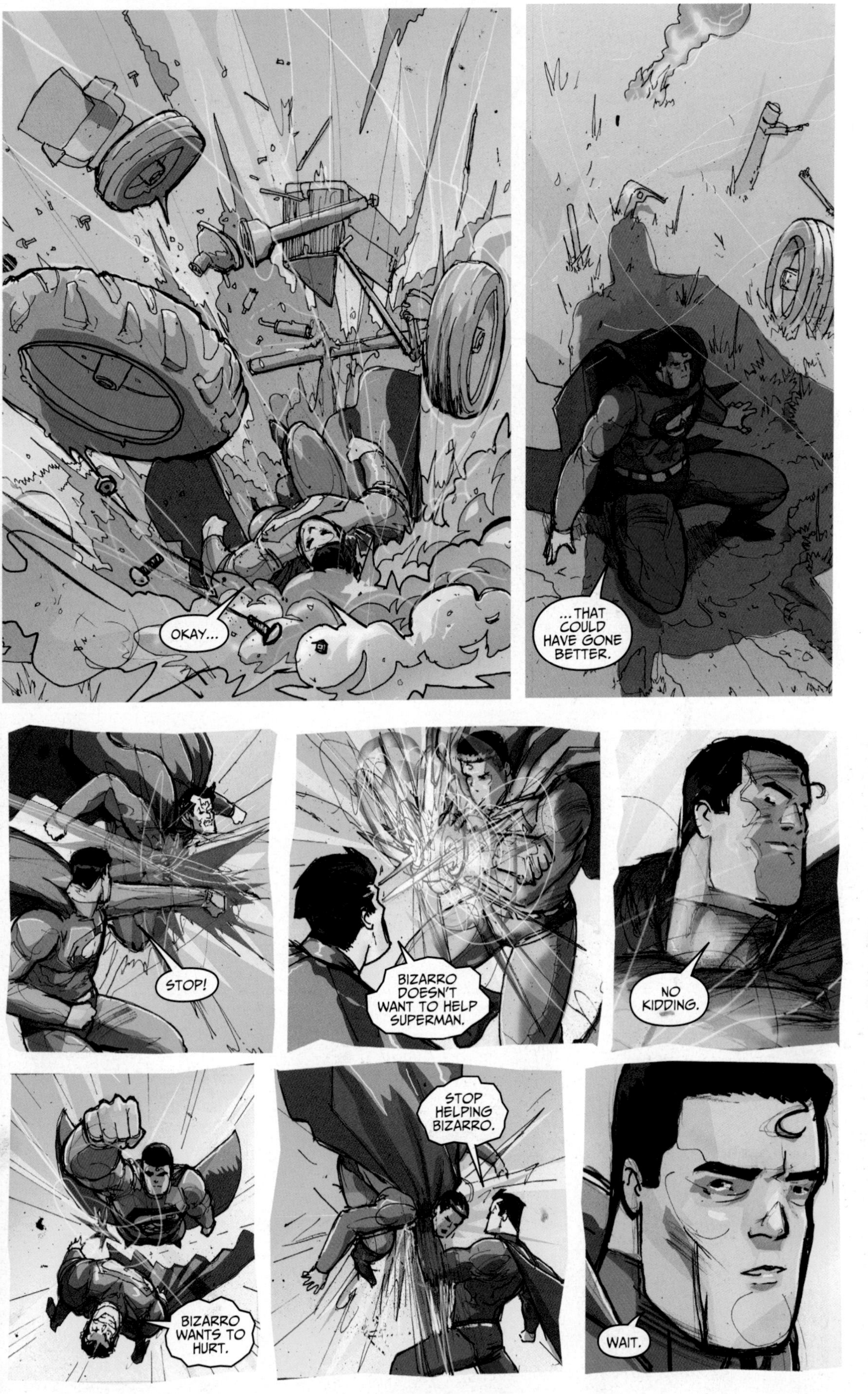
OKAY...
...THAT COULD HAVE GONE BETTER.
STOP!
BIZARRO DOESN'T WANT TO HELP SUPERMAN.
NO KIDDING.
BIZARRO WANTS TO HURT.
STOP HELPING BIZARRO.
WAIT.

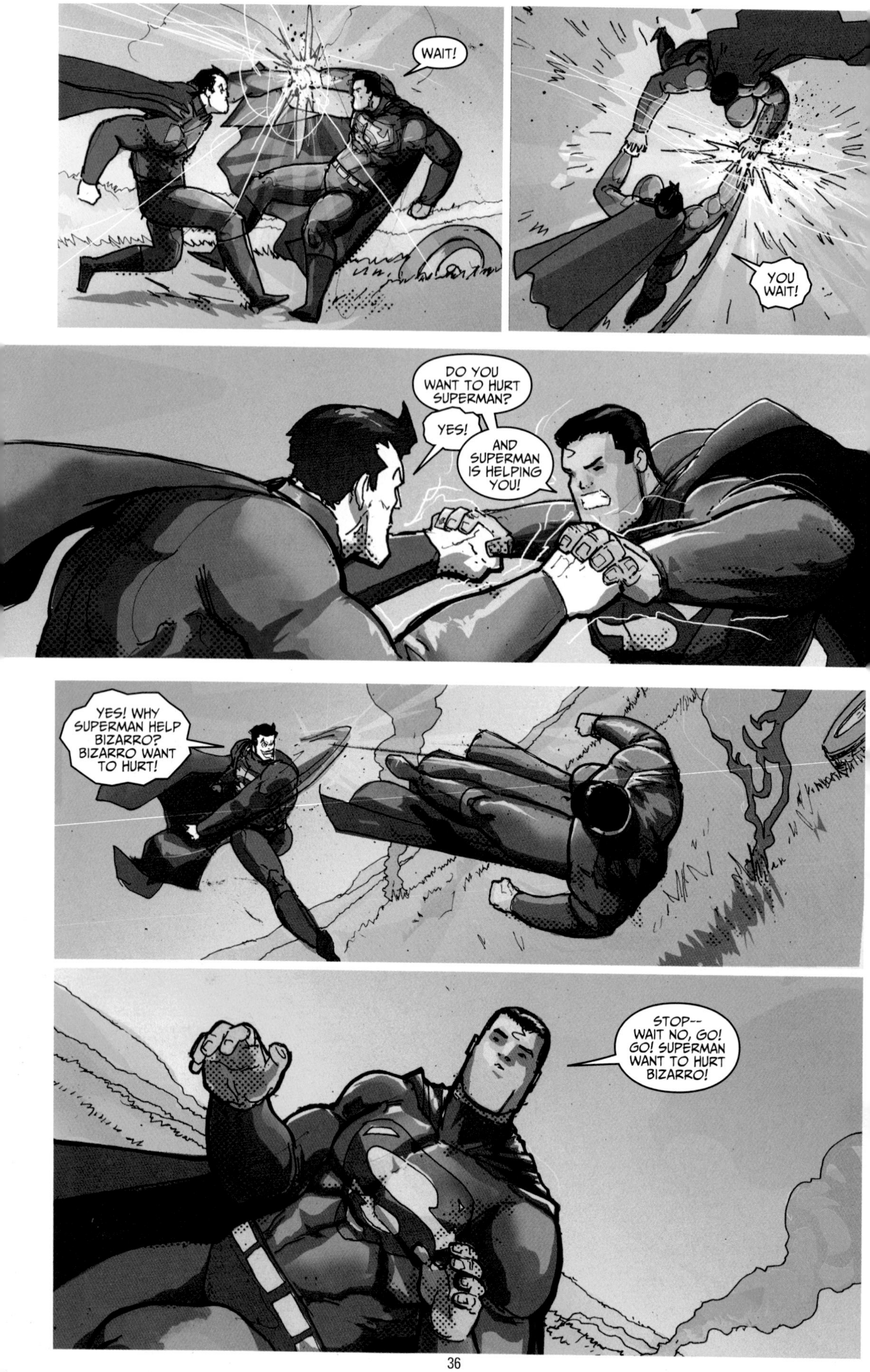
WAIT!
YOU WAIT!
DO YOU WANT TO HURT SUPERMAN?
YES!
AND SUPERMAN IS HELPING YOU!
YES! WHY SUPERMAN HELP BIZARRO? BIZARRO WANT TO HURT!
STOP-- WAIT NO, GO! GO! SUPERMAN WANT TO HURT BIZARRO!

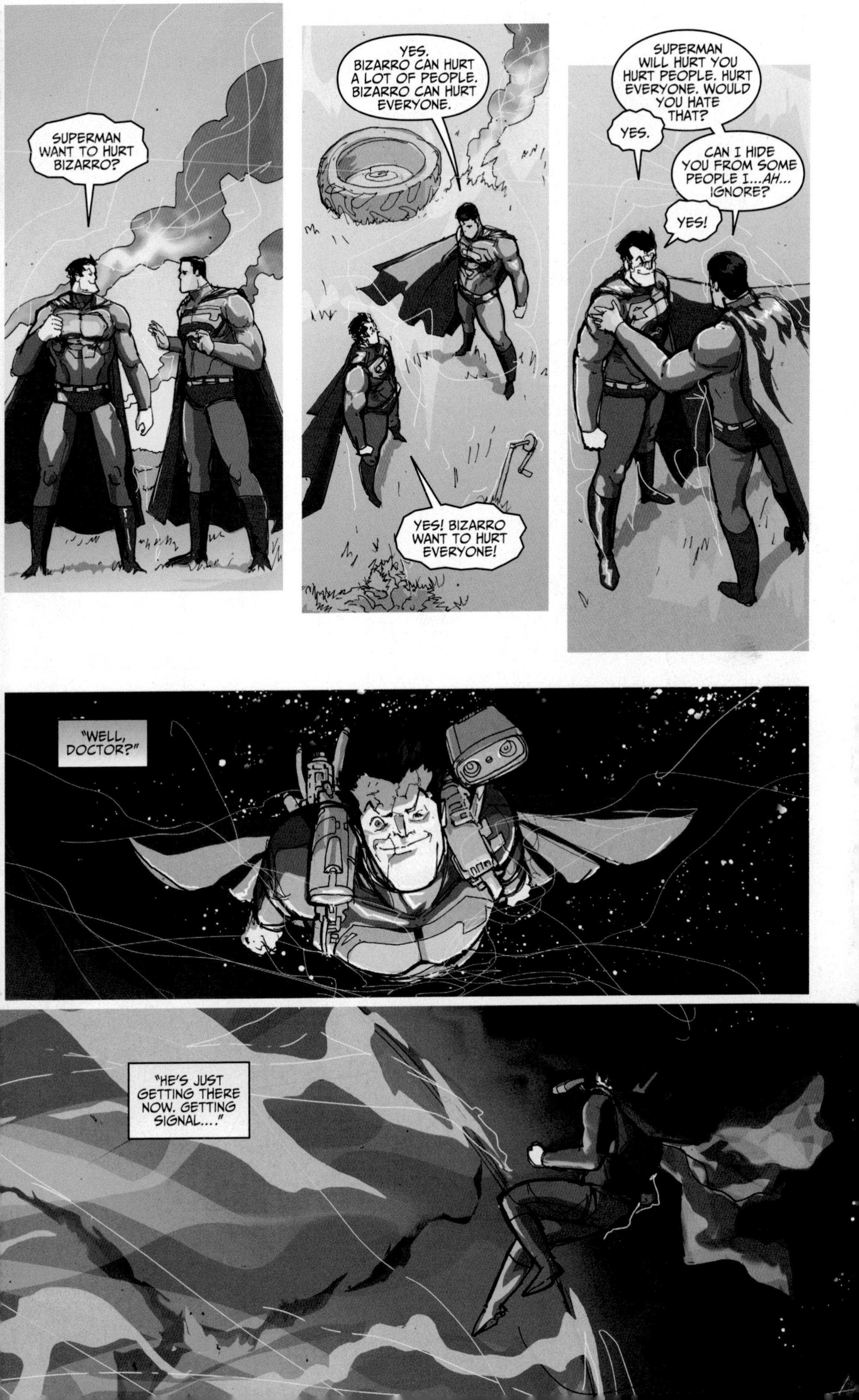
SUPERMAN WANT TO HURT BIZARRO?
YES. BIZARRO CAN HURT A LOT OF PEOPLE. BIZARRO CAN HURT EVERYONE.
YES! BIZARRO WANT TO HURT EVERYONE!
SUPERMAN WILL HURT YOU HURT PEOPLE. HURT EVERYONE. WOULD YOU HATE THAT?
YES.
CAN I HIDE YOU FROM SOME PEOPLE I...AH... IGNORE?
YES!
"WELL, DOCTOR?"
"HE'S JUST GETTING THERE NOW. GETTING SIGNAL...."

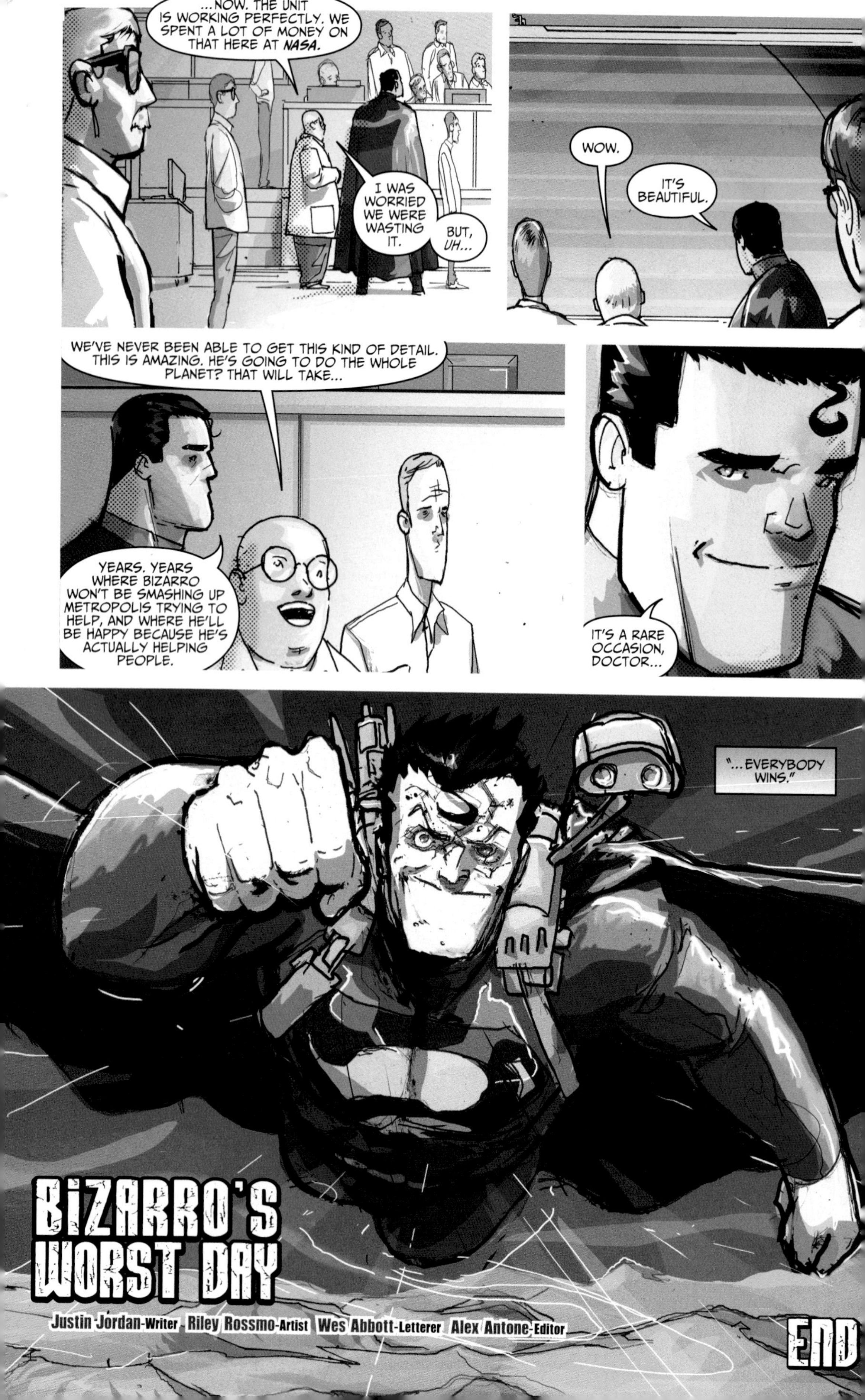
...NOW. THE UNIT IS WORKING PERFECTLY. WE SPENT A LOT OF MONEY ON THAT HERE AT NASA.
I WAS WORRIED WE WERE WASTING IT.
BUT, UH...
WOW.
IT'S BEAUTIFUL.
WE'VE NEVER BEEN ABLE TO GET THIS KIND OF DETAIL. THIS IS AMAZING. HE'S GOING TO DO THE WHOLE PLANET? THAT WILL TAKE...
YEARS. YEARS WHERE BIZARRO WON'T BE SMASHING UP METROPOLIS TRYING TO HELP, AND WHERE HE'LL BE HAPPY BECAUSE HE'S ACTUALLY HELPING PEOPLE.
IT'S A RARE OCCASION, DOCTOR...
"...EVERYBODY WINS."
BIZARRO'S WORST DAY
Justin Jordan-Writer Riley Rossmo-Artist Wes Abbott-Letterer Alex Antone-Editor
END

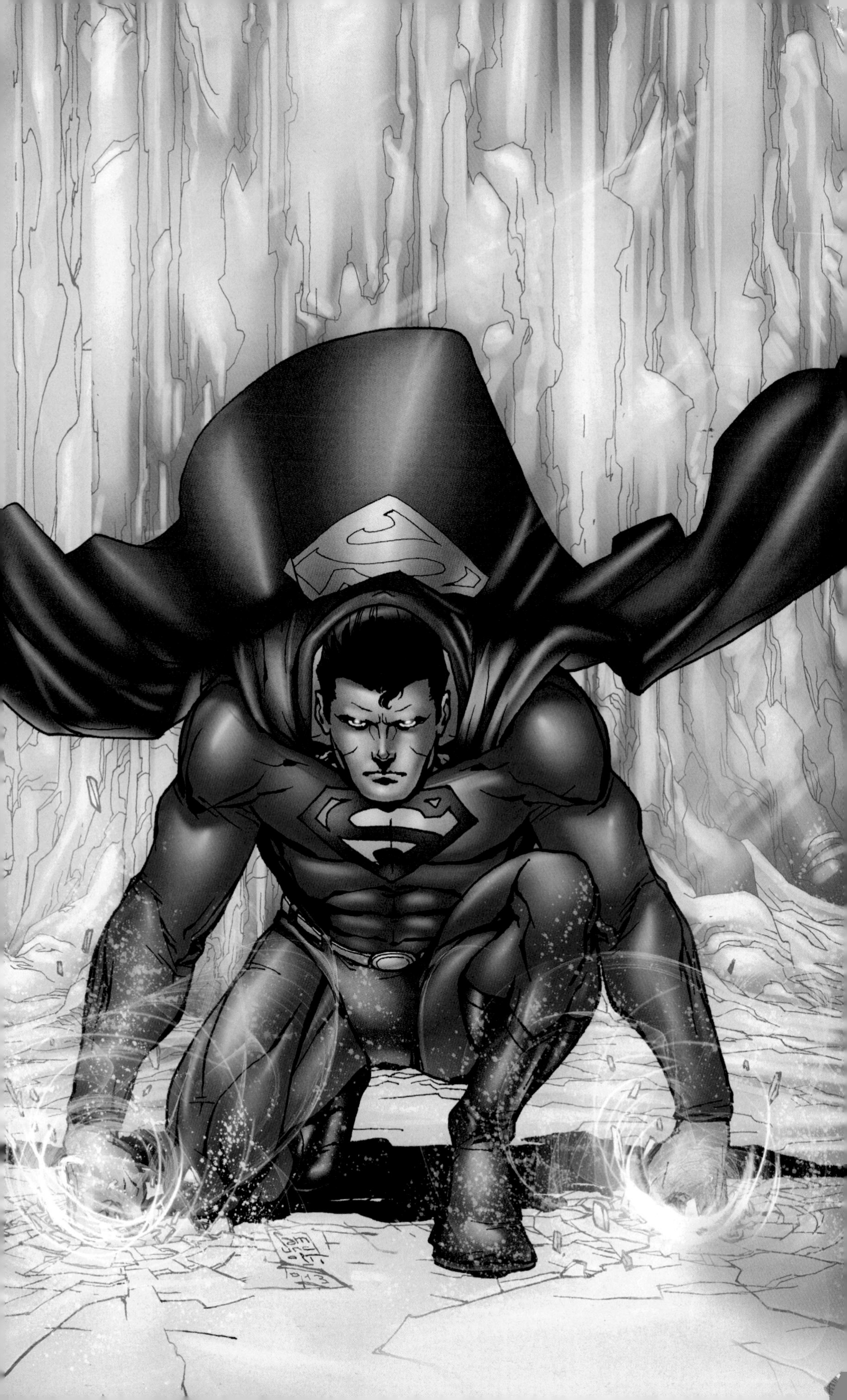

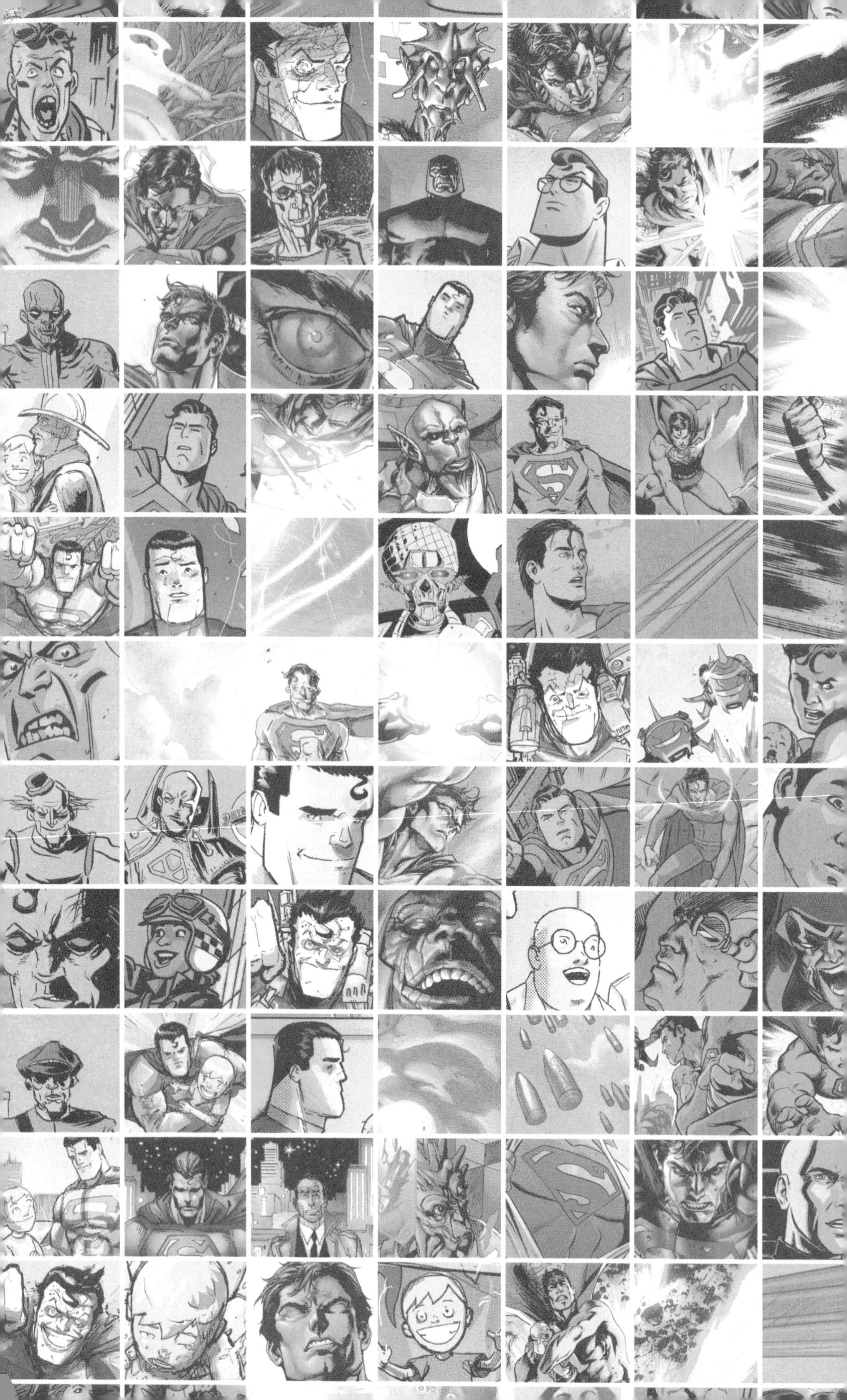

I KNOW IT'S SOMEWHAT... IMMODEST TO SAY THIS...

LOOK! UP IN THE SKY!

...BUT I LOVE BEING ME!

HERE'S A LITTLE EGO IN THAT STATEMENT, SURE--BUT THIS ISN'T ABOUT ME FEELING SELF-IMPORTANT OR BETTER THAN ANYBODY.

IT'S ABOUT THE SHEER JOY OF BEING ABLE TO MAKE A DIFFERENCE IN THIS WORLD. OF HELPING PEOPLE. DOING THE RIGHT THING.

SURE, IT HELPS THAT I'M...WHAT DO THEY LIKE TO SAY?..."MORE POWERFUL THAN A LOCOMOTIVE."

BUT MY TRUE POWER COMES FROM WHAT MY PARENTS TAUGHT ME:

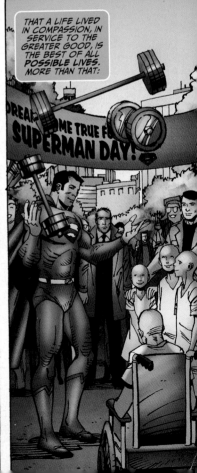

THAT A LIFE LIVED IN COMPASSION, IN SERVICE TO THE GREATER GOOD, IS THE BEST OF ALL POSSIBLE LIVES. MORE THAN THAT:

DREAM COME TRUE FOR SUPERMAN DAY!

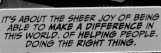

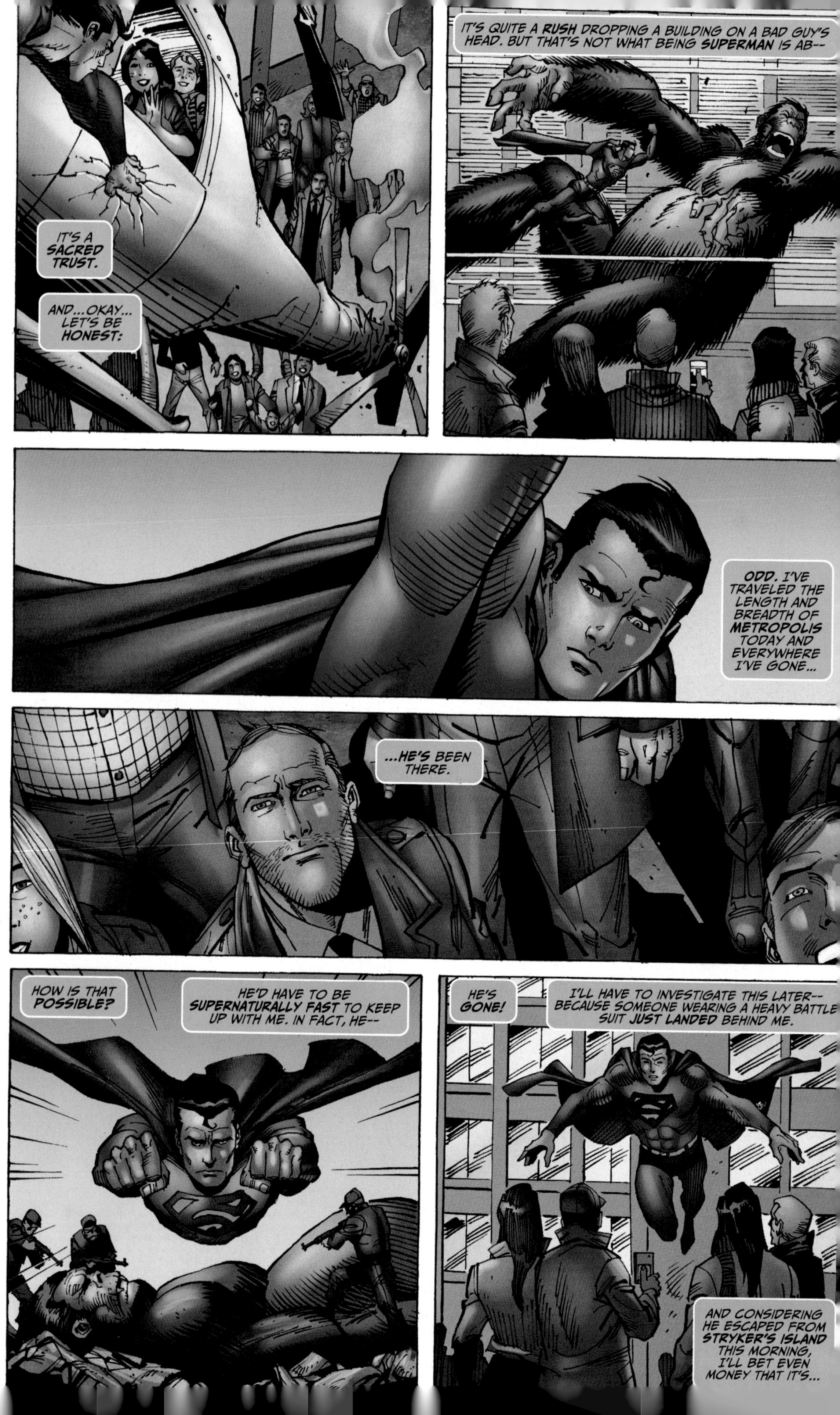
IT'S A SACRED TRUST.
AND...OKAY... LET'S BE HONEST:
IT'S QUITE A RUSH DROPPING A BUILDING ON A BAD GUY'S HEAD. BUT THAT'S NOT WHAT BEING SUPERMAN IS AB--
ODD. I'VE TRAVELED THE LENGTH AND BREADTH OF METROPOLIS TODAY AND EVERYWHERE I'VE GONE...
...HE'S BEEN THERE.
HOW IS THAT POSSIBLE?
HE'D HAVE TO BE SUPERNATURALLY FAST TO KEEP UP WITH ME. IN FACT, HE--
HE'S GONE!
I'LL HAVE TO INVESTIGATE THIS LATER--BECAUSE SOMEONE WEARING A HEAVY BATTLE SUIT JUST LANDED BEHIND ME.
AND CONSIDERING HE ESCAPED FROM STRYKER'S ISLAND THIS MORNING, I'LL BET EVEN MONEY THAT IT'S...

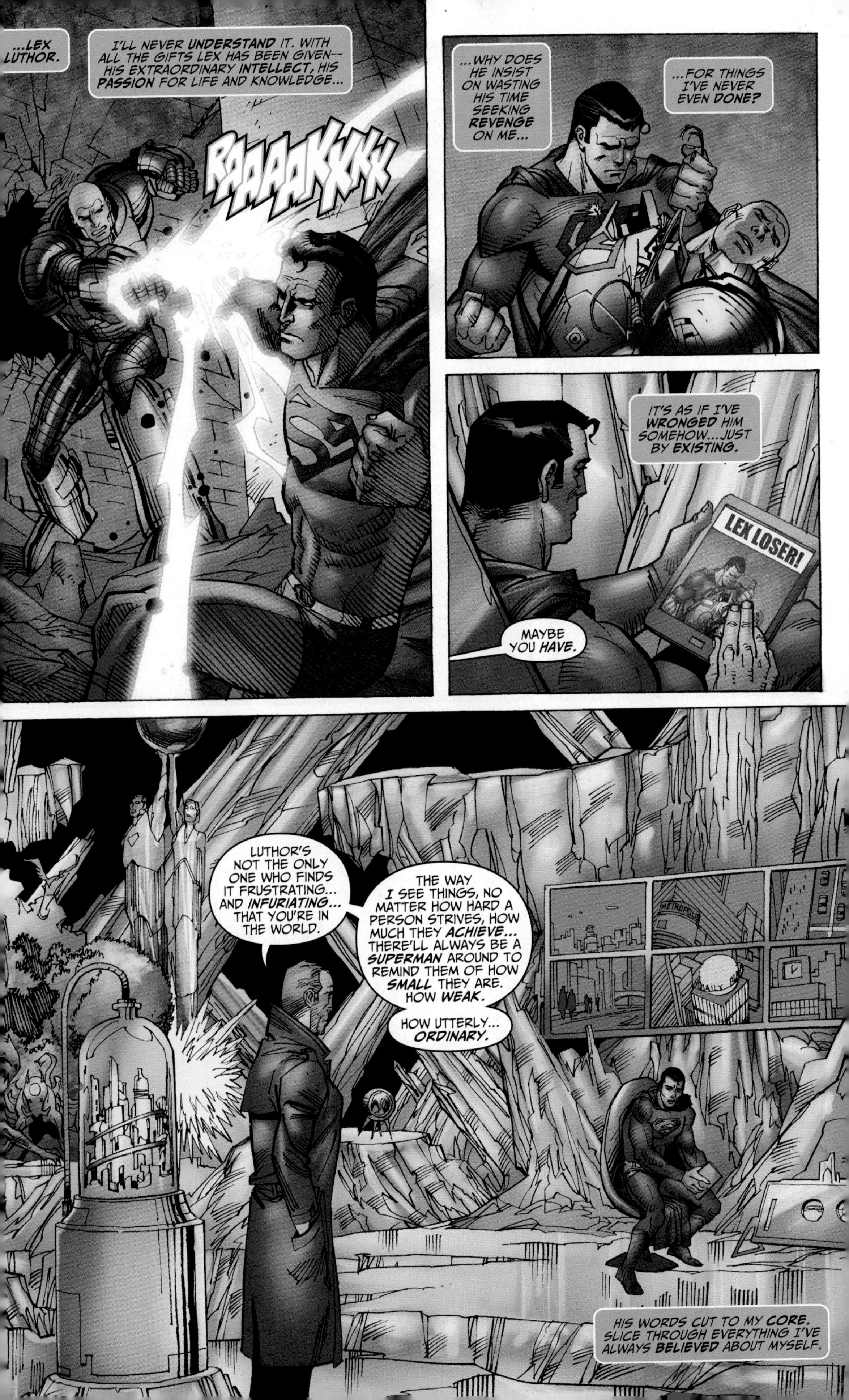

...LEX LUTHOR.
I'LL NEVER UNDERSTAND IT. WITH ALL THE GIFTS LEX HAS BEEN GIVEN-- HIS EXTRAORDINARY INTELLECT, HIS PASSION FOR LIFE AND KNOWLEDGE...
RAAAAKKKK
...WHY DOES HE INSIST ON WASTING HIS TIME SEEKING REVENGE ON ME...
...FOR THINGS I'VE NEVER EVEN DONE?
IT'S AS IF I'VE WRONGED HIM SOMEHOW...JUST BY EXISTING.
LEX LOSER!
MAYBE YOU HAVE.
LUTHOR'S NOT THE ONLY ONE WHO FINDS IT FRUSTRATING... AND INFURIATING... THAT YOU'RE IN THE WORLD.
THE WAY I SEE THINGS, NO MATTER HOW HARD A PERSON STRIVES, HOW MUCH THEY ACHIEVE... THERE'LL ALWAYS BE A SUPERMAN AROUND TO REMIND THEM OF HOW SMALL THEY ARE. HOW WEAK.
HOW UTTERLY... ORDINARY.
METROPOLIS
HIS WORDS CUT TO MY CORE. SLICE THROUGH EVERYTHING I'VE ALWAYS BELIEVED ABOUT MYSELF.

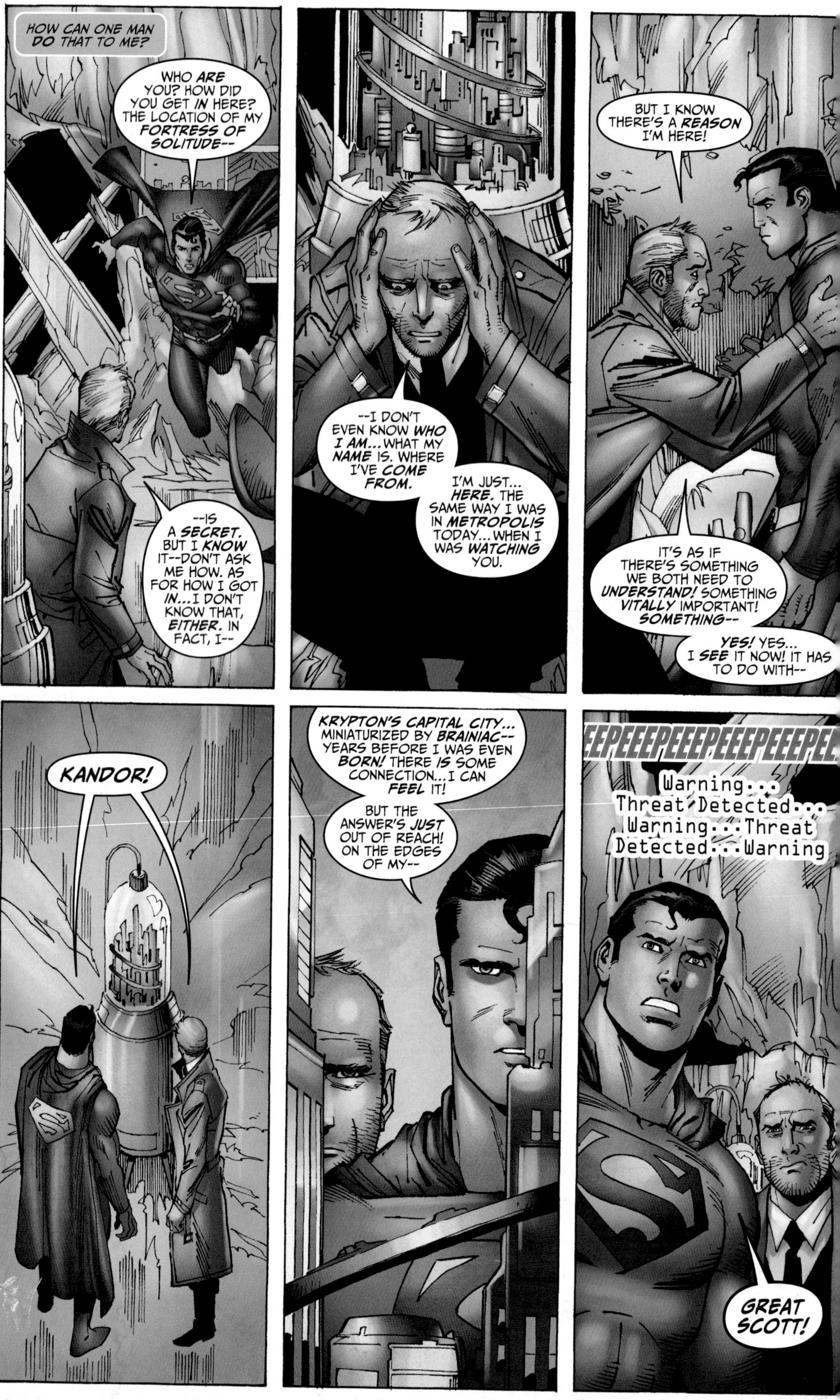
HOW CAN ONE MAN DO THAT TO ME?
WHO ARE YOU? HOW DID YOU GET IN HERE? THE LOCATION OF MY FORTRESS OF SOLITUDE--
--IS A SECRET. BUT I KNOW IT--DON'T ASK ME HOW. AS FOR HOW I GOT IN...I DON'T KNOW THAT, EITHER. IN FACT, I--
--I DON'T EVEN KNOW WHO I AM...WHAT MY NAME IS. WHERE I'VE COME FROM.
I'M JUST... HERE. THE SAME WAY I WAS IN METROPOLIS TODAY...WHEN I WAS WATCHING YOU.
BUT I KNOW THERE'S A REASON I'M HERE!
IT'S AS IF THERE'S SOMETHING WE BOTH NEED TO UNDERSTAND! SOMETHING VITALLY IMPORTANT! SOMETHING--
YES! YES... I SEE IT NOW! IT HAS TO DO WITH--
KANDOR!
KRYPTON'S CAPITAL CITY... MINIATURIZED BY BRAINIAC-- YEARS BEFORE I WAS EVEN BORN! THERE IS SOME CONNECTION...I CAN FEEL IT!
BUT THE ANSWER'S JUST OUT OF REACH! ON THE EDGES OF MY--
EEPEEEPEEEPEEEPEEEPEE
Warning... Threat Detected... Warning...Threat Detected...Warning
GREAT SCOTT!

ALIEN WARSHIPS! DOZENS OF THEM--

--HEADING STRAIGHT FOR METROPOLIS!

"GREAT SCOTT"? REALLY? WELL, GO AHEAD-- PROVE, ONCE AGAIN, THAT YOU'RE THE ONLY MAN ON EARTH WHO--

CAN...

GONE AGAIN...AND SUDDENLY THE ENTIRE WORLD FEELS LIKE IT COULD VANISH--AS QUICKLY AS HE DID.

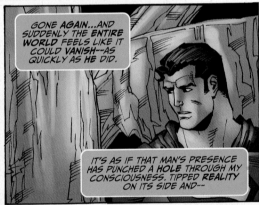

IT'S AS IF THAT MAN'S PRESENCE HAS PUNCHED A HOLE THROUGH MY CONSCIOUSNESS. TIPPED REALITY ON ITS SIDE AND--

NO! I'VE ENCOUNTERED STRANGER RIDDLES THAN THIS OVER THE YEARS...

...AND I'VE ALWAYS FOUND THE ANSWER!

NOW'S NOT THE TIME TO START DOUBTING MYSELF...OR MY SANITY.

NOW'S THE TIME TO PROTECT THE CITY AND THE PEOPLE I LOVE.

METROPOLIS IS DEPENDING ON ME. AND I DON'T INTEND TO LET HER--

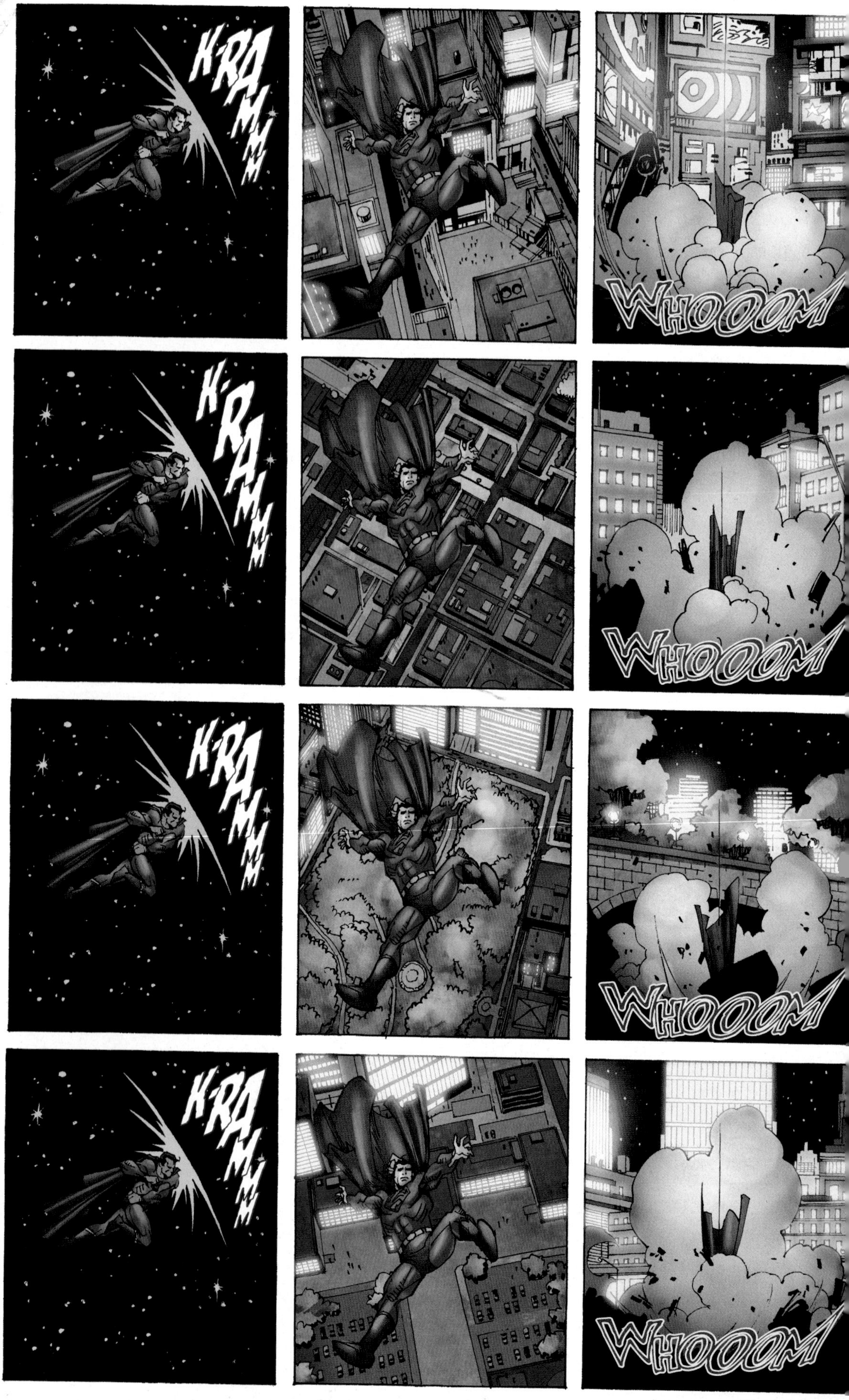
K-RAMMM
WHOOOM
K-RAMMM
WHOOOM
K-RAMMM
WHOOOM
K-RAMMM
WHOOOM

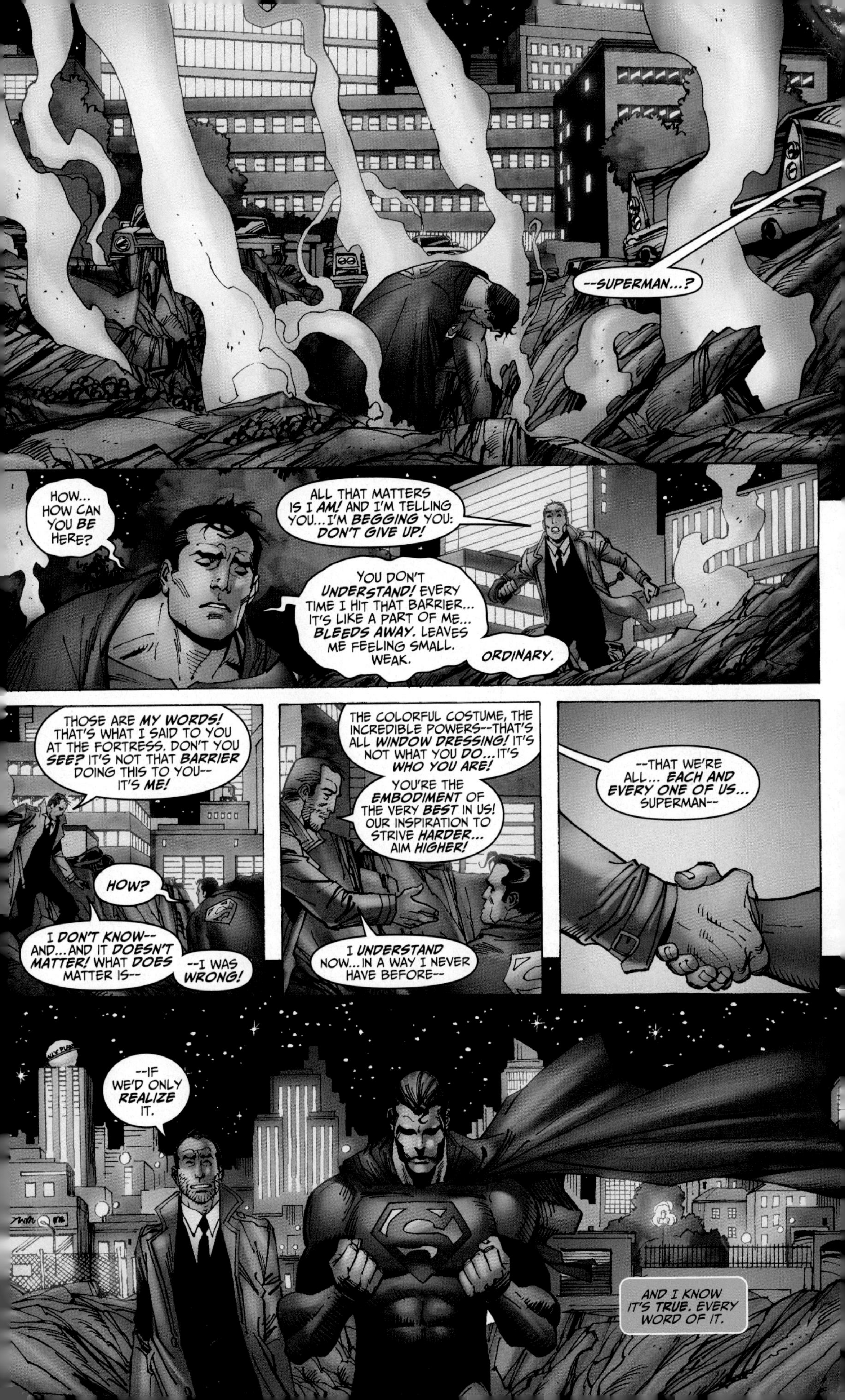
--SUPERMAN...?
HOW... HOW CAN YOU BE HERE?
ALL THAT MATTERS IS I AM! AND I'M TELLING YOU...I'M BEGGING YOU: DON'T GIVE UP!
YOU DON'T UNDERSTAND! EVERY TIME I HIT THAT BARRIER... IT'S LIKE A PART OF ME... BLEEDS AWAY. LEAVES ME FEELING SMALL. WEAK.
ORDINARY.
THOSE ARE MY WORDS! THAT'S WHAT I SAID TO YOU AT THE FORTRESS. DON'T YOU SEE? IT'S NOT THAT BARRIER DOING THIS TO YOU-- IT'S ME!
HOW?
I DON'T KNOW-- AND...AND IT DOESN'T MATTER! WHAT DOES MATTER IS--
--I WAS WRONG!
THE COLORFUL COSTUME, THE INCREDIBLE POWERS--THAT'S ALL WINDOW DRESSING! IT'S NOT WHAT YOU DO...IT'S WHO YOU ARE!
YOU'RE THE EMBODIMENT OF THE VERY BEST IN US! OUR INSPIRATION TO STRIVE HARDER... AIM HIGHER!
I UNDERSTAND NOW...IN A WAY I NEVER HAVE BEFORE--
--THAT WE'RE ALL... EACH AND EVERY ONE OF US... SUPERMAN--
--IF WE'D ONLY REALIZE IT.
AND I KNOW IT'S TRUE. EVERY WORD OF IT.

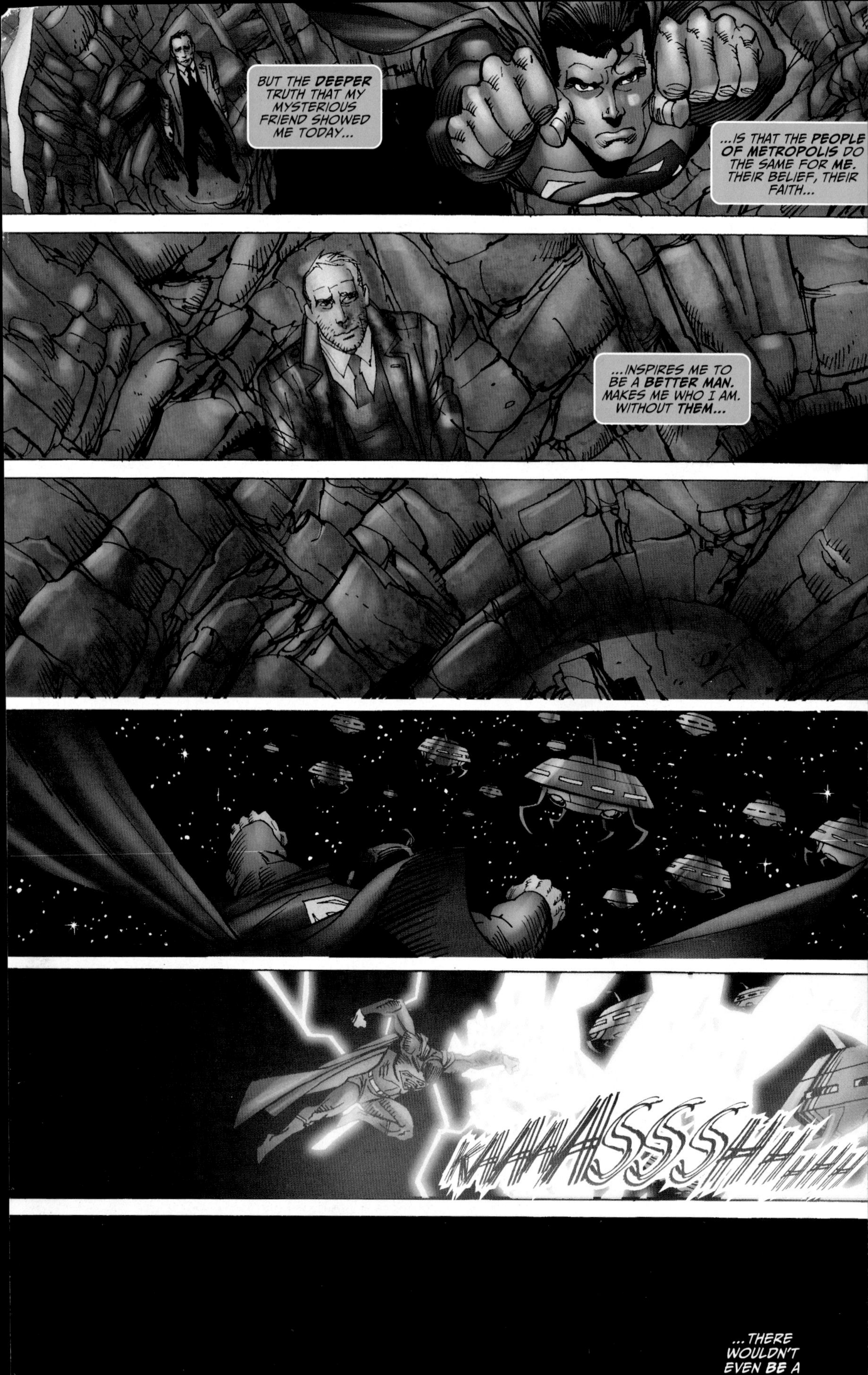
BUT THE DEEPER TRUTH THAT MY MYSTERIOUS FRIEND SHOWED ME TODAY...
...IS THAT THE PEOPLE OF METROPOLIS DO THE SAME FOR ME. THEIR BELIEF, THEIR FAITH...
...INSPIRES ME TO BE A BETTER MAN. MAKES ME WHO I AM. WITHOUT THEM...
KAHHASSSSHHHHH
...THERE WOULDN'T EVEN BE A

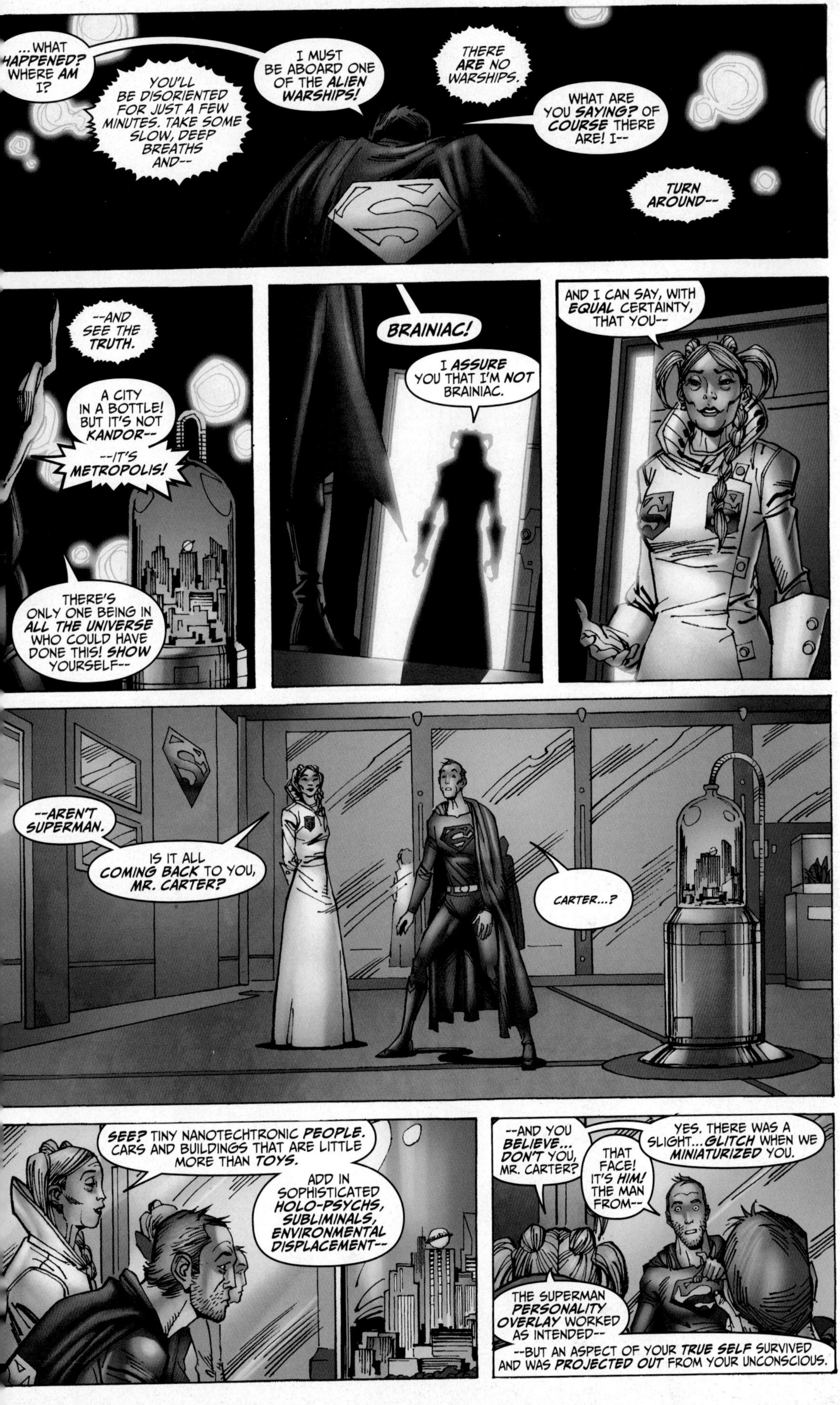
...WHAT HAPPENED? WHERE AM I?
YOU'LL BE DISORIENTED FOR JUST A FEW MINUTES. TAKE SOME SLOW, DEEP BREATHS AND--
I MUST BE ABOARD ONE OF THE ALIEN WARSHIPS!
THERE ARE NO WARSHIPS.
WHAT ARE YOU SAYING? OF COURSE THERE ARE! I--
TURN AROUND--
--AND SEE THE TRUTH.
A CITY IN A BOTTLE! BUT IT'S NOT KANDOR--
--IT'S METROPOLIS!
THERE'S ONLY ONE BEING IN ALL THE UNIVERSE WHO COULD HAVE DONE THIS! SHOW YOURSELF--
BRAINIAC!
I ASSURE YOU THAT I'M NOT BRAINIAC.
AND I CAN SAY, WITH EQUAL CERTAINTY, THAT YOU--
--AREN'T SUPERMAN.
IS IT ALL COMING BACK TO YOU, MR. CARTER?
CARTER...?
SEE? TINY NANOTECHTRONIC PEOPLE. CARS AND BUILDINGS THAT ARE LITTLE MORE THAN TOYS.
ADD IN SOPHISTICATED HOLO-PSYCHS, SUBLIMINALS, ENVIRONMENTAL DISPLACEMENT--
--AND YOU BELIEVE... DON'T YOU, MR. CARTER?
THAT FACE! IT'S HIM! THE MAN FROM--
YES. THERE WAS A SLIGHT...GLITCH WHEN WE MINIATURIZED YOU.
THE SUPERMAN PERSONALITY OVERLAY WORKED AS INTENDED--
--BUT AN ASPECT OF YOUR TRUE SELF SURVIVED AND WAS PROJECTED OUT FROM YOUR UNCONSCIOUS.

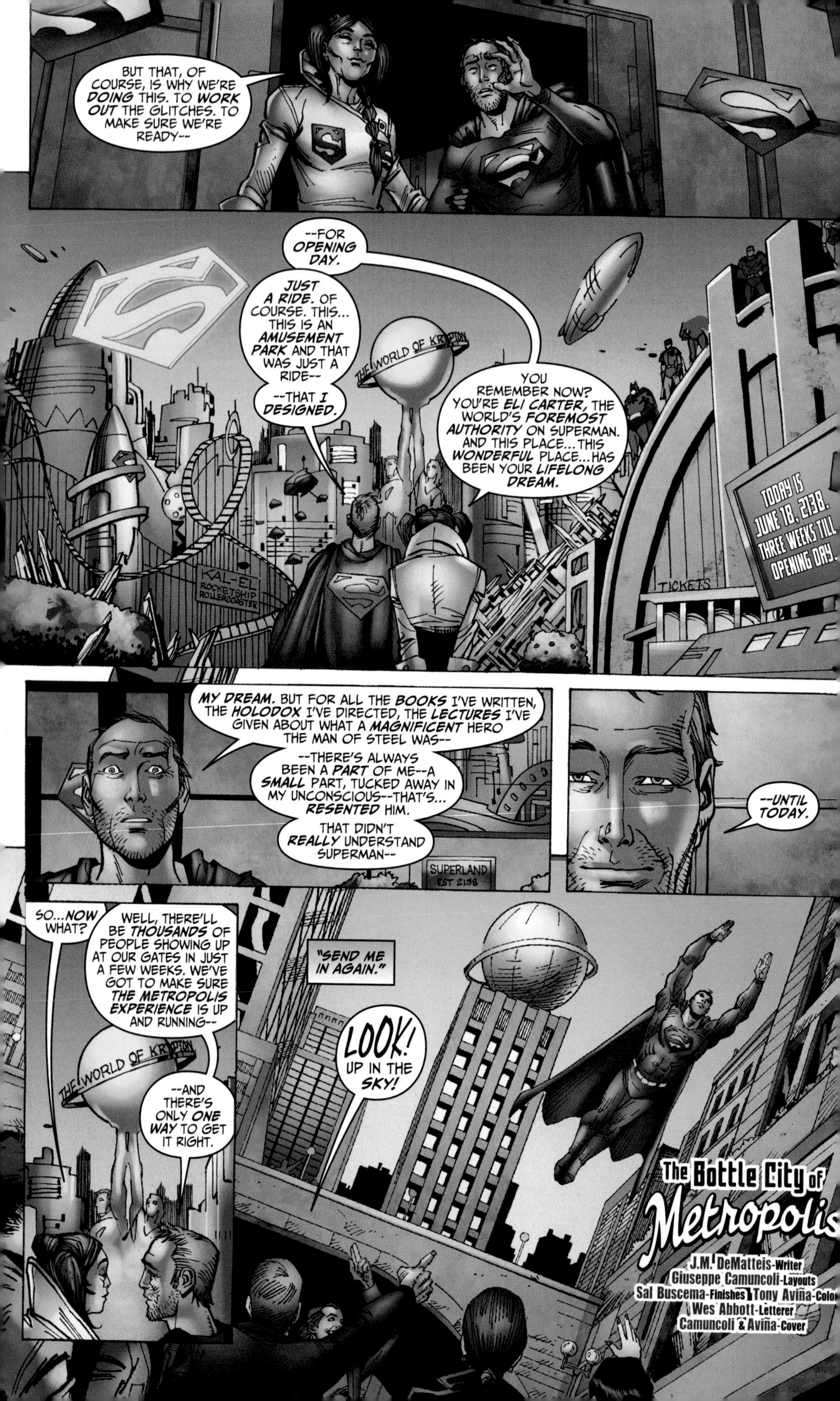

BUT THAT, OF COURSE, IS WHY WE'RE DOING THIS. TO WORK OUT THE GLITCHES. TO MAKE SURE WE'RE READY--
--FOR OPENING DAY.
JUST A RIDE. OF COURSE. THIS... THIS IS AN AMUSEMENT PARK AND THAT WAS JUST A RIDE--
--THAT I DESIGNED.
THE WORLD OF KRYPTON
YOU REMEMBER NOW? YOU'RE ELI CARTER, THE WORLD'S FOREMOST AUTHORITY ON SUPERMAN. AND THIS PLACE...THIS WONDERFUL PLACE...HAS BEEN YOUR LIFELONG DREAM.
KAL-EL ROCKETSHIP ROLLERCOASTER
TICKETS
TODAY IS JUNE 18, 2138. THREE WEEKS TILL OPENING DAY.
MY DREAM. BUT FOR ALL THE BOOKS I'VE WRITTEN, THE HOLODOX I'VE DIRECTED, THE LECTURES I'VE GIVEN ABOUT WHAT A MAGNIFICENT HERO THE MAN OF STEEL WAS--
--THERE'S ALWAYS BEEN A PART OF ME--A SMALL PART, TUCKED AWAY IN MY UNCONSCIOUS--THAT'S... RESENTED HIM.
THAT DIDN'T REALLY UNDERSTAND SUPERMAN--
SUPERLAND EST 2138
--UNTIL TODAY.
SO...NOW WHAT?
WELL, THERE'LL BE THOUSANDS OF PEOPLE SHOWING UP AT OUR GATES IN JUST A FEW WEEKS. WE'VE GOT TO MAKE SURE THE METROPOLIS EXPERIENCE IS UP AND RUNNING--
--AND THERE'S ONLY ONE WAY TO GET IT RIGHT.
THE WORLD OF KRYPTON
"SEND ME IN AGAIN."
LOOK! UP IN THE SKY!
The Bottle City of Metropolis
J.M. DeMatteis-Writer
Giuseppe Camuncoli-Layouts
Sal Buscema-Finishes Tony Aviña-Colo
Wes Abbott-Letterer
Camuncoli & Aviña-Cover

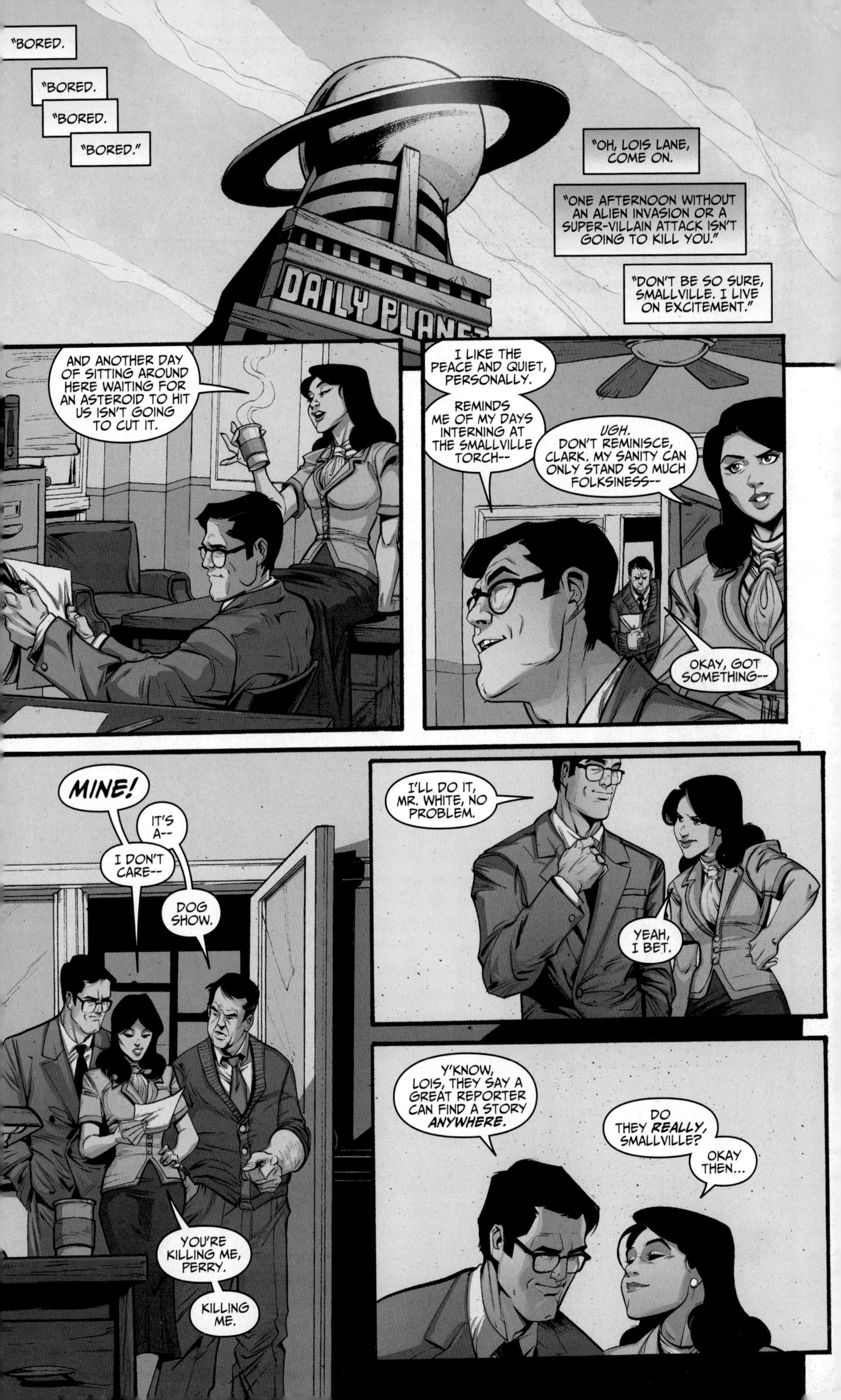
"BORED.
"BORED.
"BORED.
"BORED."
"OH, LOIS LANE, COME ON.
"ONE AFTERNOON WITHOUT AN ALIEN INVASION OR A SUPER-VILLAIN ATTACK ISN'T GOING TO KILL YOU."
"DON'T BE SO SURE, SMALLVILLE. I LIVE ON EXCITEMENT."
DAILY PLANET
AND ANOTHER DAY OF SITTING AROUND HERE WAITING FOR AN ASTEROID TO HIT US ISN'T GOING TO CUT IT.
I LIKE THE PEACE AND QUIET, PERSONALLY.
REMINDS ME OF MY DAYS INTERNING AT THE SMALLVILLE TORCH--
UGH. DON'T REMINISCE, CLARK. MY SANITY CAN ONLY STAND SO MUCH FOLKSINESS--
OKAY, GOT SOMETHING--
MINE!
IT'S A--
I DON'T CARE--
DOG SHOW.
YOU'RE KILLING ME, PERRY.
KILLING ME.
I'LL DO IT, MR. WHITE, NO PROBLEM.
YEAH, I BET.
Y'KNOW, LOIS, THEY SAY A GREAT REPORTER CAN FIND A STORY ANYWHERE.
DO THEY REALLY, SMALLVILLE?
OKAY THEN...

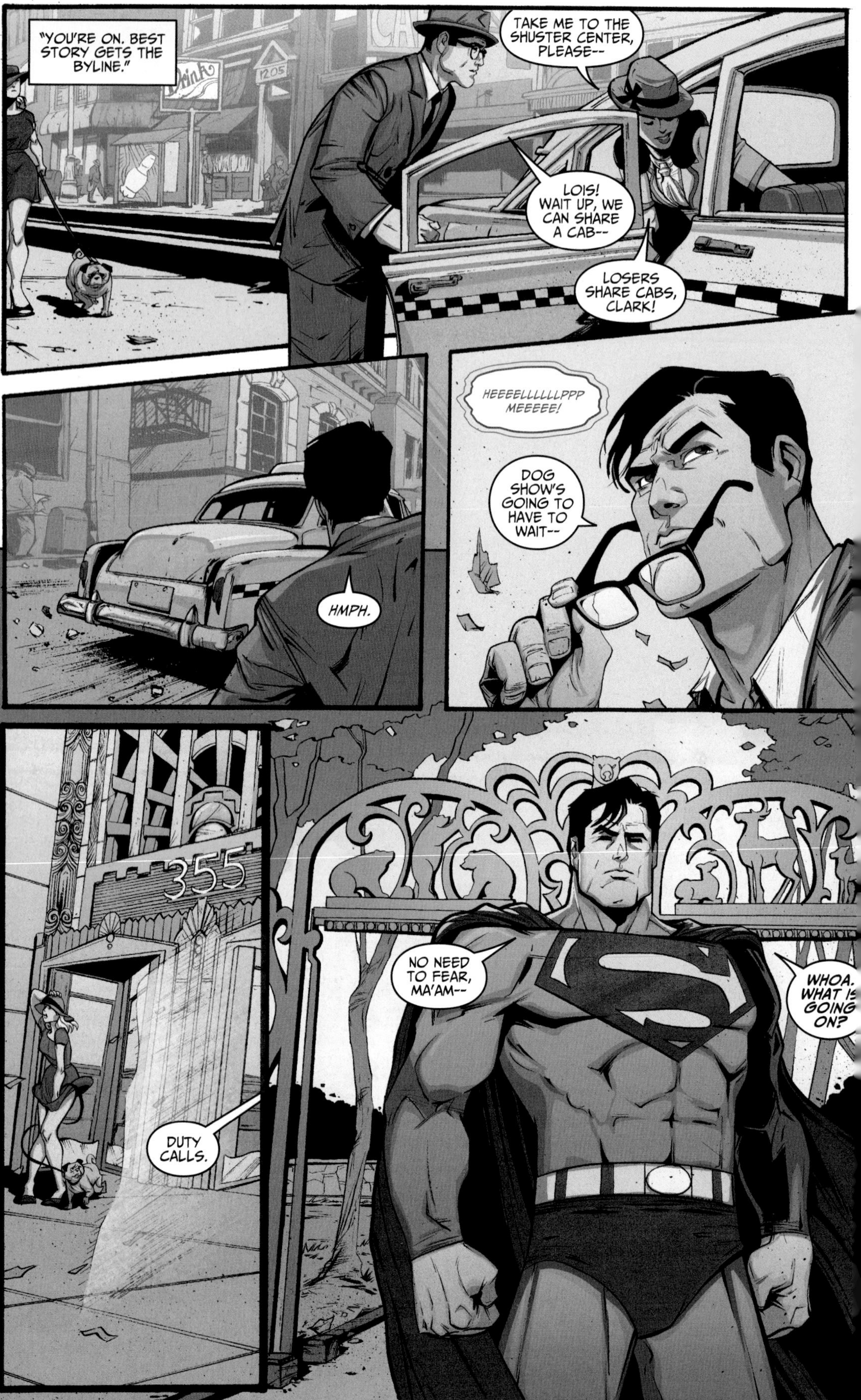
"YOU'RE ON. BEST STORY GETS THE BYLINE."
TAKE ME TO THE SHUSTER CENTER, PLEASE--
LOIS! WAIT UP, WE CAN SHARE A CAB--
LOSERS SHARE CABS, CLARK!
HMPH.
HEEEELLLLLLPPP MEEEEE!
DOG SHOW'S GOING TO HAVE TO WAIT--
DUTY CALLS.
NO NEED TO FEAR, MA'AM--
WHOA. WHAT IS GOING ON?

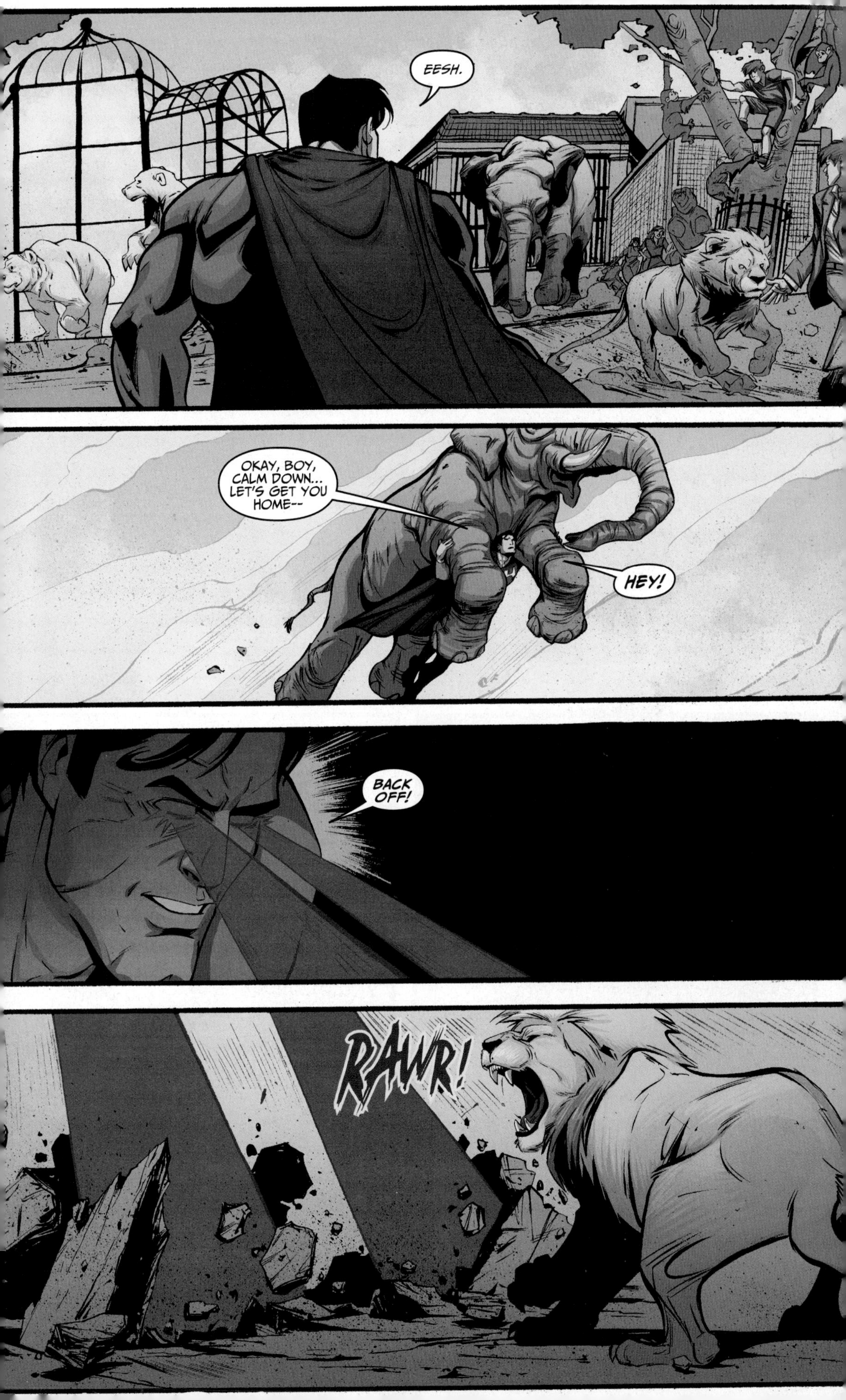
EESH.
OKAY, BOY, CALM DOWN... LET'S GET YOU HOME--
HEY!
BACK OFF!
RAWR!

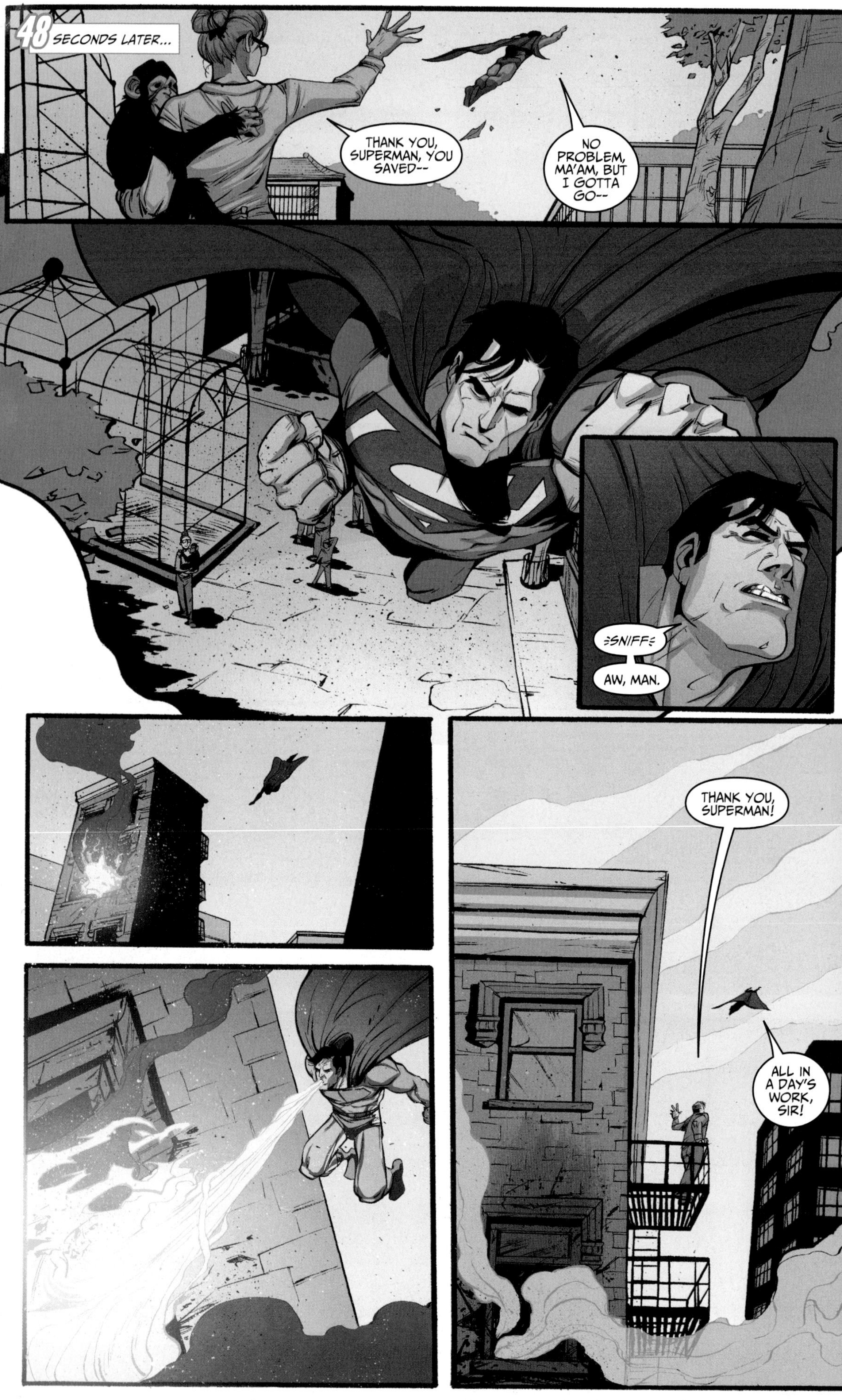
48 SECONDS LATER...
THANK YOU, SUPERMAN, YOU SAVED--
NO PROBLEM, MA'AM, BUT I GOTTA GO--
≈SNIFF≈
AW, MAN.
THANK YOU, SUPERMAN!
ALL IN A DAY'S WORK, SIR!

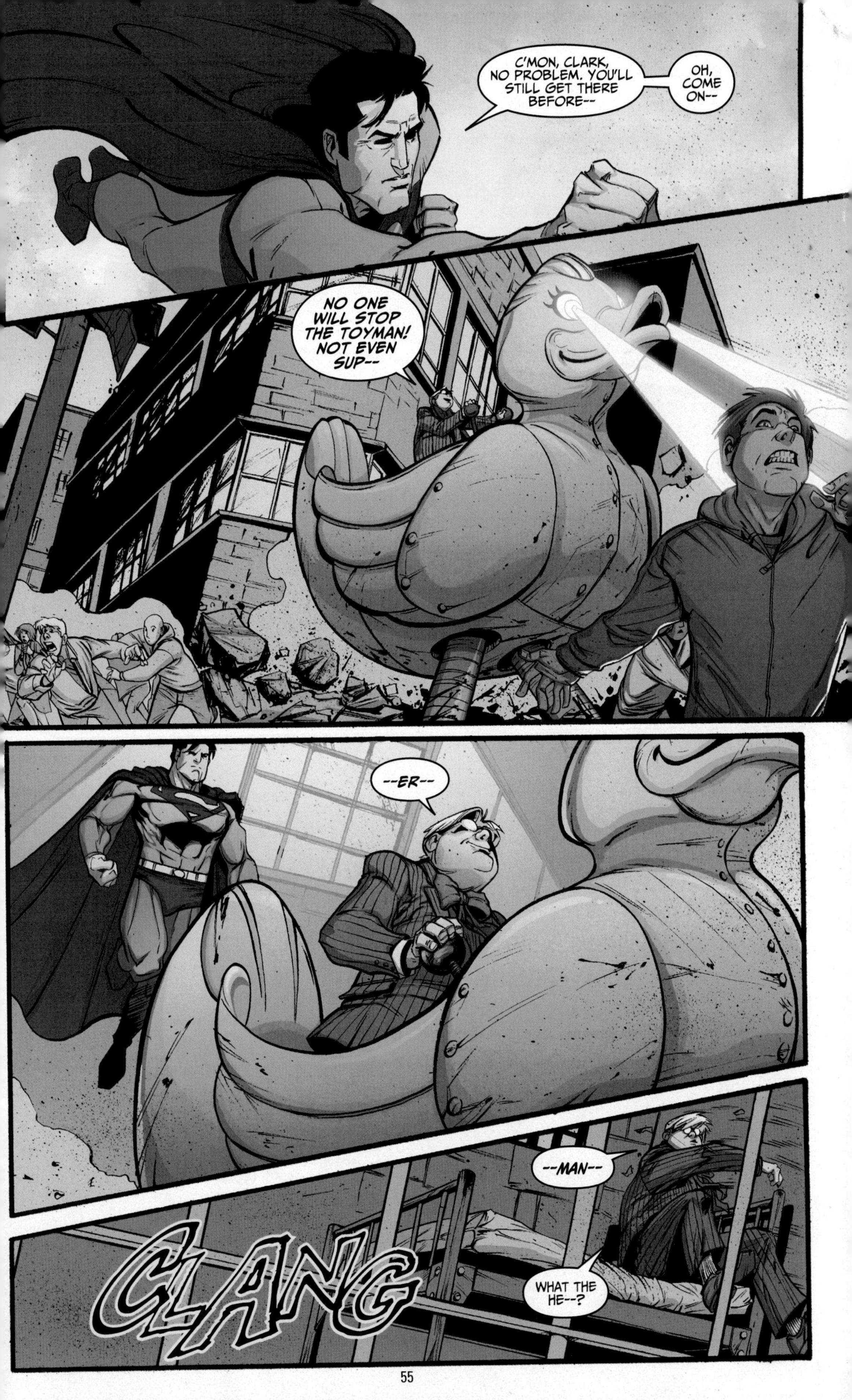

C'MON, CLARK, NO PROBLEM. YOU'LL STILL GET THERE BEFORE--
OH, COME ON--
NO ONE WILL STOP THE TOYMAN! NOT EVEN SUP--
--ER--
--MAN--
CLANG
WHAT THE HE--?

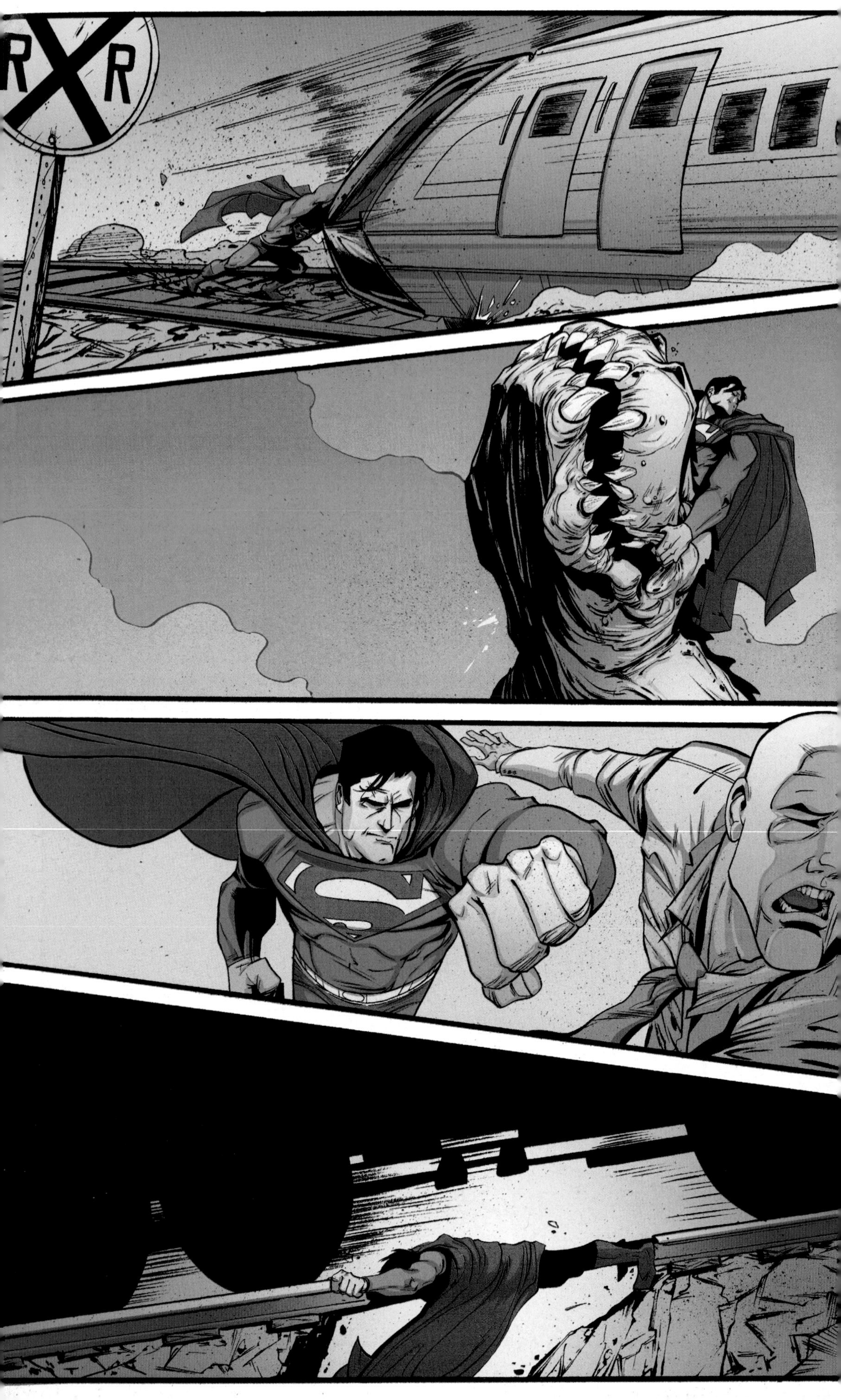
R R

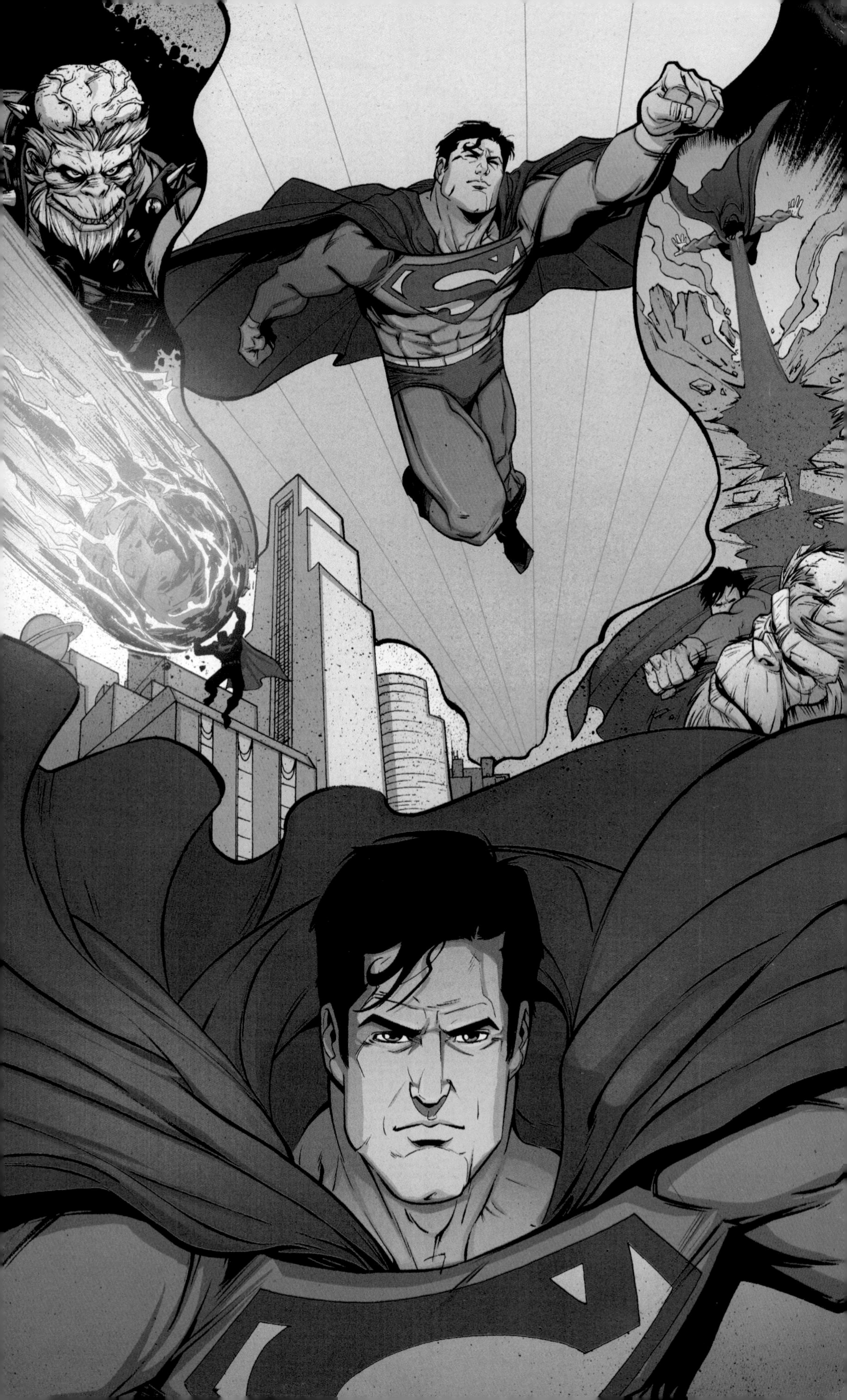

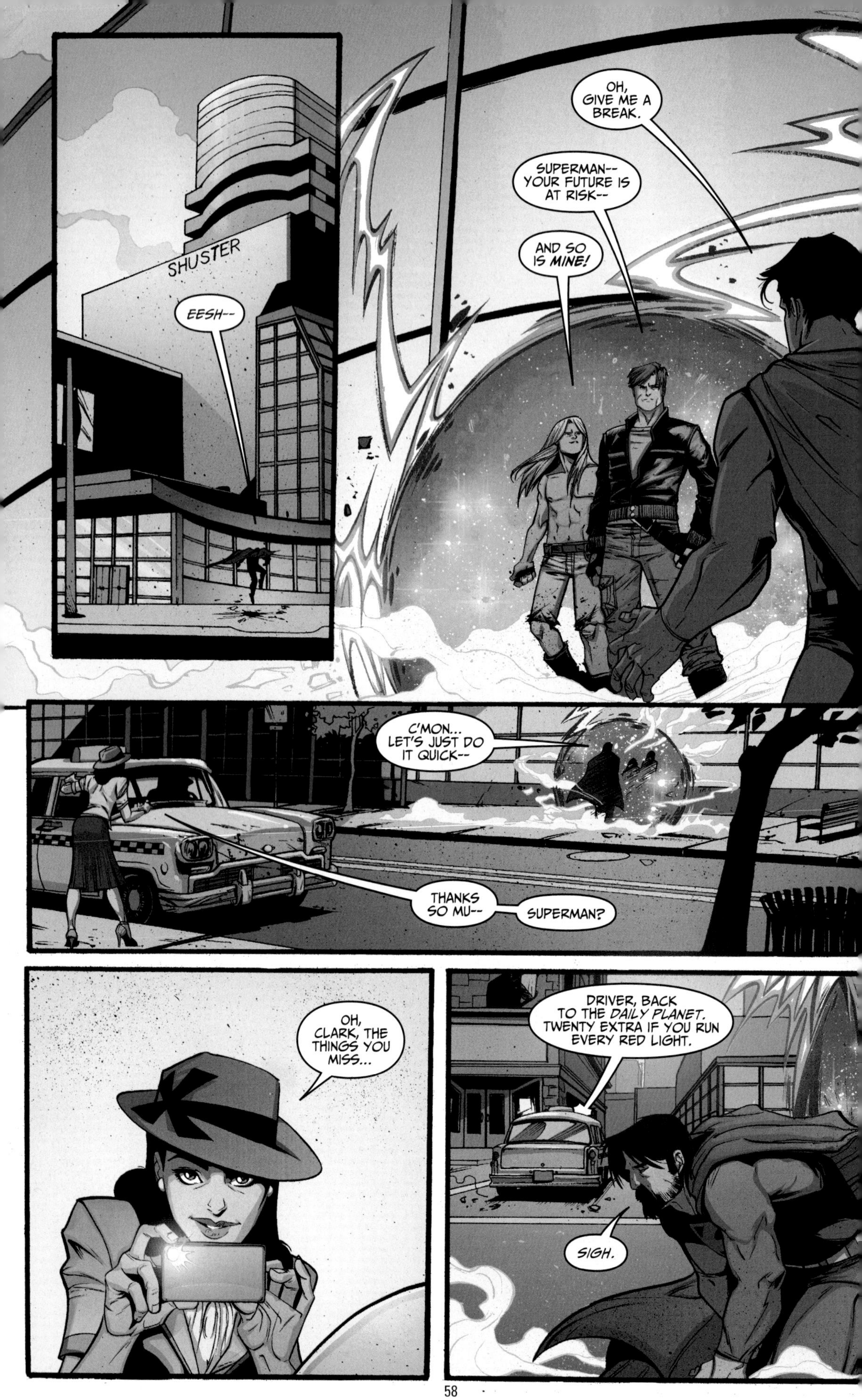

EESH--
OH, GIVE ME A BREAK.
SUPERMAN-- YOUR FUTURE IS AT RISK--
AND SO IS *MINE!*
C'MON... LET'S JUST DO IT QUICK--
THANKS SO MU--
SUPERMAN?
OH, CLARK, THE THINGS YOU MISS...
DRIVER, BACK TO THE *DAILY PLANET.* TWENTY EXTRA IF YOU RUN EVERY RED LIGHT.
SIGH.

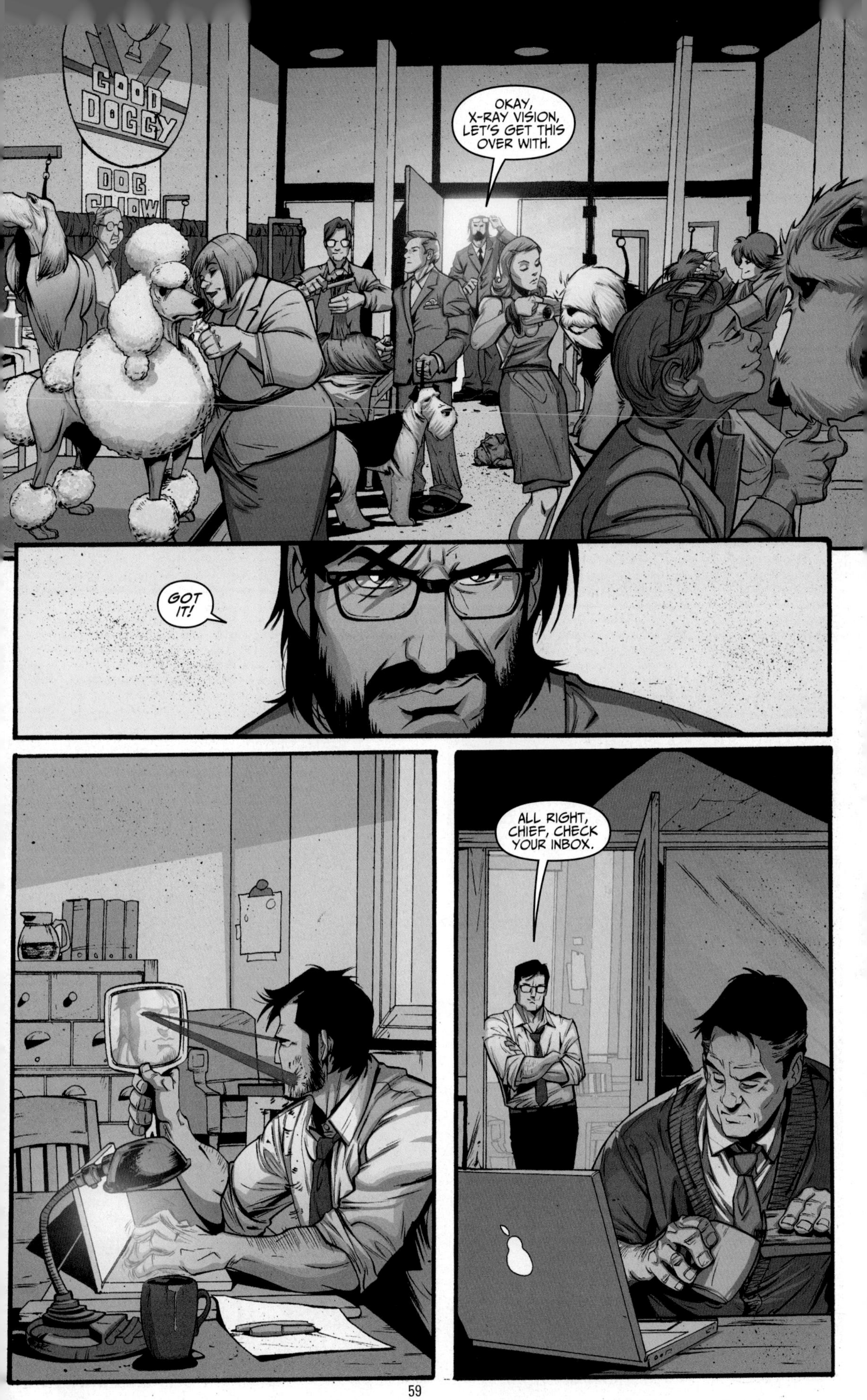
GOOD DOGGY
DOG
OKAY, X-RAY VISION, LET'S GET THIS OVER WITH.
GOT IT!
ALL RIGHT, CHIEF, CHECK YOUR INBOX.

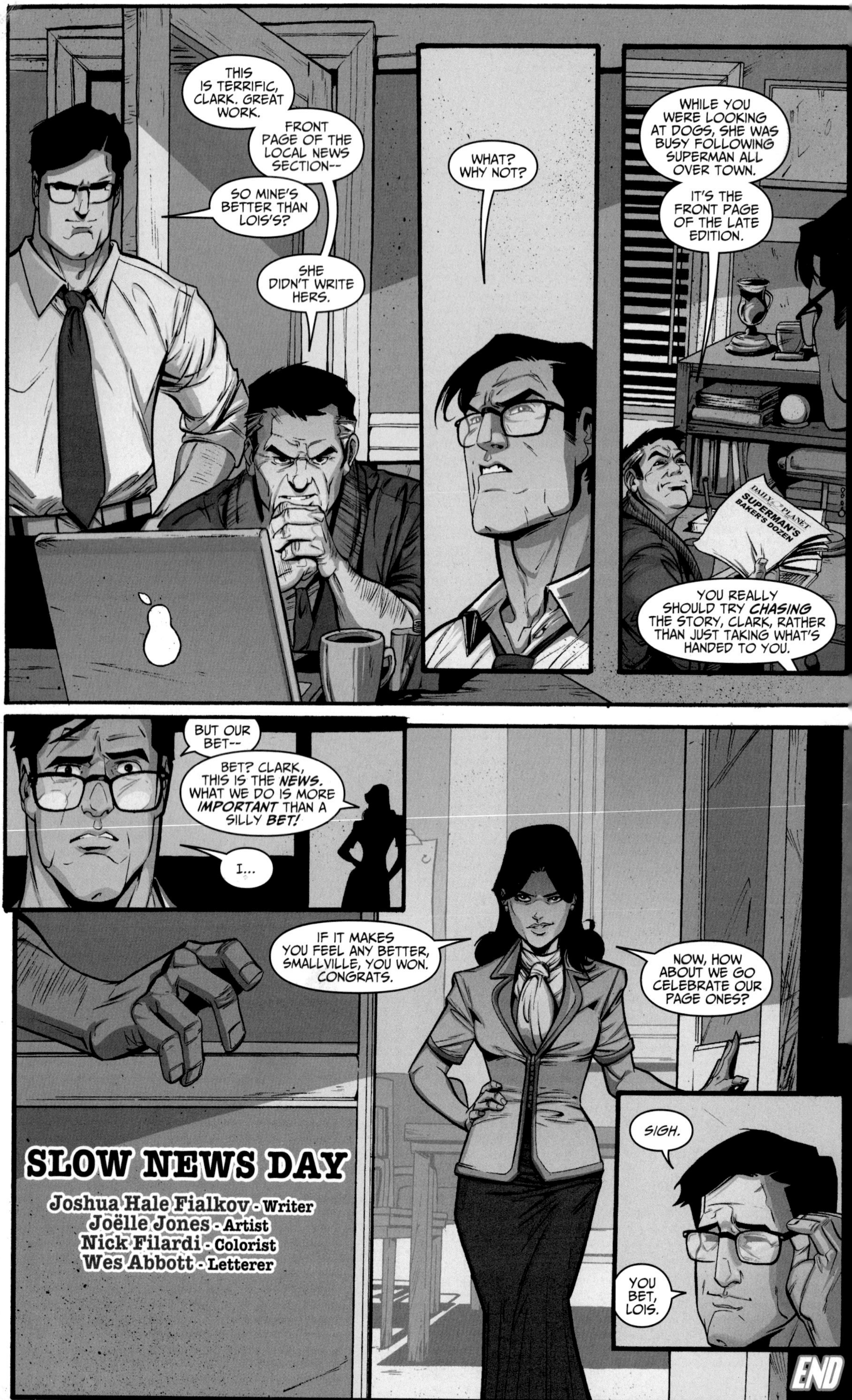
THIS IS TERRIFIC, CLARK. GREAT WORK.
FRONT PAGE OF THE LOCAL NEWS SECTION--
SO MINE'S BETTER THAN LOIS'S?
SHE DIDN'T WRITE HERS.
WHAT? WHY NOT?
WHILE YOU WERE LOOKING AT DOGS, SHE WAS BUSY FOLLOWING SUPERMAN ALL OVER TOWN.
IT'S THE FRONT PAGE OF THE LATE EDITION.
DAILY PLANET
SUPERMAN'S BAKER'S DOZEN
YOU REALLY SHOULD TRY CHASING THE STORY, CLARK, RATHER THAN JUST TAKING WHAT'S HANDED TO YOU.
BUT OUR BET--
BET? CLARK, THIS IS THE NEWS. WHAT WE DO IS MORE IMPORTANT THAN A SILLY BET!
I...
IF IT MAKES YOU FEEL ANY BETTER, SMALLVILLE, YOU WON. CONGRATS.
NOW, HOW ABOUT WE GO CELEBRATE OUR PAGE ONES?
SLOW NEWS DAY
Joshua Hale Fialkov - Writer
Joëlle Jones - Artist
Nick Filardi - Colorist
Wes Abbott - Letterer
SIGH.
YOU BET, LOIS.
END

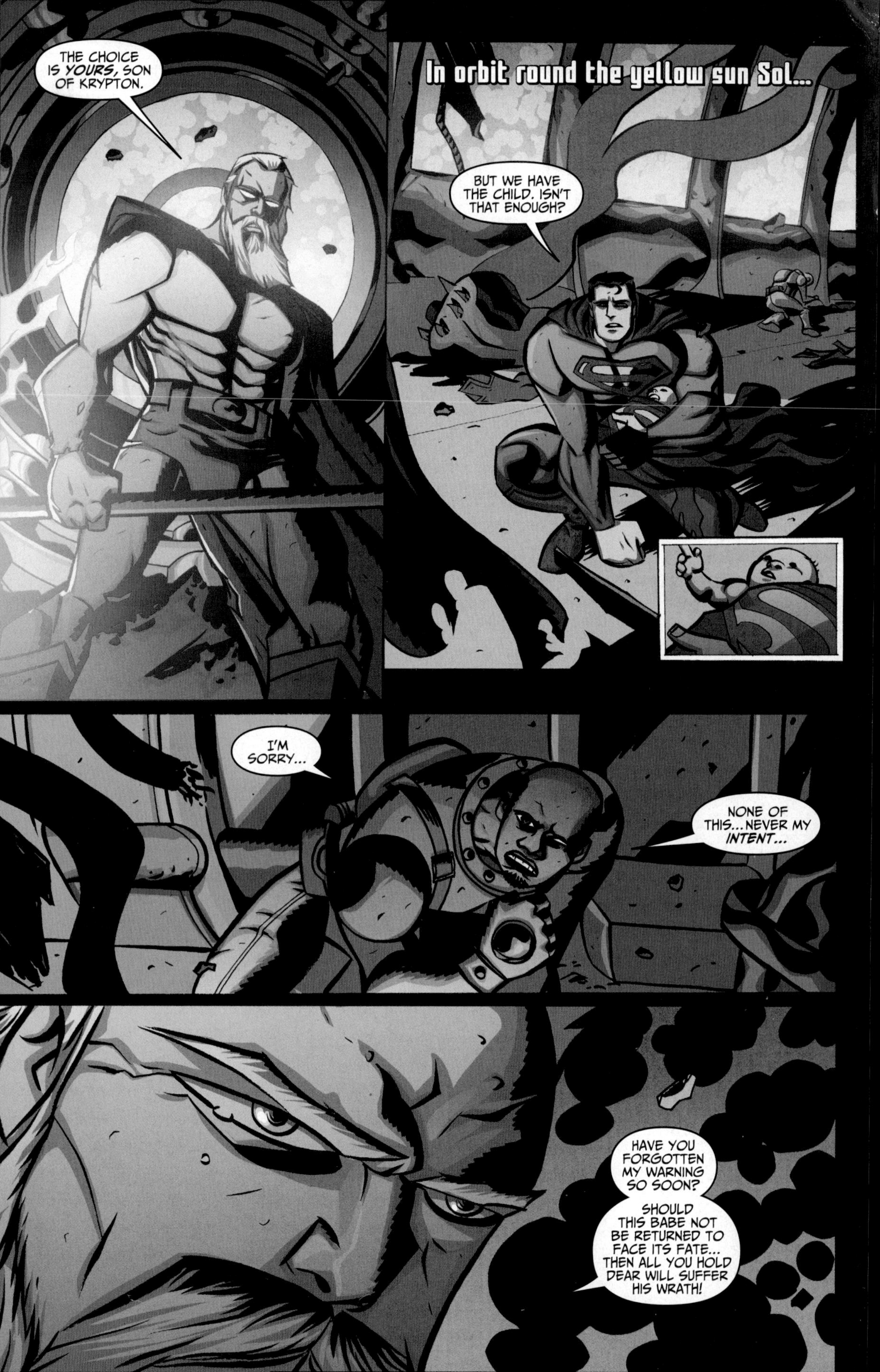
THE CHOICE IS YOURS, SON OF KRYPTON.
In orbit round the yellow sun Sol...
BUT WE HAVE THE CHILD. ISN'T THAT ENOUGH?
I'M SORRY...
NONE OF THIS...NEVER MY INTENT...
HAVE YOU FORGOTTEN MY WARNING SO SOON?
SHOULD THIS BABE NOT BE RETURNED TO FACE ITS FATE... THEN ALL YOU HOLD DEAR WILL SUFFER HIS WRATH!

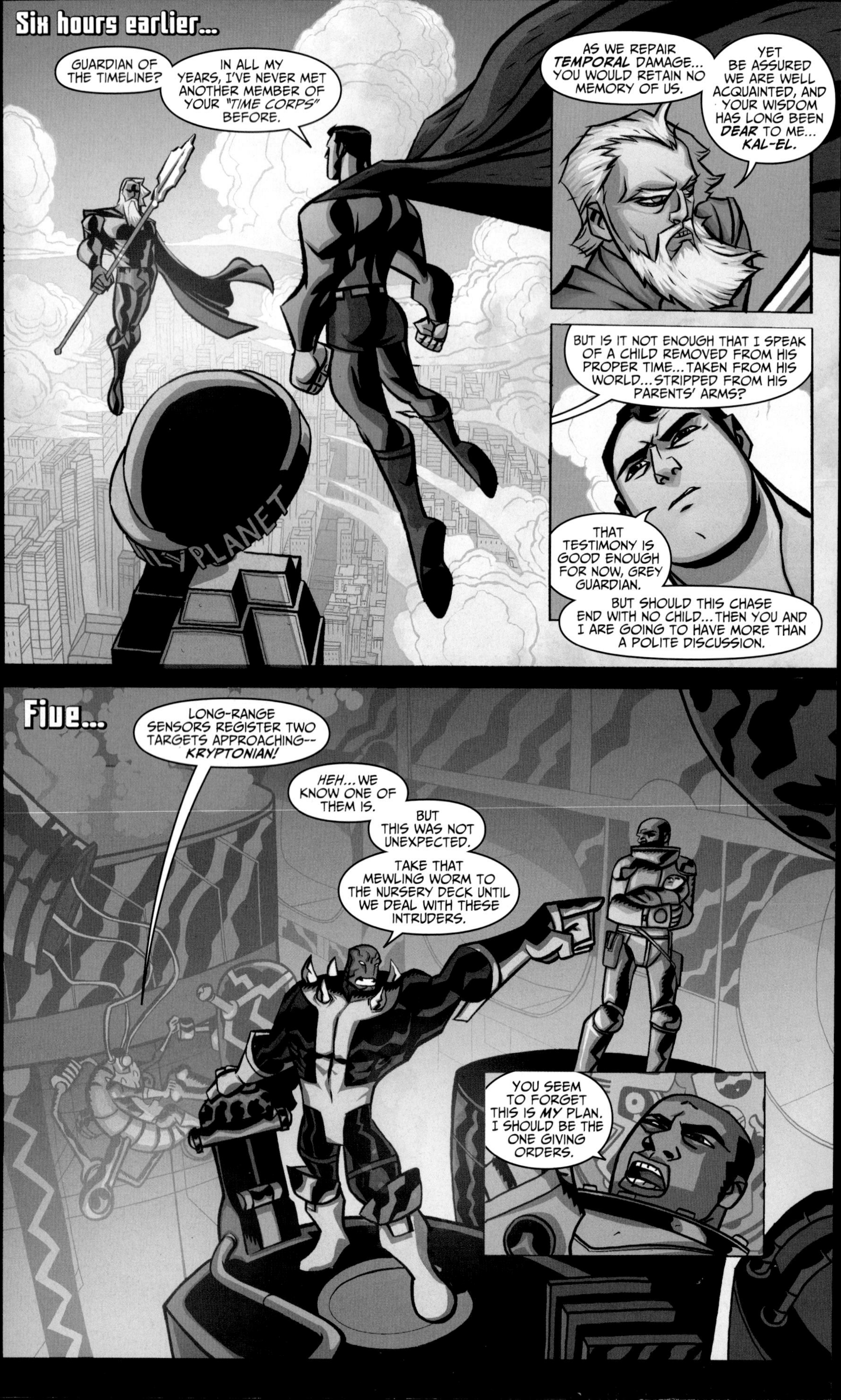
Six hours earlier...
GUARDIAN OF THE TIMELINE?
IN ALL MY YEARS, I'VE NEVER MET ANOTHER MEMBER OF YOUR "TIME CORPS" BEFORE.
AS WE REPAIR TEMPORAL DAMAGE... YOU WOULD RETAIN NO MEMORY OF US.
YET BE ASSURED WE ARE WELL ACQUAINTED, AND YOUR WISDOM HAS LONG BEEN DEAR TO ME... KAL-EL.
BUT IS IT NOT ENOUGH THAT I SPEAK OF A CHILD REMOVED FROM HIS PROPER TIME...TAKEN FROM HIS WORLD...STRIPPED FROM HIS PARENTS' ARMS?
THAT TESTIMONY IS GOOD ENOUGH FOR NOW, GREY GUARDIAN.
BUT SHOULD THIS CHASE END WITH NO CHILD...THEN YOU AND I ARE GOING TO HAVE MORE THAN A POLITE DISCUSSION.
PLANET
Five...
LONG-RANGE SENSORS REGISTER TWO TARGETS APPROACHING-- KRYPTONIAN!
HEH...WE KNOW ONE OF THEM IS.
BUT THIS WAS NOT UNEXPECTED.
TAKE THAT MEWLING WORM TO THE NURSERY DECK UNTIL WE DEAL WITH THESE INTRUDERS.
YOU SEEM TO FORGET THIS IS MY PLAN. I SHOULD BE THE ONE GIVING ORDERS.

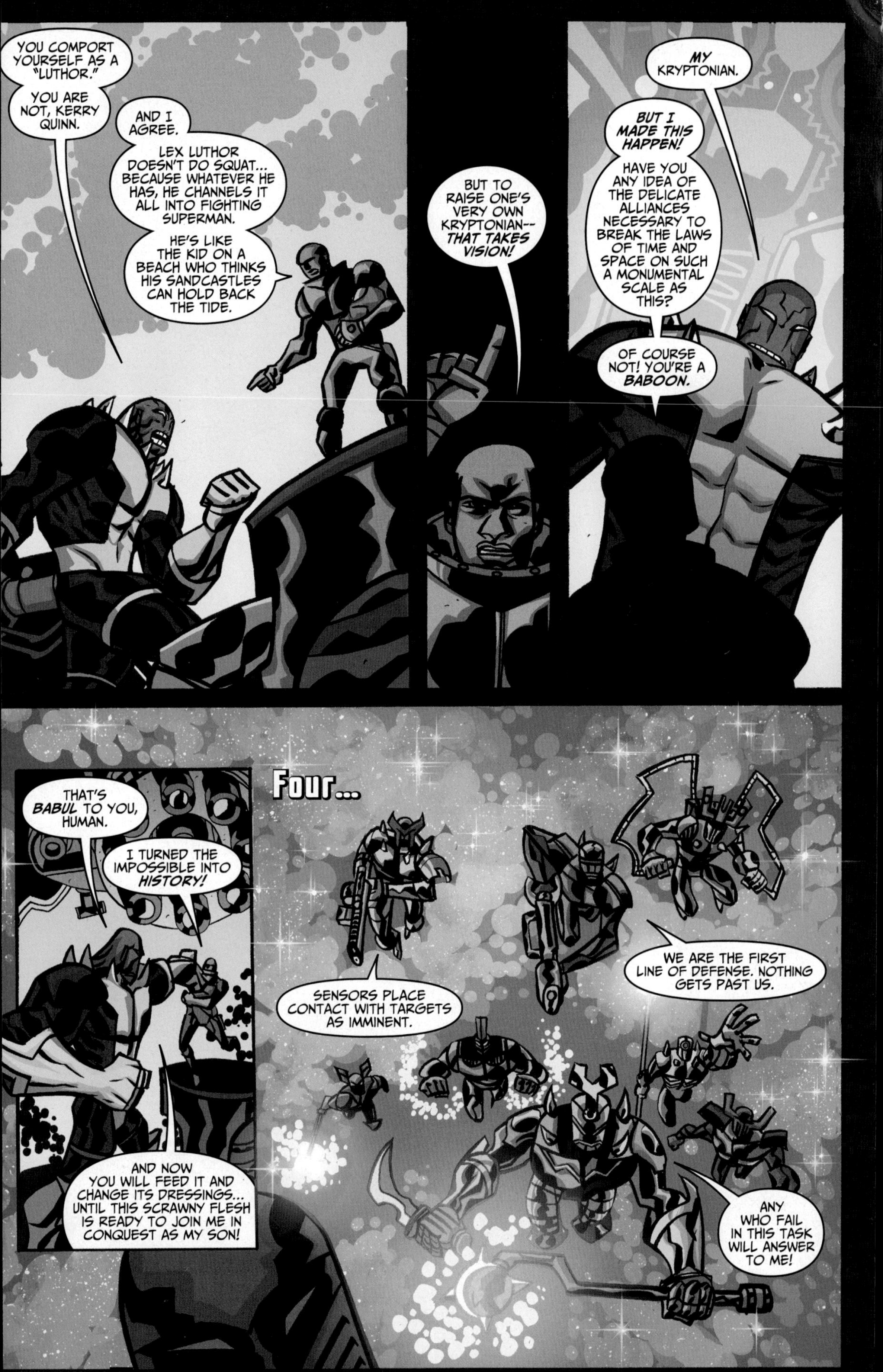
YOU COMPORT YOURSELF AS A "LUTHOR."
YOU ARE NOT, KERRY QUINN.
AND I AGREE.
LEX LUTHOR DOESN'T DO SQUAT... BECAUSE WHATEVER HE HAS, HE CHANNELS IT ALL INTO FIGHTING SUPERMAN.
HE'S LIKE THE KID ON A BEACH WHO THINKS HIS SANDCASTLES CAN HOLD BACK THE TIDE.
BUT TO RAISE ONE'S VERY OWN KRYPTONIAN-- THAT TAKES VISION!
MY KRYPTONIAN.
BUT I MADE THIS HAPPEN!
HAVE YOU ANY IDEA OF THE DELICATE ALLIANCES NECESSARY TO BREAK THE LAWS OF TIME AND SPACE ON SUCH A MONUMENTAL SCALE AS THIS?
OF COURSE NOT! YOU'RE A BABOON.
THAT'S BABUL TO YOU, HUMAN.
I TURNED THE IMPOSSIBLE INTO HISTORY!
AND NOW YOU WILL FEED IT AND CHANGE ITS DRESSINGS... UNTIL THIS SCRAWNY FLESH IS READY TO JOIN ME IN CONQUEST AS MY SON!
Four...
SENSORS PLACE CONTACT WITH TARGETS AS IMMINENT.
WE ARE THE FIRST LINE OF DEFENSE. NOTHING GETS PAST US.
ANY WHO FAIL IN THIS TASK WILL ANSWER TO ME!

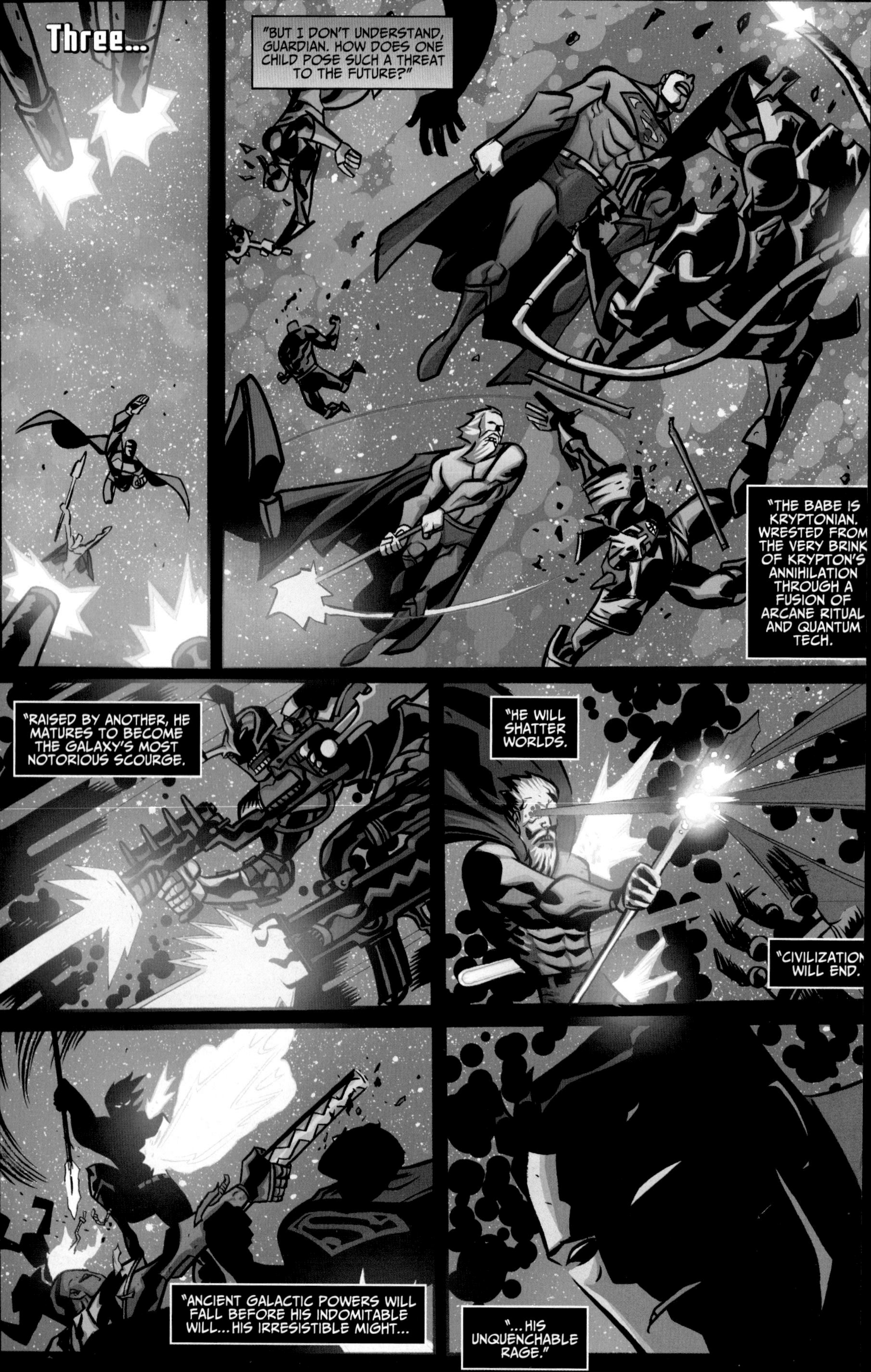
Three...
"BUT I DON'T UNDERSTAND, GUARDIAN. HOW DOES ONE CHILD POSE SUCH A THREAT TO THE FUTURE?"
"THE BABE IS KRYPTONIAN. WRESTED FROM THE VERY BRINK OF KRYPTON'S ANNIHILATION THROUGH A FUSION OF ARCANE RITUAL AND QUANTUM TECH.
"RAISED BY ANOTHER, HE MATURES TO BECOME THE GALAXY'S MOST NOTORIOUS SCOURGE.
"HE WILL SHATTER WORLDS.
"CIVILIZATION WILL END.
"ANCIENT GALACTIC POWERS WILL FALL BEFORE HIS INDOMITABLE WILL...HIS IRRESISTIBLE MIGHT...
"...HIS UNQUENCHABLE RAGE."

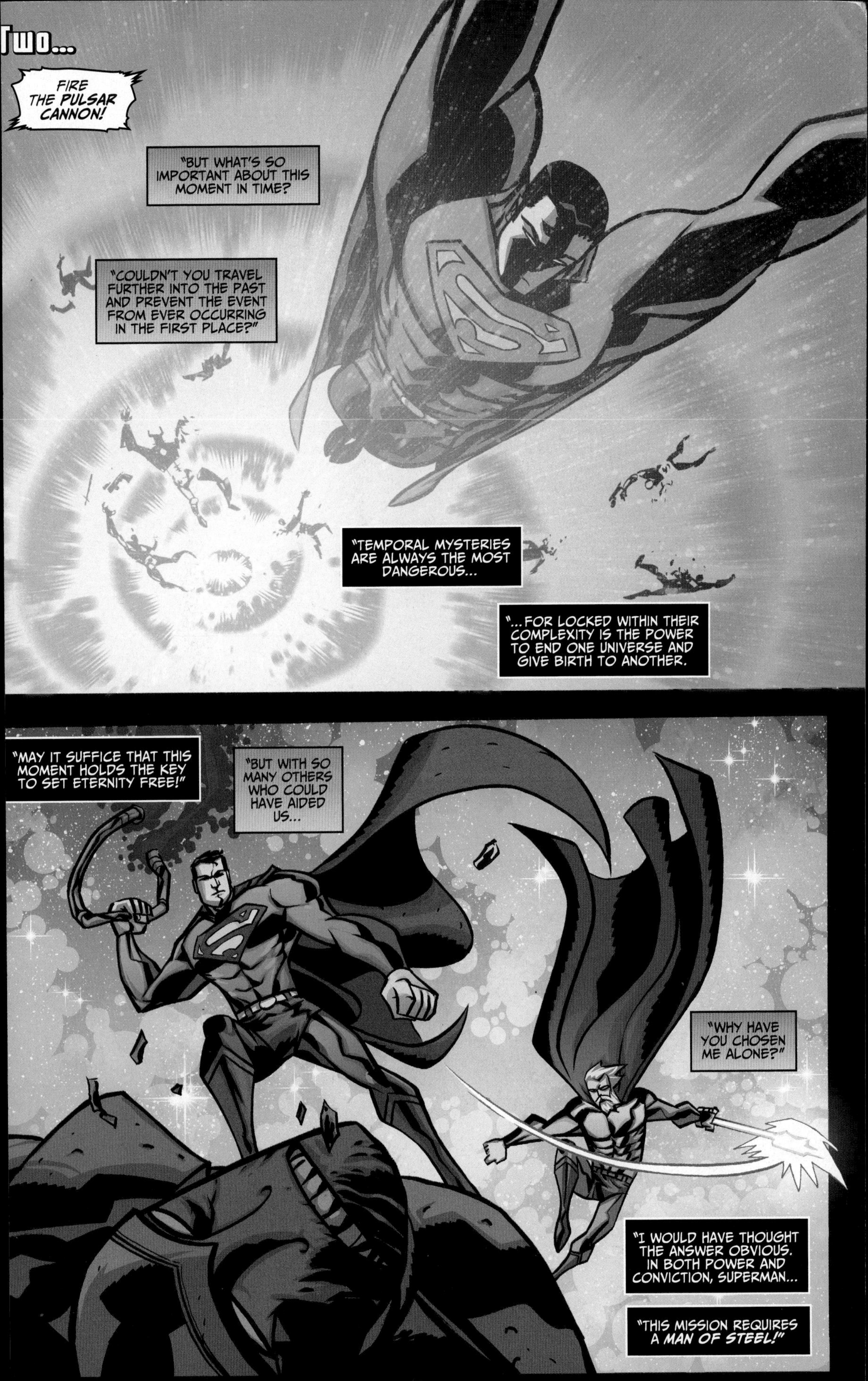
Two...
FIRE THE PULSAR CANNON!
"BUT WHAT'S SO IMPORTANT ABOUT THIS MOMENT IN TIME?
"COULDN'T YOU TRAVEL FURTHER INTO THE PAST AND PREVENT THE EVENT FROM EVER OCCURRING IN THE FIRST PLACE?"
"TEMPORAL MYSTERIES ARE ALWAYS THE MOST DANGEROUS...
"...FOR LOCKED WITHIN THEIR COMPLEXITY IS THE POWER TO END ONE UNIVERSE AND GIVE BIRTH TO ANOTHER.
"MAY IT SUFFICE THAT THIS MOMENT HOLDS THE KEY TO SET ETERNITY FREE!"
"BUT WITH SO MANY OTHERS WHO COULD HAVE AIDED US...
"WHY HAVE YOU CHOSEN ME ALONE?"
"I WOULD HAVE THOUGHT THE ANSWER OBVIOUS. IN BOTH POWER AND CONVICTION, SUPERMAN...
"THIS MISSION REQUIRES A MAN OF STEEL!"

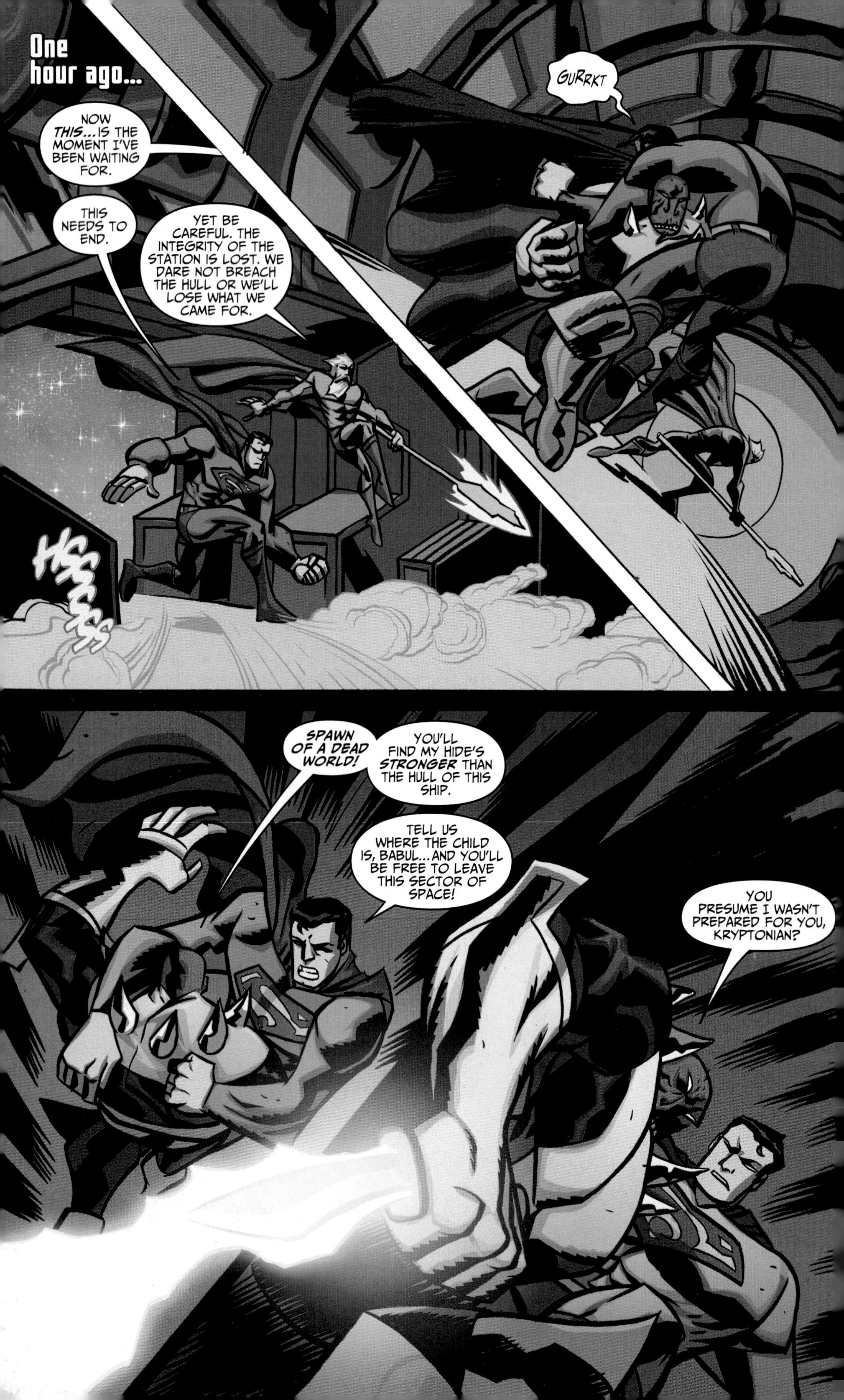
One hour ago...
GURRKT
NOW THIS...IS THE MOMENT I'VE BEEN WAITING FOR.
THIS NEEDS TO END.
YET BE CAREFUL. THE INTEGRITY OF THE STATION IS LOST. WE DARE NOT BREACH THE HULL OR WE'LL LOSE WHAT WE CAME FOR.
HSSSSS
SPAWN OF A DEAD WORLD!
YOU'LL FIND MY HIDE'S STRONGER THAN THE HULL OF THIS SHIP.
TELL US WHERE THE CHILD IS, BABUL...AND YOU'LL BE FREE TO LEAVE THIS SECTOR OF SPACE!
YOU PRESUME I WASN'T PREPARED FOR YOU, KRYPTONIAN?

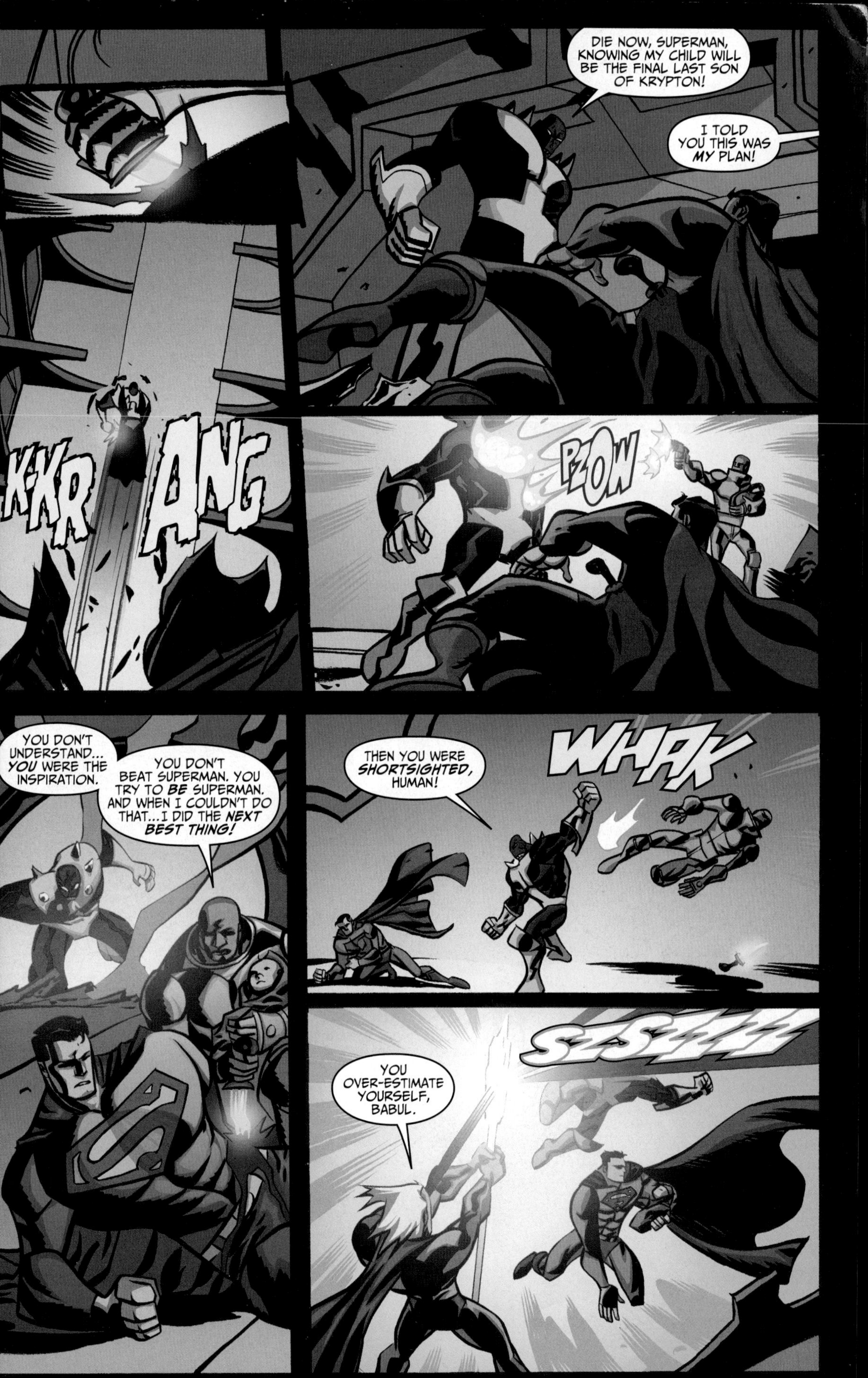
DIE NOW, SUPERMAN, KNOWING MY CHILD WILL BE THE FINAL LAST SON OF KRYPTON!
I TOLD YOU THIS WAS MY PLAN!
K-KRANG
PZOW
YOU DON'T UNDERSTAND... YOU WERE THE INSPIRATION.
YOU DON'T BEAT SUPERMAN. YOU TRY TO BE SUPERMAN. AND WHEN I COULDN'T DO THAT...I DID THE NEXT BEST THING!
THEN YOU WERE SHORTSIGHTED, HUMAN!
WHAK
SZSZSZ
YOU OVER-ESTIMATE YOURSELF, BABUL.

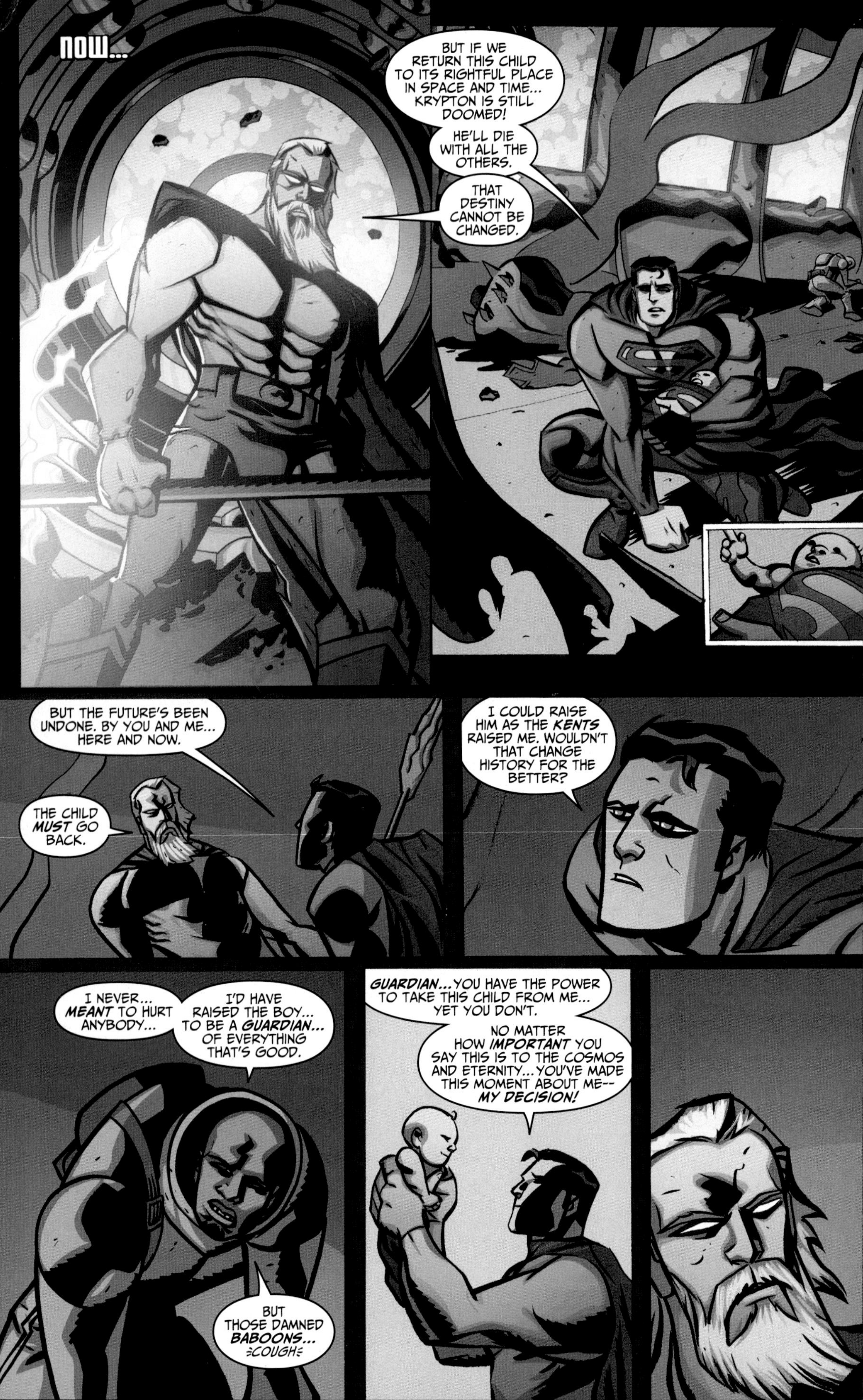
NOW...
BUT IF WE RETURN THIS CHILD TO ITS RIGHTFUL PLACE IN SPACE AND TIME... KRYPTON IS STILL DOOMED!
HE'LL DIE WITH ALL THE OTHERS.
THAT DESTINY CANNOT BE CHANGED.
BUT THE FUTURE'S BEEN UNDONE. BY YOU AND ME... HERE AND NOW.
THE CHILD MUST GO BACK.
I COULD RAISE HIM AS THE KENTS RAISED ME. WOULDN'T THAT CHANGE HISTORY FOR THE BETTER?
I NEVER... MEANT TO HURT ANYBODY...
I'D HAVE RAISED THE BOY... TO BE A GUARDIAN... OF EVERYTHING THAT'S GOOD.
BUT THOSE DAMNED BABOONS... COUGH
GUARDIAN... YOU HAVE THE POWER TO TAKE THIS CHILD FROM ME... YET YOU DON'T.
NO MATTER HOW IMPORTANT YOU SAY THIS IS TO THE COSMOS AND ETERNITY... YOU'VE MADE THIS MOMENT ABOUT ME-- MY DECISION!

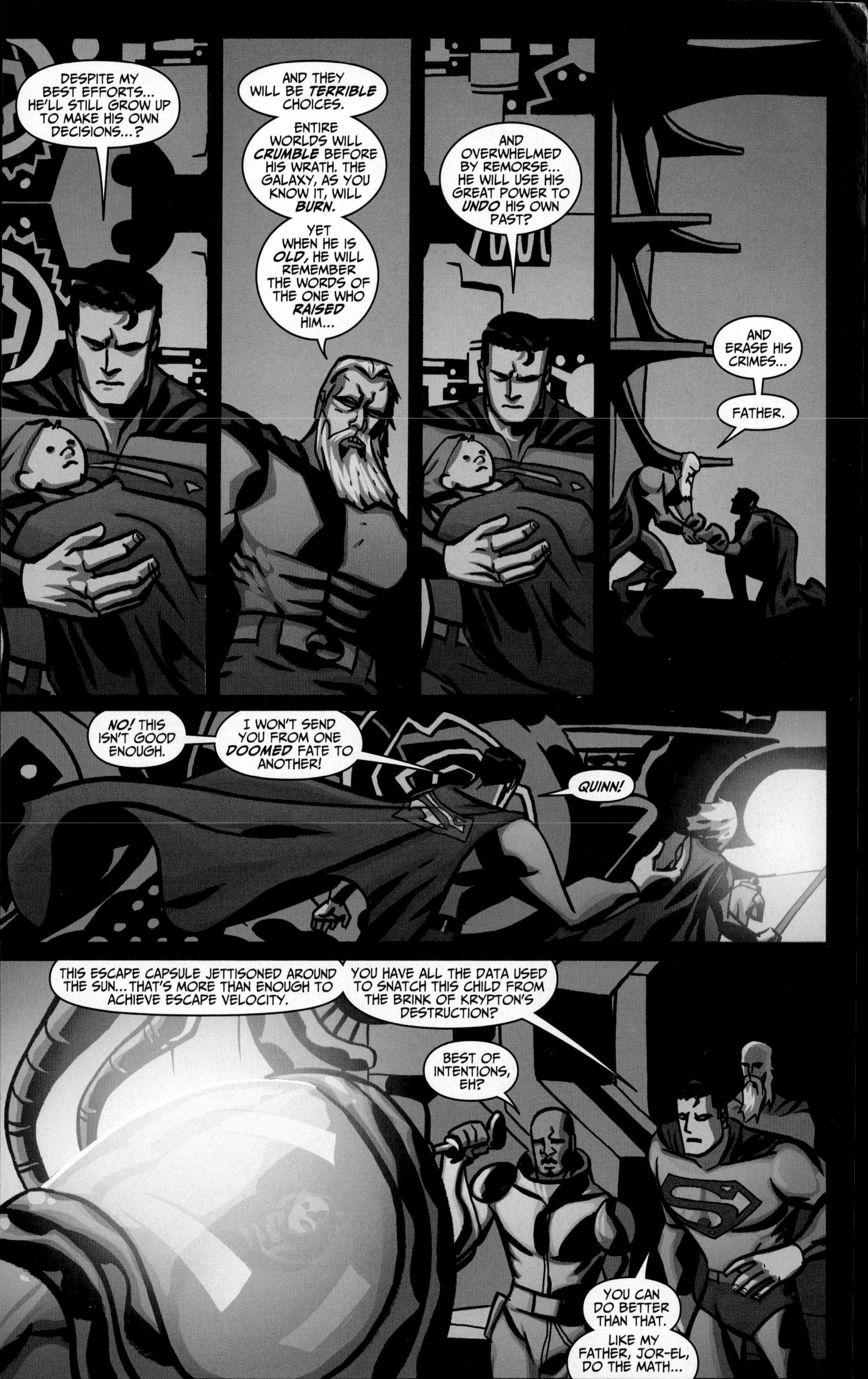
DESPITE MY BEST EFFORTS... HE'LL STILL GROW UP TO MAKE HIS OWN DECISIONS...?
AND THEY WILL BE TERRIBLE CHOICES.
ENTIRE WORLDS WILL CRUMBLE BEFORE HIS WRATH. THE GALAXY, AS YOU KNOW IT, WILL BURN.
YET WHEN HE IS OLD, HE WILL REMEMBER THE WORDS OF THE ONE WHO RAISED HIM...
AND OVERWHELMED BY REMORSE... HE WILL USE HIS GREAT POWER TO UNDO HIS OWN PAST?
AND ERASE HIS CRIMES...
FATHER.
NO! THIS ISN'T GOOD ENOUGH.
I WON'T SEND YOU FROM ONE DOOMED FATE TO ANOTHER!
QUINN!
THIS ESCAPE CAPSULE JETTISONED AROUND THE SUN...THAT'S MORE THAN ENOUGH TO ACHIEVE ESCAPE VELOCITY.
YOU HAVE ALL THE DATA USED TO SNATCH THIS CHILD FROM THE BRINK OF KRYPTON'S DESTRUCTION?
BEST OF INTENTIONS, EH?
YOU CAN DO BETTER THAN THAT.
LIKE MY FATHER, JOR-EL, DO THE MATH...

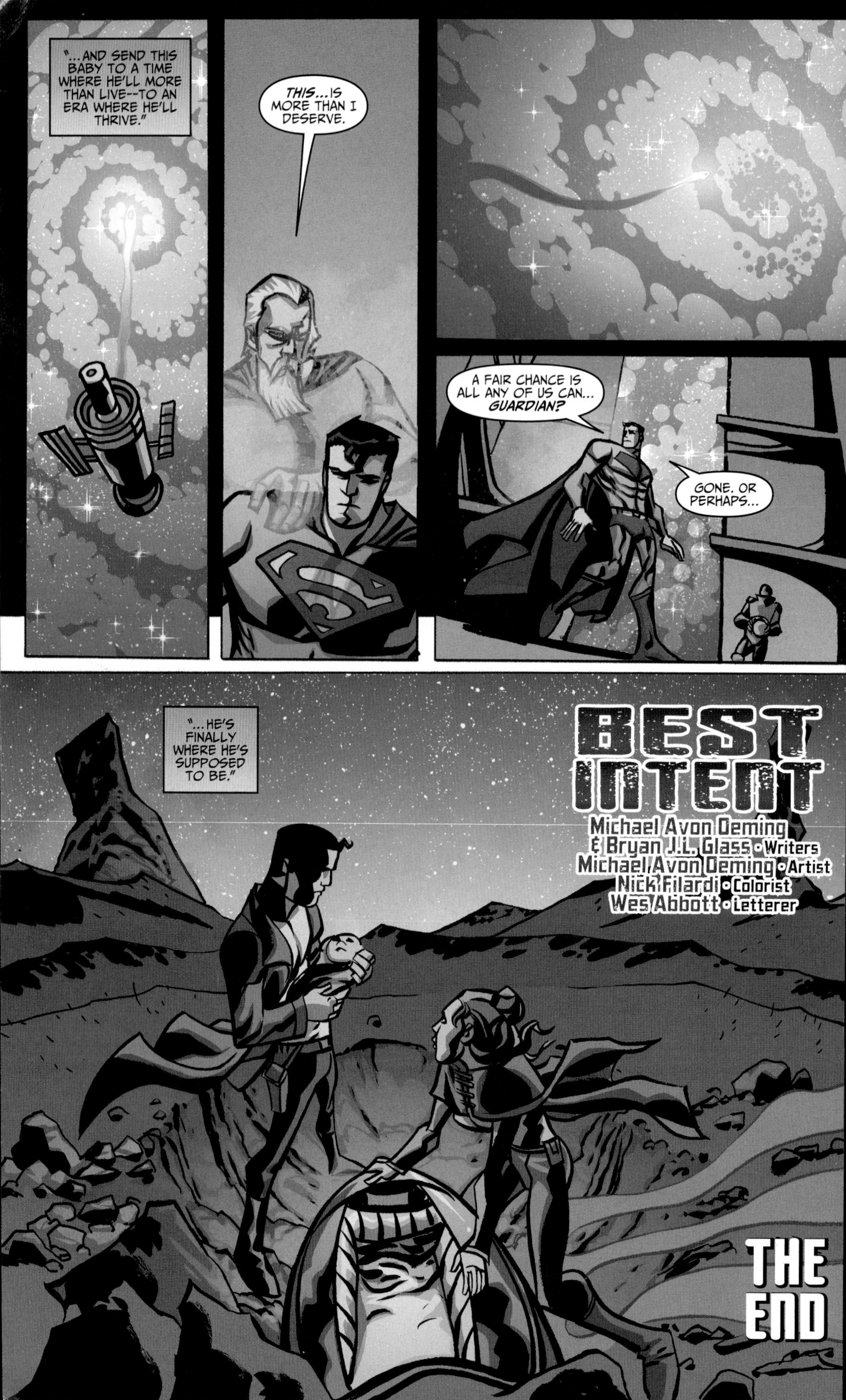
"...AND SEND THIS BABY TO A TIME WHERE HE'LL MORE THAN LIVE--TO AN ERA WHERE HE'LL THRIVE."
THIS...IS MORE THAN I DESERVE.
A FAIR CHANCE IS ALL ANY OF US CAN... GUARDIAN?
GONE. OR PERHAPS...
"...HE'S FINALLY WHERE HE'S SUPPOSED TO BE."
BEST INTENT
Michael Avon Oeming & Bryan J.L. Glass • Writers
Michael Avon Oeming • Artist
Nick Filardi • Colorist
Wes Abbott • Letterer
THE END

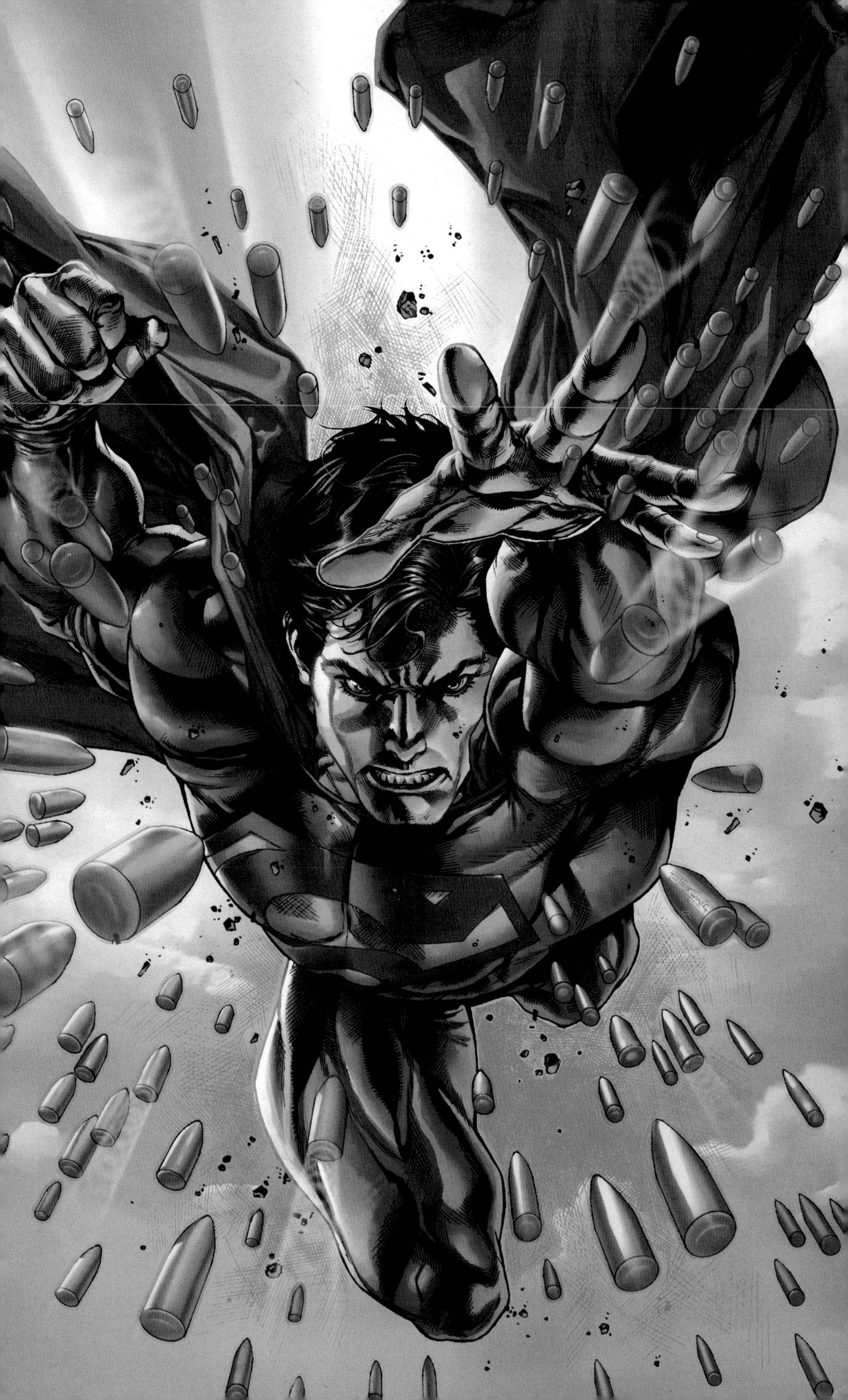

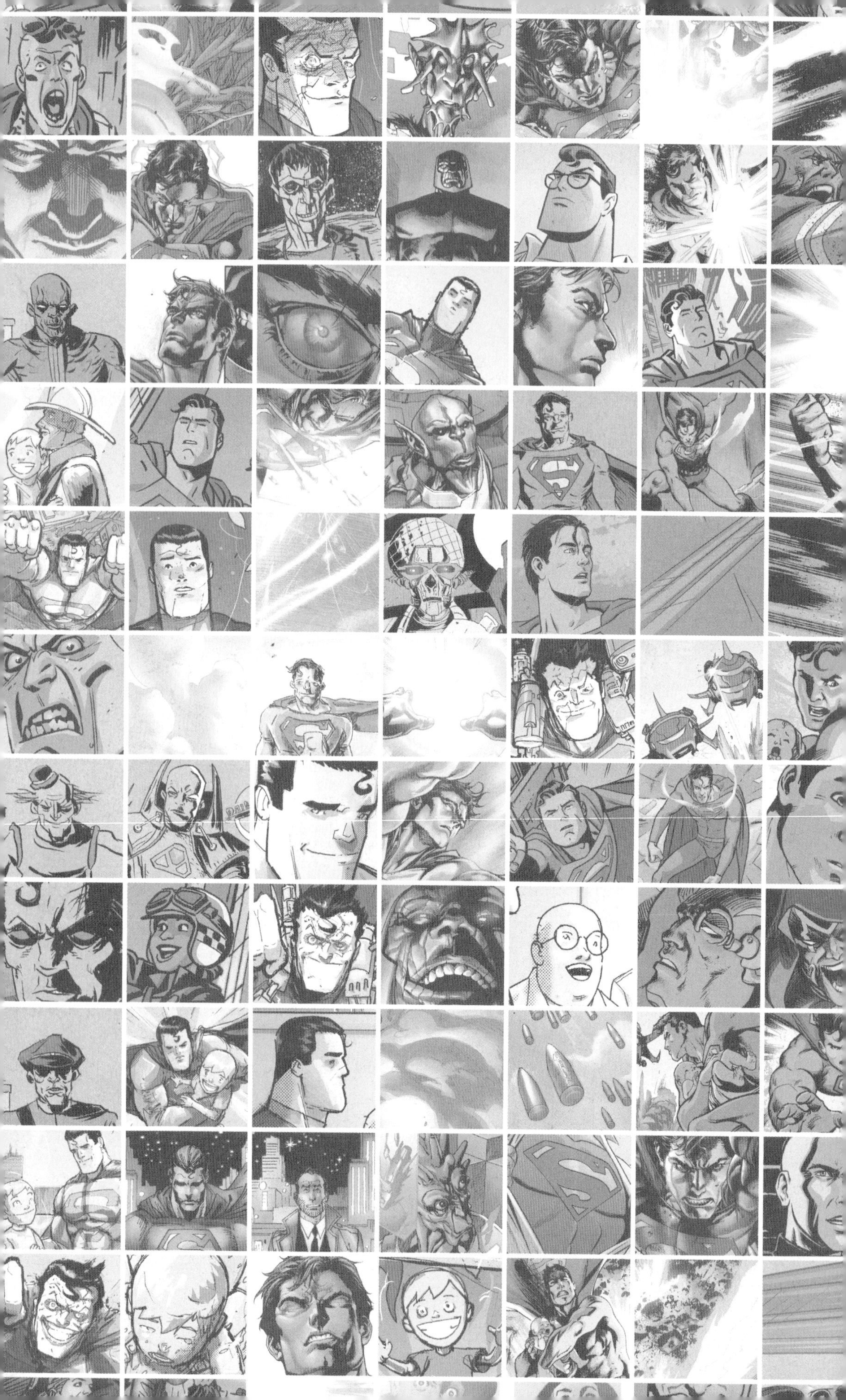

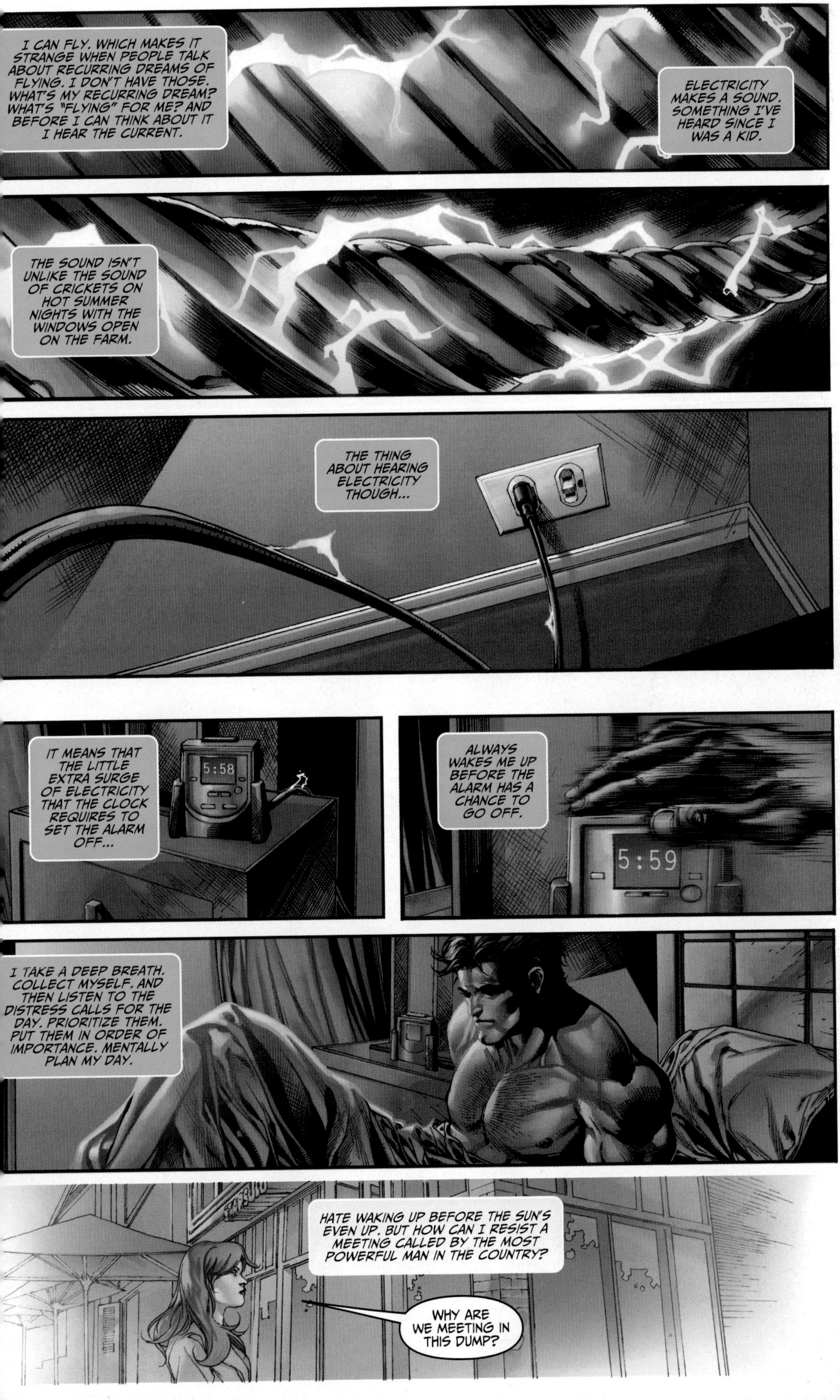

I CAN FLY. WHICH MAKES IT STRANGE WHEN PEOPLE TALK ABOUT RECURRING DREAMS OF FLYING. I DON'T HAVE THOSE. WHAT'S MY RECURRING DREAM? WHAT'S "FLYING" FOR ME? AND BEFORE I CAN THINK ABOUT IT I HEAR THE CURRENT.
ELECTRICITY MAKES A SOUND. SOMETHING I'VE HEARD SINCE I WAS A KID.
THE SOUND ISN'T UNLIKE THE SOUND OF CRICKETS ON HOT SUMMER NIGHTS WITH THE WINDOWS OPEN ON THE FARM.
THE THING ABOUT HEARING ELECTRICITY THOUGH...
IT MEANS THAT THE LITTLE EXTRA SURGE OF ELECTRICITY THAT THE CLOCK REQUIRES TO SET THE ALARM OFF...
5:58
ALWAYS WAKES ME UP BEFORE THE ALARM HAS A CHANCE TO GO OFF.
5:59
I TAKE A DEEP BREATH. COLLECT MYSELF. AND THEN LISTEN TO THE DISTRESS CALLS FOR THE DAY. PRIORITIZE THEM. PUT THEM IN ORDER OF IMPORTANCE. MENTALLY PLAN MY DAY.
HATE WAKING UP BEFORE THE SUN'S EVEN UP. BUT HOW CAN I RESIST A MEETING CALLED BY THE MOST POWERFUL MAN IN THE COUNTRY?
WHY ARE WE MEETING IN THIS DUMP?

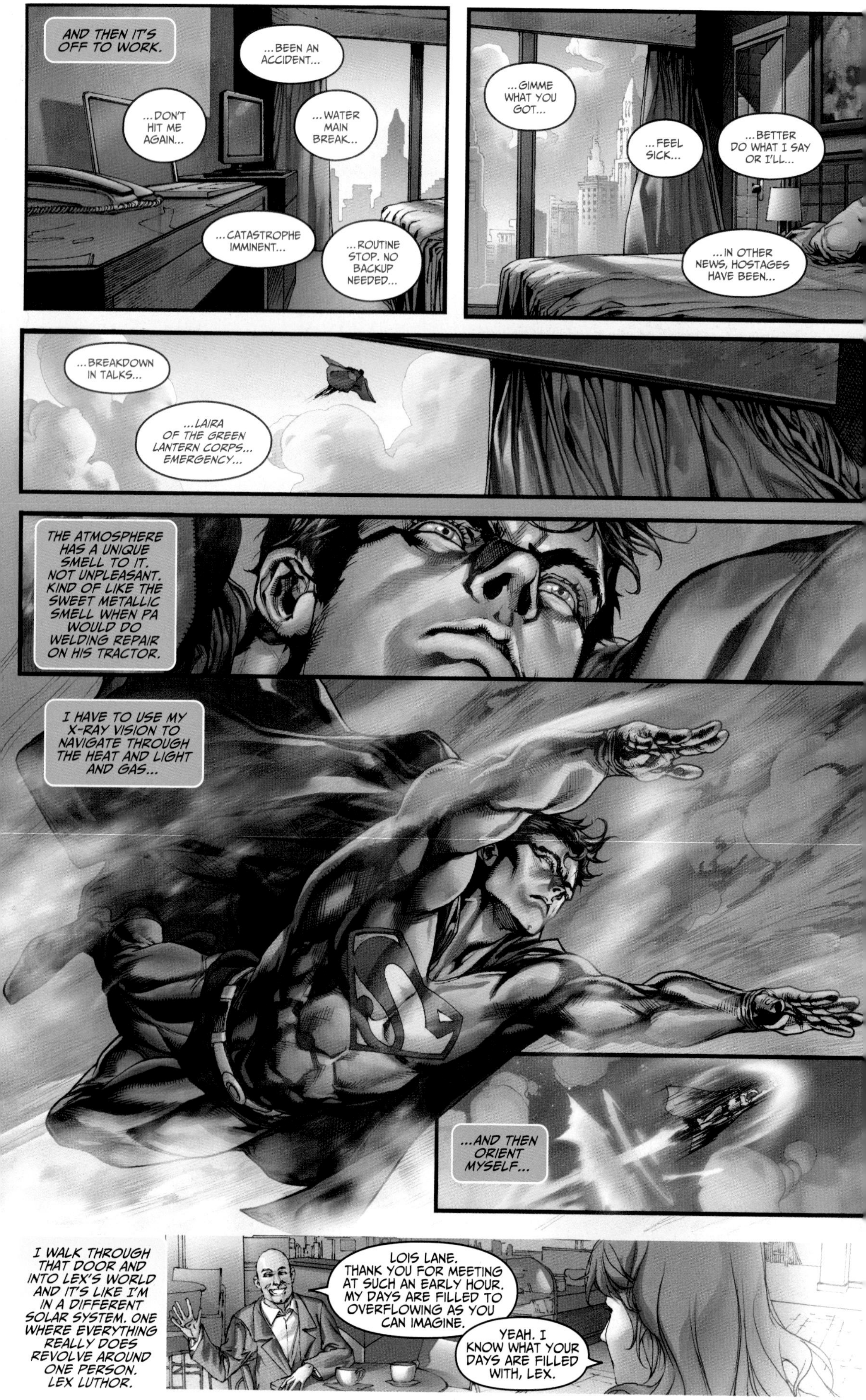
AND THEN IT'S OFF TO WORK.
...BEEN AN ACCIDENT...
...DON'T HIT ME AGAIN...
...WATER MAIN BREAK...
...CATASTROPHE IMMINENT...
...ROUTINE STOP. NO BACKUP NEEDED...
...GIMME WHAT YOU GOT...
...FEEL SICK...
...BETTER DO WHAT I SAY OR I'LL...
...IN OTHER NEWS, HOSTAGES HAVE BEEN...
...BREAKDOWN IN TALKS...
...LAIRA OF THE GREEN LANTERN CORPS... EMERGENCY...
THE ATMOSPHERE HAS A UNIQUE SMELL TO IT. NOT UNPLEASANT. KIND OF LIKE THE SWEET METALLIC SMELL WHEN PA WOULD DO WELDING REPAIR ON HIS TRACTOR.
I HAVE TO USE MY X-RAY VISION TO NAVIGATE THROUGH THE HEAT AND LIGHT AND GAS...
...AND THEN ORIENT MYSELF...
I WALK THROUGH THAT DOOR AND INTO LEX'S WORLD AND IT'S LIKE I'M IN A DIFFERENT SOLAR SYSTEM. ONE WHERE EVERYTHING REALLY DOES REVOLVE AROUND ONE PERSON. LEX LUTHOR.
LOIS LANE. THANK YOU FOR MEETING AT SUCH AN EARLY HOUR. MY DAYS ARE FILLED TO OVERFLOWING AS YOU CAN IMAGINE.
YEAH. I KNOW WHAT YOUR DAYS ARE FILLED WITH, LEX.

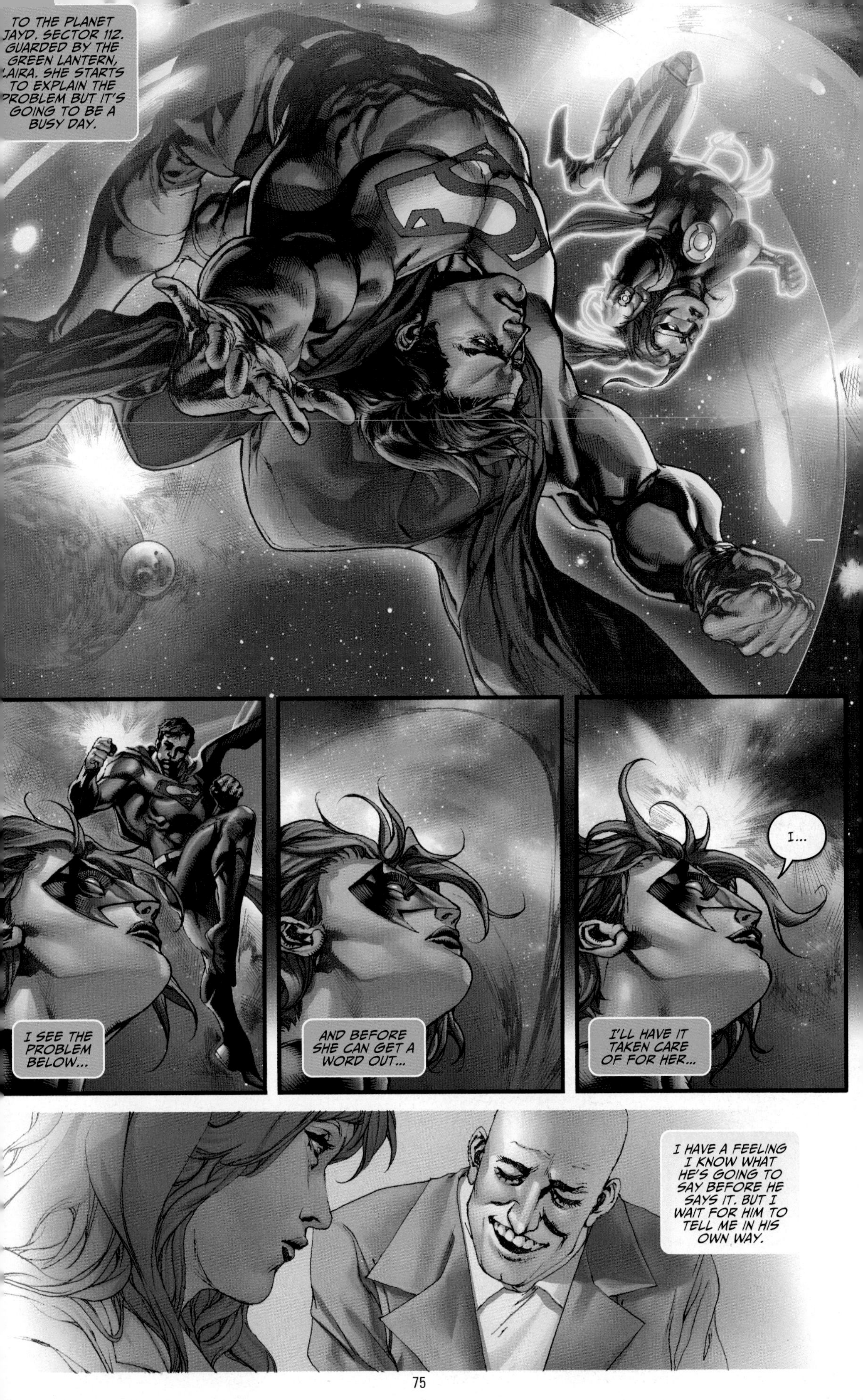
TO THE PLANET JAYD. SECTOR 112. GUARDED BY THE GREEN LANTERN, LAIRA. SHE STARTS TO EXPLAIN THE PROBLEM BUT IT'S GOING TO BE A BUSY DAY.
I SEE THE PROBLEM BELOW...
AND BEFORE SHE CAN GET A WORD OUT...
I...
I'LL HAVE IT TAKEN CARE OF FOR HER...
I HAVE A FEELING I KNOW WHAT HE'S GOING TO SAY BEFORE HE SAYS IT. BUT I WAIT FOR HIM TO TELL ME IN HIS OWN WAY.

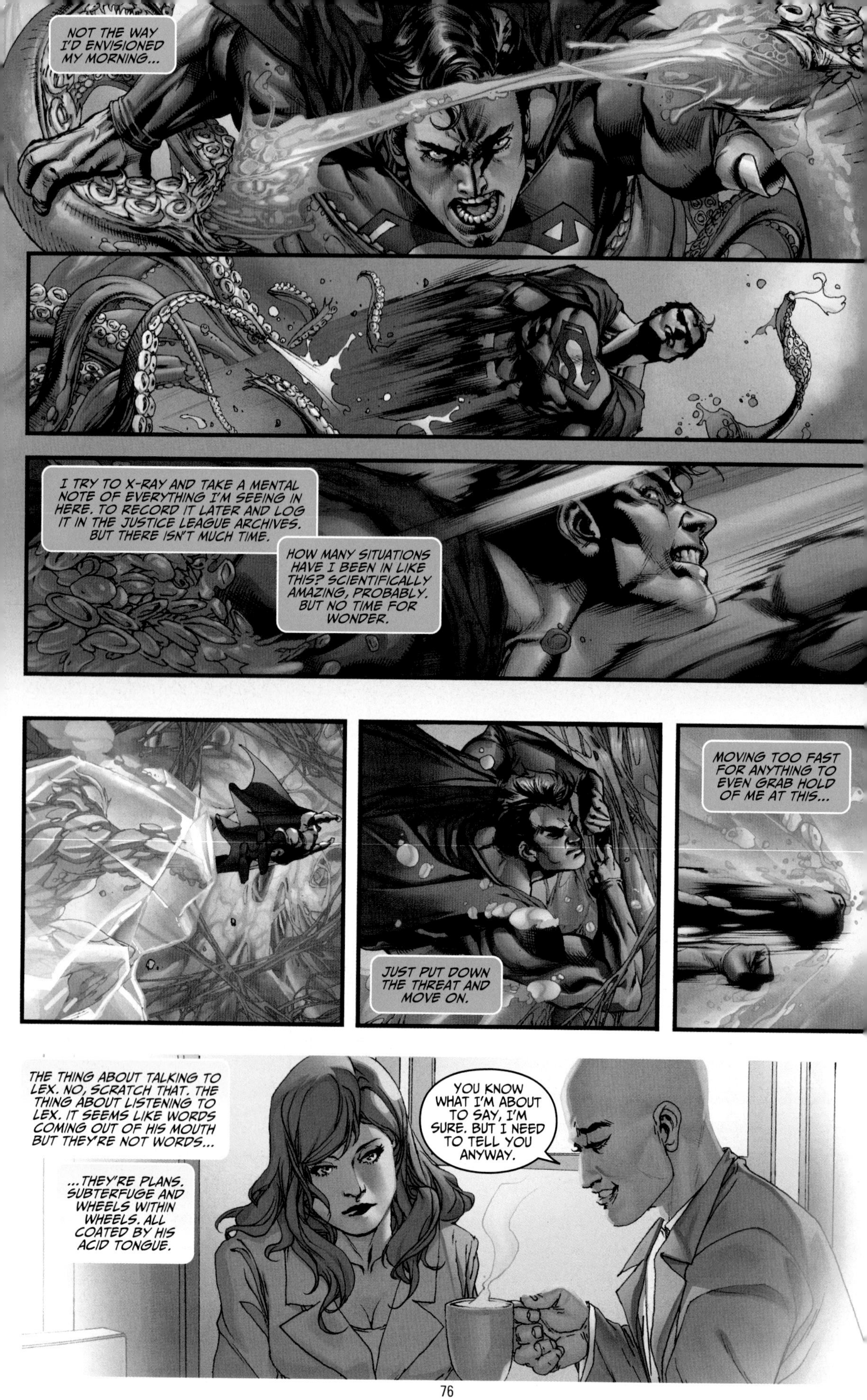
NOT THE WAY I'D ENVISIONED MY MORNING...
I TRY TO X-RAY AND TAKE A MENTAL NOTE OF EVERYTHING I'M SEEING IN HERE. TO RECORD IT LATER AND LOG IT IN THE JUSTICE LEAGUE ARCHIVES. BUT THERE ISN'T MUCH TIME.
HOW MANY SITUATIONS HAVE I BEEN IN LIKE THIS? SCIENTIFICALLY AMAZING, PROBABLY. BUT NO TIME FOR WONDER.
JUST PUT DOWN THE THREAT AND MOVE ON.
MOVING TOO FAST FOR ANYTHING TO EVEN GRAB HOLD OF ME AT THIS...
THE THING ABOUT TALKING TO LEX. NO, SCRATCH THAT. THE THING ABOUT LISTENING TO LEX. IT SEEMS LIKE WORDS COMING OUT OF HIS MOUTH BUT THEY'RE NOT WORDS...
...THEY'RE PLANS. SUBTERFUGE AND WHEELS WITHIN WHEELS. ALL COATED BY HIS ACID TONGUE.
YOU KNOW WHAT I'M ABOUT TO SAY, I'M SURE. BUT I NEED TO TELL YOU ANYWAY.

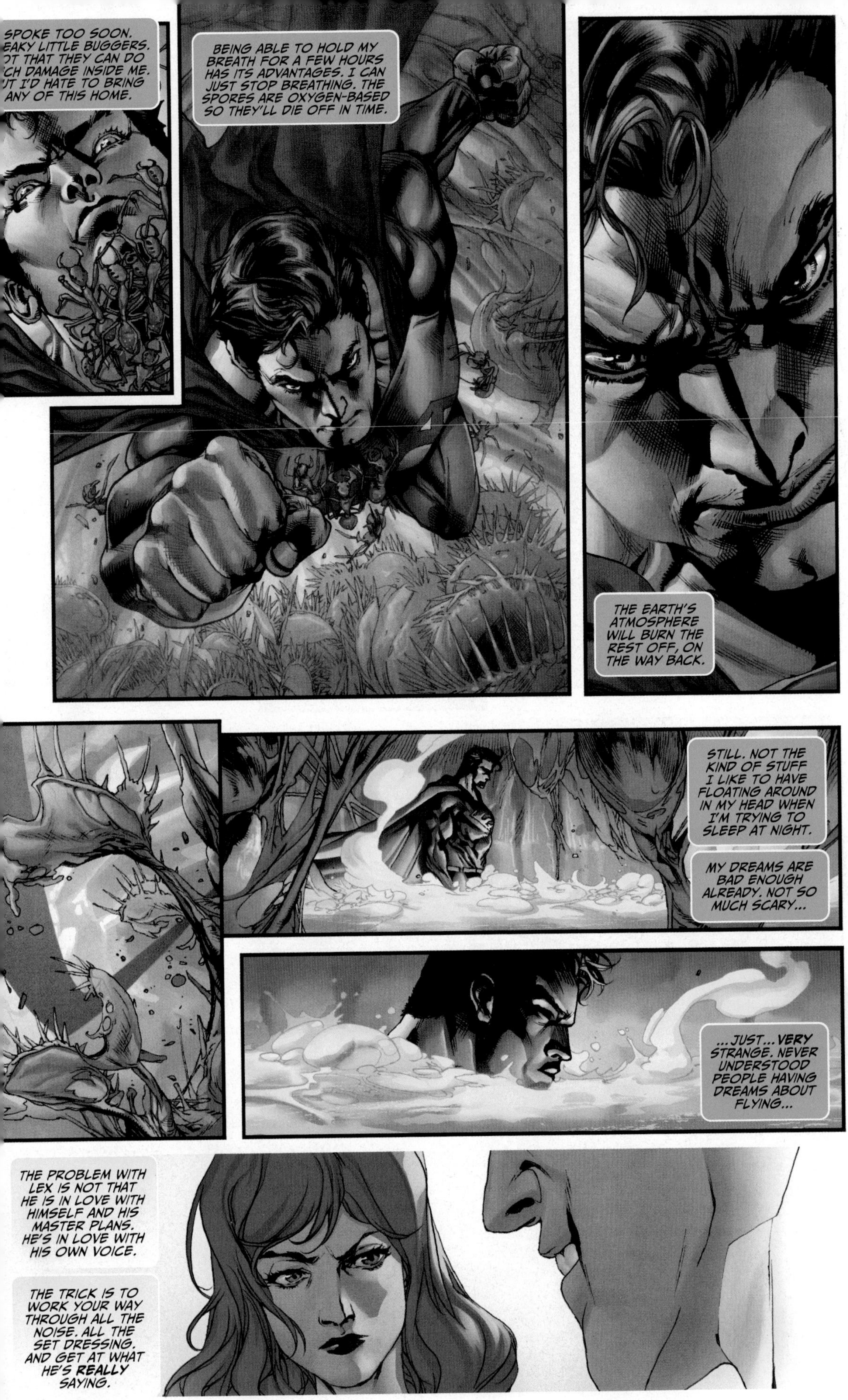
SPOKE TOO SOON. EAKY LITTLE BUGGERS. OT THAT THEY CAN DO CH DAMAGE INSIDE ME. UT I'D HATE TO BRING ANY OF THIS HOME.
BEING ABLE TO HOLD MY BREATH FOR A FEW HOURS HAS ITS ADVANTAGES. I CAN JUST STOP BREATHING. THE SPORES ARE OXYGEN-BASED SO THEY'LL DIE OFF IN TIME.
THE EARTH'S ATMOSPHERE WILL BURN THE REST OFF, ON THE WAY BACK.
STILL. NOT THE KIND OF STUFF I LIKE TO HAVE FLOATING AROUND IN MY HEAD WHEN I'M TRYING TO SLEEP AT NIGHT.
MY DREAMS ARE BAD ENOUGH ALREADY. NOT SO MUCH SCARY...
...JUST...VERY STRANGE. NEVER UNDERSTOOD PEOPLE HAVING DREAMS ABOUT FLYING...
THE PROBLEM WITH LEX IS NOT THAT HE IS IN LOVE WITH HIMSELF AND HIS MASTER PLANS. HE'S IN LOVE WITH HIS OWN VOICE.
THE TRICK IS TO WORK YOUR WAY THROUGH ALL THE NOISE. ALL THE SET DRESSING. AND GET AT WHAT HE'S REALLY SAYING.

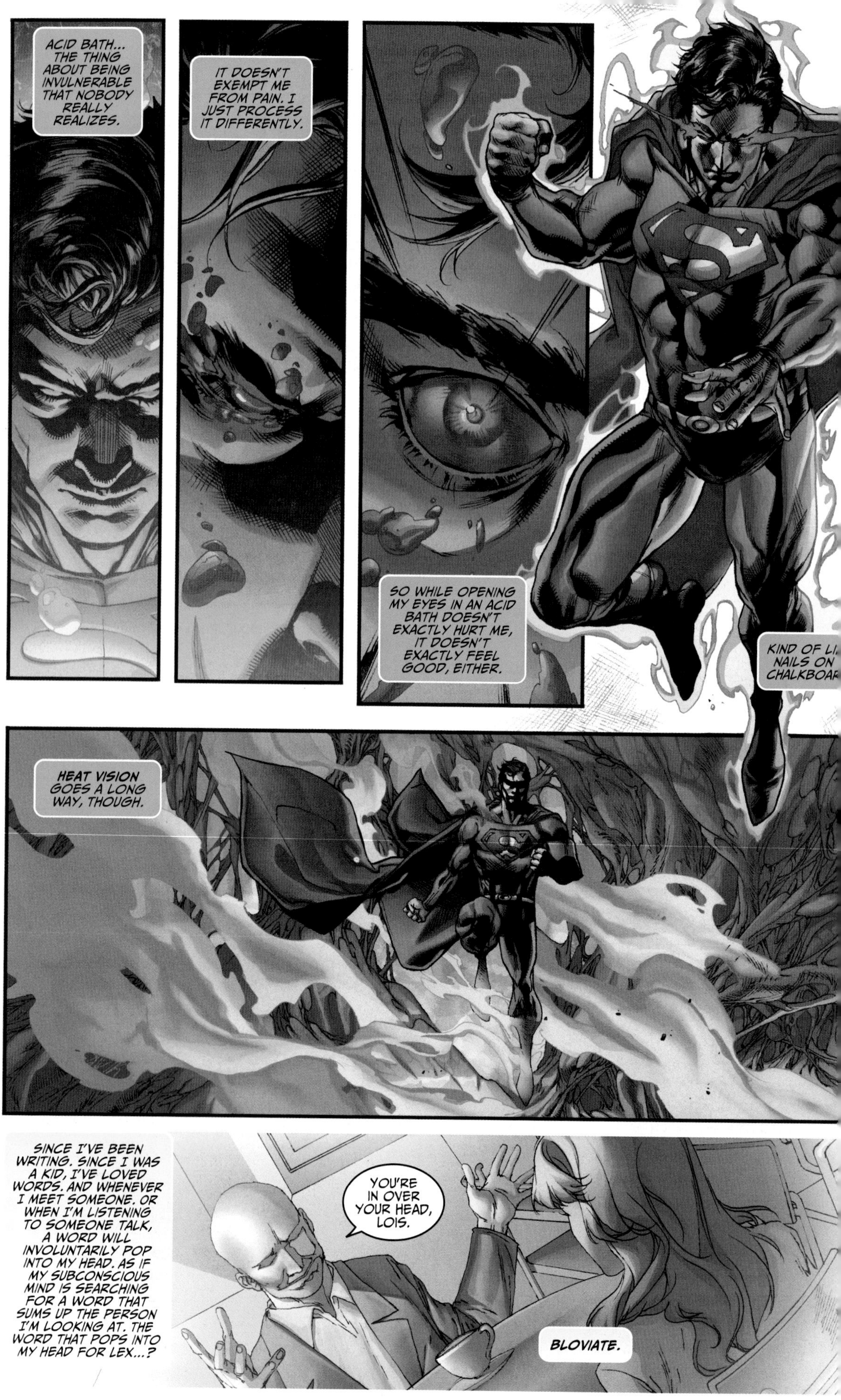
ACID BATH... THE THING ABOUT BEING INVULNERABLE THAT NOBODY REALLY REALIZES.
IT DOESN'T EXEMPT ME FROM PAIN. I JUST PROCESS IT DIFFERENTLY.
SO WHILE OPENING MY EYES IN AN ACID BATH DOESN'T EXACTLY HURT ME, IT DOESN'T EXACTLY FEEL GOOD, EITHER.
KIND OF LI NAILS ON CHALKBOAR
HEAT VISION GOES A LONG WAY, THOUGH.
SINCE I'VE BEEN WRITING. SINCE I WAS A KID, I'VE LOVED WORDS. AND WHENEVER I MEET SOMEONE. OR WHEN I'M LISTENING TO SOMEONE TALK, A WORD WILL INVOLUNTARILY POP INTO MY HEAD. AS IF MY SUBCONSCIOUS MIND IS SEARCHING FOR A WORD THAT SUMS UP THE PERSON I'M LOOKING AT. THE WORD THAT POPS INTO MY HEAD FOR LEX...?
YOU'RE IN OVER YOUR HEAD, LOIS.
BLOVIATE.

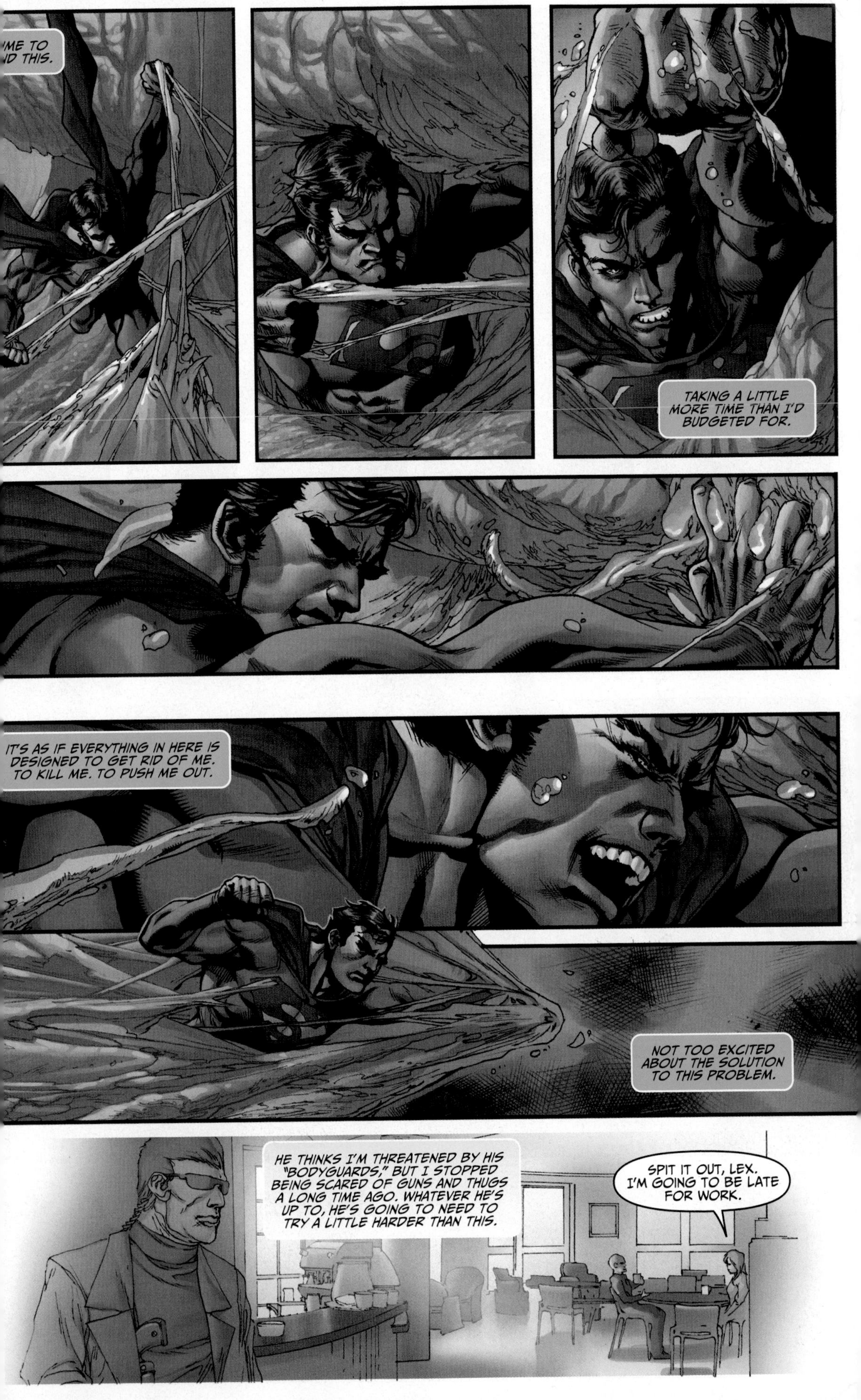

...ME TO
...D THIS.
TAKING A LITTLE MORE TIME THAN I'D BUDGETED FOR.
IT'S AS IF EVERYTHING IN HERE IS DESIGNED TO GET RID OF ME. TO KILL ME. TO PUSH ME OUT.
NOT TOO EXCITED ABOUT THE SOLUTION TO THIS PROBLEM.
HE THINKS I'M THREATENED BY HIS "BODYGUARDS," BUT I STOPPED BEING SCARED OF GUNS AND THUGS A LONG TIME AGO. WHATEVER HE'S UP TO, HE'S GOING TO NEED TO TRY A LITTLE HARDER THAN THIS.
SPIT IT OUT, LEX. I'M GOING TO BE LATE FOR WORK.

BUT LAIRA'S CITY IS BEING DESTROYED AND A FEW MORE WILL BE IF I DON'T GET GOING HERE.

NOT AN EXACT SCIENCE HERE, BUT INFRARED VISION WILL SHOW ME THE HOTSPOTS FOR THE VIOLENT ACTIVITY...

AND WITH A LITTLE LUCK...

...AND SOME BRAIN SURGERY...

...ONE GIANT INTERSTELLAR WORM...

I AM GOING TO RUN FOR OFFICE.

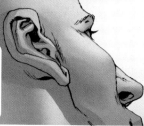

EVEN AS HE SAYS THE WORDS, IT'S AS IF I HAVE X-RAY VISION. I CAN SEE RIGHT INTO HIS SKULL. I CAN SEE THE TWISTED WORMS OF SCHEMES AND EVIL TWISTING AROUND IN THERE.

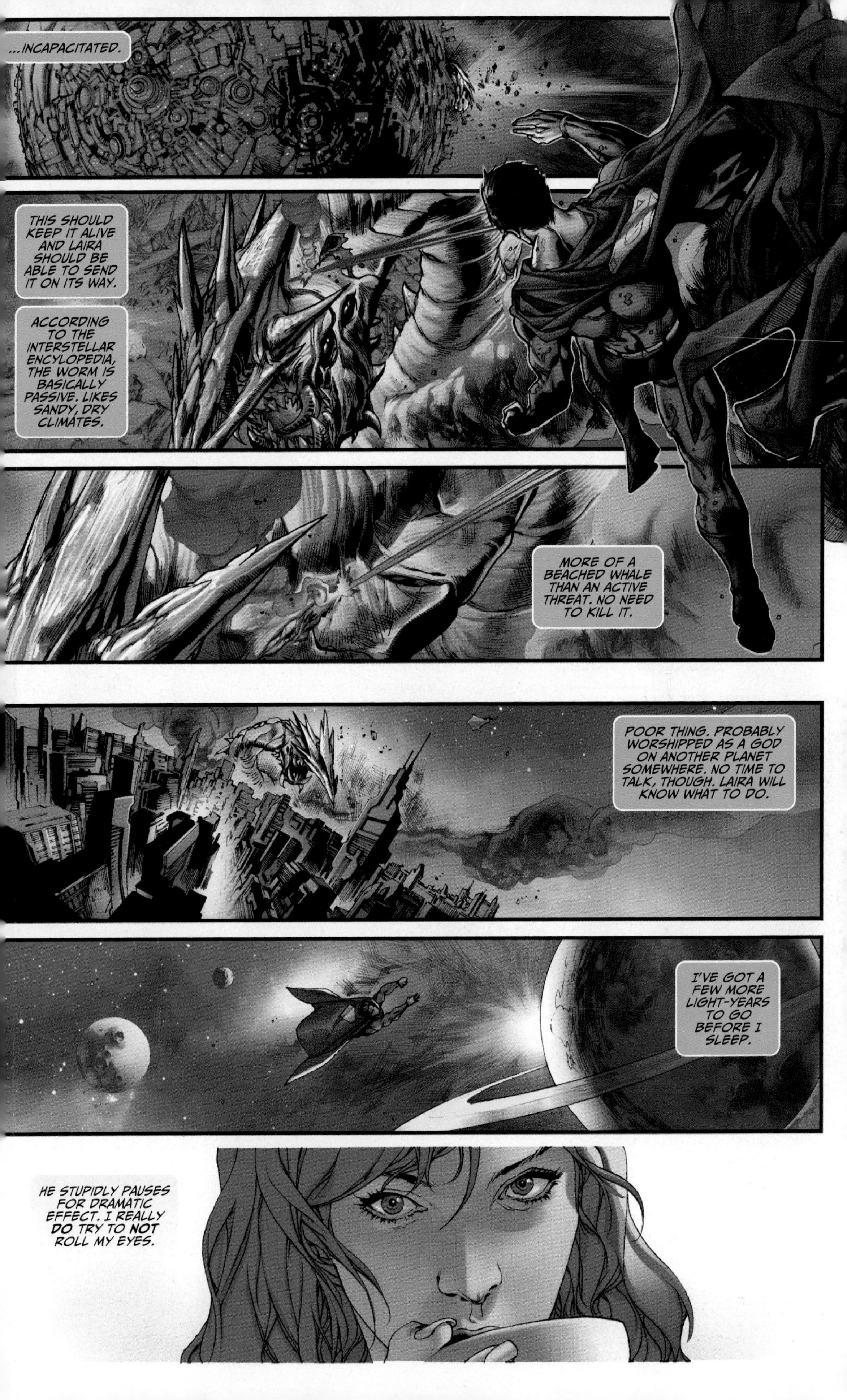
...INCAPACITATED.
THIS SHOULD KEEP IT ALIVE AND LAIRA SHOULD BE ABLE TO SEND IT ON ITS WAY.
ACCORDING TO THE INTERSTELLAR ENCYLOPEDIA, THE WORM IS BASICALLY PASSIVE. LIKES SANDY, DRY CLIMATES.
MORE OF A BEACHED WHALE THAN AN ACTIVE THREAT. NO NEED TO KILL IT.
POOR THING. PROBABLY WORSHIPPED AS A GOD ON ANOTHER PLANET SOMEWHERE. NO TIME TO TALK, THOUGH. LAIRA WILL KNOW WHAT TO DO.
I'VE GOT A FEW MORE LIGHT-YEARS TO GO BEFORE I SLEEP.
HE STUPIDLY PAUSES FOR DRAMATIC EFFECT. I REALLY **DO** TRY TO **NOT** ROLL MY EYES.

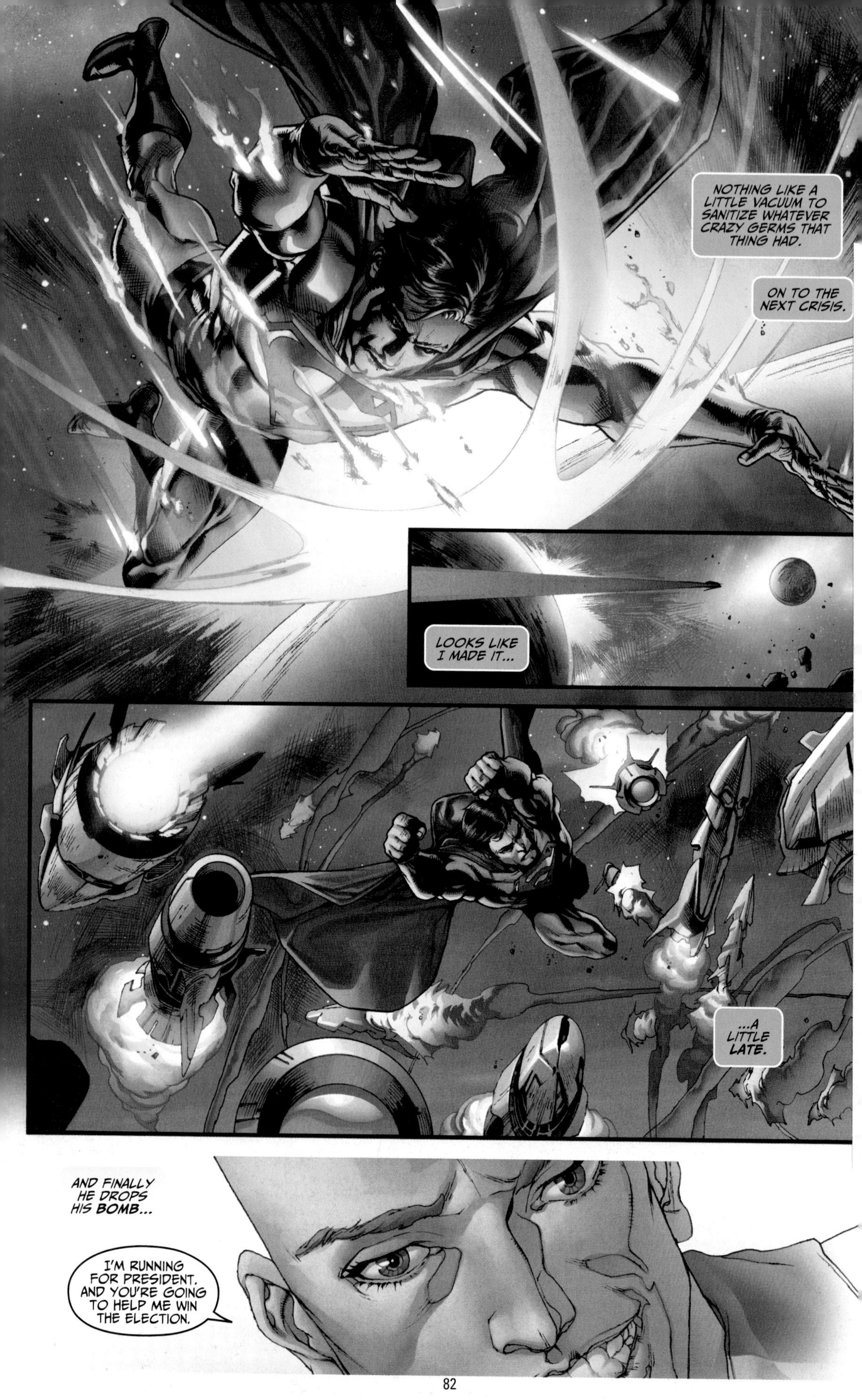
NOTHING LIKE A LITTLE VACUUM TO SANITIZE WHATEVER CRAZY GERMS THAT THING HAD.
ON TO THE NEXT CRISIS.
LOOKS LIKE I MADE IT...
...A LITTLE LATE.
AND FINALLY HE DROPS HIS BOMB...
I'M RUNNING FOR PRESIDENT. AND YOU'RE GOING TO HELP ME WIN THE ELECTION.

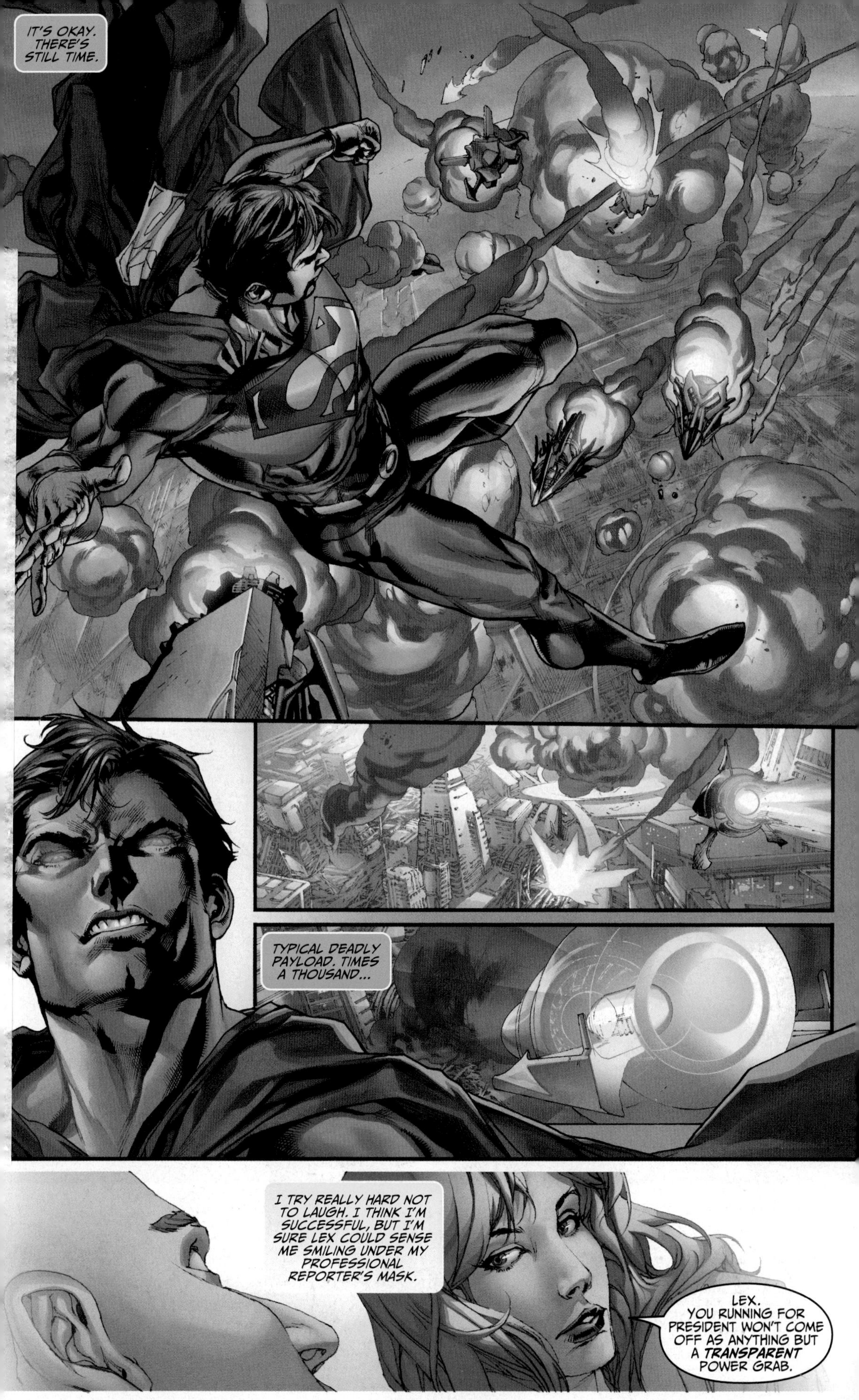
IT'S OKAY. THERE'S STILL TIME.
TYPICAL DEADLY PAYLOAD. TIMES A THOUSAND...
I TRY REALLY HARD NOT TO LAUGH. I THINK I'M SUCCESSFUL, BUT I'M SURE LEX COULD SENSE ME SMILING UNDER MY PROFESSIONAL REPORTER'S MASK.
LEX. YOU RUNNING FOR PRESIDENT WON'T COME OFF AS ANYTHING BUT A TRANSPARENT POWER GRAB.

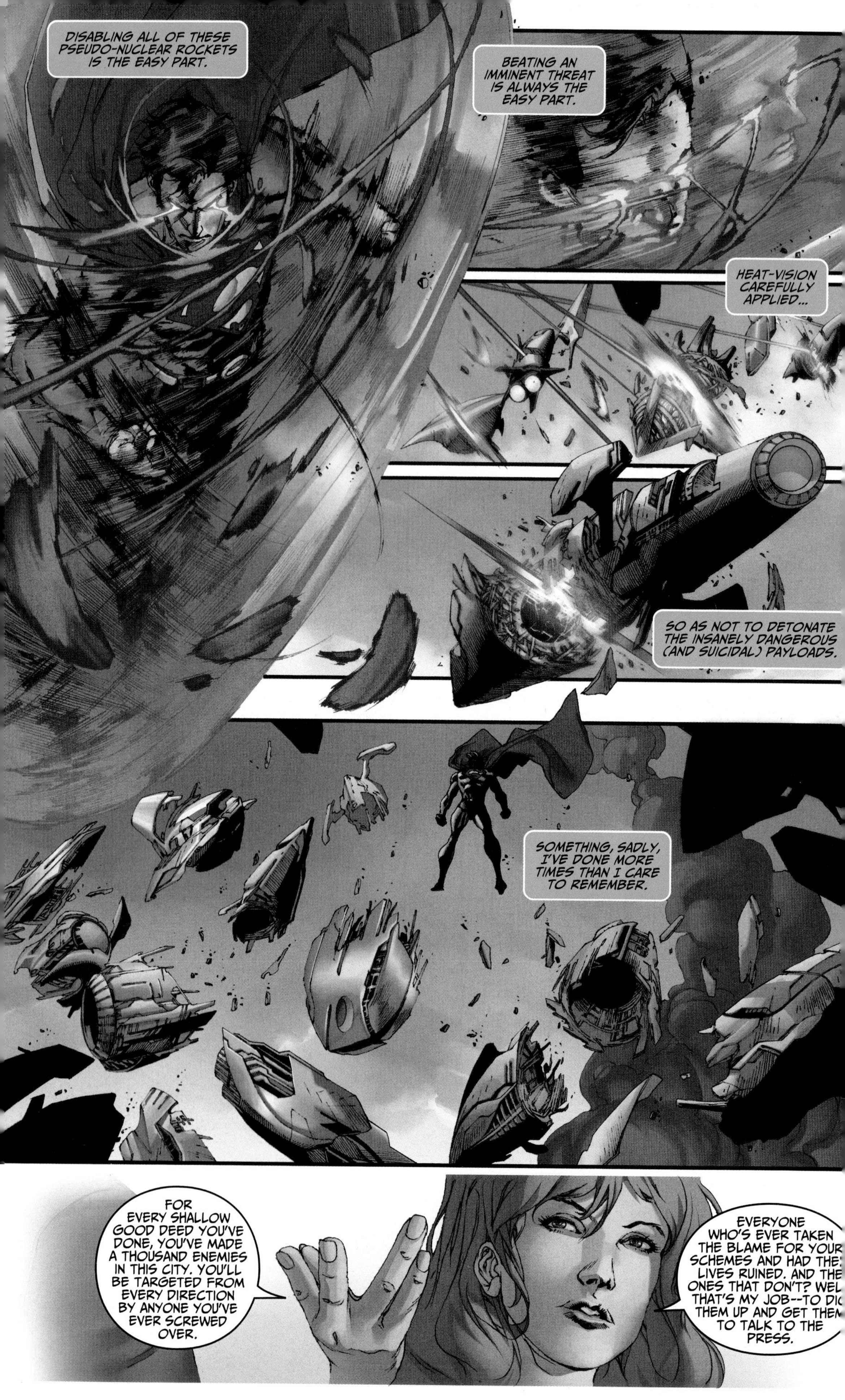
DISABLING ALL OF THESE PSEUDO-NUCLEAR ROCKETS IS THE EASY PART.
BEATING AN IMMINENT THREAT IS ALWAYS THE EASY PART.
HEAT-VISION CAREFULLY APPLIED...
SO AS NOT TO DETONATE THE INSANELY DANGEROUS (AND SUICIDAL) PAYLOADS.
SOMETHING, SADLY, I'VE DONE MORE TIMES THAN I CARE TO REMEMBER.
FOR EVERY SHALLOW GOOD DEED YOU'VE DONE, YOU'VE MADE A THOUSAND ENEMIES IN THIS CITY. YOU'LL BE TARGETED FROM EVERY DIRECTION BY ANYONE YOU'VE EVER SCREWED OVER.
EVERYONE WHO'S EVER TAKEN THE BLAME FOR YOUR SCHEMES AND HAD THE LIVES RUINED. AND THE ONES THAT DON'T? WEL THAT'S MY JOB--TO DI THEM UP AND GET THEM TO TALK TO THE PRESS.

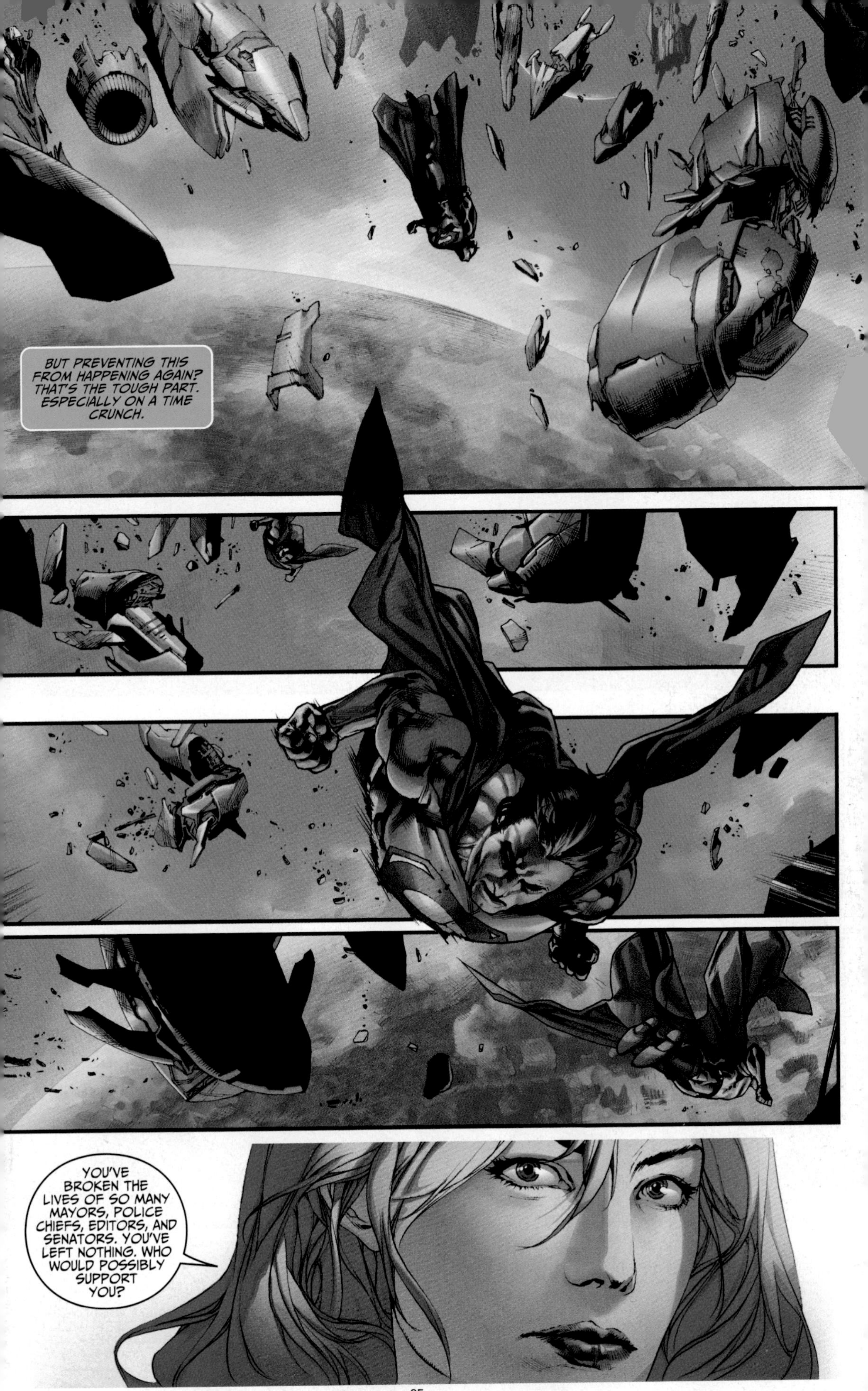
BUT PREVENTING THIS FROM HAPPENING AGAIN? THAT'S THE TOUGH PART. ESPECIALLY ON A TIME CRUNCH.
YOU'VE BROKEN THE LIVES OF SO MANY MAYORS, POLICE CHIEFS, EDITORS, AND SENATORS. YOU'VE LEFT NOTHING. WHO WOULD POSSIBLY SUPPORT YOU?

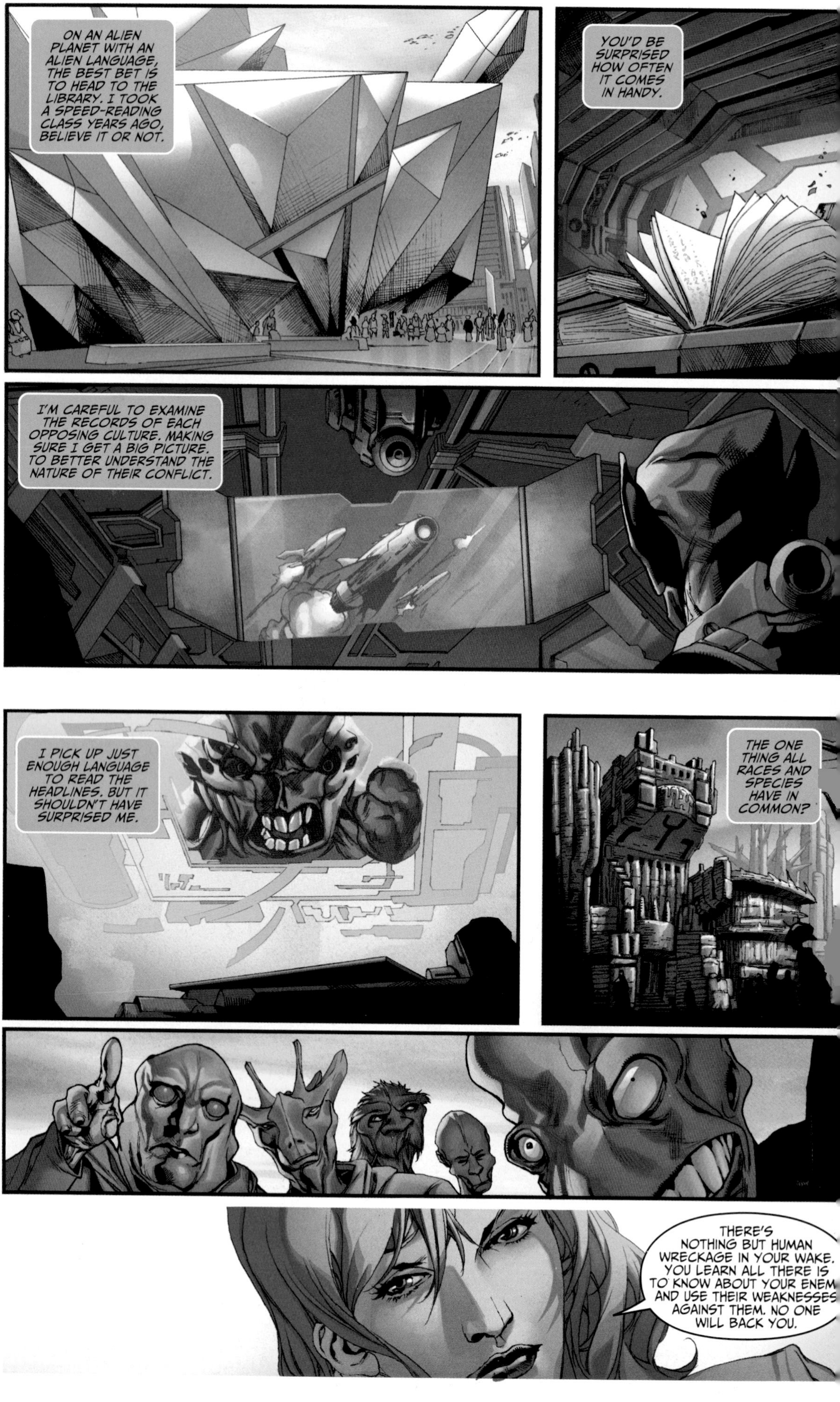
ON AN ALIEN PLANET WITH AN ALIEN LANGUAGE, THE BEST BET IS TO HEAD TO THE LIBRARY. I TOOK A SPEED-READING CLASS YEARS AGO, BELIEVE IT OR NOT.
YOU'D BE SURPRISED HOW OFTEN IT COMES IN HANDY.
I'M CAREFUL TO EXAMINE THE RECORDS OF EACH OPPOSING CULTURE. MAKING SURE I GET A BIG PICTURE. TO BETTER UNDERSTAND THE NATURE OF THEIR CONFLICT.
I PICK UP JUST ENOUGH LANGUAGE TO READ THE HEADLINES. BUT IT SHOULDN'T HAVE SURPRISED ME.
THE ONE THING ALL RACES AND SPECIES HAVE IN COMMON?
THERE'S NOTHING BUT HUMAN WRECKAGE IN YOUR WAKE. YOU LEARN ALL THERE IS TO KNOW ABOUT YOUR ENEM AND USE THEIR WEAKNESSES AGAINST THEM. NO ONE WILL BACK YOU.

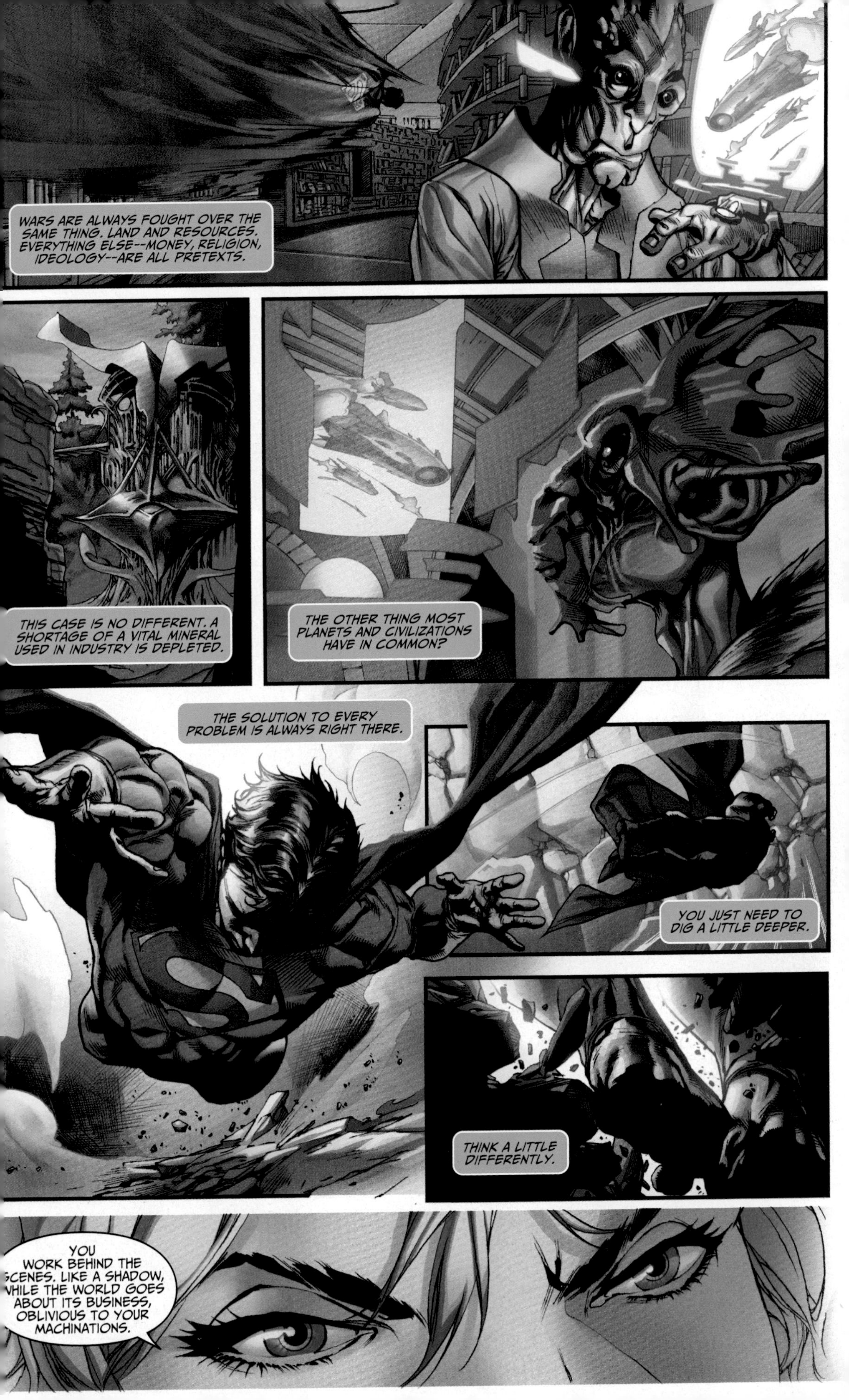
WARS ARE ALWAYS FOUGHT OVER THE SAME THING. LAND AND RESOURCES. EVERYTHING ELSE--MONEY, RELIGION, IDEOLOGY--ARE ALL PRETEXTS.
THIS CASE IS NO DIFFERENT. A SHORTAGE OF A VITAL MINERAL USED IN INDUSTRY IS DEPLETED.
THE OTHER THING MOST PLANETS AND CIVILIZATIONS HAVE IN COMMON?
THE SOLUTION TO EVERY PROBLEM IS ALWAYS RIGHT THERE.
YOU JUST NEED TO DIG A LITTLE DEEPER.
THINK A LITTLE DIFFERENTLY.
YOU WORK BEHIND THE SCENES. LIKE A SHADOW, WHILE THE WORLD GOES ABOUT ITS BUSINESS, OBLIVIOUS TO YOUR MACHINATIONS.

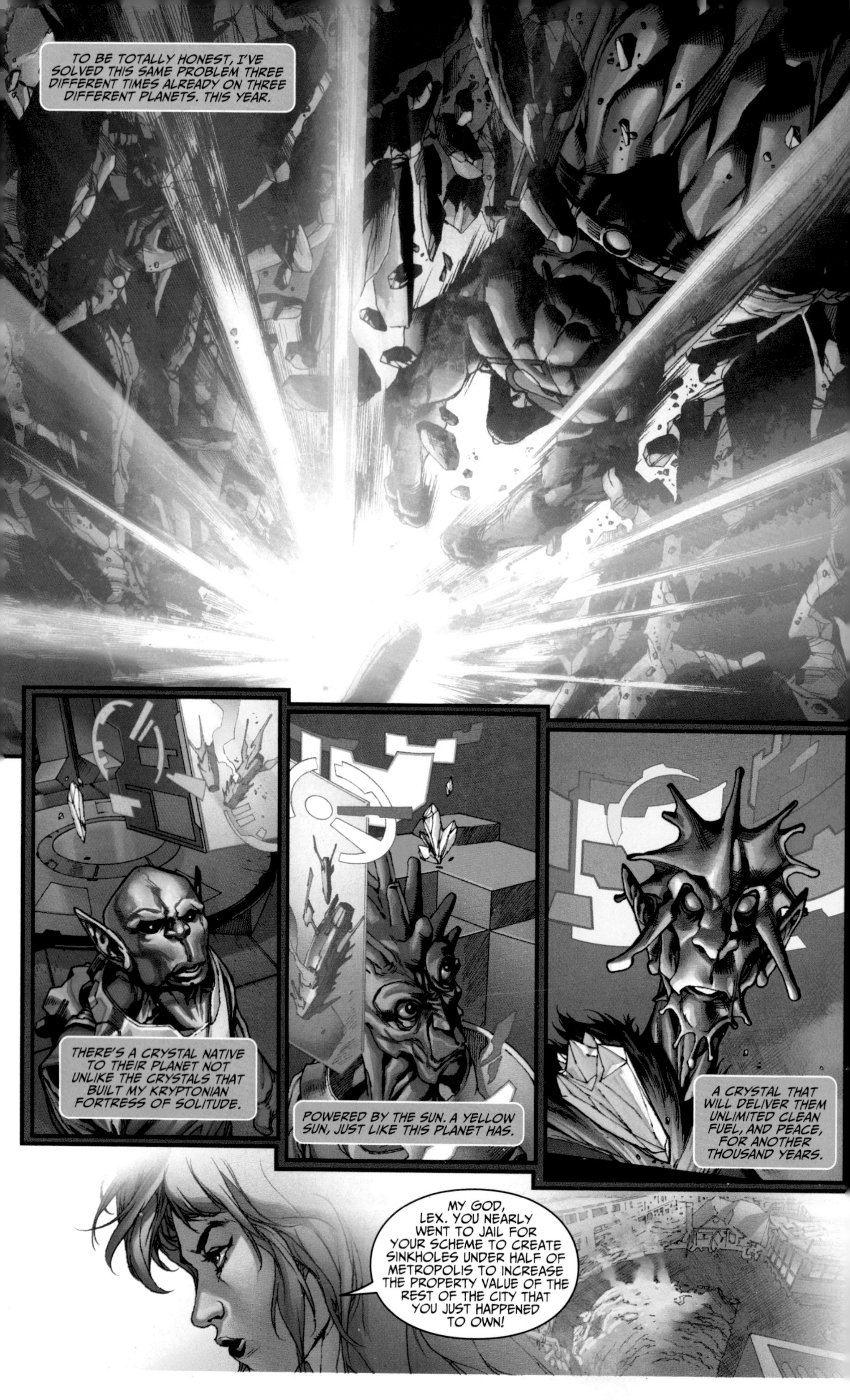
TO BE TOTALLY HONEST, I'VE SOLVED THIS SAME PROBLEM THREE DIFFERENT TIMES ALREADY ON THREE DIFFERENT PLANETS. THIS YEAR.
THERE'S A CRYSTAL NATIVE TO THEIR PLANET NOT UNLIKE THE CRYSTALS THAT BUILT MY KRYPTONIAN FORTRESS OF SOLITUDE.
POWERED BY THE SUN. A YELLOW SUN, JUST LIKE THIS PLANET HAS.
A CRYSTAL THAT WILL DELIVER THEM UNLIMITED CLEAN FUEL, AND PEACE, FOR ANOTHER THOUSAND YEARS.
MY GOD, LEX. YOU NEARLY WENT TO JAIL FOR YOUR SCHEME TO CREATE SINKHOLES UNDER HALF OF METROPOLIS TO INCREASE THE PROPERTY VALUE OF THE REST OF THE CITY THAT YOU JUST HAPPENED TO OWN!

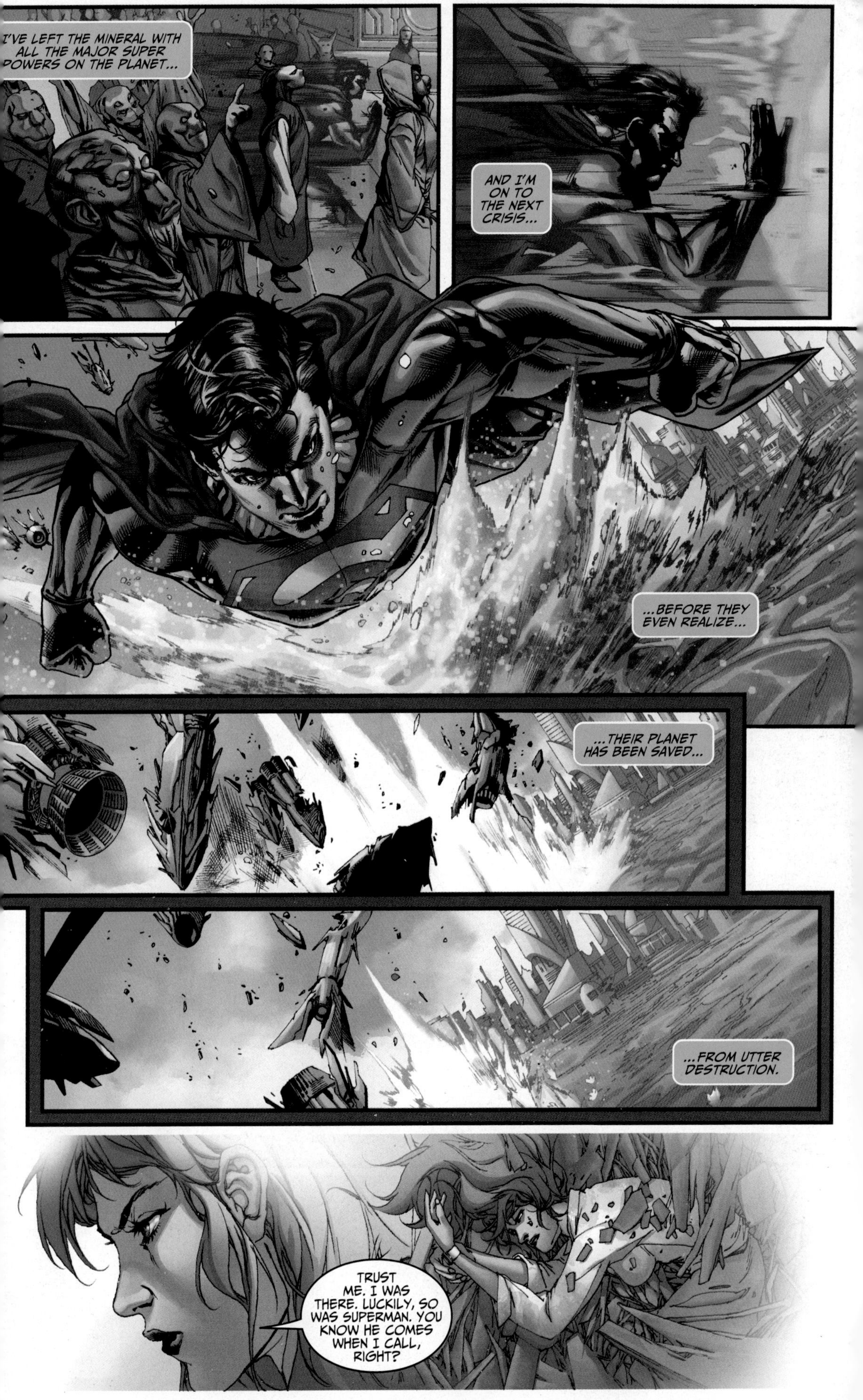
I'VE LEFT THE MINERAL WITH ALL THE MAJOR SUPER POWERS ON THE PLANET...
AND I'M ON TO THE NEXT CRISIS...
...BEFORE THEY EVEN REALIZE...
...THEIR PLANET HAS BEEN SAVED...
...FROM UTTER DESTRUCTION.
TRUST ME. I WAS THERE. LUCKILY, SO WAS SUPERMAN. YOU KNOW HE COMES WHEN I CALL, RIGHT?

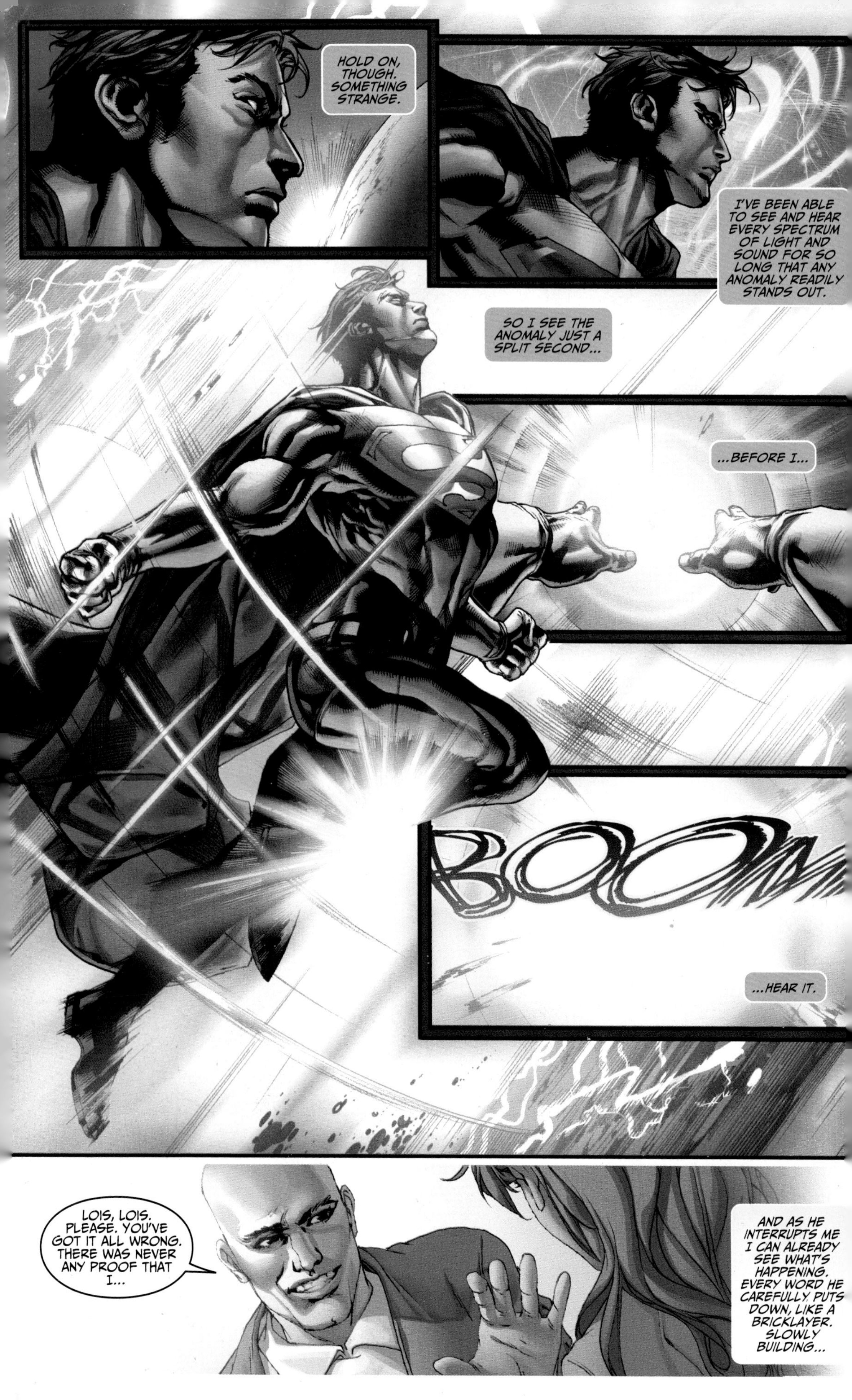
HOLD ON, THOUGH. SOMETHING STRANGE.
I'VE BEEN ABLE TO SEE AND HEAR EVERY SPECTRUM OF LIGHT AND SOUND FOR SO LONG THAT ANY ANOMALY READILY STANDS OUT.
SO I SEE THE ANOMALY JUST A SPLIT SECOND...
...BEFORE I...
BOOM
...HEAR IT.
LOIS, LOIS. PLEASE. YOU'VE GOT IT ALL WRONG. THERE WAS NEVER ANY PROOF THAT I...
AND AS HE INTERRUPTS ME I CAN ALREADY SEE WHAT'S HAPPENING. EVERY WORD HE CAREFULLY PUTS DOWN, LIKE A BRICKLAYER. SLOWLY BUILDING...

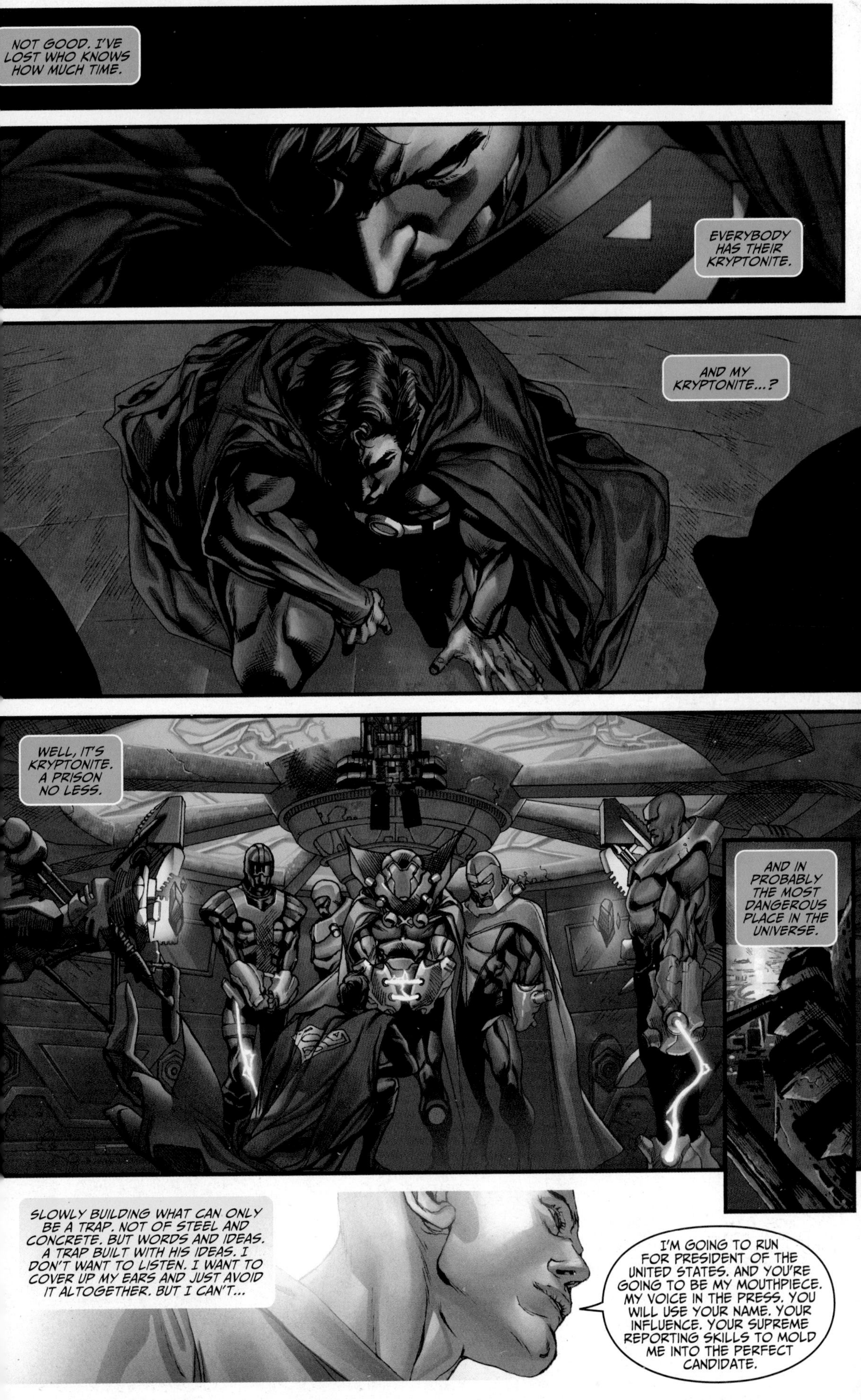
NOT GOOD. I'VE LOST WHO KNOWS HOW MUCH TIME.
EVERYBODY HAS THEIR KRYPTONITE.
AND MY KRYPTONITE...?
WELL, IT'S KRYPTONITE. A PRISON NO LESS.
AND IN PROBABLY THE MOST DANGEROUS PLACE IN THE UNIVERSE.
SLOWLY BUILDING WHAT CAN ONLY BE A TRAP. NOT OF STEEL AND CONCRETE. BUT WORDS AND IDEAS. A TRAP BUILT WITH HIS IDEAS. I DON'T WANT TO LISTEN. I WANT TO COVER UP MY EARS AND JUST AVOID IT ALTOGETHER. BUT I CAN'T...
I'M GOING TO RUN FOR PRESIDENT OF THE UNITED STATES. AND YOU'RE GOING TO BE MY MOUTHPIECE. MY VOICE IN THE PRESS. YOU WILL USE YOUR NAME. YOUR INFLUENCE. YOUR SUPREME REPORTING SKILLS TO MOLD ME INTO THE PERFECT CANDIDATE.

APOKOLIPS.

I DON'T HAVE TIME FOR THIS DETOUR.

MY FAULT FOR GOING TOO FAST, I GUESS.

DIDN'T SEE THE BOOM-TUBE TRAP SET BY *DARKSEID* UNTIL IT WAS TOO LATE. TOO LATE.

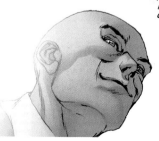

THAT'S IT? THAT'S THE MASTER PLAN? WELL, IF THAT'S IT, HE CAN JUST BLOW IT OUT HIS--

AND IF YOU DON'T DO AS I SAY, YOU AND ALL OF YOUR FAMILY AND FRIENDS WILL DISAPPEAR FROM THE FACE OF THE EARTH. WITHIN THE HOUR.

OH.

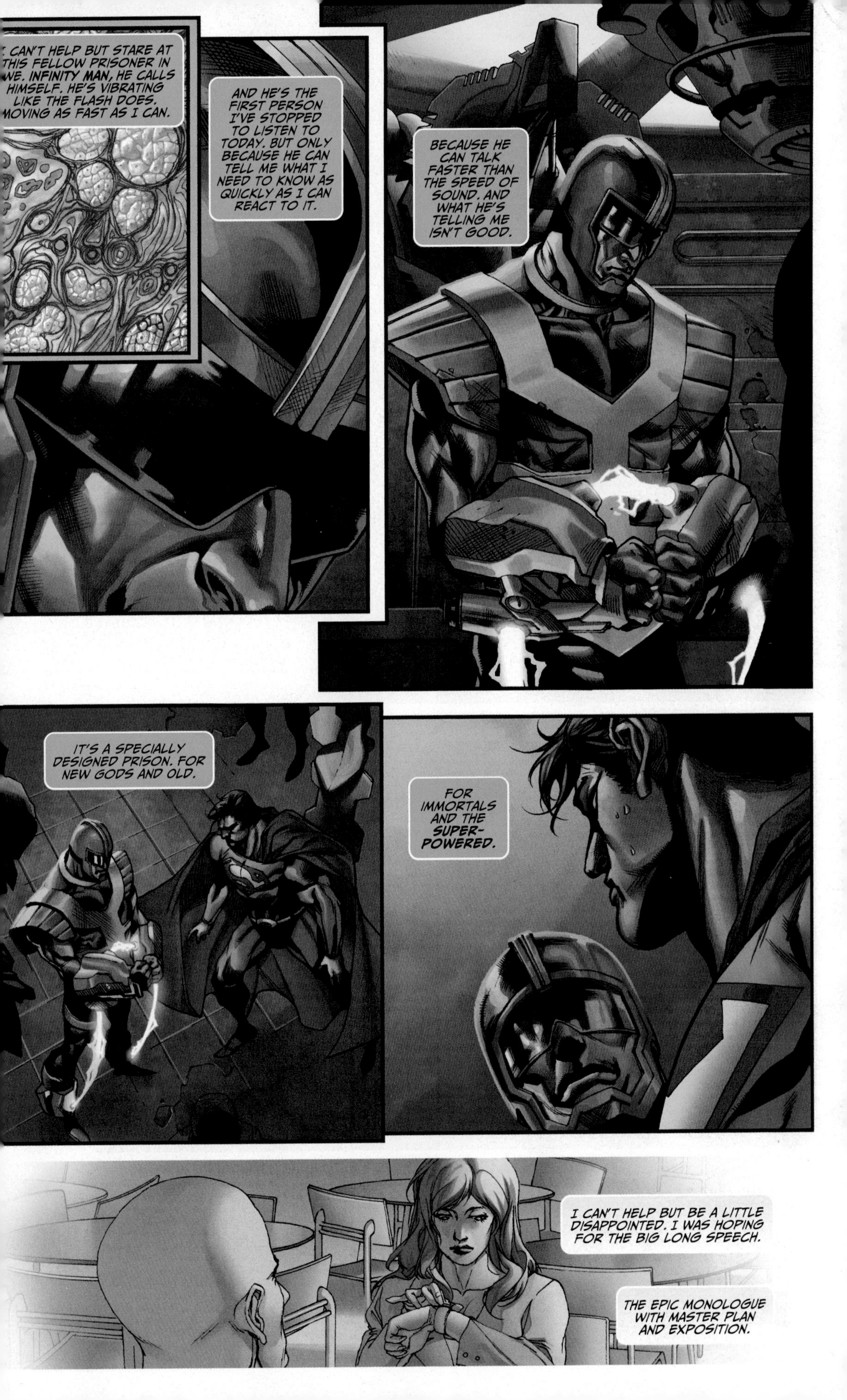
I CAN'T HELP BUT STARE AT THIS FELLOW PRISONER IN AWE. INFINITY MAN, HE CALLS HIMSELF. HE'S VIBRATING LIKE THE FLASH DOES. MOVING AS FAST AS I CAN.
AND HE'S THE FIRST PERSON I'VE STOPPED TO LISTEN TO TODAY. BUT ONLY BECAUSE HE CAN TELL ME WHAT I NEED TO KNOW AS QUICKLY AS I CAN REACT TO IT.
BECAUSE HE CAN TALK FASTER THAN THE SPEED OF SOUND. AND WHAT HE'S TELLING ME ISN'T GOOD.
IT'S A SPECIALLY DESIGNED PRISON. FOR NEW GODS AND OLD.
FOR IMMORTALS AND THE SUPER-POWERED.
I CAN'T HELP BUT BE A LITTLE DISAPPOINTED. I WAS HOPING FOR THE BIG LONG SPEECH.
THE EPIC MONOLOGUE WITH MASTER PLAN AND EXPOSITION.

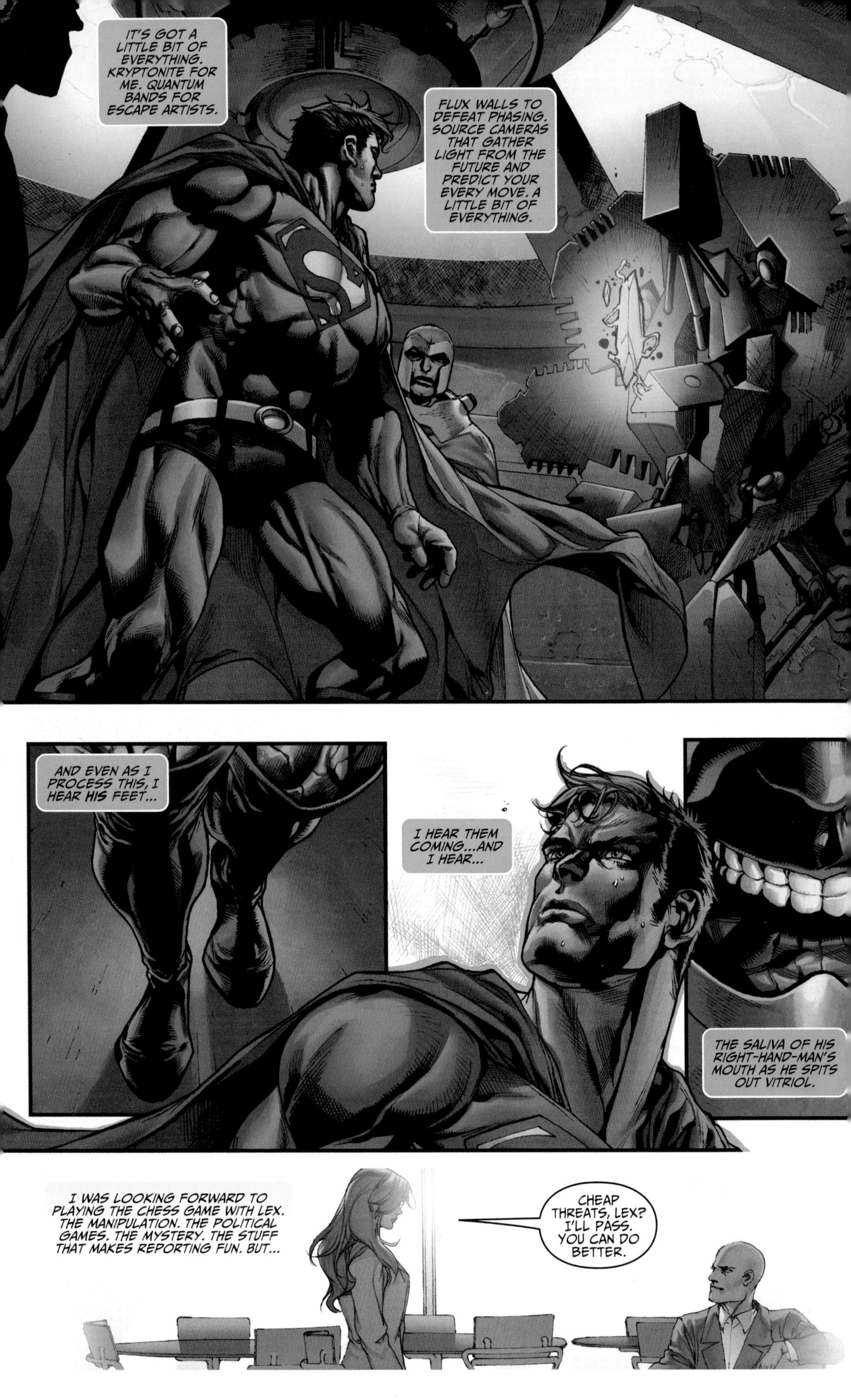
IT'S GOT A LITTLE BIT OF EVERYTHING. KRYPTONITE FOR ME. QUANTUM BANDS FOR ESCAPE ARTISTS.
FLUX WALLS TO DEFEAT PHASING. SOURCE CAMERAS THAT GATHER LIGHT FROM THE FUTURE AND PREDICT YOUR EVERY MOVE. A LITTLE BIT OF EVERYTHING.
AND EVEN AS I PROCESS THIS, I HEAR HIS FEET...
I HEAR THEM COMING...AND I HEAR...
THE SALIVA OF HIS RIGHT-HAND-MAN'S MOUTH AS HE SPITS OUT VITRIOL.
I WAS LOOKING FORWARD TO PLAYING THE CHESS GAME WITH LEX. THE MANIPULATION. THE POLITICAL GAMES. THE MYSTERY. THE STUFF THAT MAKES REPORTING FUN. BUT...
CHEAP THREATS, LEX? I'LL PASS. YOU CAN DO BETTER.

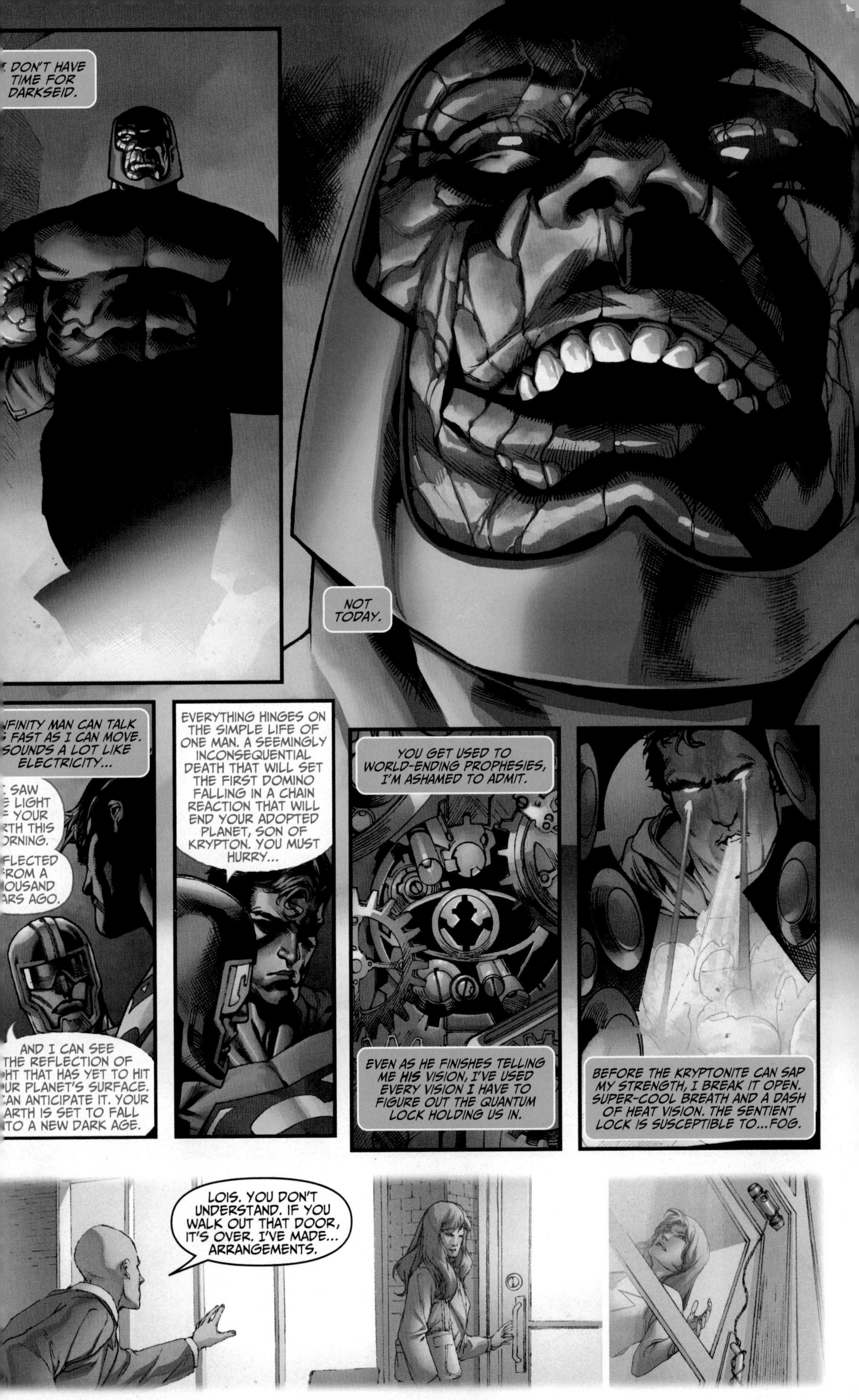

DON'T HAVE TIME FOR DARKSEID.
NOT TODAY.
NFINITY MAN CAN TALK FAST AS I CAN MOVE. SOUNDS A LOT LIKE ELECTRICITY...
SAW LIGHT YOUR RTH THIS ORNING.
FLECTED FROM A HOUSAND ARS AGO.
AND I CAN SEE THE REFLECTION OF HT THAT HAS YET TO HIT UR PLANET'S SURFACE. CAN ANTICIPATE IT. YOUR ARTH IS SET TO FALL NTO A NEW DARK AGE.
EVERYTHING HINGES ON THE SIMPLE LIFE OF ONE MAN. A SEEMINGLY INCONSEQUENTIAL DEATH THAT WILL SET THE FIRST DOMINO FALLING IN A CHAIN REACTION THAT WILL END YOUR ADOPTED PLANET, SON OF KRYPTON. YOU MUST HURRY...
YOU GET USED TO WORLD-ENDING PROPHESIES, I'M ASHAMED TO ADMIT.
EVEN AS HE FINISHES TELLING ME HIS VISION, I'VE USED EVERY VISION I HAVE TO FIGURE OUT THE QUANTUM LOCK HOLDING US IN.
BEFORE THE KRYPTONITE CAN SAP MY STRENGTH, I BREAK IT OPEN. SUPER-COOL BREATH AND A DASH OF HEAT VISION. THE SENTIENT LOCK IS SUSCEPTIBLE TO...FOG.
LOIS. YOU DON'T UNDERSTAND. IF YOU WALK OUT THAT DOOR, IT'S OVER. I'VE MADE... ARRANGEMENTS.

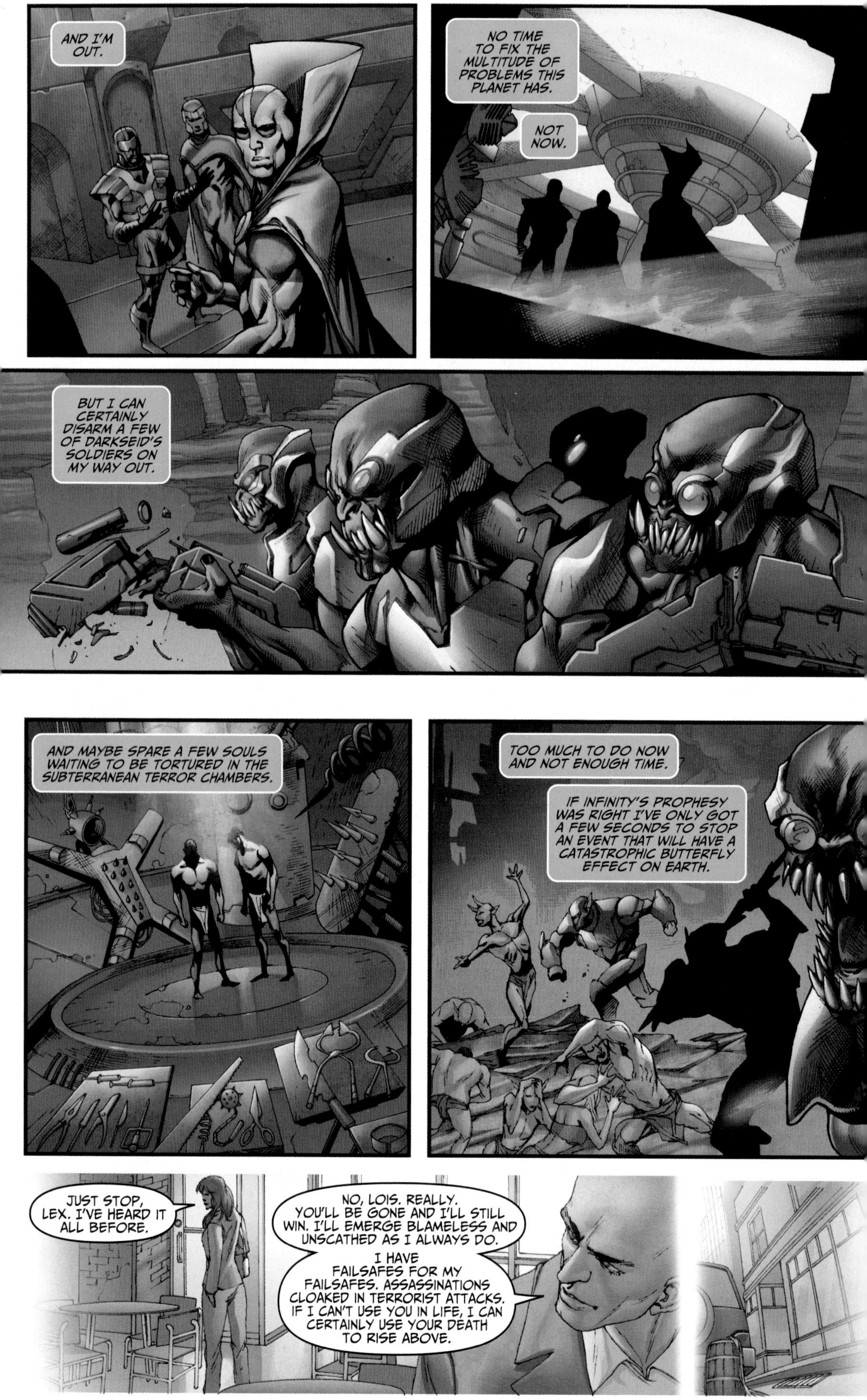
AND I'M OUT.
NO TIME TO FIX THE MULTITUDE OF PROBLEMS THIS PLANET HAS.
NOT NOW.
BUT I CAN CERTAINLY DISARM A FEW OF DARKSEID'S SOLDIERS ON MY WAY OUT.
AND MAYBE SPARE A FEW SOULS WAITING TO BE TORTURED IN THE SUBTERRANEAN TERROR CHAMBERS.
TOO MUCH TO DO NOW AND NOT ENOUGH TIME.
IF INFINITY'S PROPHESY WAS RIGHT I'VE ONLY GOT A FEW SECONDS TO STOP AN EVENT THAT WILL HAVE A CATASTROPHIC BUTTERFLY EFFECT ON EARTH.
JUST STOP, LEX. I'VE HEARD IT ALL BEFORE.
NO, LOIS. REALLY. YOU'LL BE GONE AND I'LL STILL WIN. I'LL EMERGE BLAMELESS AND UNSCATHED AS I ALWAYS DO.
I HAVE FAILSAFES FOR MY FAILSAFES. ASSASSINATIONS CLOAKED IN TERRORIST ATTACKS. IF I CAN'T USE YOU IN LIFE, I CAN CERTAINLY USE YOUR DEATH TO RISE ABOVE.

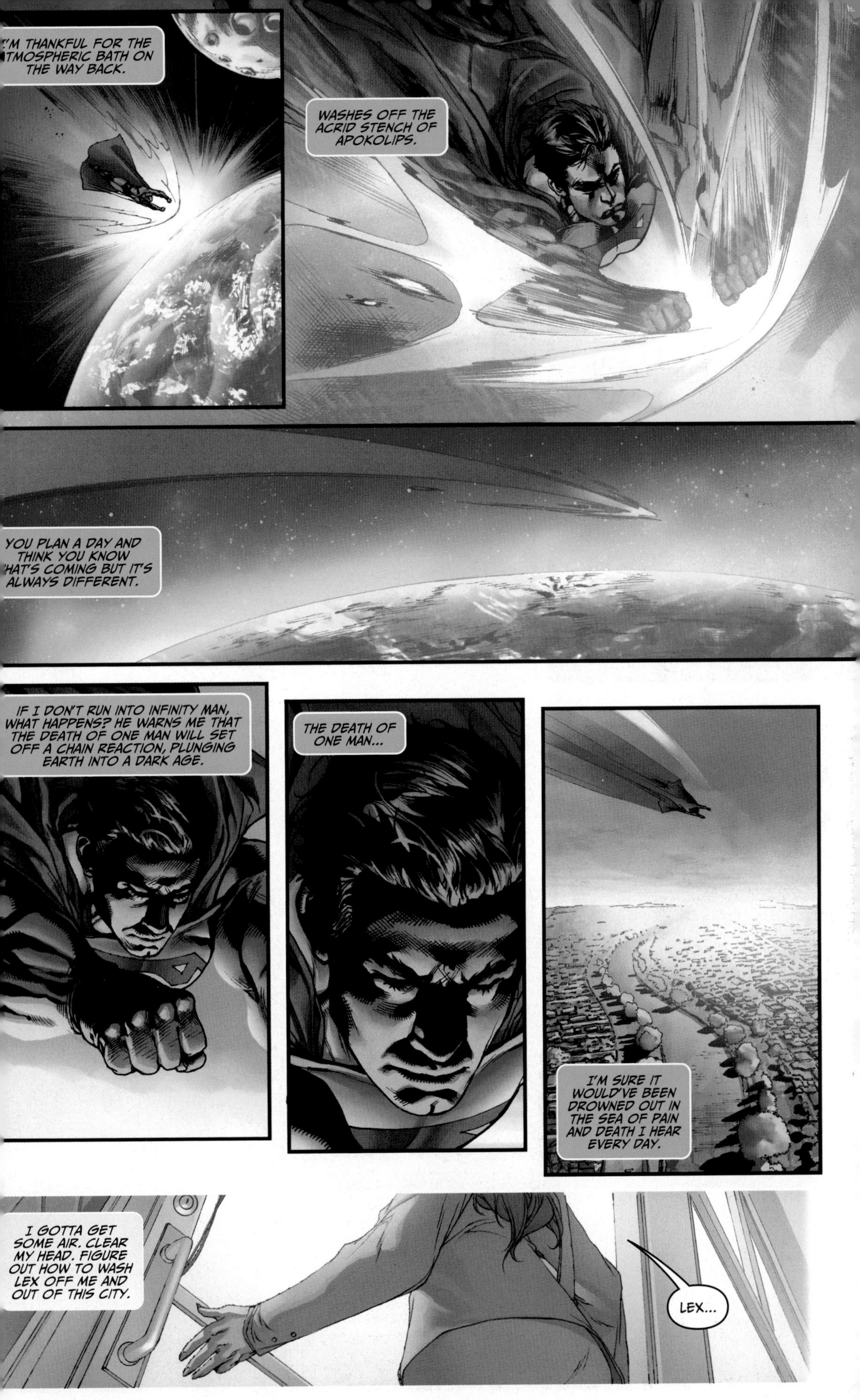
I'M THANKFUL FOR THE ATMOSPHERIC BATH ON THE WAY BACK.
WASHES OFF THE ACRID STENCH OF APOKOLIPS.
YOU PLAN A DAY AND THINK YOU KNOW WHAT'S COMING BUT IT'S ALWAYS DIFFERENT.
IF I DON'T RUN INTO INFINITY MAN, WHAT HAPPENS? HE WARNS ME THAT THE DEATH OF ONE MAN WILL SET OFF A CHAIN REACTION, PLUNGING EARTH INTO A DARK AGE.
THE DEATH OF ONE MAN...
I'M SURE IT WOULD'VE BEEN DROWNED OUT IN THE SEA OF PAIN AND DEATH I HEAR EVERY DAY.
I GOTTA GET SOME AIR. CLEAR MY HEAD. FIGURE OUT HOW TO WASH LEX OFF ME AND OUT OF THIS CITY.
LEX...

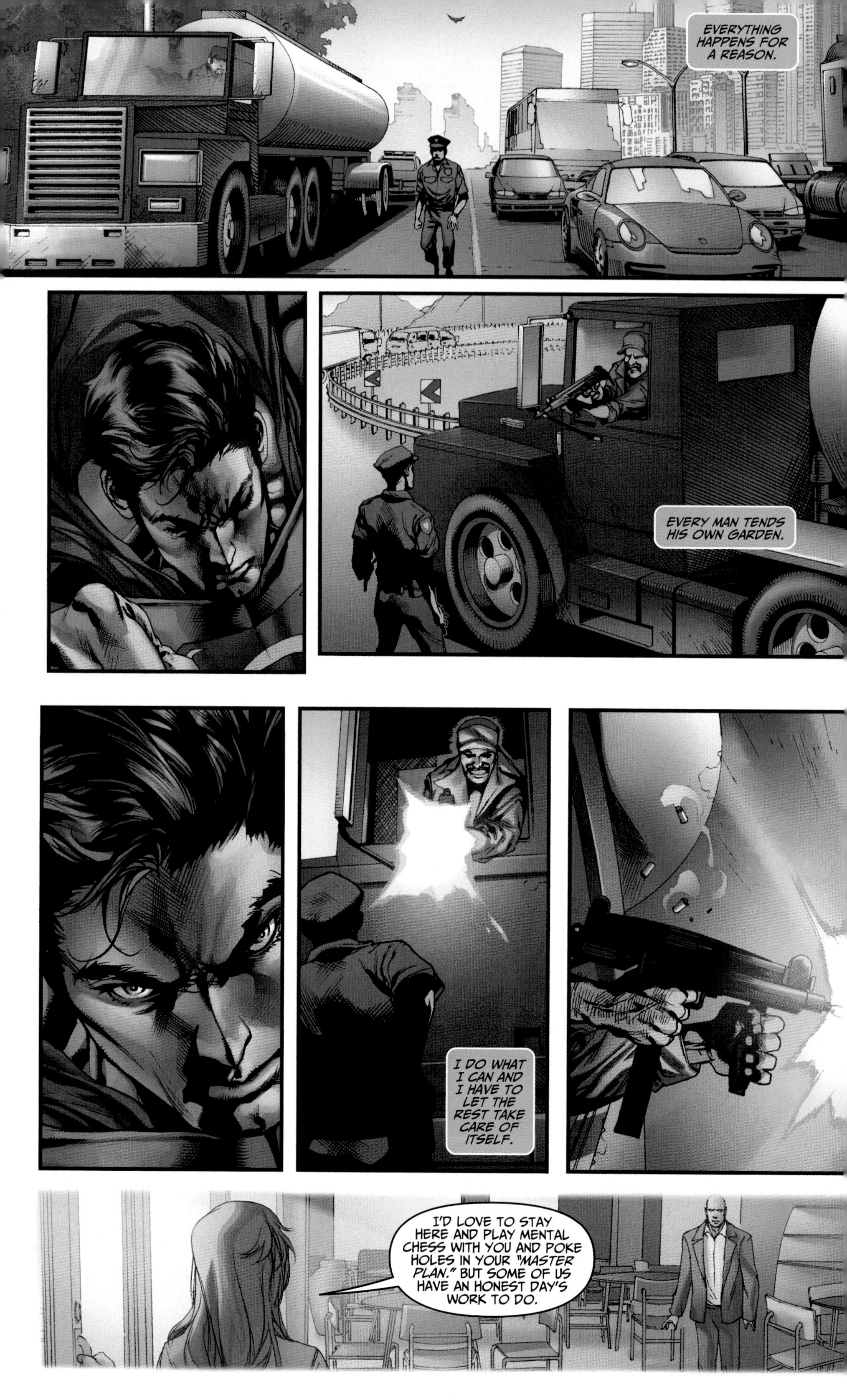
EVERYTHING HAPPENS FOR A REASON.
EVERY MAN TENDS HIS OWN GARDEN.
I DO WHAT I CAN AND I HAVE TO LET THE REST TAKE CARE OF ITSELF.
I'D LOVE TO STAY HERE AND PLAY MENTAL CHESS WITH YOU AND POKE HOLES IN YOUR "MASTER PLAN." BUT SOME OF US HAVE AN HONEST DAY'S WORK TO DO.

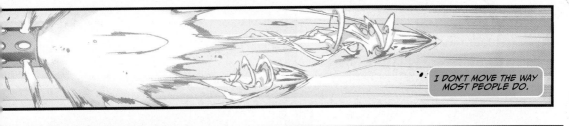

I DON'T MOVE THE WAY MOST PEOPLE DO.

I'M FASTER. I CAN DO MORE.

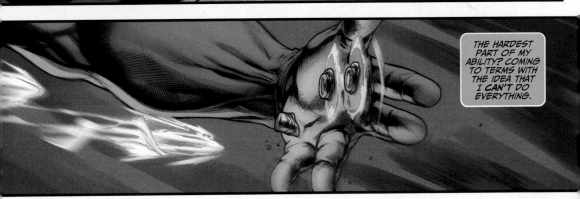

THE HARDEST PART OF MY ABILITY? COMING TO TERMS WITH THE IDEA THAT I CAN'T DO EVERYTHING.

YOU CAN ONLY DODGE BULLETS FOR SO LONG, LEX. EVENTUALLY YOU'RE GOING TO CATCH ONE.

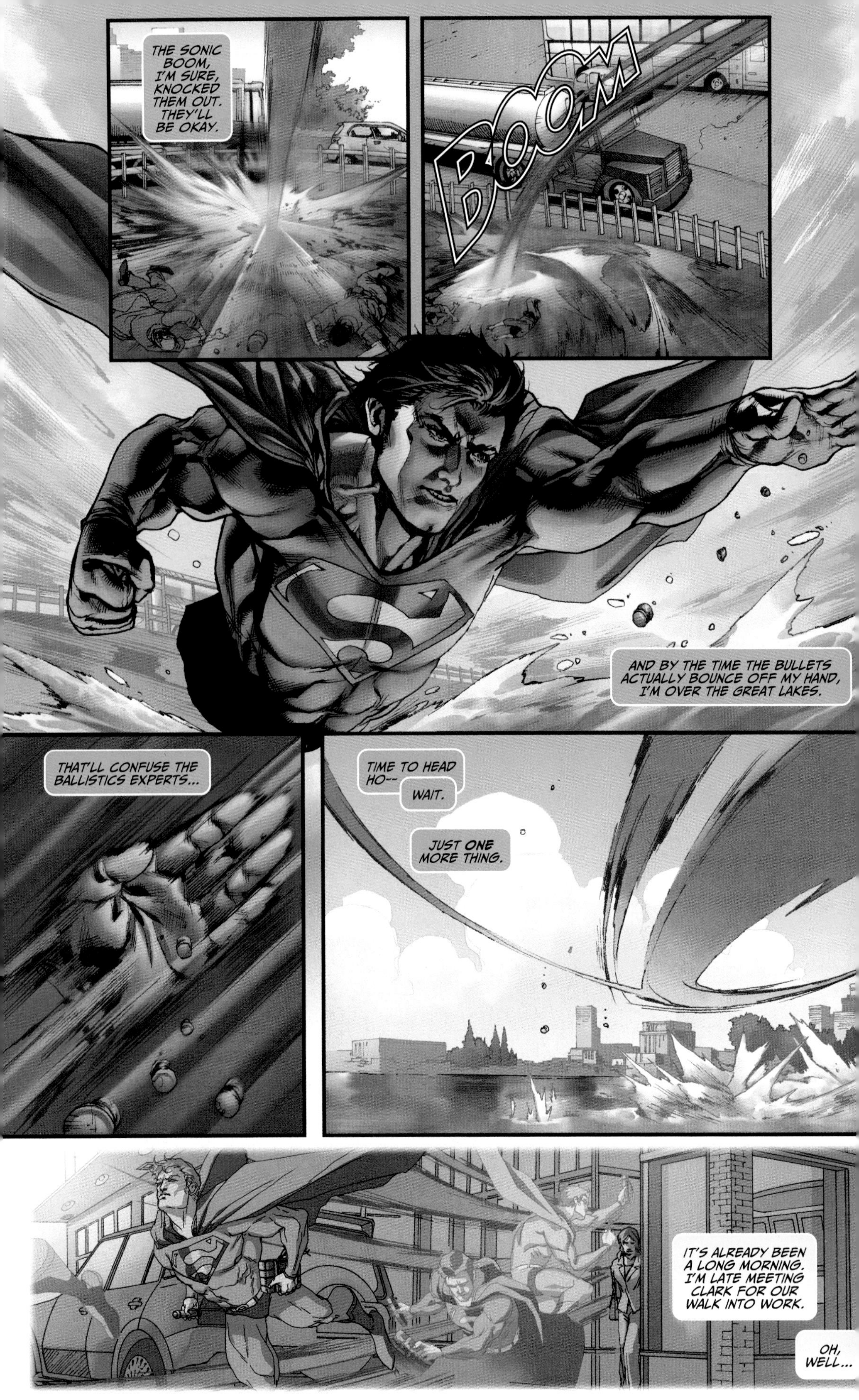
THE SONIC BOOM, I'M SURE, KNOCKED THEM OUT. THEY'LL BE OKAY.
BOOM
AND BY THE TIME THE BULLETS ACTUALLY BOUNCE OFF MY HAND, I'M OVER THE GREAT LAKES.
THAT'LL CONFUSE THE BALLISTICS EXPERTS...
TIME TO HEAD HO--
WAIT.
JUST ONE MORE THING.
IT'S ALREADY BEEN A LONG MORNING. I'M LATE MEETING CLARK FOR OUR WALK INTO WORK.
OH, WELL...

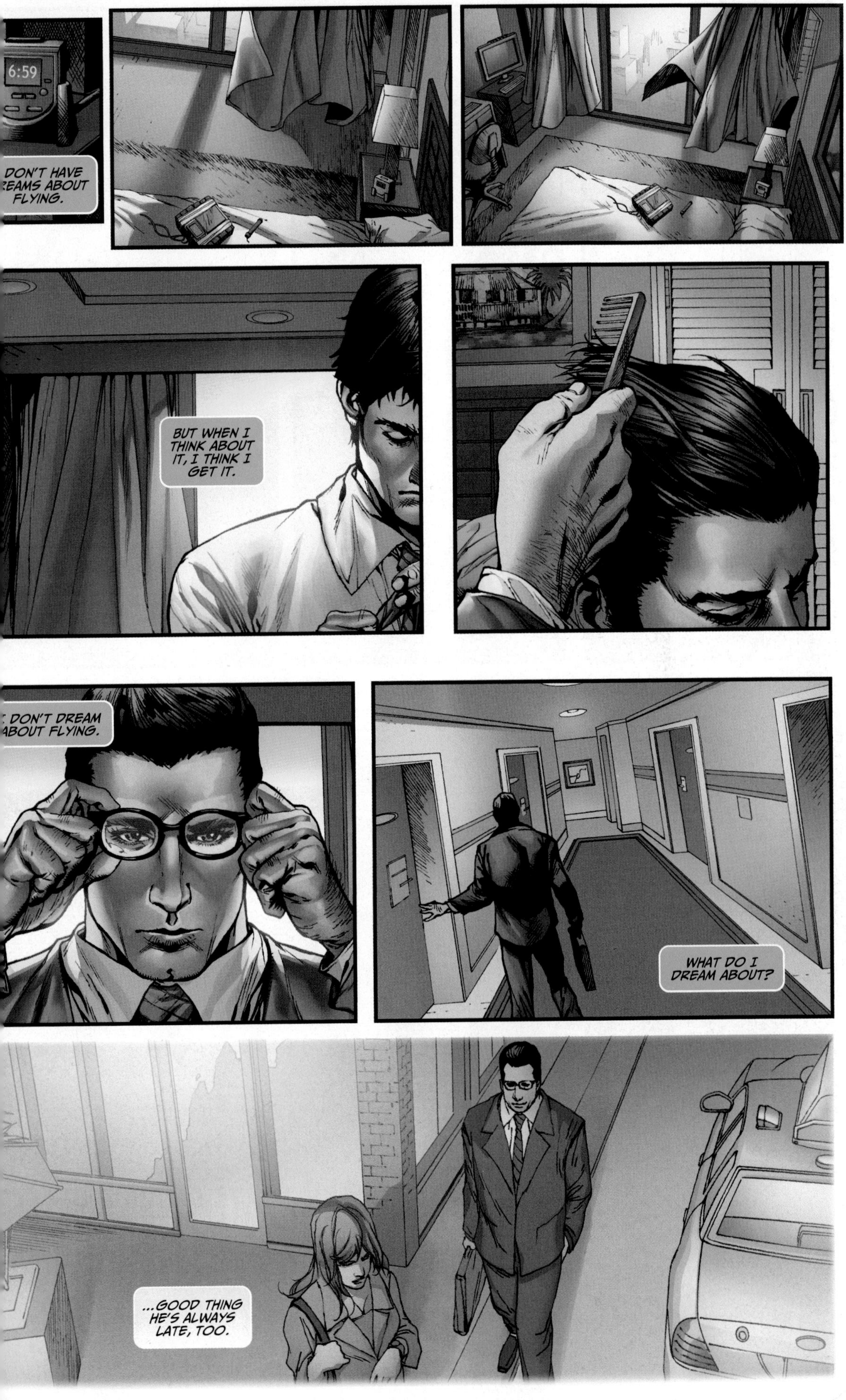
6:59
DON'T HAVE
REAMS ABOUT
FLYING.
BUT WHEN I
THINK ABOUT
IT, I THINK I
GET IT.
DON'T DREAM
ABOUT FLYING.
WHAT DO I
DREAM ABOUT?
...GOOD THING
HE'S ALWAYS
LATE, TOO.

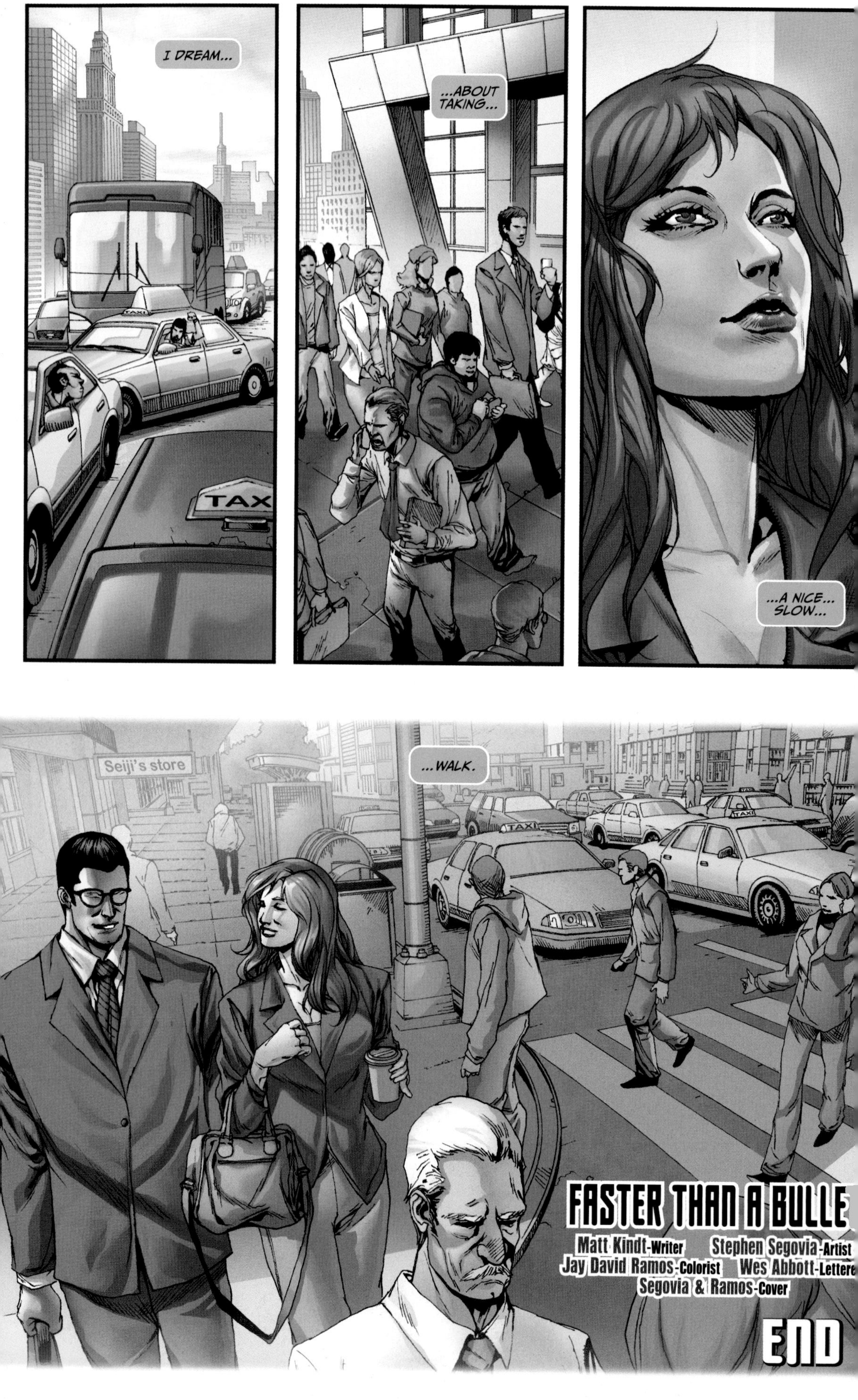
I DREAM...
TAX
...ABOUT TAKING...
...A NICE... SLOW...
Seiji's store
...WALK.
TAXI
FASTER THAN A BULLE
Matt Kindt-Writer
Stephen Segovia-Artist
Jay David Ramos-Colorist
Wes Abbott-Lettere
Segovia & Ramos-Cover
END

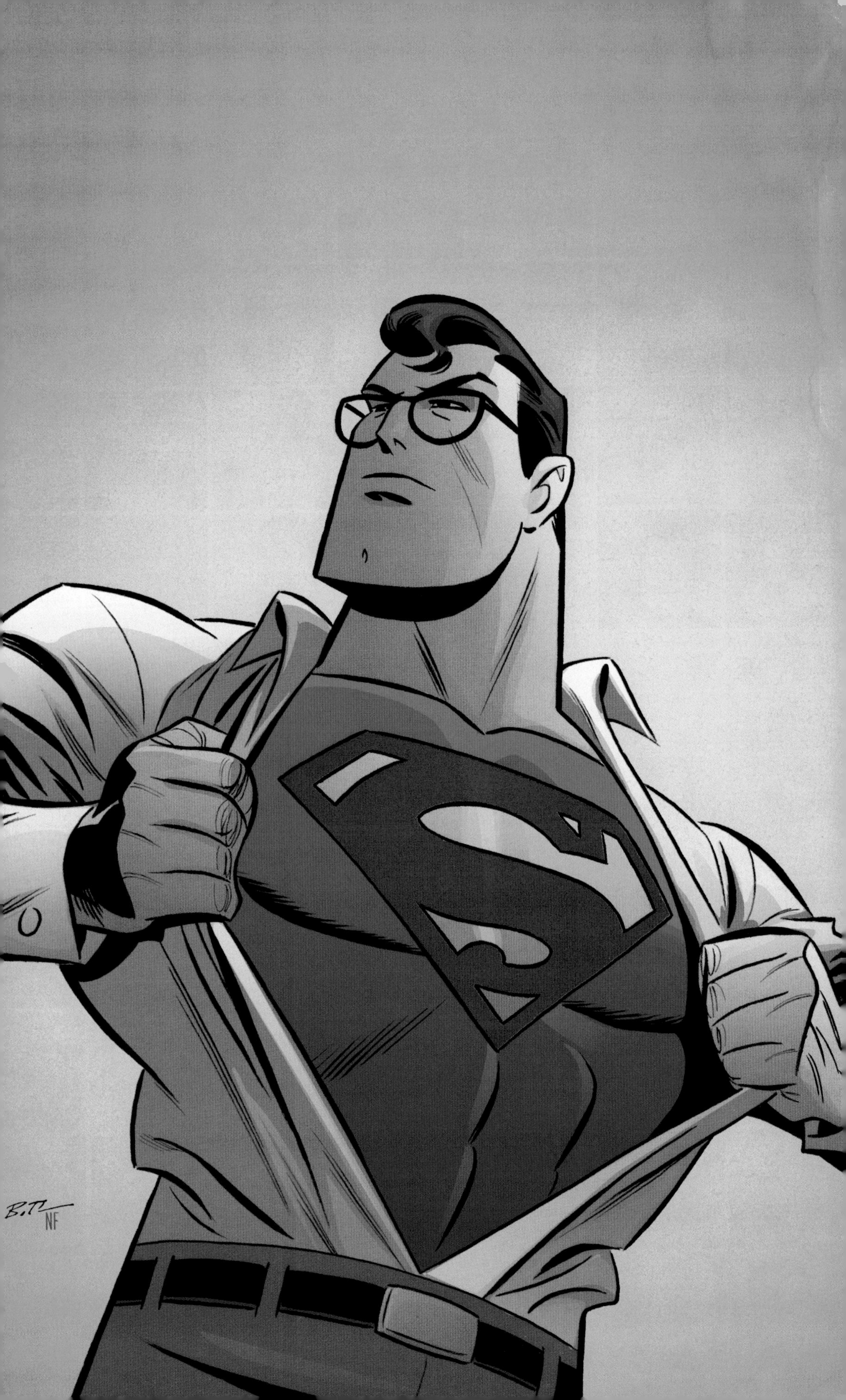

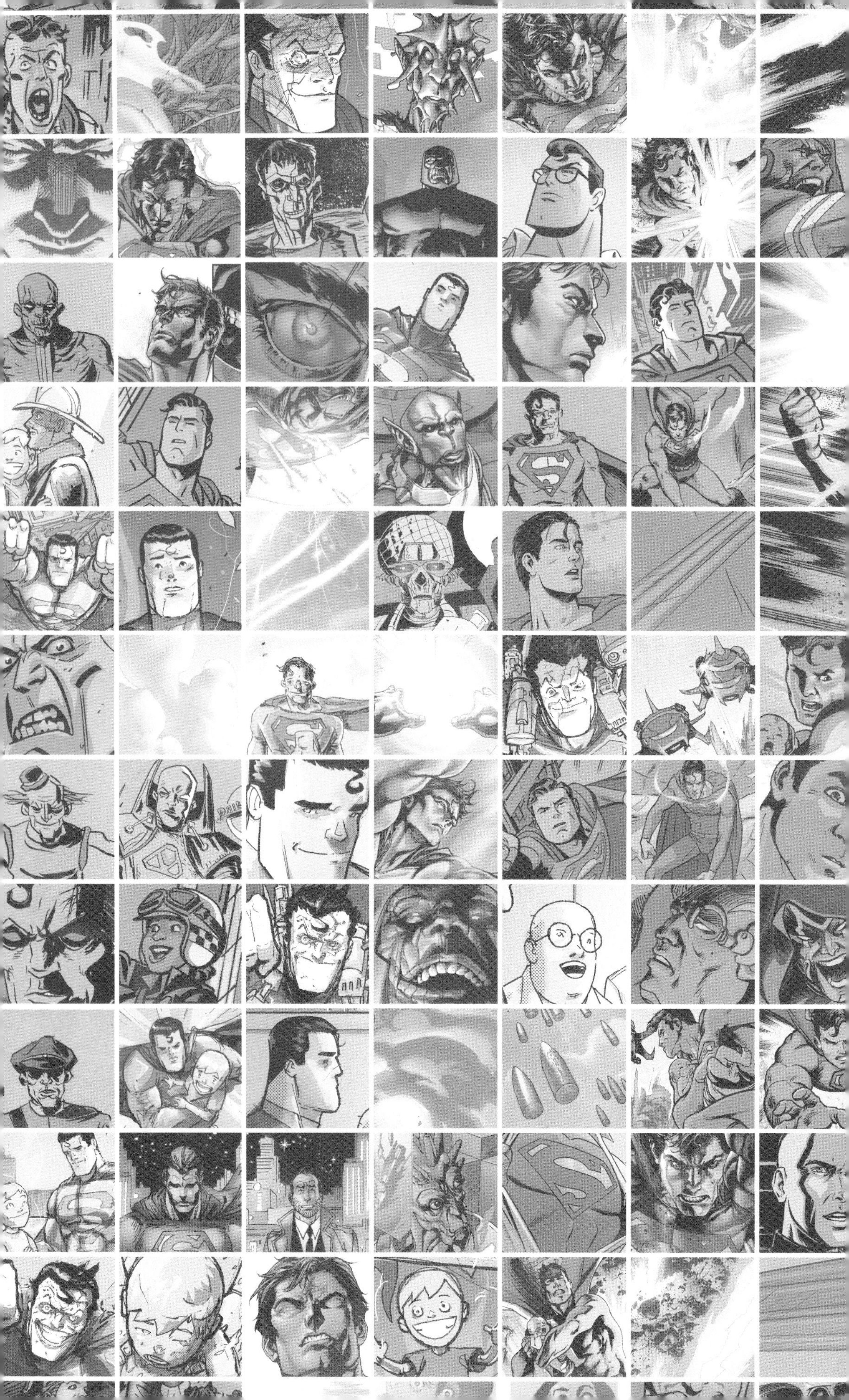

MY IDEA NOTEBOOK IS AN *ACTUAL* NOTEBOOK. PEN AND PAPER. OLD SCHOOL, *YES*, BUT *UNHACKABLE.*

DIGITAL TECHNOLOGY HAS COME SO FAR IT'S ESSENTIALLY *UNRELIABLE.* I SHOULD KNOW.

I ALWAYS LIKE TO START THE DAY WITH A LITTLE BRAINSTORMING. THEN TO BUSINESS...

HOW TO KILL SUPERMAN
IDEA #78013

PROBLEM= KRYPTONIAN SKIN IMPERVIOUS TO PHYSIC
WEAKEST PART OF SUPERMAN IS HIS

7:30 AM – PRE-BREAKFAST MEETING

M-MR. LUTHOR! YOU CAN'T JUST... *BUY OUT MY COMPANY!*

YES, I *CAN,* AND ALL BEFORE BREAKFAST. IT'S CALLED A *"HOSTILE TAKEOVER,"* MR. ANDRIDGE.

I REFUSE TO--

OH NO. NO, NO.

LET'S REVIEW THE *DIRT* I HAVE ON YOU, ANDRIDGE.

KNOWING THAT I *WON'T GO PUBLIC* WITH IT WILL MAKE YOUR COMPLIANCE WITH THE TAKEOVER SEEM LIKE THE *SWEETEST* DEAL YOU *EVER* GOT.

Dan Abnett & Andy Lanning
Writers

Wes Craig
Penciller

Craig Yeung
Inker

Lee Loughridge
Colorist

Wes Abbott
Letterer

Bruce Timm & Nick Filardi
Cover

A DAY IN THE LIFE

I SEE WE'RE STARTING *EARLY* TODAY...

UGHNN!

B OO M

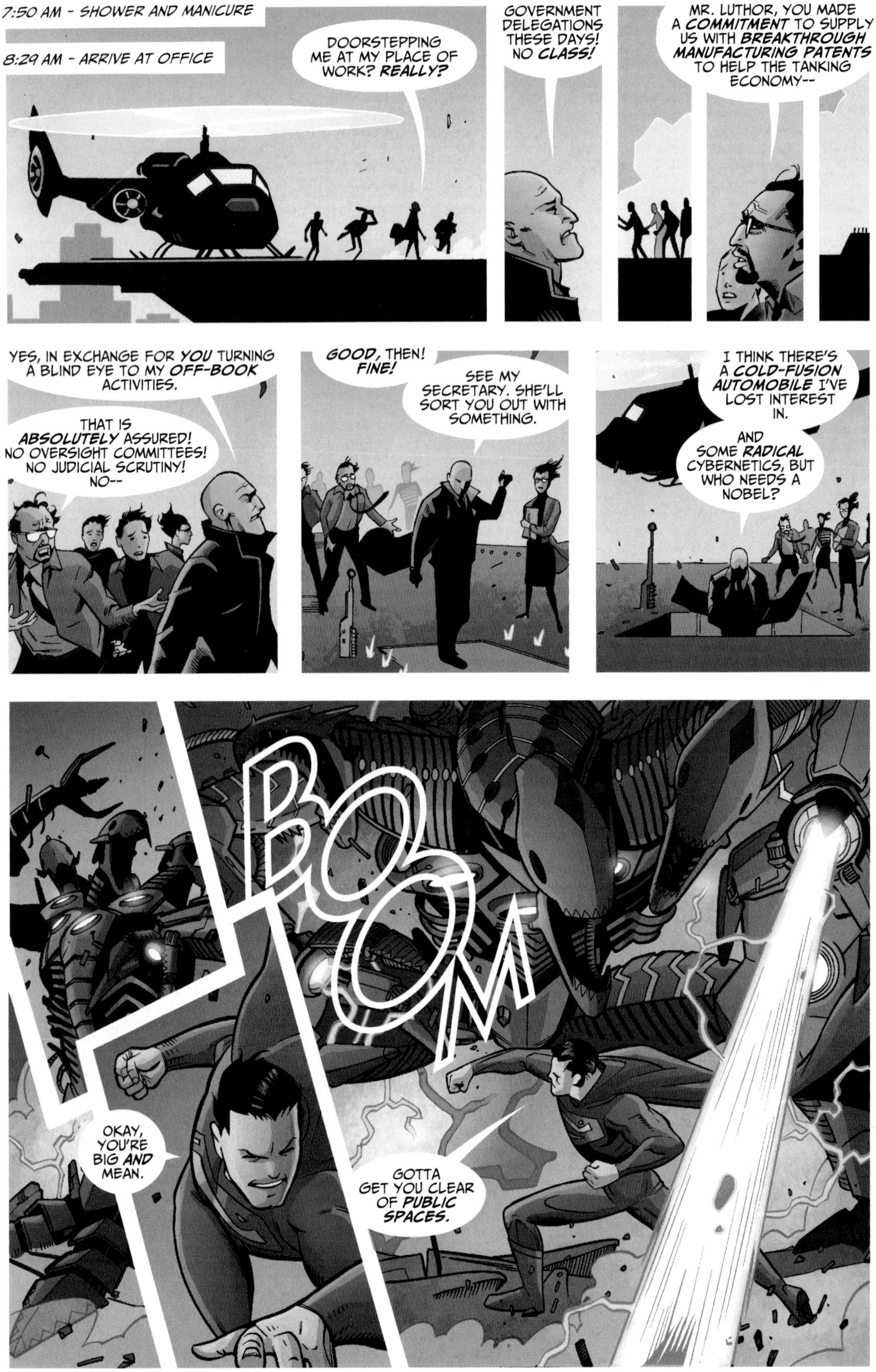
7:50 AM - SHOWER AND MANICURE
8:29 AM - ARRIVE AT OFFICE
DOORSTEPPING ME AT MY PLACE OF WORK? REALLY?
GOVERNMENT DELEGATIONS THESE DAYS! NO CLASS!
MR. LUTHOR, YOU MADE A COMMITMENT TO SUPPLY US WITH BREAKTHROUGH MANUFACTURING PATENTS TO HELP THE TANKING ECONOMY--
YES, IN EXCHANGE FOR YOU TURNING A BLIND EYE TO MY OFF-BOOK ACTIVITIES.
THAT IS ABSOLUTELY ASSURED! NO OVERSIGHT COMMITTEES! NO JUDICIAL SCRUTINY! NO--
GOOD, THEN! FINE!
SEE MY SECRETARY. SHE'LL SORT YOU OUT WITH SOMETHING.
I THINK THERE'S A COLD-FUSION AUTOMOBILE I'VE LOST INTEREST IN.
AND SOME RADICAL CYBERNETICS, BUT WHO NEEDS A NOBEL?
BOOOM
OKAY, YOU'RE BIG AND MEAN.
GOTTA GET YOU CLEAR OF PUBLIC SPACES.

9:01 AM - AT-DESK WORK REVIEW
--FIGHTING AN OUT-OF-CONTROL GIANT ROBOT IN DOWNTOWN METROPOLIS--
--GLOBAL SHARES PRICES NOW--
--AND CUTTING TO WORLD NEWS--
ARE YOU READY FOR YOUR 9:15, SIR? YOU SAID YOU WANTED TO HANDLE THE GENOME DIVISION THING PERSONALLY?
OH, YEAH. GET THOSE GUYS IN HERE!
OKAY, PEOPLE. GOOD TO SEE YOU.
BIG HONOR, I KNOW, TO COME UP HERE FOR SOME FACE-TIME. YOU'VE BEEN WORKING FOR ME FOR SEVEN YEARS NOW. WE'VE NEVER MET.
NOW I KNOW I CAN EASILY DELEGATE THIS TO HUMAN RESOURCES, BECAUSE I AM VERY BUSY, BUT FOR ME THIS IS A BRIGHT SPOT IN THE DAY.
I JUST LOVE TO BE ABLE TO SEE YOUR FACES. IT'S A PERSONAL THING.
SO HERE IT IS. YOU'RE ALL FIRED.
OH, I LOVE THAT!
LEAVE YOUR BOXES. LEAVE THE ROOM. LEAVE THE BUILDING.
5142
SUPES HAS BEEN FIGHTING THAT THING ALL MORNIN'!
IT KEEPS TAKING EVERYTHING HE THROWS AT IT! GETS UP AND COMES BACK FOR MORE!

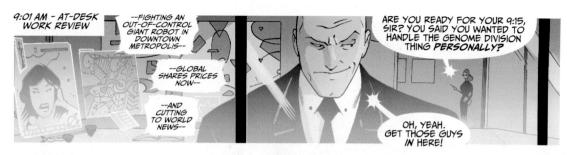

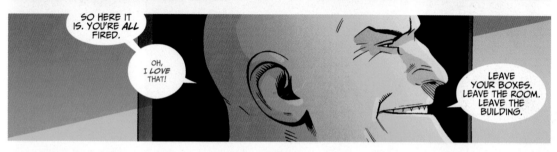

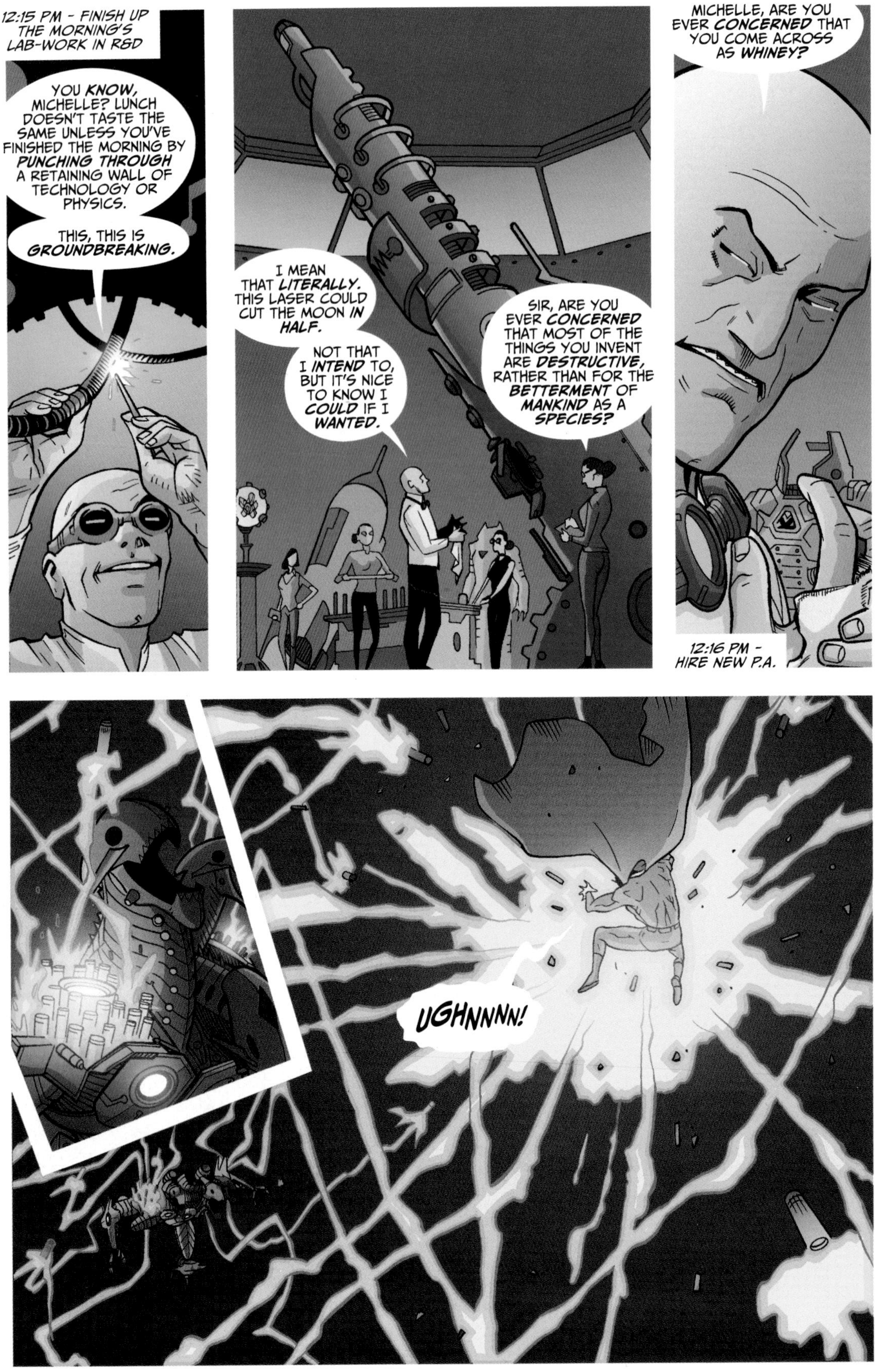
12:15 PM - FINISH UP THE MORNING'S LAB-WORK IN R&D
YOU KNOW, MICHELLE? LUNCH DOESN'T TASTE THE SAME UNLESS YOU'VE FINISHED THE MORNING BY PUNCHING THROUGH A RETAINING WALL OF TECHNOLOGY OR PHYSICS.
THIS, THIS IS GROUNDBREAKING.
I MEAN THAT LITERALLY. THIS LASER COULD CUT THE MOON IN HALF.
NOT THAT I INTEND TO, BUT IT'S NICE TO KNOW I COULD IF I WANTED.
SIR, ARE YOU EVER CONCERNED THAT MOST OF THE THINGS YOU INVENT ARE DESTRUCTIVE, RATHER THAN FOR THE BETTERMENT OF MANKIND AS A SPECIES?
MICHELLE, ARE YOU EVER CONCERNED THAT YOU COME ACROSS AS WHINEY?
12:16 PM - HIRE NEW P.A.
UGHNNNN!

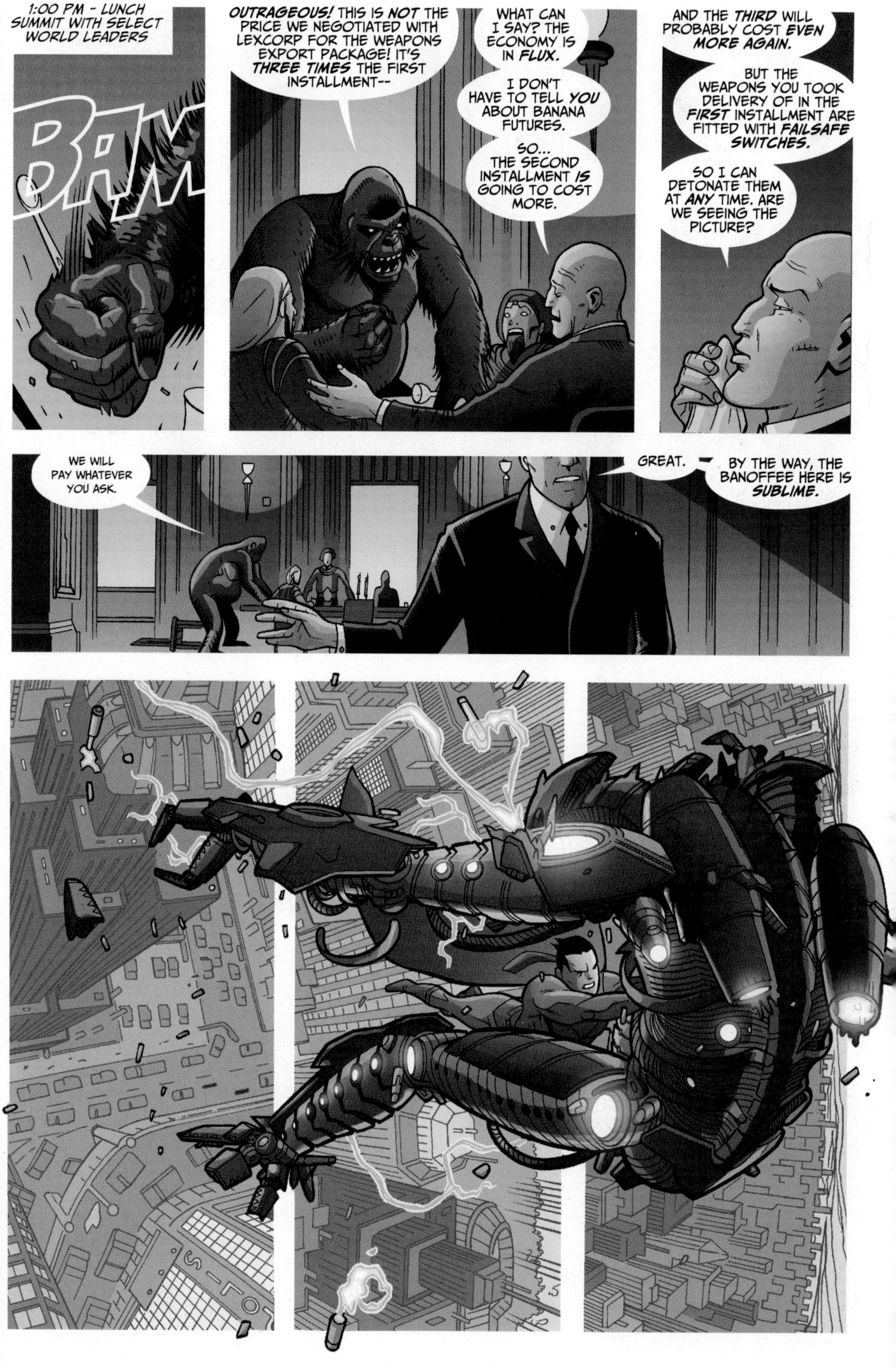
1:00 PM - LUNCH SUMMIT WITH SELECT WORLD LEADERS
BAM
OUTRAGEOUS! THIS IS NOT THE PRICE WE NEGOTIATED WITH LEXCORP FOR THE WEAPONS EXPORT PACKAGE! IT'S THREE TIMES THE FIRST INSTALLMENT--
WHAT CAN I SAY? THE ECONOMY IS IN FLUX.
I DON'T HAVE TO TELL YOU ABOUT BANANA FUTURES.
SO... THE SECOND INSTALLMENT IS GOING TO COST MORE.
AND THE THIRD WILL PROBABLY COST EVEN MORE AGAIN.
BUT THE WEAPONS YOU TOOK DELIVERY OF IN THE FIRST INSTALLMENT ARE FITTED WITH FAILSAFE SWITCHES.
SO I CAN DETONATE THEM AT ANY TIME. ARE WE SEEING THE PICTURE?
WE WILL PAY WHATEVER YOU ASK.
GREAT.
BY THE WAY, THE BANOFFEE HERE IS SUBLIME.

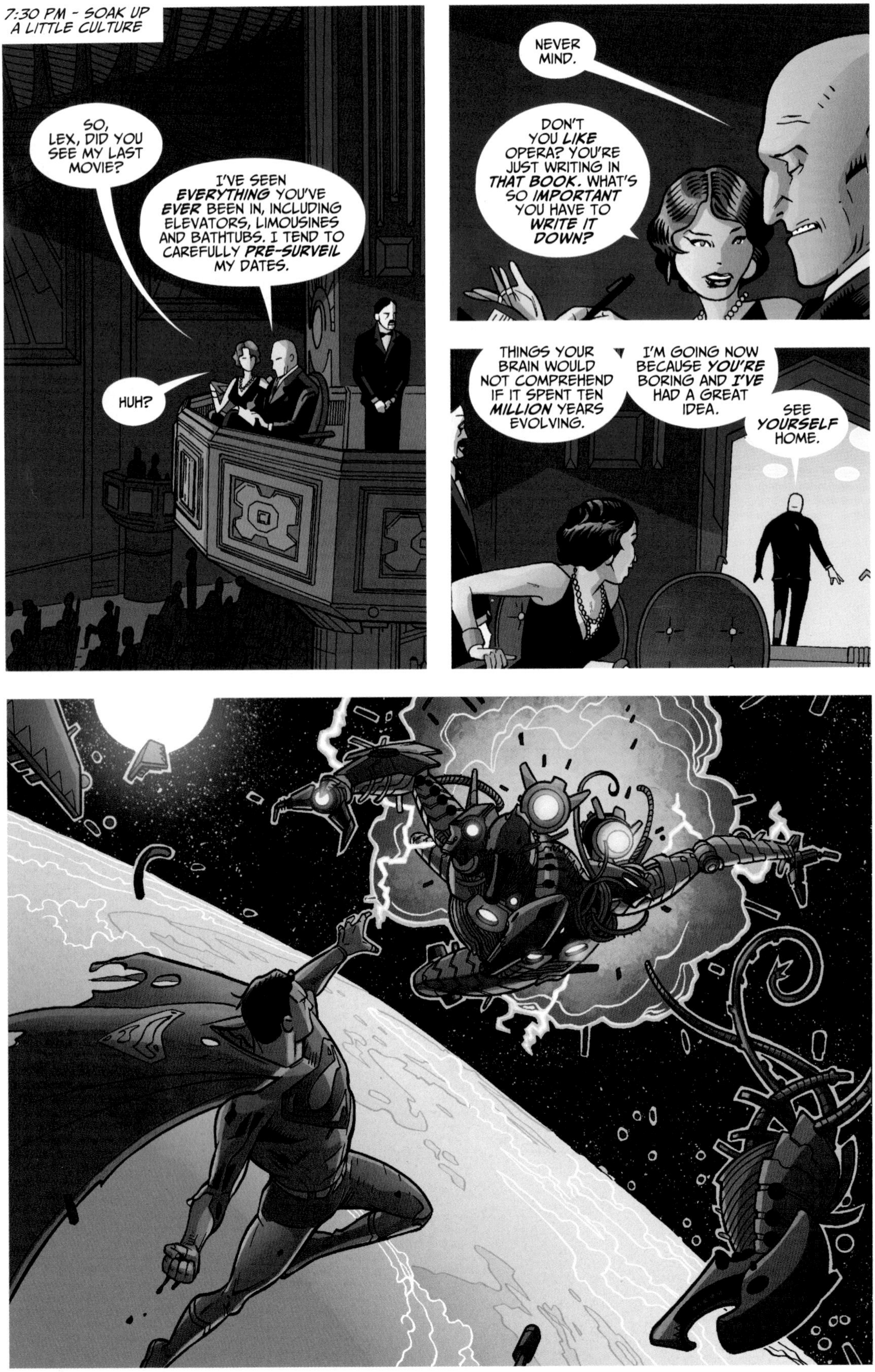
7:30 PM - SOAK UP A LITTLE CULTURE
SO, LEX, DID YOU SEE MY LAST MOVIE?
I'VE SEEN EVERYTHING YOU'VE EVER BEEN IN, INCLUDING ELEVATORS, LIMOUSINES AND BATHTUBS. I TEND TO CAREFULLY PRE-SURVEIL MY DATES.
HUH?
NEVER MIND.
DON'T YOU LIKE OPERA? YOU'RE JUST WRITING IN THAT BOOK. WHAT'S SO IMPORTANT YOU HAVE TO WRITE IT DOWN?
THINGS YOUR BRAIN WOULD NOT COMPREHEND IF IT SPENT TEN MILLION YEARS EVOLVING.
I'M GOING NOW BECAUSE YOU'RE BORING AND I'VE HAD A GREAT IDEA.
SEE YOURSELF HOME.

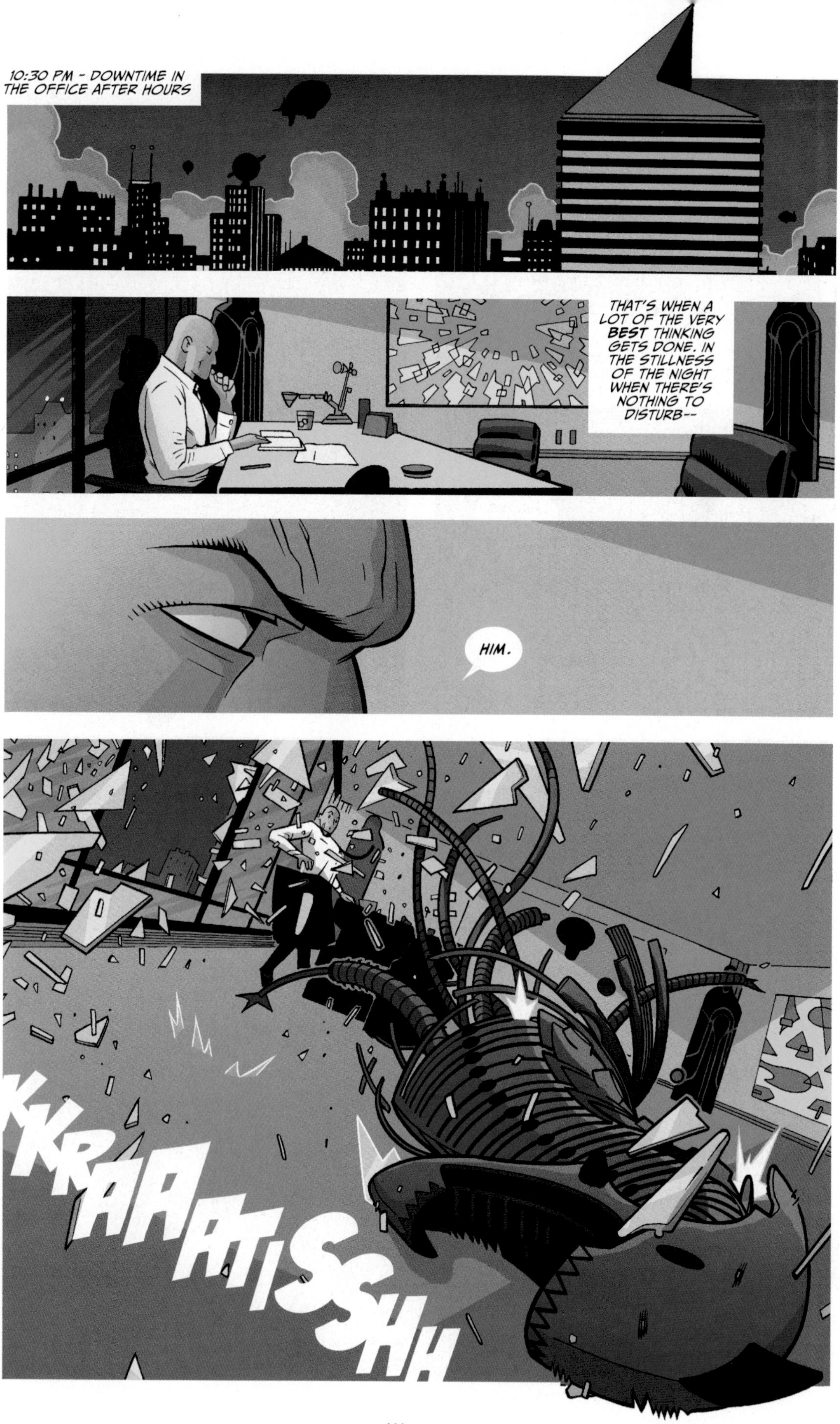
10:30 PM - DOWNTIME IN THE OFFICE AFTER HOURS
THAT'S WHEN A LOT OF THE VERY BEST THINKING GETS DONE. IN THE STILLNESS OF THE NIGHT WHEN THERE'S NOTHING TO DISTURB--
HIM.
KKRAAATISSHH

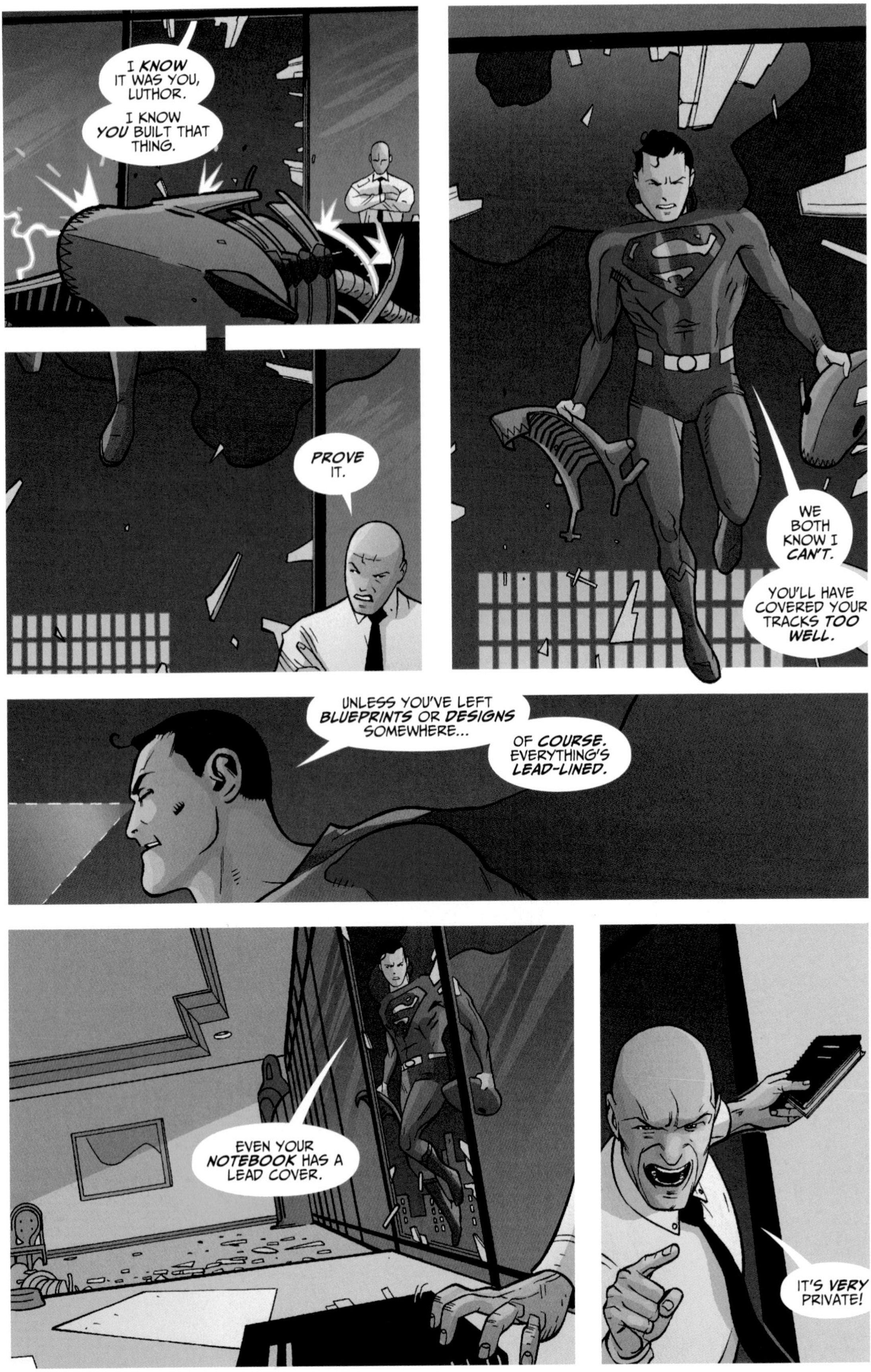
I KNOW IT WAS YOU, LUTHOR.
I KNOW YOU BUILT THAT THING.
PROVE IT.
WE BOTH KNOW I CAN'T.
YOU'LL HAVE COVERED YOUR TRACKS TOO WELL.
UNLESS YOU'VE LEFT BLUEPRINTS OR DESIGNS SOMEWHERE...
OF COURSE. EVERYTHING'S LEAD-LINED.
EVEN YOUR NOTEBOOK HAS A LEAD COVER.
IT'S VERY PRIVATE!

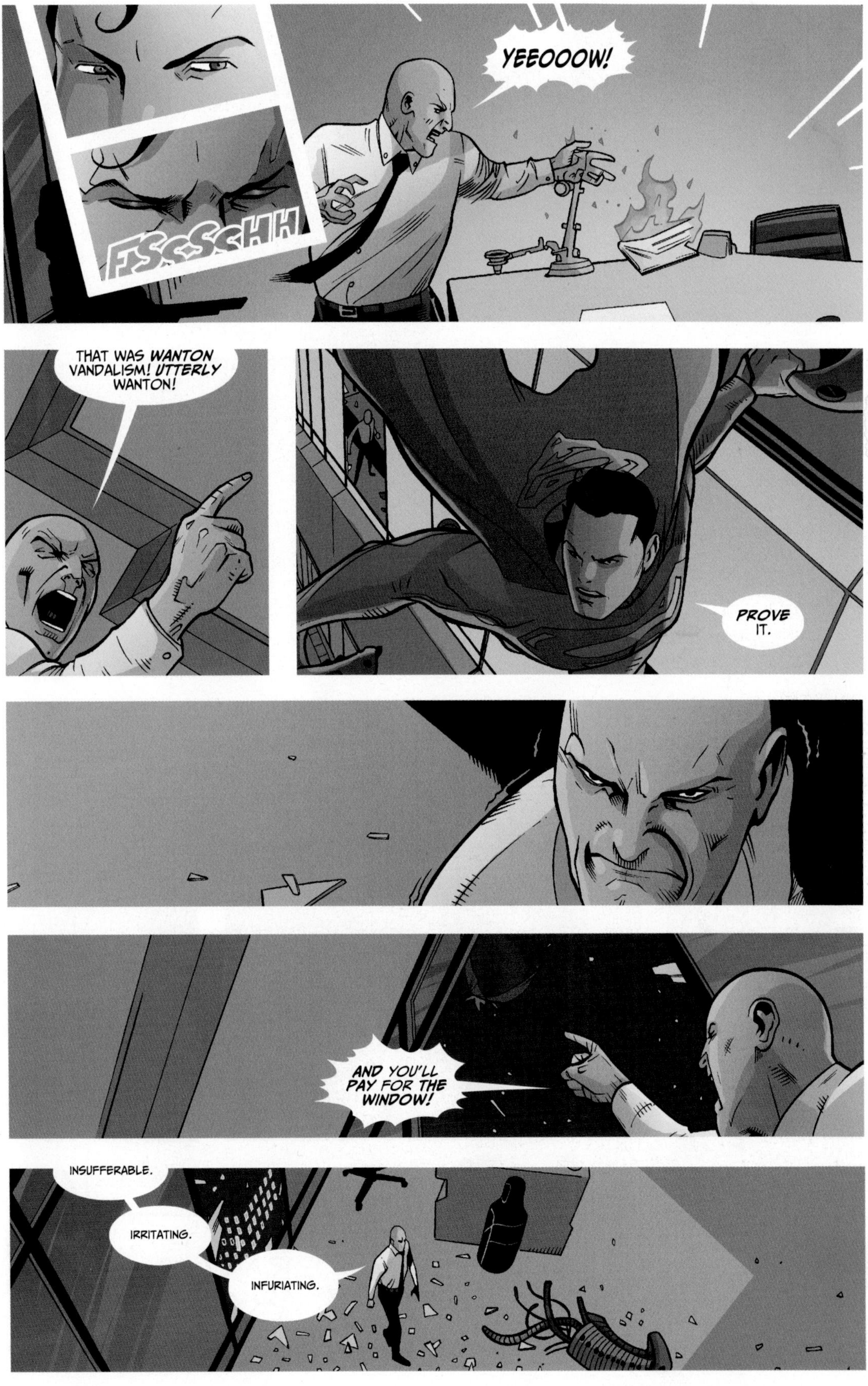
FSSSSHH
YEEOOOW!
THAT WAS WANTON VANDALISM! UTTERLY WANTON!
PROVE IT.
AND YOU'LL PAY FOR THE WINDOW!
INSUFFERABLE.
IRRITATING.
INFURIATING.

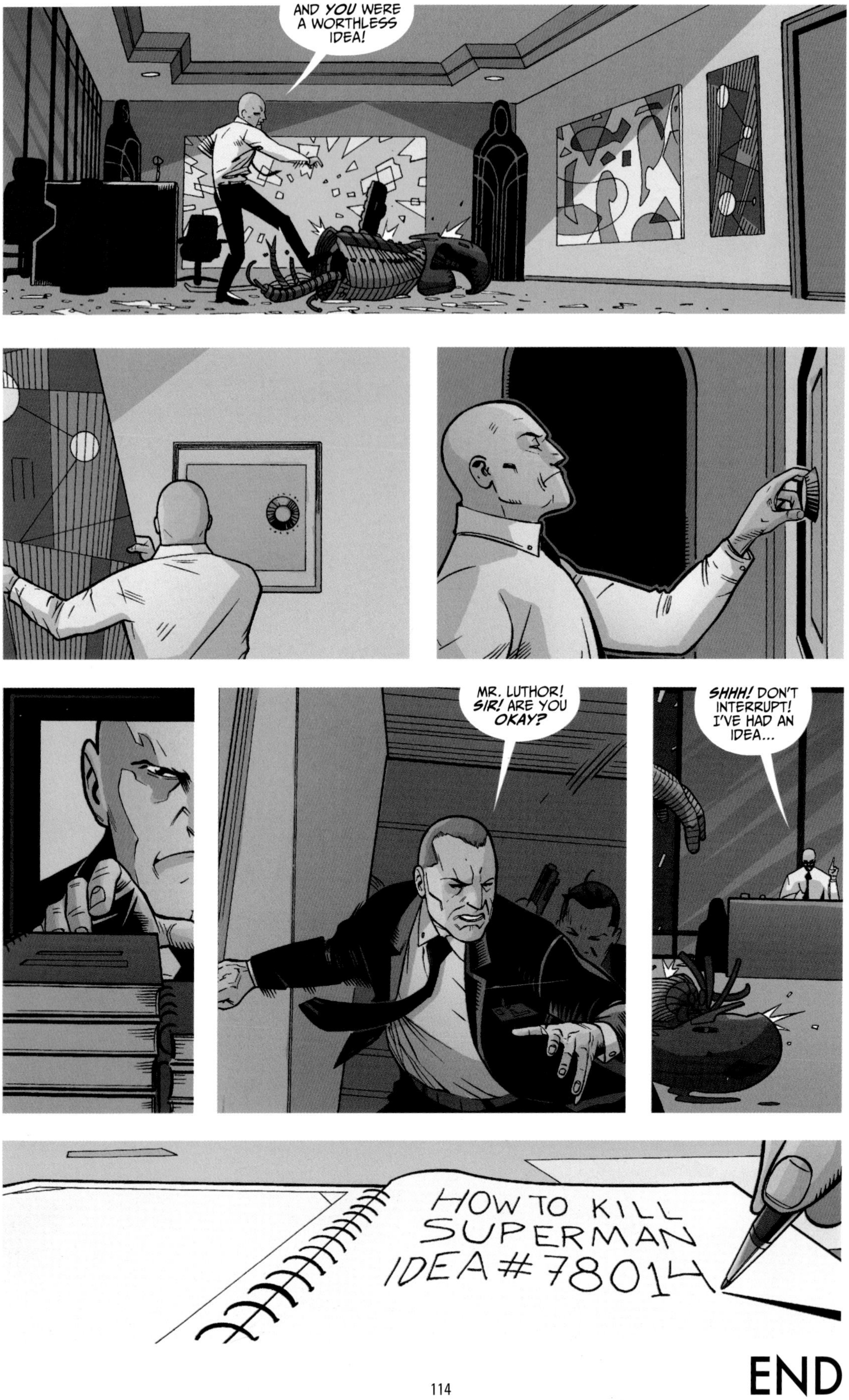
AND YOU WERE A WORTHLESS IDEA!
MR. LUTHOR! SIR! ARE YOU OKAY?
SHHH! DON'T INTERRUPT! I'VE HAD AN IDEA...
HOW TO KILL SUPERMAN IDEA #78014
END

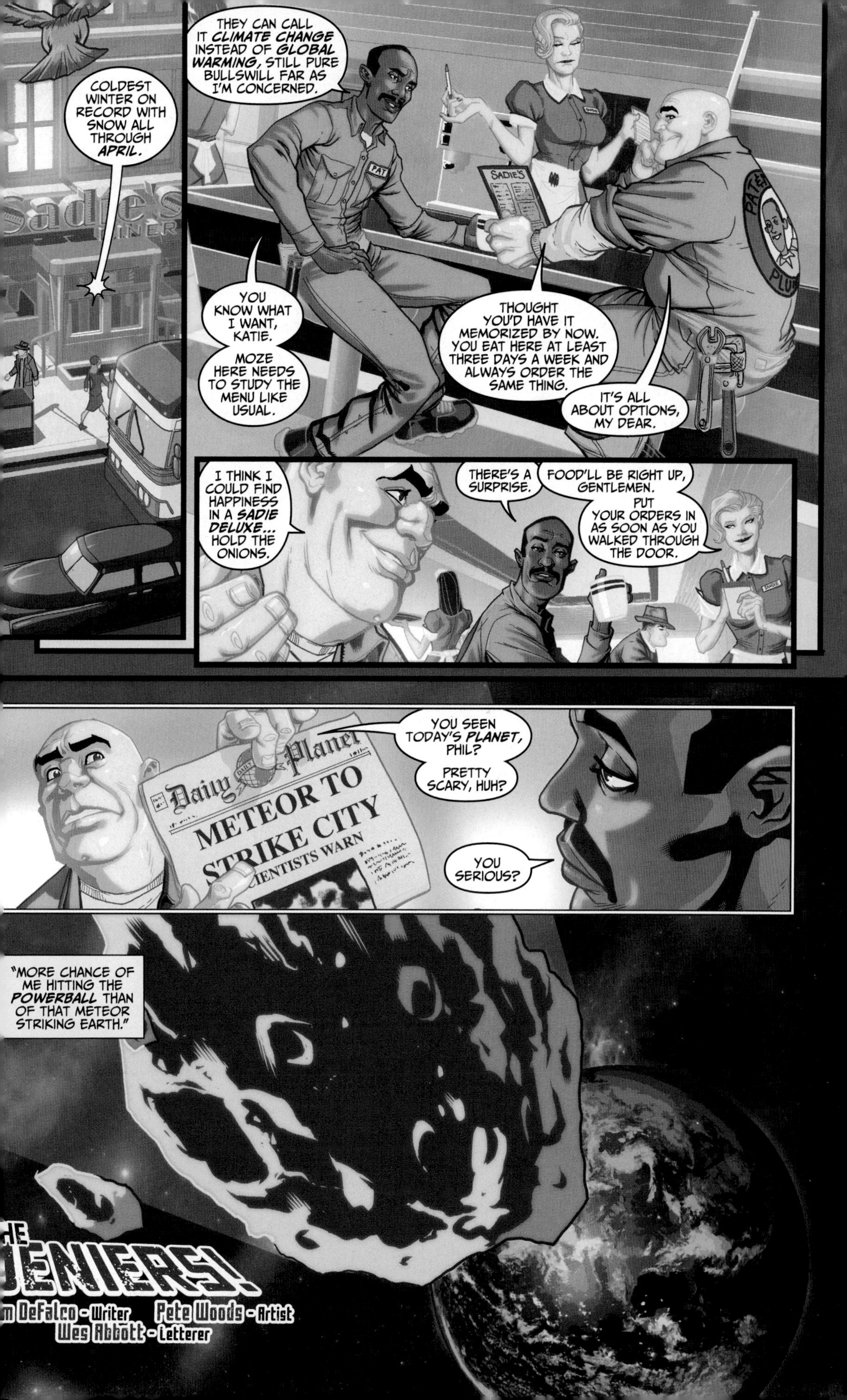
COLDEST WINTER ON RECORD WITH SNOW ALL THROUGH APRIL.
THEY CAN CALL IT CLIMATE CHANGE INSTEAD OF GLOBAL WARMING, STILL PURE BULLSWILL FAR AS I'M CONCERNED.
PAT
SADIE'S
YOU KNOW WHAT I WANT, KATIE.
MOZE HERE NEEDS TO STUDY THE MENU LIKE USUAL.
THOUGHT YOU'D HAVE IT MEMORIZED BY NOW. YOU EAT HERE AT LEAST THREE DAYS A WEEK AND ALWAYS ORDER THE SAME THING.
IT'S ALL ABOUT OPTIONS, MY DEAR.
I THINK I COULD FIND HAPPINESS IN A SADIE DELUXE... HOLD THE ONIONS.
THERE'S A SURPRISE.
FOOD'LL BE RIGHT UP, GENTLEMEN.
PUT YOUR ORDERS IN AS SOON AS YOU WALKED THROUGH THE DOOR.
YOU SEEN TODAY'S PLANET, PHIL?
PRETTY SCARY, HUH?
Daily Planet
METEOR TO
STRIKE CITY
YOU SERIOUS?
"MORE CHANCE OF ME HITTING THE POWERBALL THAN OF THAT METEOR STRIKING EARTH."
DeFalco - Writer
Pete Woods - Artist
Wes Abbott - Letterer

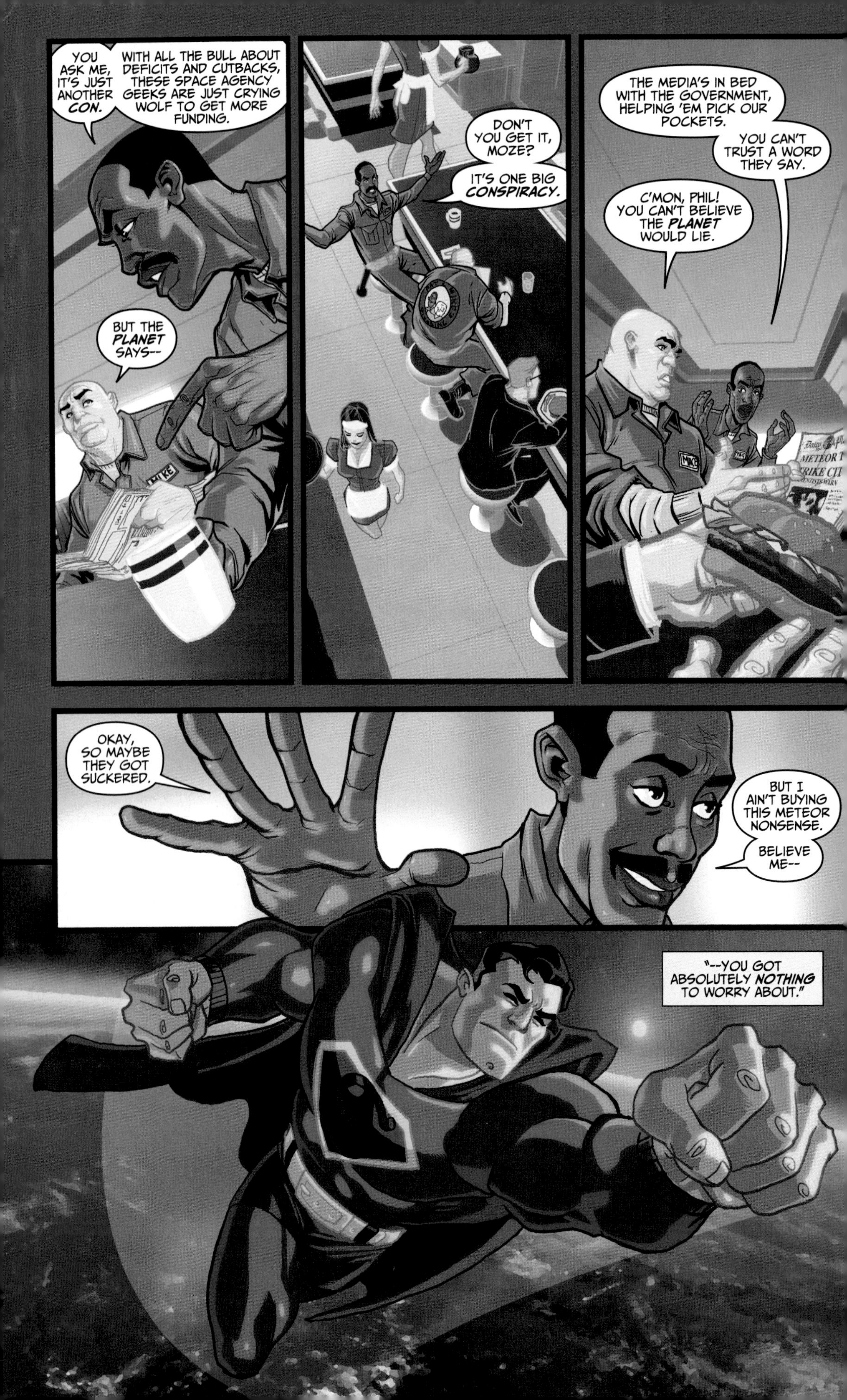
YOU ASK ME, IT'S JUST ANOTHER CON.
WITH ALL THE BULL ABOUT DEFICITS AND CUTBACKS, THESE SPACE AGENCY GEEKS ARE JUST CRYING WOLF TO GET MORE FUNDING.
BUT THE PLANET SAYS--
DON'T YOU GET IT, MOZE?
IT'S ONE BIG CONSPIRACY.
THE MEDIA'S IN BED WITH THE GOVERNMENT, HELPING 'EM PICK OUR POCKETS.
YOU CAN'T TRUST A WORD THEY SAY.
C'MON, PHIL! YOU CAN'T BELIEVE THE PLANET WOULD LIE.
OKAY, SO MAYBE THEY GOT SUCKERED.
BUT I AIN'T BUYING THIS METEOR NONSENSE.
BELIEVE ME--
"--YOU GOT ABSOLUTELY NOTHING TO WORRY ABOUT."

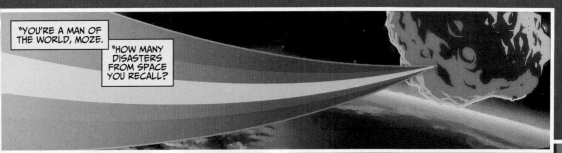

"YOU'RE A MAN OF THE WORLD, MOZE.

"HOW MANY DISASTERS FROM SPACE YOU RECALL?

"EXACTLY *NONE*, RIGHT?

"THAT'S 'CAUSE THEY ONLY EXIST IN *MOVIES* AND *COMIC BOOKS* AND STUFF LIKE THAT.

"PURE *FICTION*, I TELL YOU.

"JUST LIKE *SUPERMAN*."

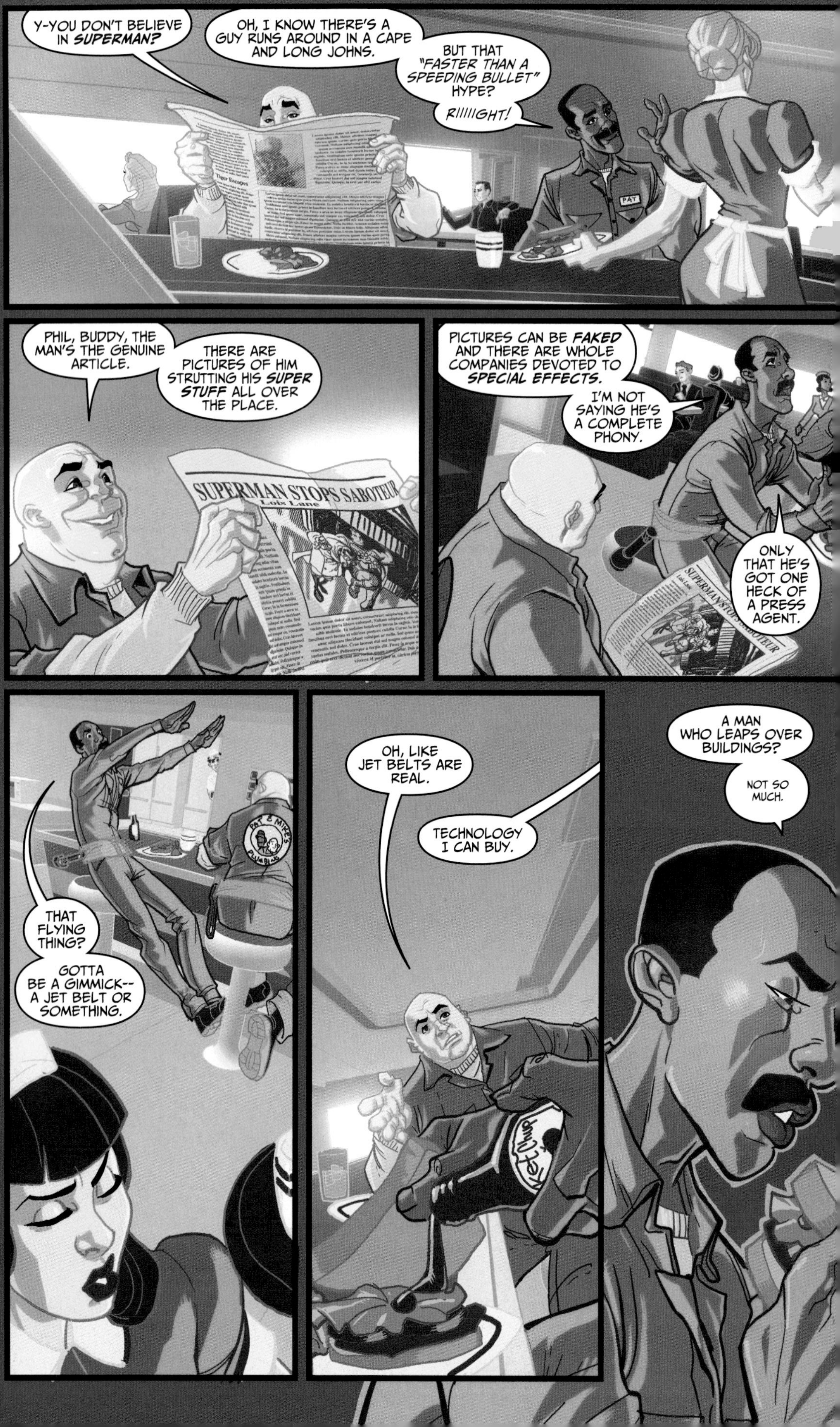
Y-YOU DON'T BELIEVE IN *SUPERMAN?*
OH, I KNOW THERE'S A GUY RUNS AROUND IN A CAPE AND LONG JOHNS.
BUT THAT *"FASTER THAN A SPEEDING BULLET"* HYPE?
RIIIIGHT!
Tiger Escapes
PAT
PHIL, BUDDY, THE MAN'S THE GENUINE ARTICLE.
THERE ARE PICTURES OF HIM STRUTTING HIS ***SUPER STUFF*** ALL OVER THE PLACE.
SUPERMAN STOPS SABOTEUR
Lois Lane
PICTURES CAN BE ***FAKED*** AND THERE ARE WHOLE COMPANIES DEVOTED TO ***SPECIAL EFFECTS.***
I'M NOT SAYING HE'S A COMPLETE PHONY.
ONLY THAT HE'S GOT ONE HECK OF A PRESS AGENT.
THAT FLYING THING?
GOTTA BE A GIMMICK-- A JET BELT OR SOMETHING.
PAT & MIKE'S PLUMBING
OH, LIKE JET BELTS ARE REAL.
TECHNOLOGY I CAN BUY.
A MAN WHO LEAPS OVER BUILDINGS?
NOT SO MUCH.

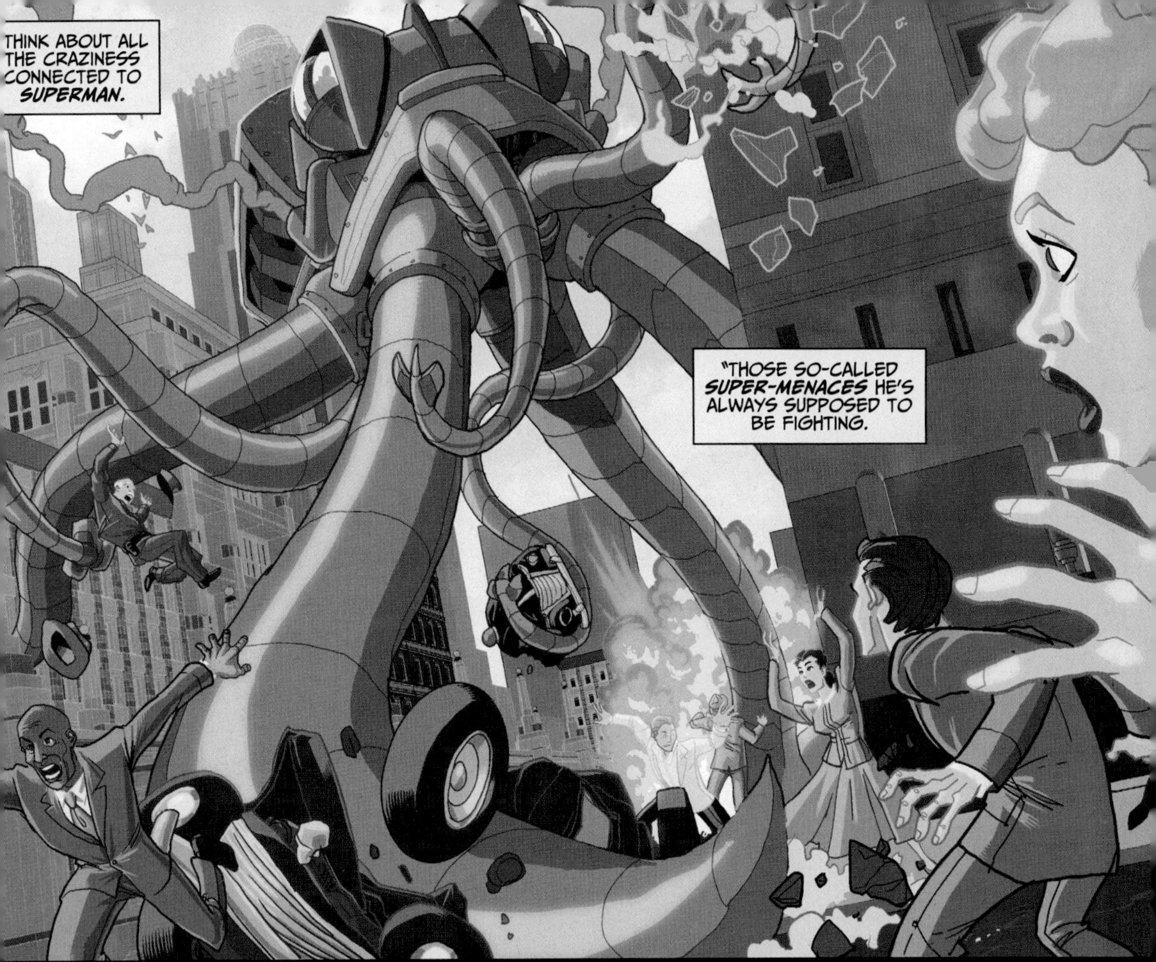
THINK ABOUT ALL THE CRAZINESS CONNECTED TO *SUPERMAN.*
"THOSE SO-CALLED *SUPER-MENACES* HE'S ALWAYS SUPPOSED TO BE FIGHTING.

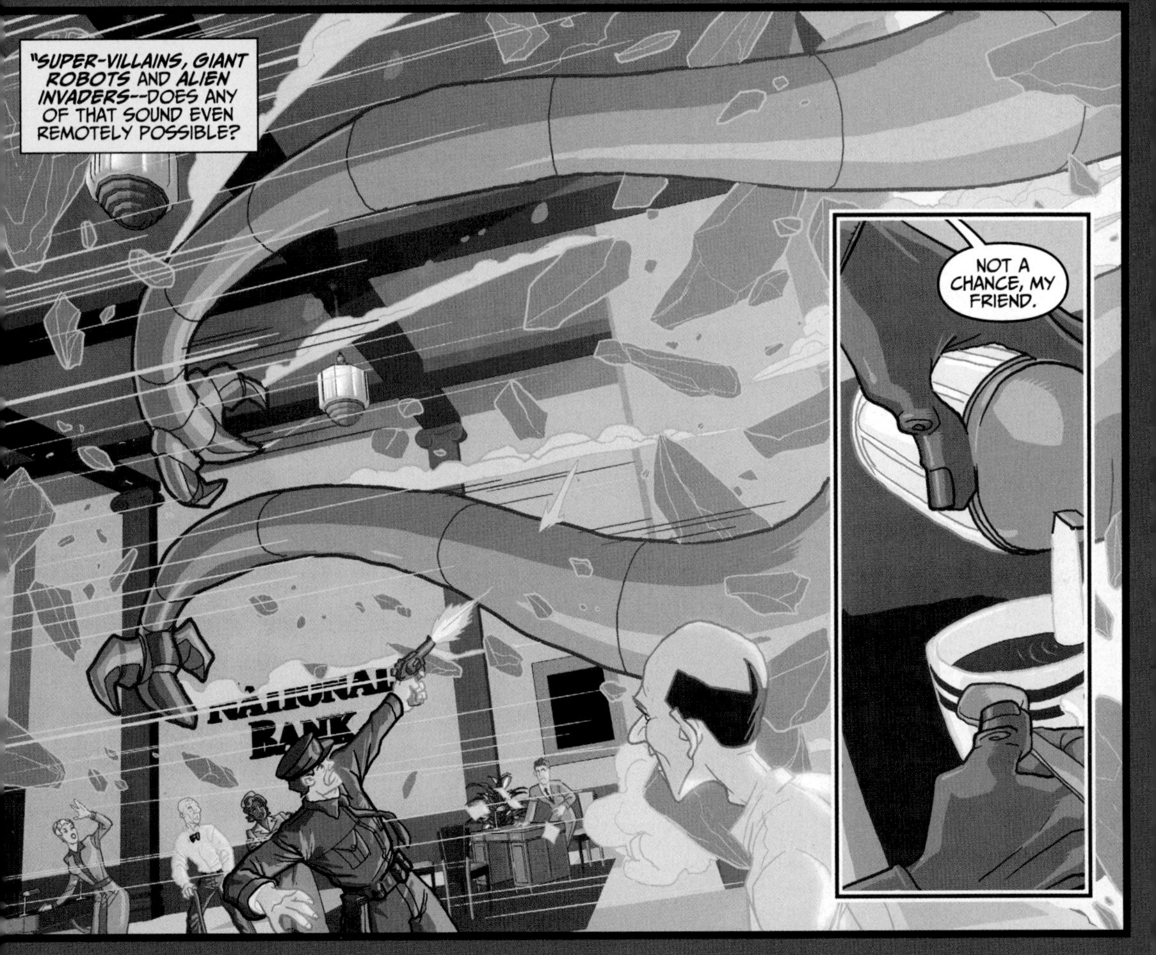
"*SUPER-VILLAINS, GIANT ROBOTS* AND *ALIEN INVADERS*--DOES ANY OF THAT SOUND EVEN REMOTELY POSSIBLE?
NOT A CHANCE, MY FRIEND.
NATIONAL BANK

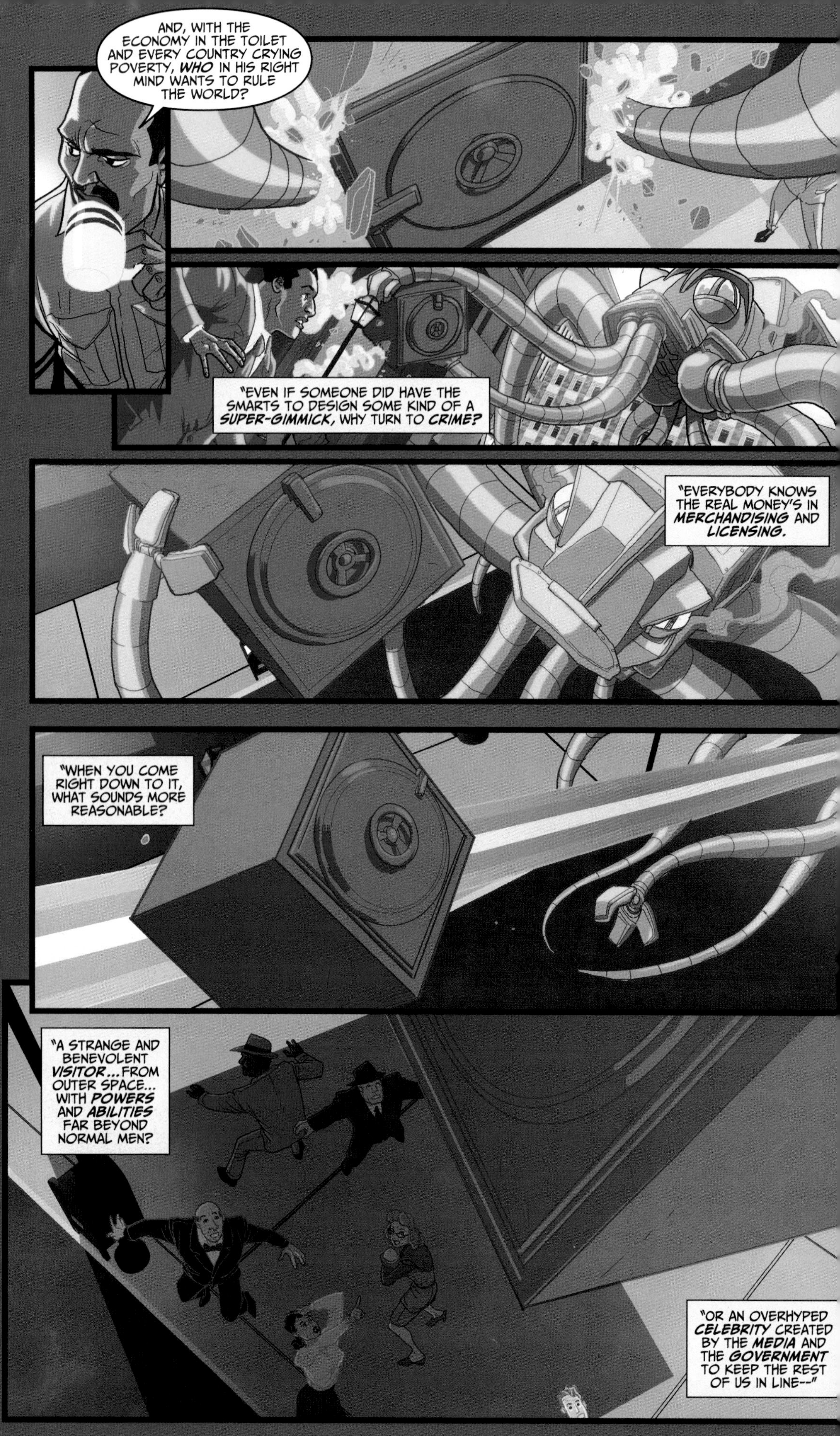
AND, WITH THE ECONOMY IN THE TOILET AND EVERY COUNTRY CRYING POVERTY, **WHO** IN HIS RIGHT MIND WANTS TO RULE THE WORLD?
"EVEN IF SOMEONE DID HAVE THE SMARTS TO DESIGN SOME KIND OF A **SUPER-GIMMICK**, WHY TURN TO **CRIME?**
"EVERYBODY KNOWS THE REAL MONEY'S IN **MERCHANDISING** AND **LICENSING.**
"WHEN YOU COME RIGHT DOWN TO IT, WHAT SOUNDS MORE REASONABLE?
"A STRANGE AND BENEVOLENT **VISITOR...** FROM OUTER SPACE... WITH **POWERS** AND **ABILITIES** FAR BEYOND NORMAL MEN?
"OR AN OVERHYPED **CELEBRITY** CREATED BY THE **MEDIA** AND THE **GOVERNMENT** TO KEEP THE REST OF US IN LINE--"

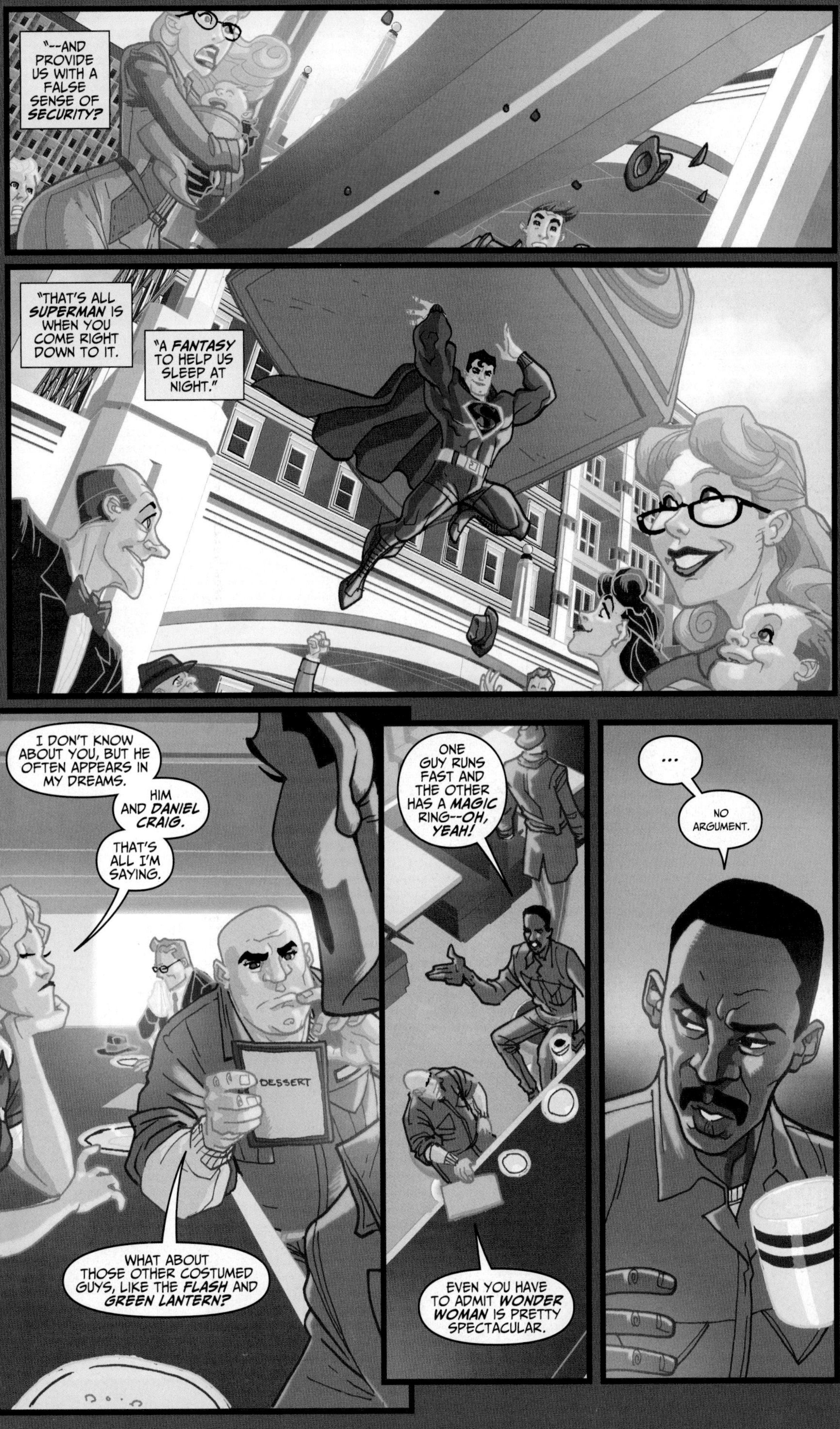
"--AND PROVIDE US WITH A FALSE SENSE OF SECURITY?
"THAT'S ALL SUPERMAN IS WHEN YOU COME RIGHT DOWN TO IT.
"A FANTASY TO HELP US SLEEP AT NIGHT."
I DON'T KNOW ABOUT YOU, BUT HE OFTEN APPEARS IN MY DREAMS.
HIM AND DANIEL CRAIG.
THAT'S ALL I'M SAYING.
WHAT ABOUT THOSE OTHER COSTUMED GUYS, LIKE THE FLASH AND GREEN LANTERN?
DESSERT
ONE GUY RUNS FAST AND THE OTHER HAS A MAGIC RING--OH, YEAH!
EVEN YOU HAVE TO ADMIT WONDER WOMAN IS PRETTY SPECTACULAR.
...
NO ARGUMENT.

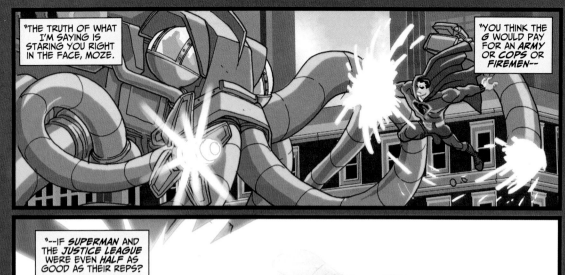

"THE TRUTH OF WHAT I'M SAYING IS STARING YOU RIGHT IN THE FACE, MOZE.

"YOU THINK THE *G* WOULD PAY FOR AN *ARMY* OR *COPS* OR *FIREMEN*--

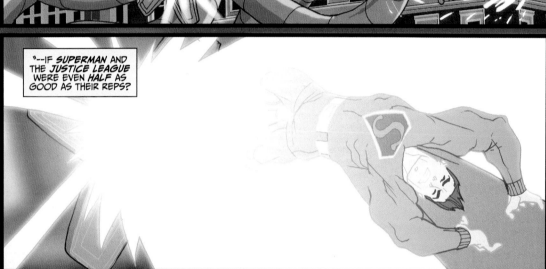

"--IF *SUPERMAN* AND THE *JUSTICE LEAGUE* WERE EVEN *HALF* AS GOOD AS THEIR REPS?

"BESIDES, I'VE LIVED MY ENTIRE LIFE IN *METROPOLIS* AND OFTEN LOOK UP IN THE SKY.

"I AIN'T NEVER ONCE SEEN *SUPERMAN* FLY OVERHEAD. HAVE YOU?"

YOU MEAN IN THE FLESH? NO.

BUT I'VE NEVER SEEN THE *PRESIDENT* OR ANY OF OUR *MAYORS* IN REAL LIFE, EITHER--ONLY ON TELEVISION.

THAT'S DIFFERENT. WE KNOW POLITICIANS EXIST--

--AND WISH THEY DIDN'T...

"LET ME BOTTOM-LINE IT, MOZE...

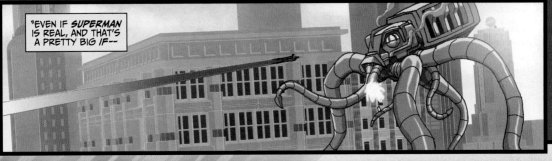

"EVEN IF *SUPERMAN* IS REAL, AND THAT'S A PRETTY BIG *IF*--

"--NO WAY HE'S ALL HE'S CRACKED UP TO BE!"

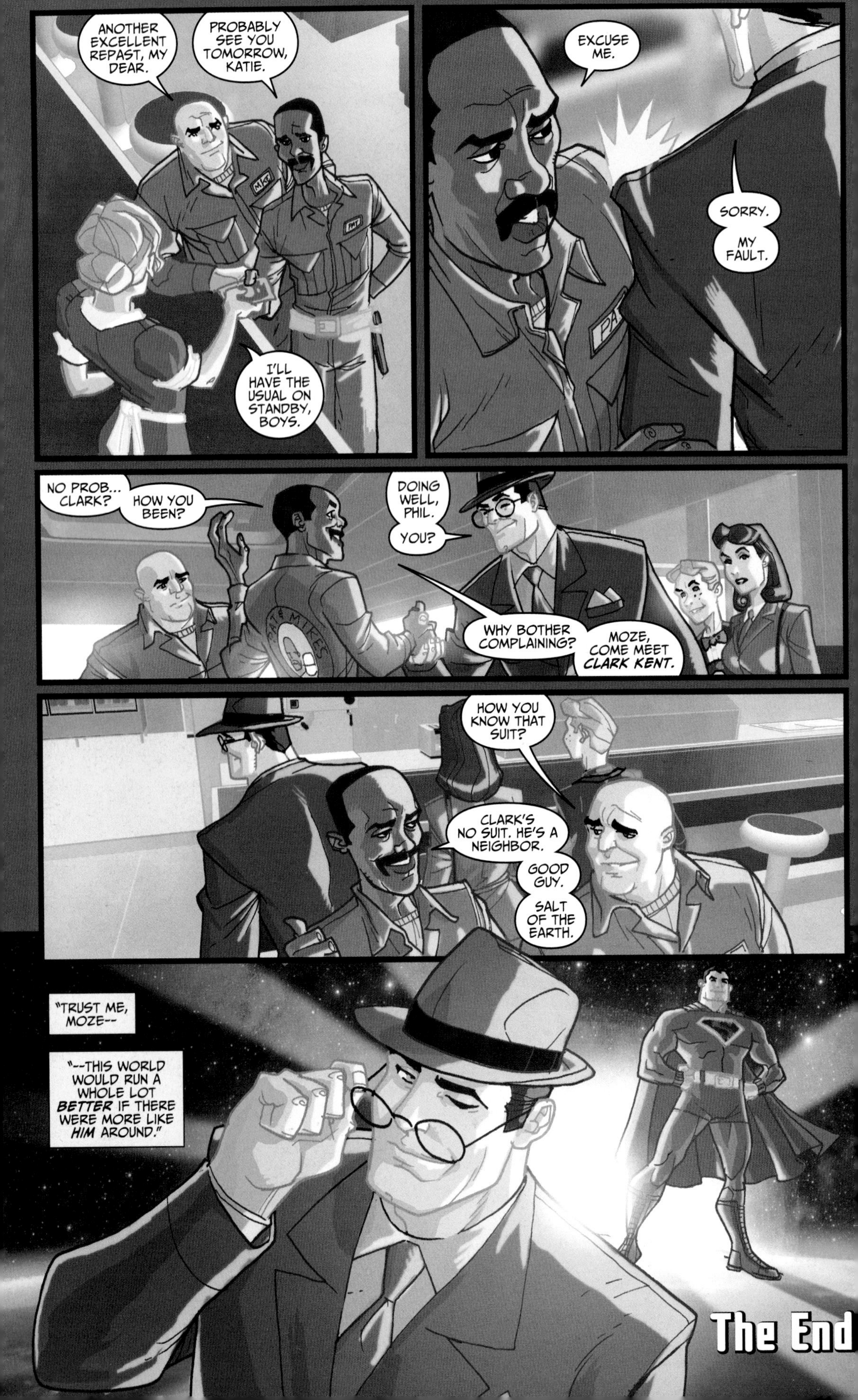
ANOTHER EXCELLENT REPAST, MY DEAR.
PROBABLY SEE YOU TOMORROW, KATIE.
I'LL HAVE THE USUAL ON STANDBY, BOYS.
EXCUSE ME.
SORRY.
MY FAULT.
NO PROB... CLARK?
HOW YOU BEEN?
DOING WELL, PHIL.
YOU?
WHY BOTHER COMPLAINING?
MOZE, COME MEET CLARK KENT.
HOW YOU KNOW THAT SUIT?
CLARK'S NO SUIT. HE'S A NEIGHBOR.
GOOD GUY.
SALT OF THE EARTH.
"TRUST ME, MOZE--
"--THIS WORLD WOULD RUN A WHOLE LOT BETTER IF THERE WERE MORE LIKE HIM AROUND."
The End

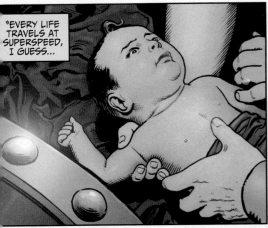

"EVERY LIFE TRAVELS AT SUPERSPEED, I GUESS...

"ONE MINUTE YOUR CHILD'S A BABY.

"NOT A CARE IN THE WHOLE WIDE WORLD.

"THEN ONE DAY YOU BLINK AND...

"...WELL...

"...I DO SO WORRY ABOUT MY BOY, LET ME JUST SAY THAT."

SAVIOR

Rob Williams · Writer   Chris Weston · Artist
Wes Abbott · Letterer

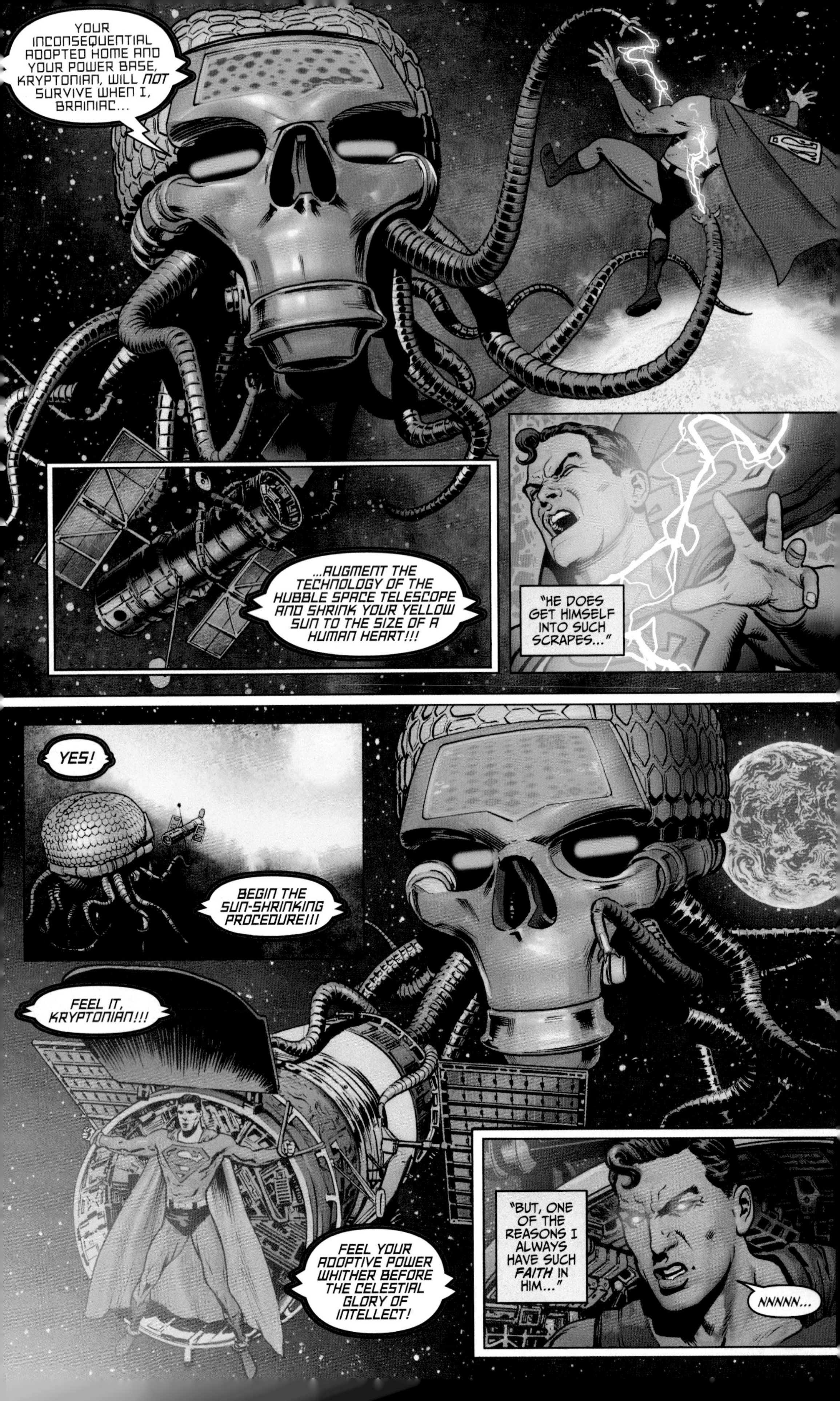
YOUR INCONSEQUENTIAL ADOPTED HOME AND YOUR POWER BASE, KRYPTONIAN, WILL *NOT* SURVIVE WHEN I, BRAINIAC...
...AUGMENT THE TECHNOLOGY OF THE HUBBLE SPACE TELESCOPE AND SHRINK YOUR YELLOW SUN TO THE SIZE OF A HUMAN HEART!!!
"HE DOES GET HIMSELF INTO SUCH SCRAPES..."
YES!
BEGIN THE SUN-SHRINKING PROCEDURE!!!
FEEL IT, KRYPTONIAN!!!
FEEL YOUR ADOPTIVE POWER WHITHER BEFORE THE CELESTIAL GLORY OF INTELLECT!
"BUT, ONE OF THE REASONS I ALWAYS HAVE SUCH *FAITH* IN HIM..."
NNNNN...

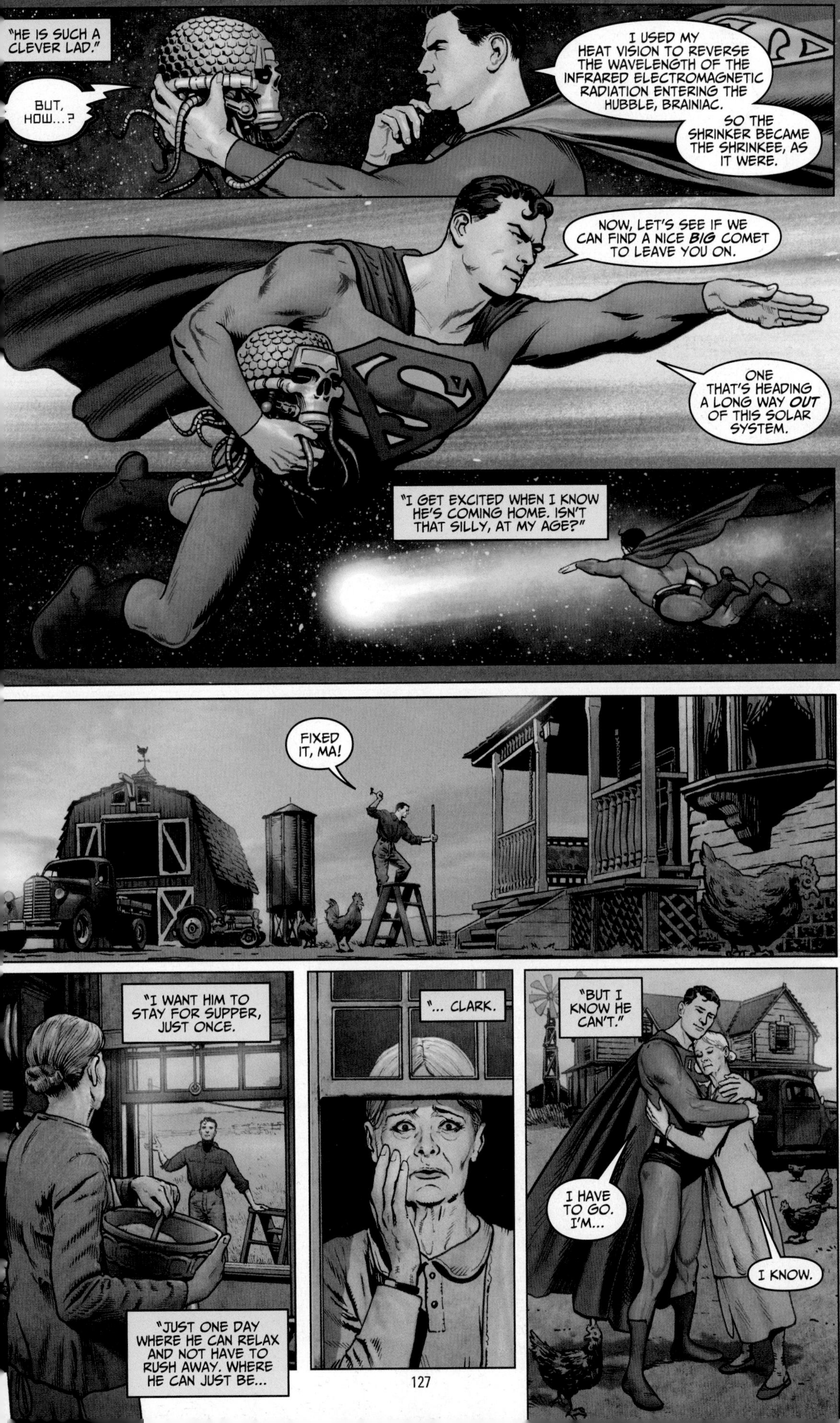
"HE IS SUCH A CLEVER LAD."
BUT, HOW...?
I USED MY HEAT VISION TO REVERSE THE WAVELENGTH OF THE INFRARED ELECTROMAGNETIC RADIATION ENTERING THE HUBBLE, BRAINIAC.
SO THE SHRINKER BECAME THE SHRINKEE, AS IT WERE.
NOW, LET'S SEE IF WE CAN FIND A NICE BIG COMET TO LEAVE YOU ON.
ONE THAT'S HEADING A LONG WAY OUT OF THIS SOLAR SYSTEM.
"I GET EXCITED WHEN I KNOW HE'S COMING HOME. ISN'T THAT SILLY, AT MY AGE?"
FIXED IT, MA!
"I WANT HIM TO STAY FOR SUPPER, JUST ONCE.
"JUST ONE DAY WHERE HE CAN RELAX AND NOT HAVE TO RUSH AWAY. WHERE HE CAN JUST BE...
"... CLARK.
"BUT I KNOW HE CAN'T."
I HAVE TO GO. I'M...
I KNOW.

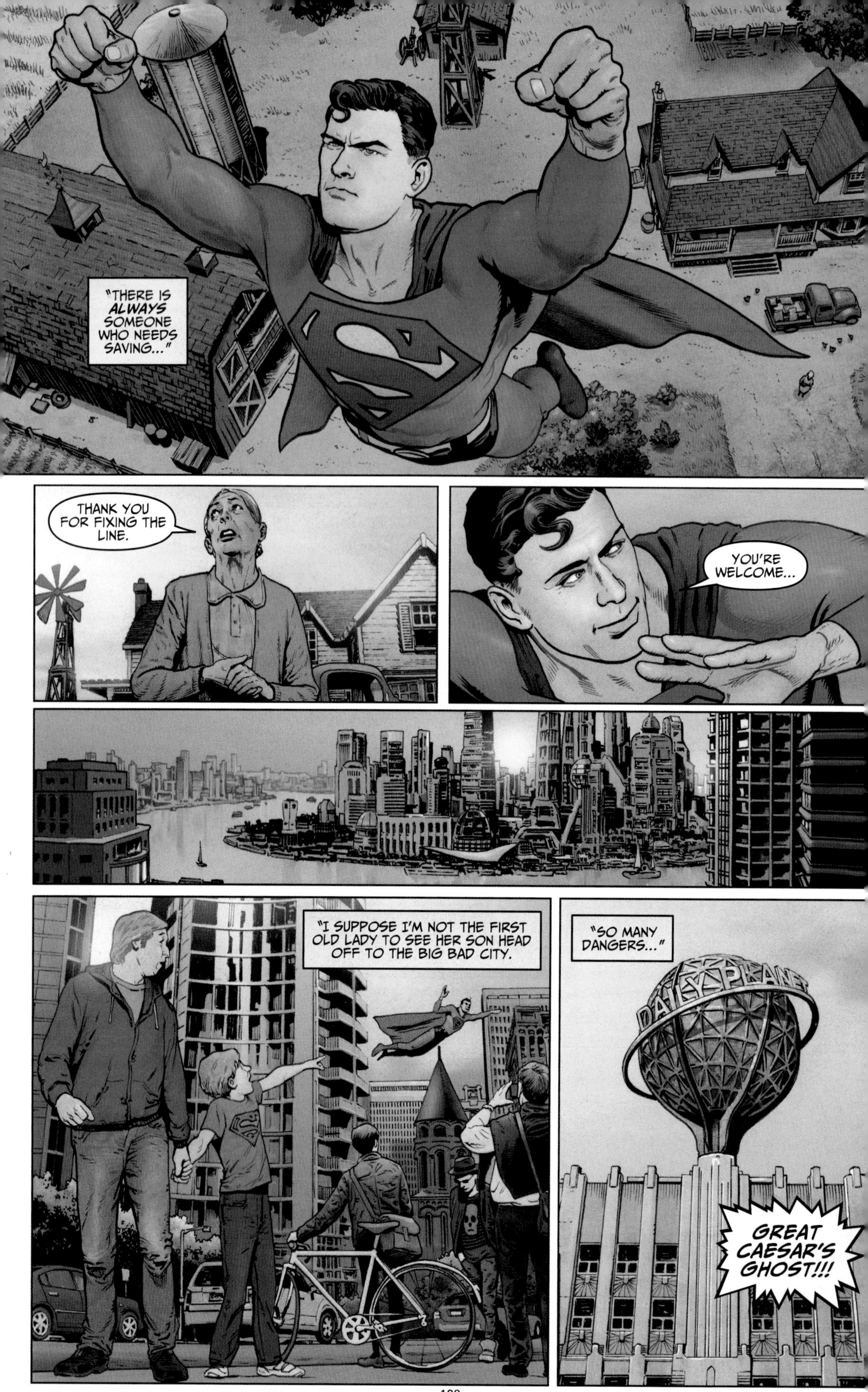
"THERE IS *ALWAYS* SOMEONE WHO NEEDS SAVING..."
THANK YOU FOR FIXING THE LINE.
YOU'RE WELCOME...
"I SUPPOSE I'M NOT THE FIRST OLD LADY TO SEE HER SON HEAD OFF TO THE BIG BAD CITY.
"SO MANY DANGERS..."
DAILY PLANET
GREAT CAESAR'S GHOST!!!

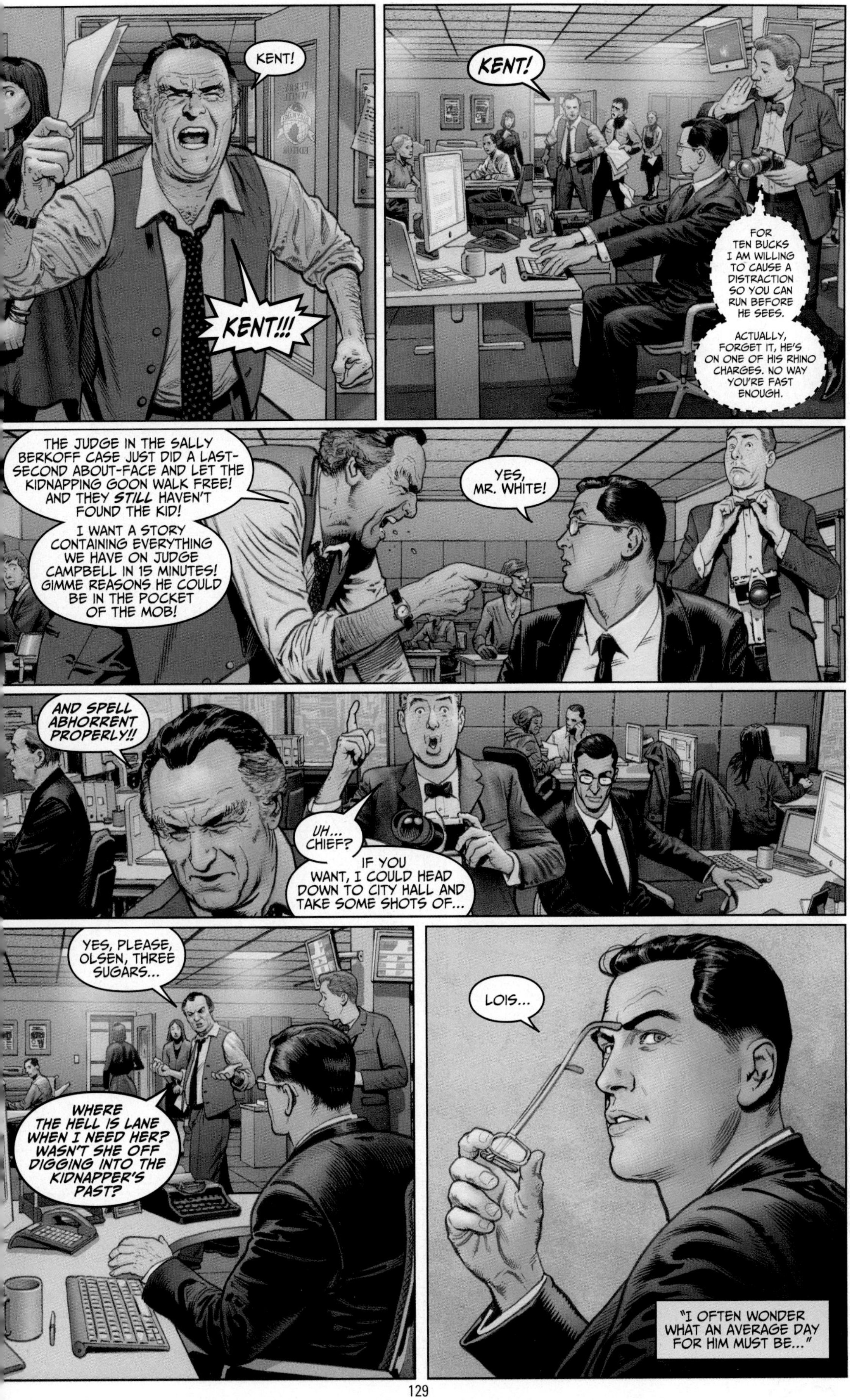

KENT!
KENT!!!
KENT!
FOR TEN BUCKS I AM WILLING TO CAUSE A DISTRACTION SO YOU CAN RUN BEFORE HE SEES.
ACTUALLY, FORGET IT, HE'S ON ONE OF HIS RHINO CHARGES. NO WAY YOU'RE FAST ENOUGH.
THE JUDGE IN THE SALLY BERKOFF CASE JUST DID A LAST-SECOND ABOUT-FACE AND LET THE KIDNAPPING GOON WALK FREE! AND THEY STILL HAVEN'T FOUND THE KID!
I WANT A STORY CONTAINING EVERYTHING WE HAVE ON JUDGE CAMPBELL IN 15 MINUTES! GIMME REASONS HE COULD BE IN THE POCKET OF THE MOB!
YES, MR. WHITE!
AND SPELL ABHORRENT PROPERLY!!
UH... CHIEF?
IF YOU WANT, I COULD HEAD DOWN TO CITY HALL AND TAKE SOME SHOTS OF...
YES, PLEASE, OLSEN, THREE SUGARS...
WHERE THE HELL IS LANE WHEN I NEED HER? WASN'T SHE OFF DIGGING INTO THE KIDNAPPER'S PAST?
LOIS...
"I OFTEN WONDER WHAT AN AVERAGE DAY FOR HIM MUST BE..."

"HOW MANY PEOPLE MUST CRY OUT TO HIM."

STAY ABOVE THE... NNNNFF... WATER... SALLY...

I'M TRYING, MISS LANE!

STUPID... LOUSY... LEAD-LINED PIT!

YOU SHOULDN'T 'A COME SNOOPING, LADY!

STICK IT IN YOUR EAR!!

MISS LANE... ARE YOU OKAY?

"DESPITE EVERYTHING. ALL HIS GIFTS. HE'S STILL JUST ONE MAN.

"HE CAN'T BE EVERYWHERE..."

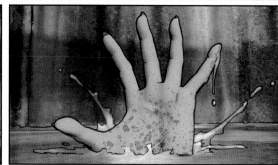

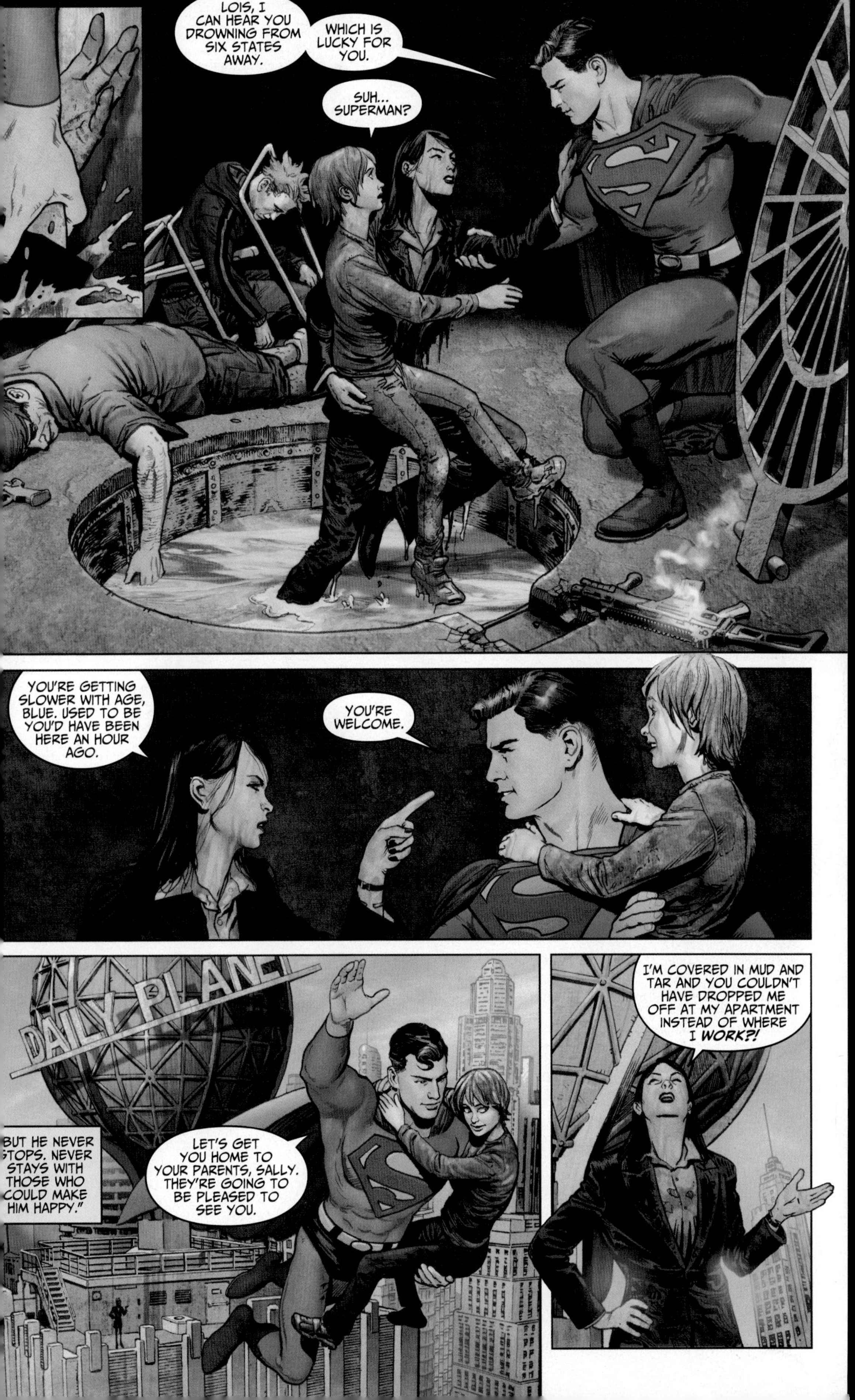
LOIS, I CAN HEAR YOU DROWNING FROM SIX STATES AWAY.
WHICH IS LUCKY FOR YOU.
SUH... SUPERMAN?
YOU'RE GETTING SLOWER WITH AGE, BLUE. USED TO BE YOU'D HAVE BEEN HERE AN HOUR AGO.
YOU'RE WELCOME.
DAILY PLAN
BUT HE NEVER STOPS. NEVER STAYS WITH THOSE WHO COULD MAKE HIM HAPPY."
LET'S GET YOU HOME TO YOUR PARENTS, SALLY. THEY'RE GOING TO BE PLEASED TO SEE YOU.
I'M COVERED IN MUD AND TAR AND YOU COULDN'T HAVE DROPPED ME OFF AT MY APARTMENT INSTEAD OF WHERE I WORK?!

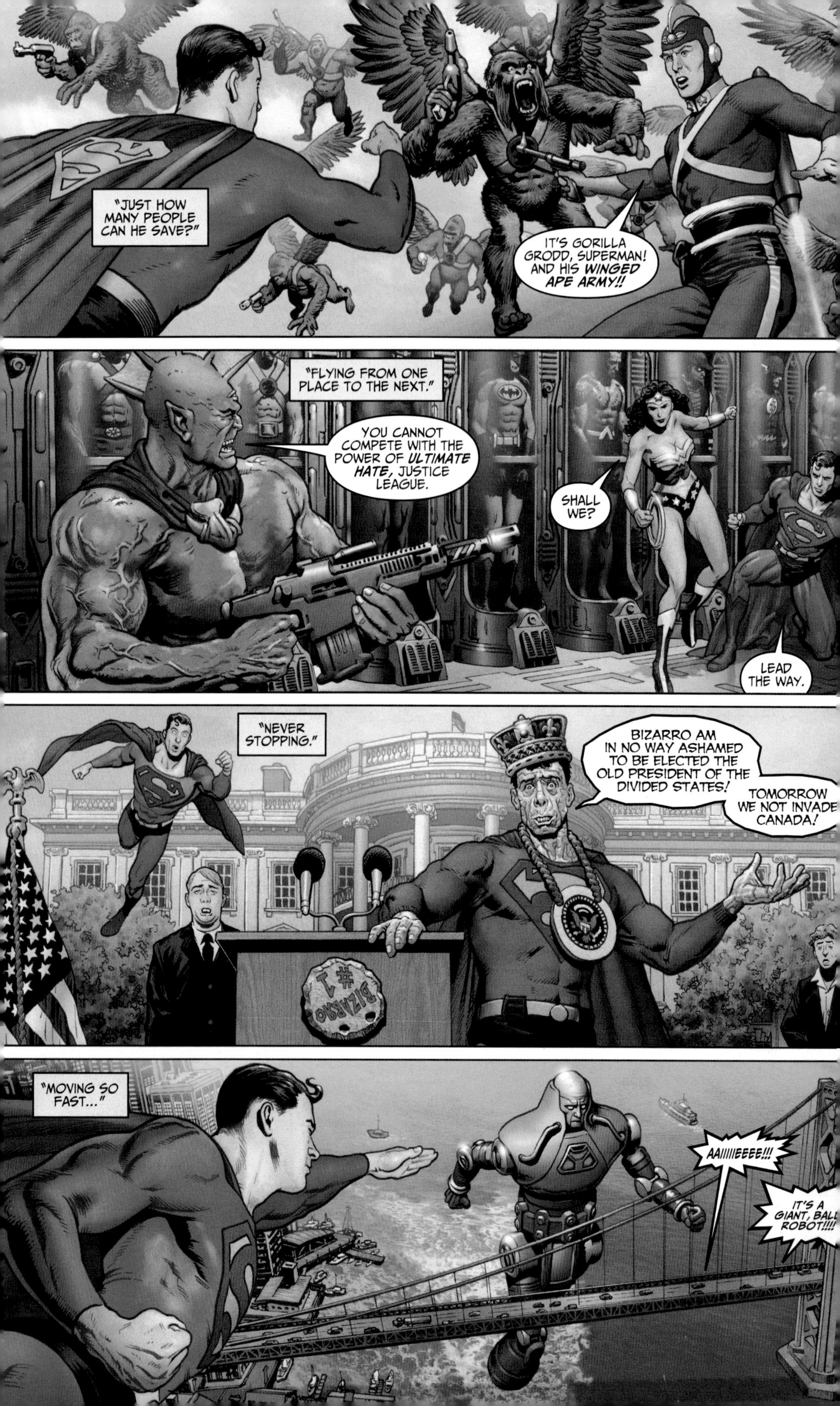

"JUST HOW MANY PEOPLE CAN HE SAVE?"
IT'S GORILLA GRODD, SUPERMAN! AND HIS *WINGED APE ARMY!!*
"FLYING FROM ONE PLACE TO THE NEXT."
YOU CANNOT COMPETE WITH THE POWER OF *ULTIMATE HATE,* JUSTICE LEAGUE.
SHALL WE?
LEAD THE WAY.
"NEVER STOPPING."
BIZARRO AM IN NO WAY ASHAMED TO BE ELECTED THE OLD PRESIDENT OF THE DIVIDED STATES!
TOMORROW WE NOT INVADE CANADA!
"MOVING SO FAST..."
AAIIIIIEEEE!!!
IT'S A GIANT, BAL ROBOT!!!!

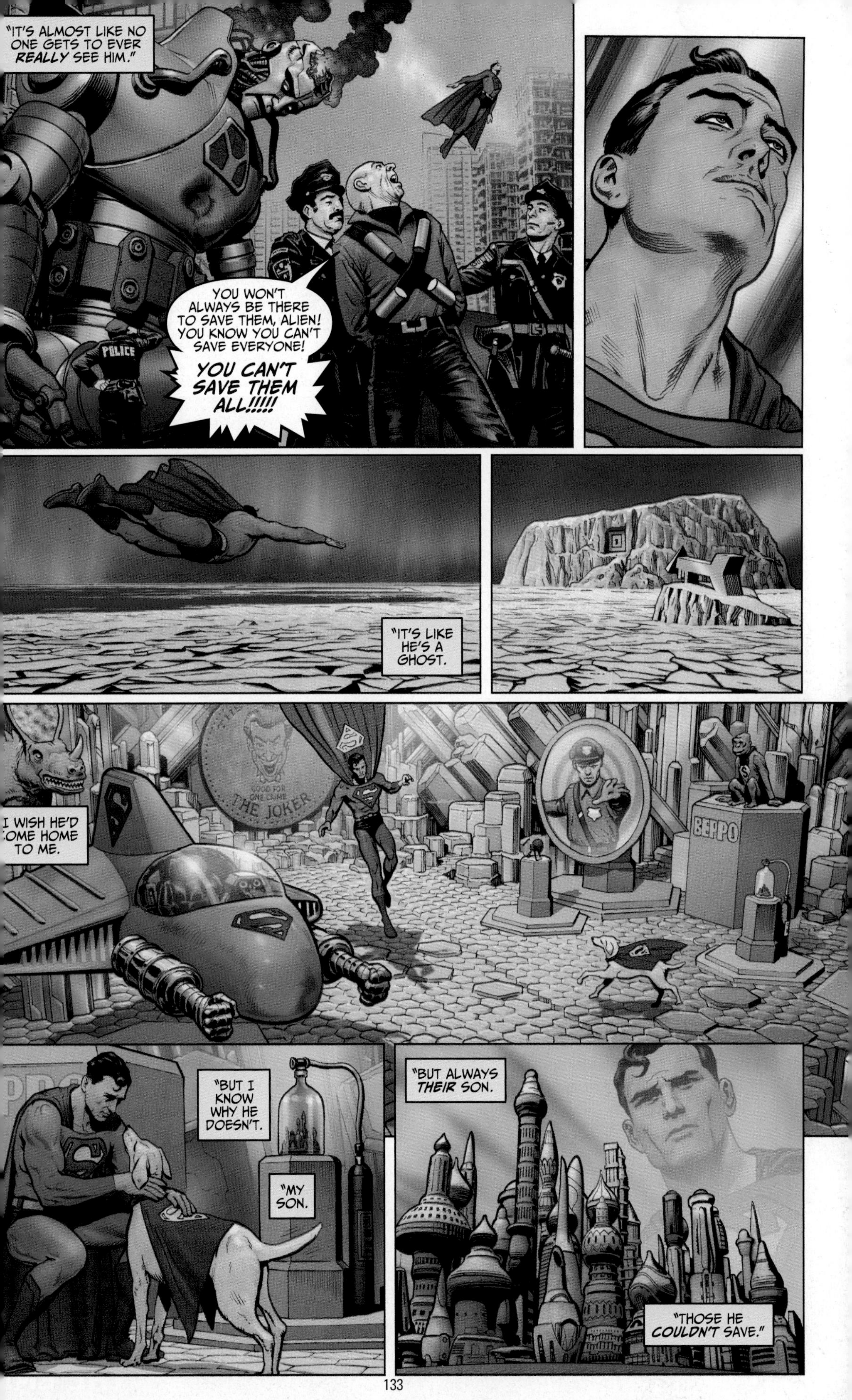
"IT'S ALMOST LIKE NO ONE GETS TO EVER REALLY SEE HIM."
YOU WON'T ALWAYS BE THERE TO SAVE THEM, ALIEN! YOU KNOW YOU CAN'T SAVE EVERYONE!
YOU CAN'T SAVE THEM ALL!!!!!
POLICE
"IT'S LIKE HE'S A GHOST.
I WISH HE'D COME HOME TO ME.
GOOD FOR ONE CRIME
THE JOKER
BEPPO
"BUT I KNOW WHY HE DOESN'T.
"MY SON.
"BUT ALWAYS THEIR SON.
"THOSE HE COULDN'T SAVE."

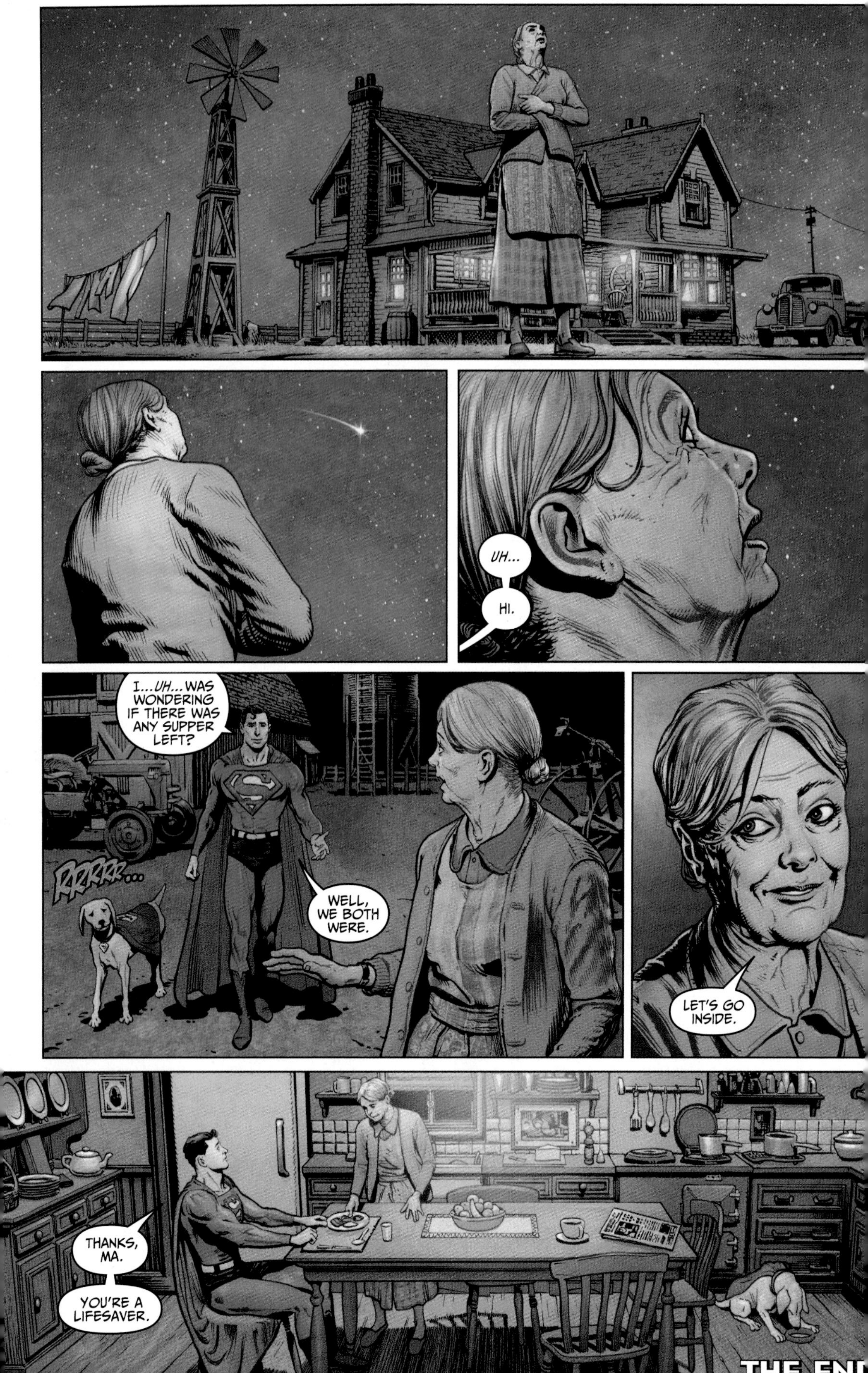

UH...
HI.
I...UH...WAS WONDERING IF THERE WAS ANY SUPPER LEFT?
RARRRR...
WELL, WE BOTH WERE.
LET'S GO INSIDE.
THANKS, MA.
YOU'RE A LIFESAVER.
THE END

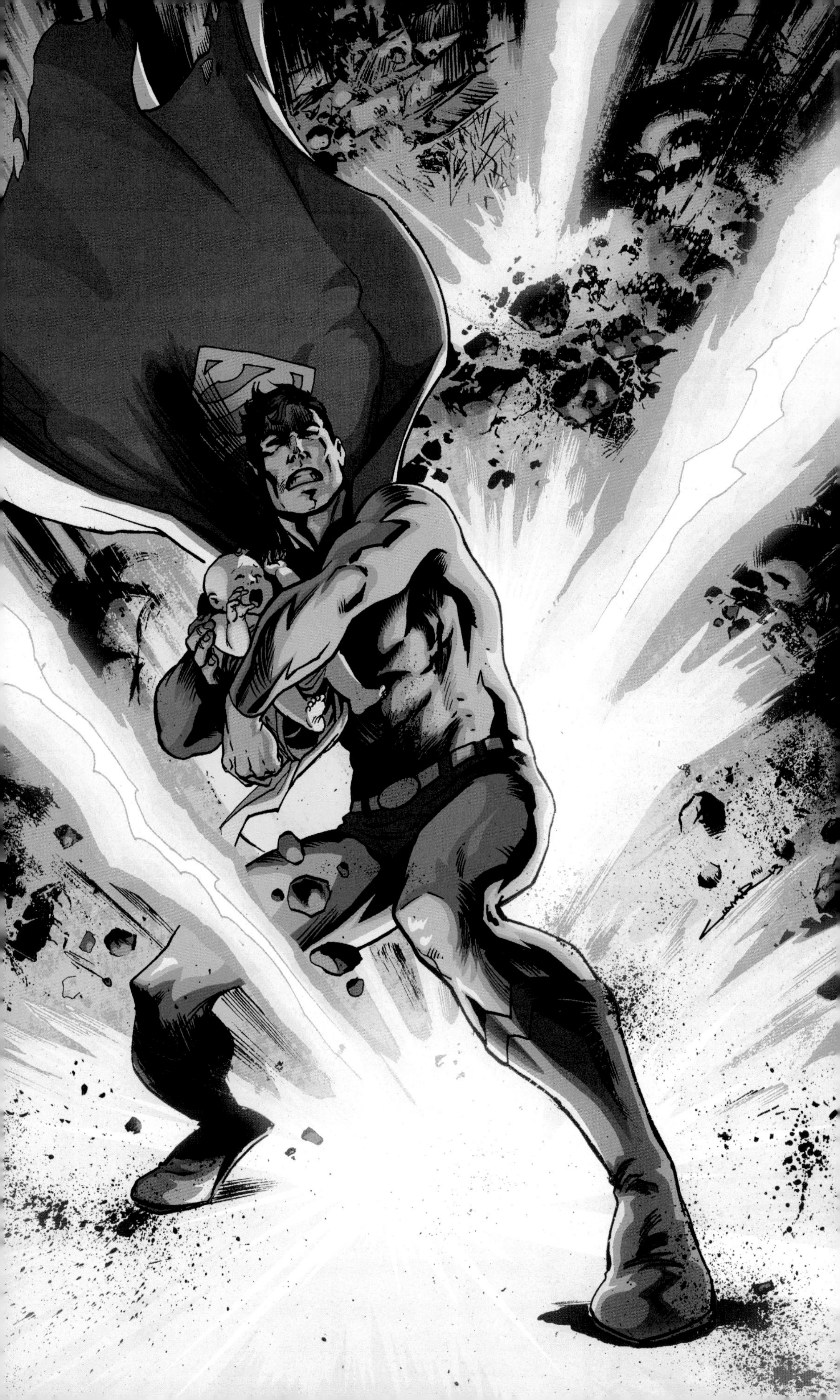

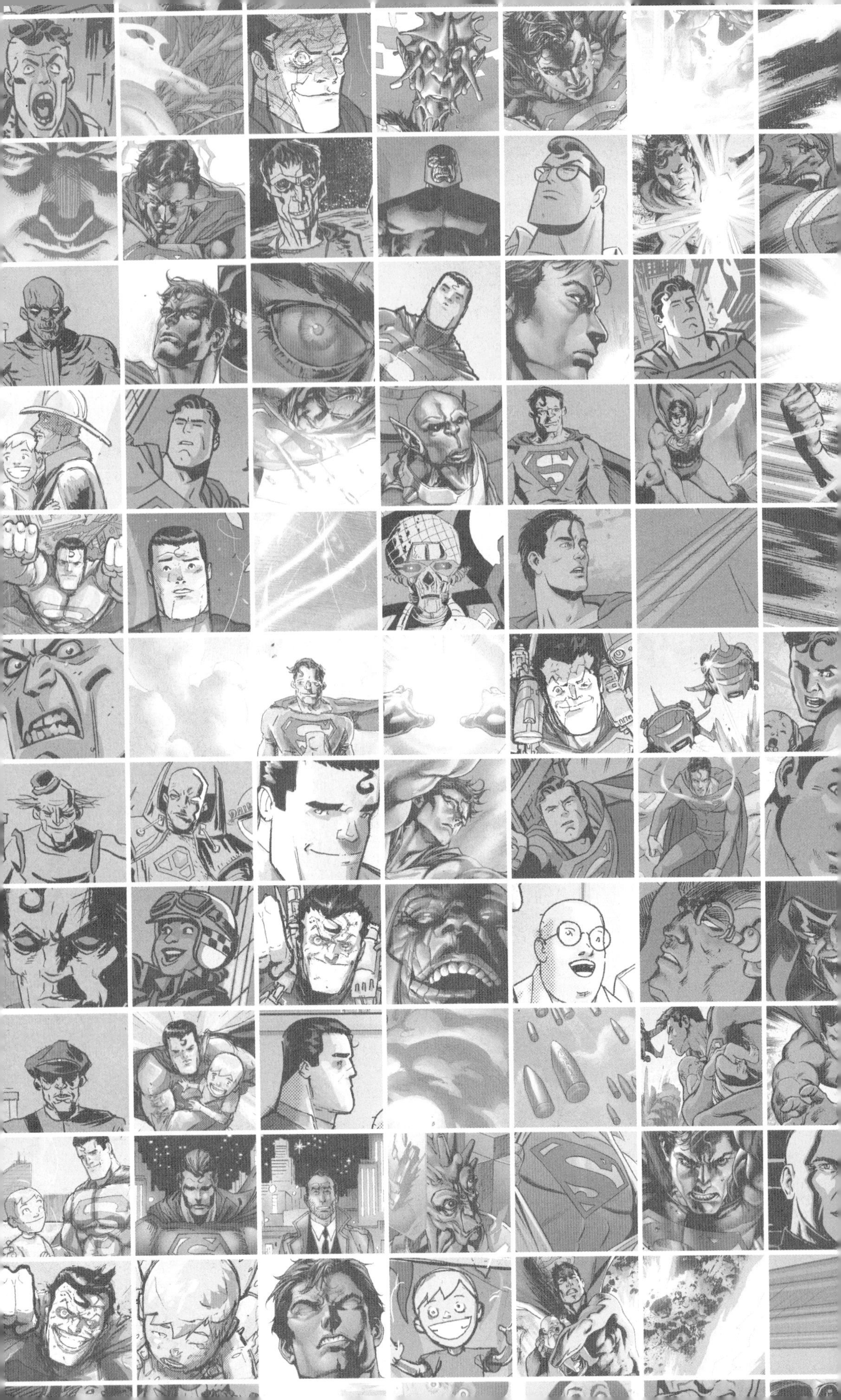

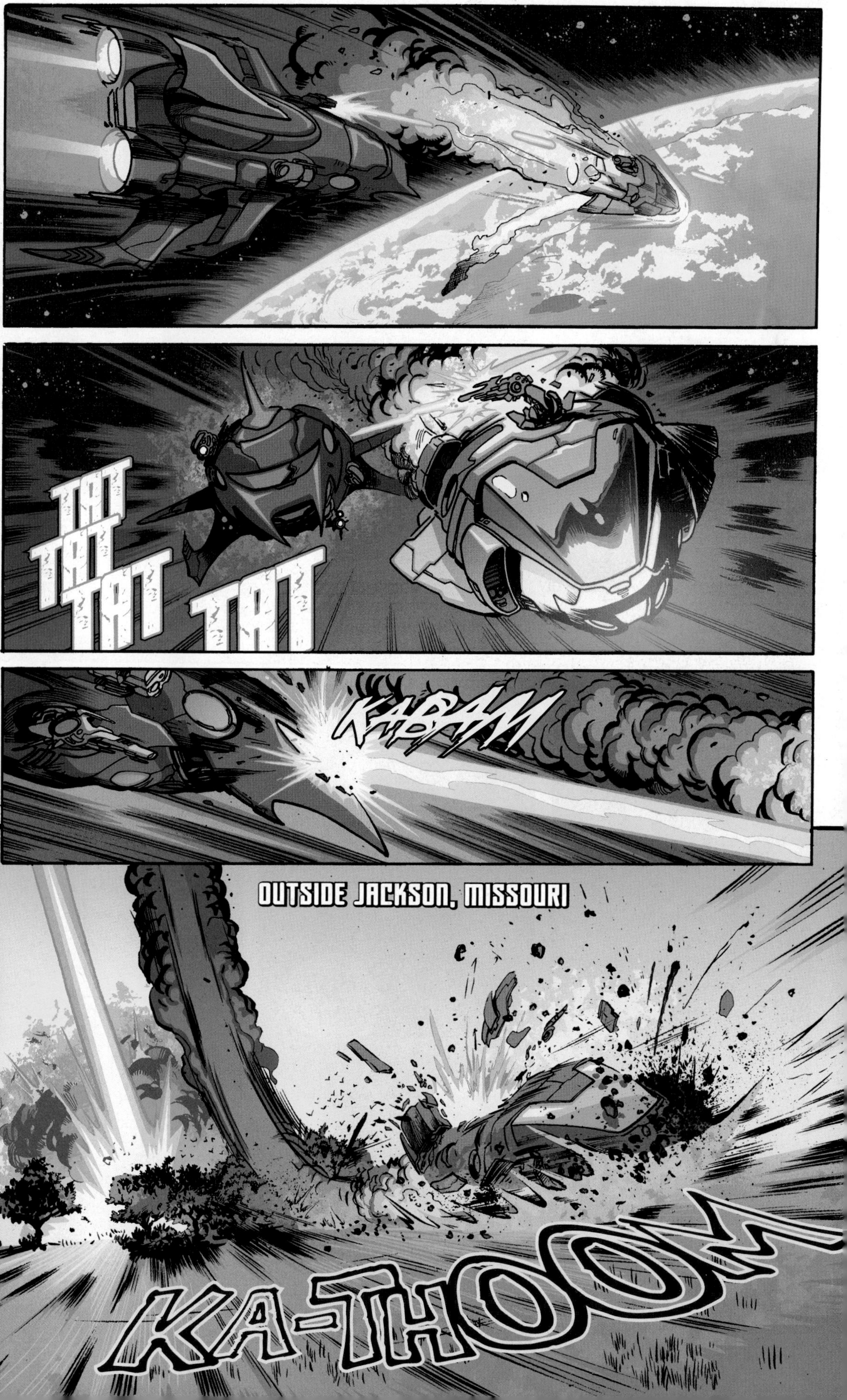
TAT
TAT
TAT
TAT
KABAM
OUTSIDE JACKSON, MISSOURI
KA-THOOOM

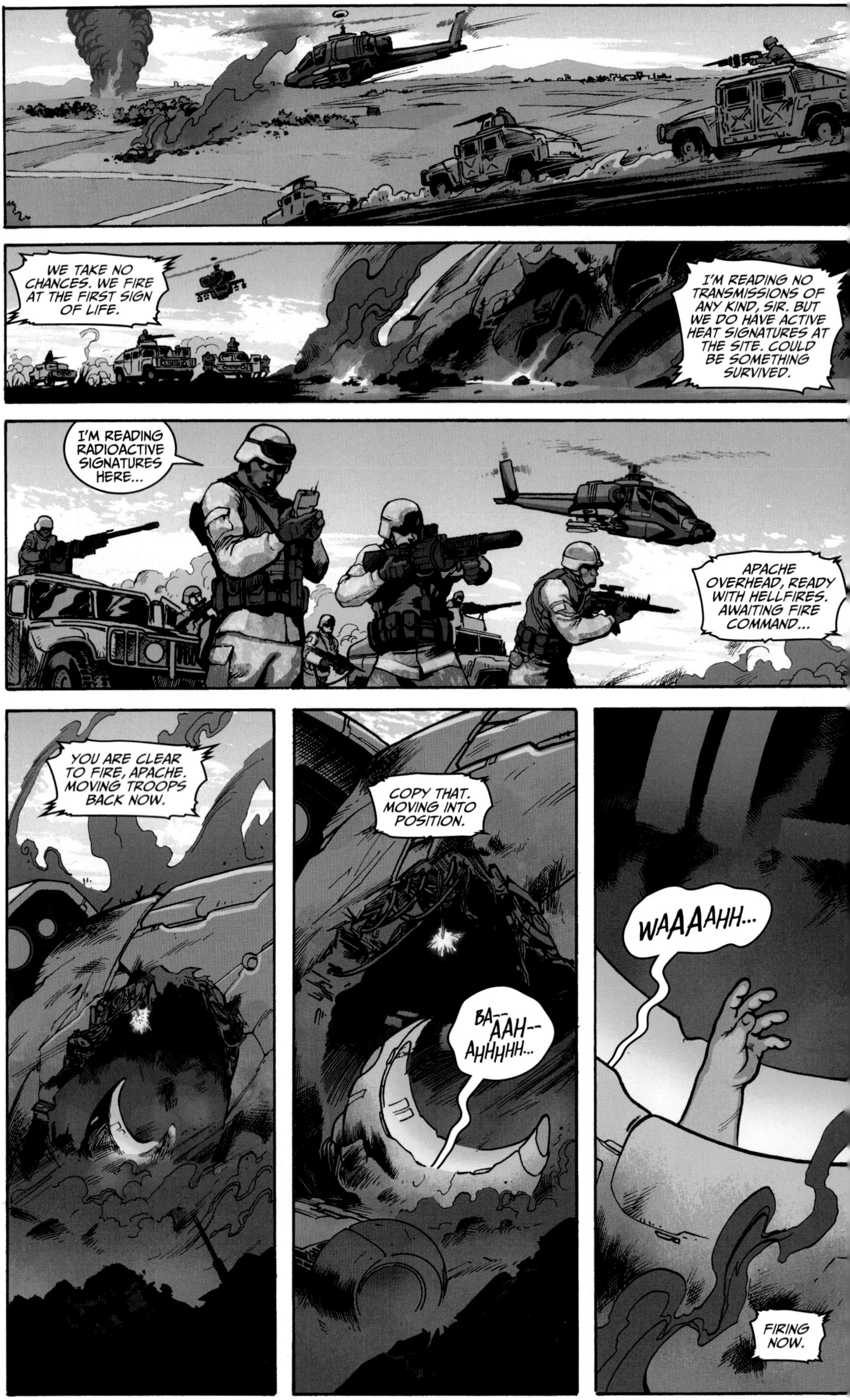
WE TAKE NO CHANCES. WE FIRE AT THE FIRST SIGN OF LIFE.
I'M READING NO TRANSMISSIONS OF ANY KIND, SIR. BUT WE DO HAVE ACTIVE HEAT SIGNATURES AT THE SITE. COULD BE SOMETHING SURVIVED.
I'M READING RADIOACTIVE SIGNATURES HERE...
APACHE OVERHEAD, READY WITH HELLFIRES. AWAITING FIRE COMMAND...
YOU ARE CLEAR TO FIRE, APACHE. MOVING TROOPS BACK NOW.
COPY THAT. MOVING INTO POSITION.
BA--AAH--AHHHHH...
WAAAAHH...
FIRING NOW.

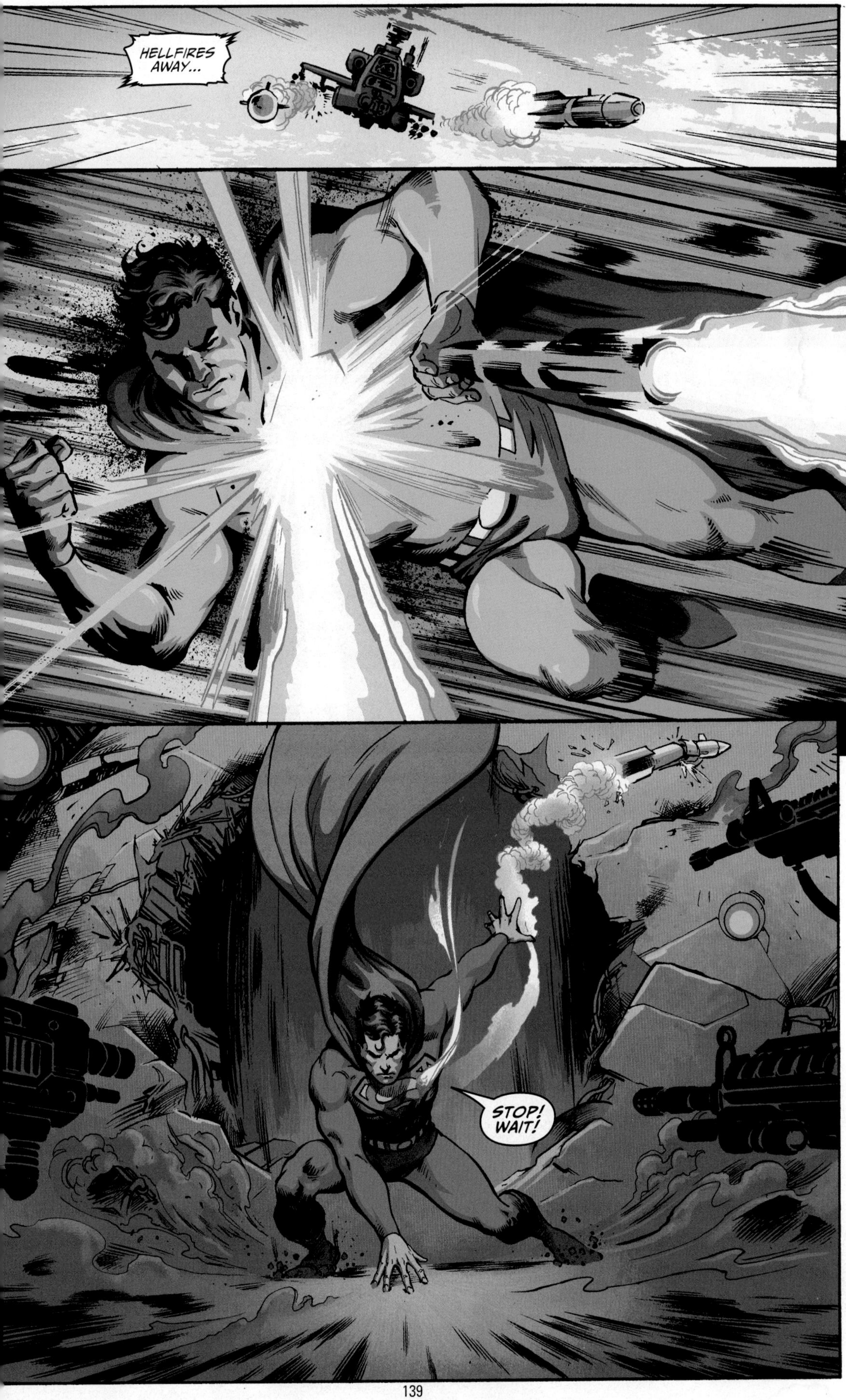
HELLFIRES AWAY...
STOP! WAIT!

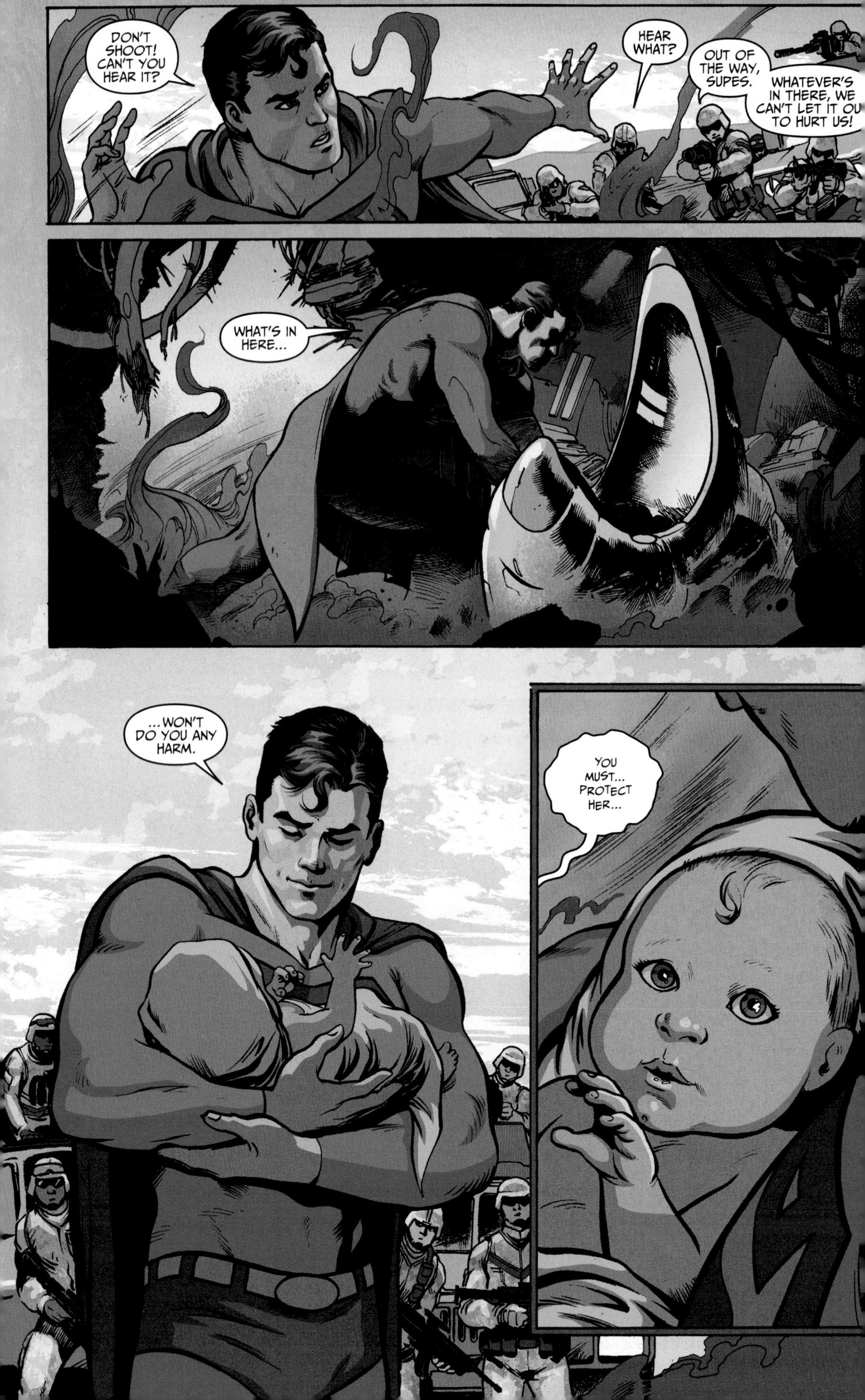
DON'T SHOOT! CAN'T YOU HEAR IT?
HEAR WHAT?
OUT OF THE WAY, SUPES.
WHATEVER'S IN THERE, WE CAN'T LET IT OU TO HURT US!
WHAT'S IN HERE...
...WON'T DO YOU ANY HARM.
YOU MUST... PROTECT HER...

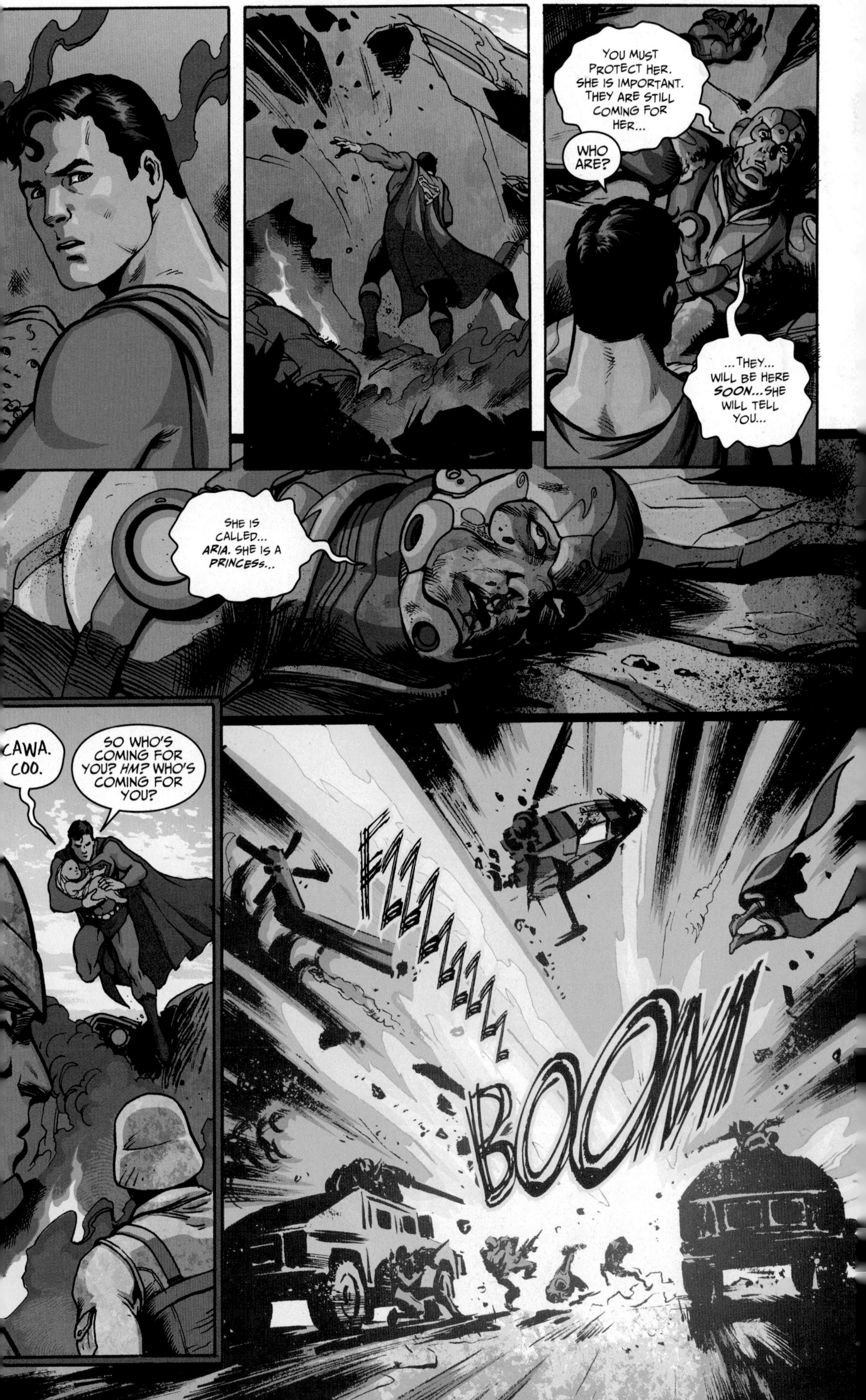
YOU MUST PROTECT HER. SHE IS IMPORTANT. THEY ARE STILL COMING FOR HER...
WHO ARE?
...THEY... WILL BE HERE SOON...SHE WILL TELL YOU...
SHE IS CALLED... ARIA. SHE IS A PRINCESS...
CAWA. COO.
SO WHO'S COMING FOR YOU? HM? WHO'S COMING FOR YOU?
FZZZZZZZZ
BOOM!

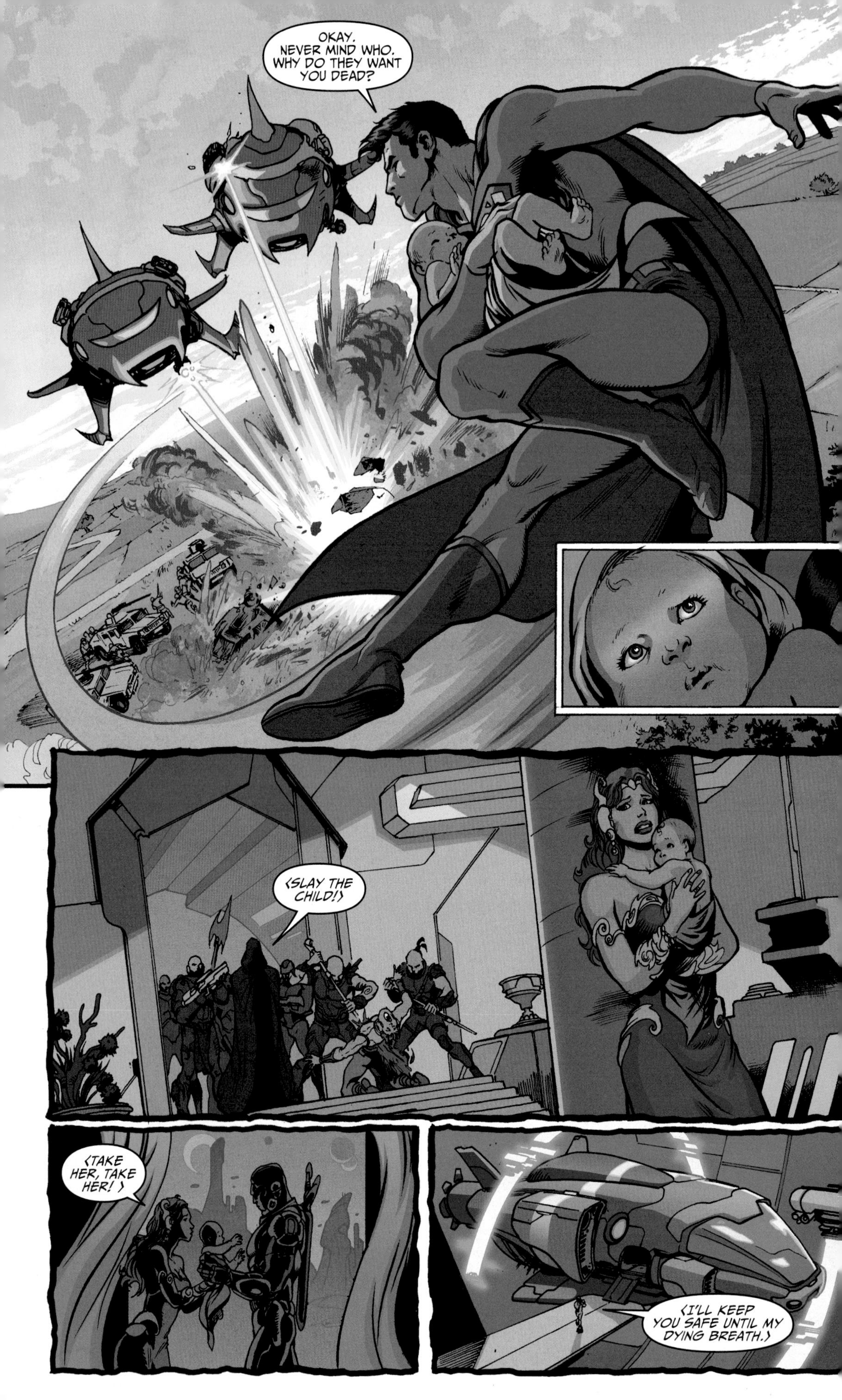
OKAY. NEVER MIND WHO. WHY DO THEY WANT YOU DEAD?
‹SLAY THE CHILD!›
‹TAKE HER, TAKE HER! ›
‹I'LL KEEP YOU SAFE UNTIL MY DYING BREATH.›

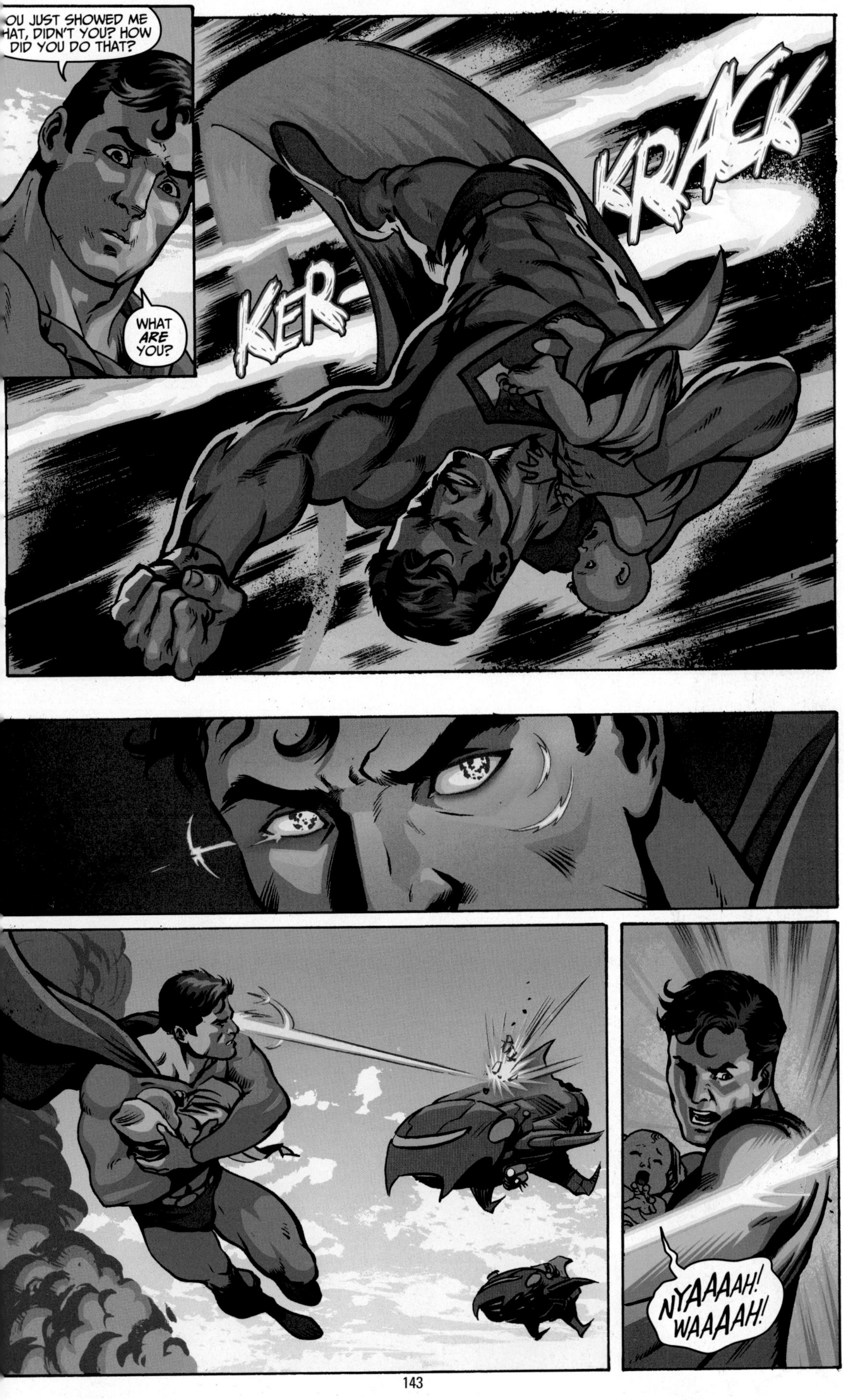
OU JUST SHOWED ME HAT, DIDN'T YOU? HOW DID YOU DO THAT?
WHAT ARE YOU?
KER-
KRACK
NYAAAAH! WAAAAH!

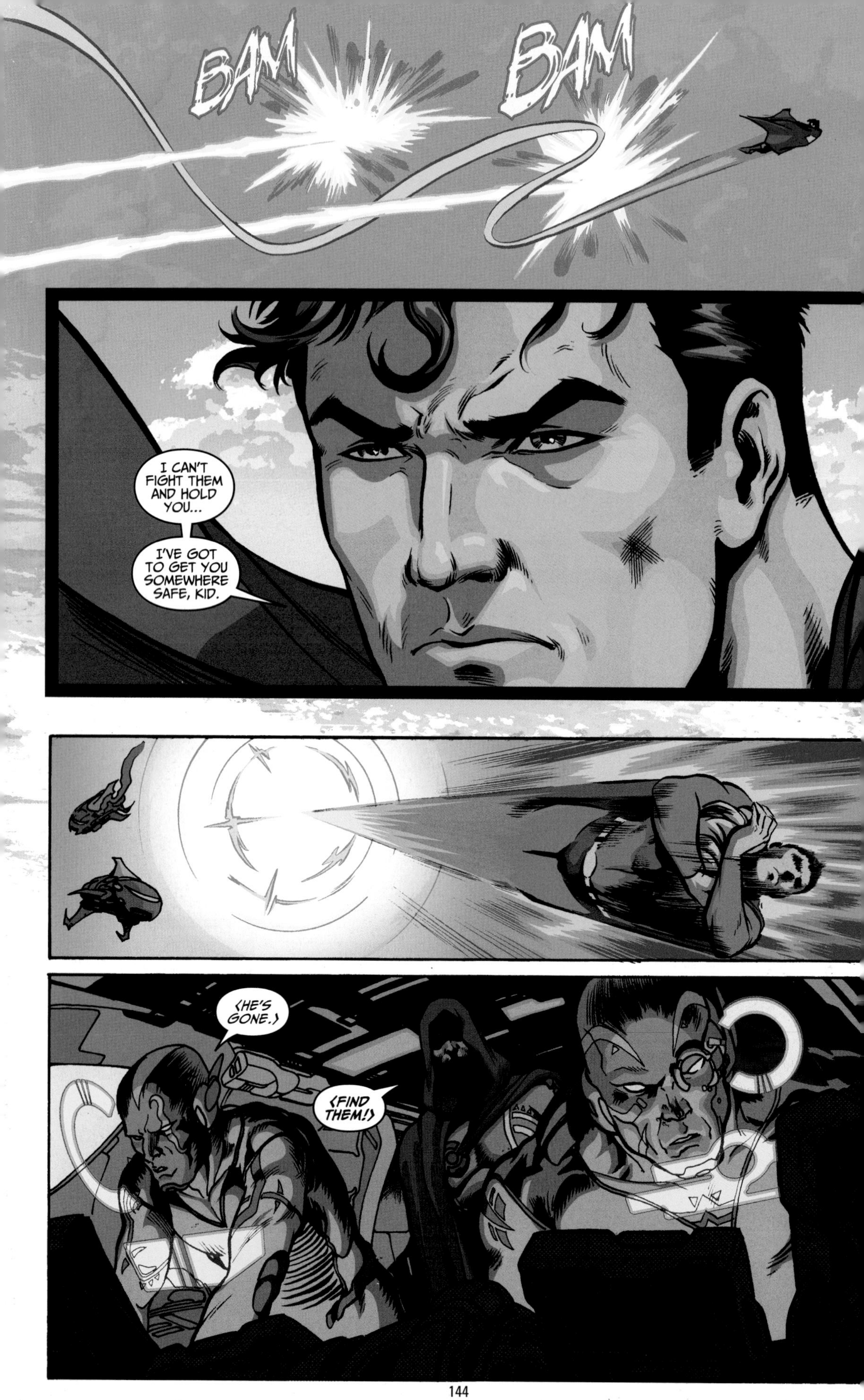
BAM
BAM
I CAN'T FIGHT THEM AND HOLD YOU...
I'VE GOT TO GET YOU SOMEWHERE SAFE, KID.
‹HE'S GONE.›
‹FIND THEM!›

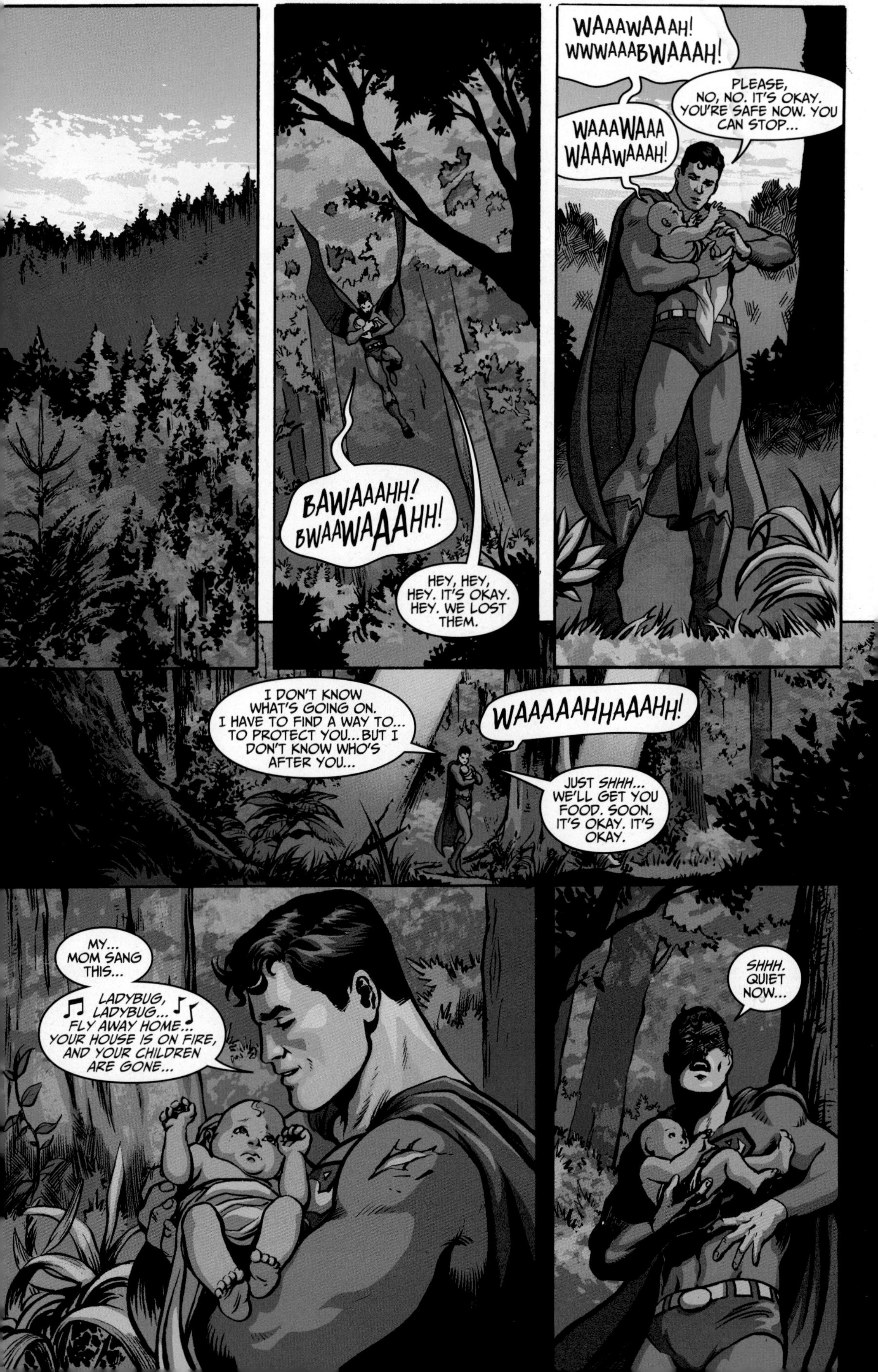
BAWAAAHH! BWAAWAAAHH!
HEY, HEY, HEY. IT'S OKAY. HEY. WE LOST THEM.
WAAAWAAAH! WWWAAABWAAAH!
WAAAWAAA WAAAWAAAH!
PLEASE, NO, NO. IT'S OKAY. YOU'RE SAFE NOW. YOU CAN STOP...
I DON'T KNOW WHAT'S GOING ON. I HAVE TO FIND A WAY TO... TO PROTECT YOU...BUT I DON'T KNOW WHO'S AFTER YOU...
WAAAAAHHAAAHH!
JUST SHHH... WE'LL GET YOU FOOD. SOON. IT'S OKAY. IT'S OKAY.
MY... MOM SANG THIS...
♫ LADYBUG, LADYBUG... ♫ FLY AWAY HOME... YOUR HOUSE IS ON FIRE, AND YOUR CHILDREN ARE GONE...
SHHH. QUIET NOW...

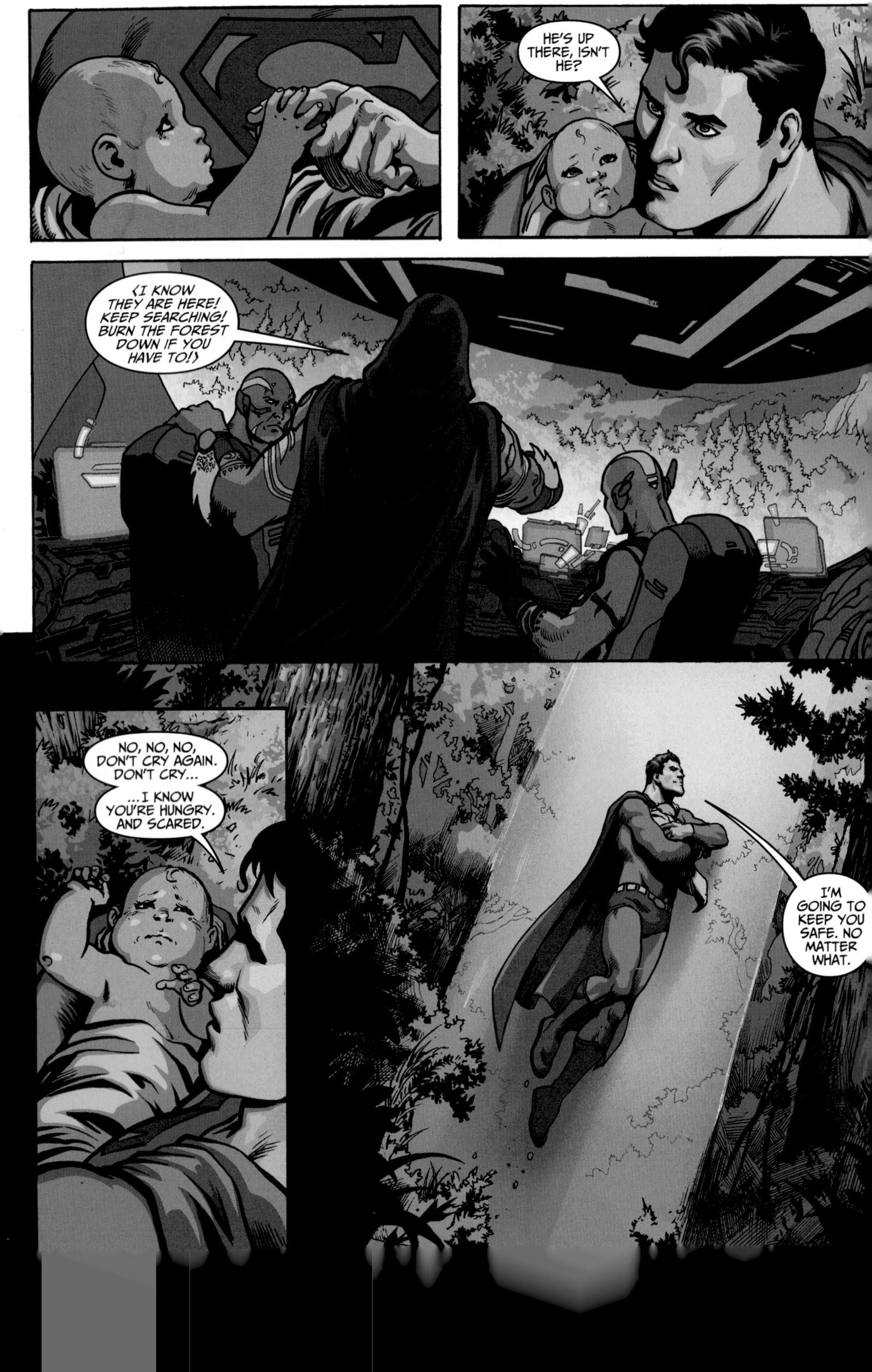
HE'S UP THERE, ISN'T HE?
‹I KNOW THEY ARE HERE! KEEP SEARCHING! BURN THE FOREST DOWN IF YOU HAVE TO!›
NO, NO, NO, DON'T CRY AGAIN. DON'T CRY...
...I KNOW YOU'RE HUNGRY. AND SCARED.
I'M GOING TO KEEP YOU SAFE. NO MATTER WHAT.

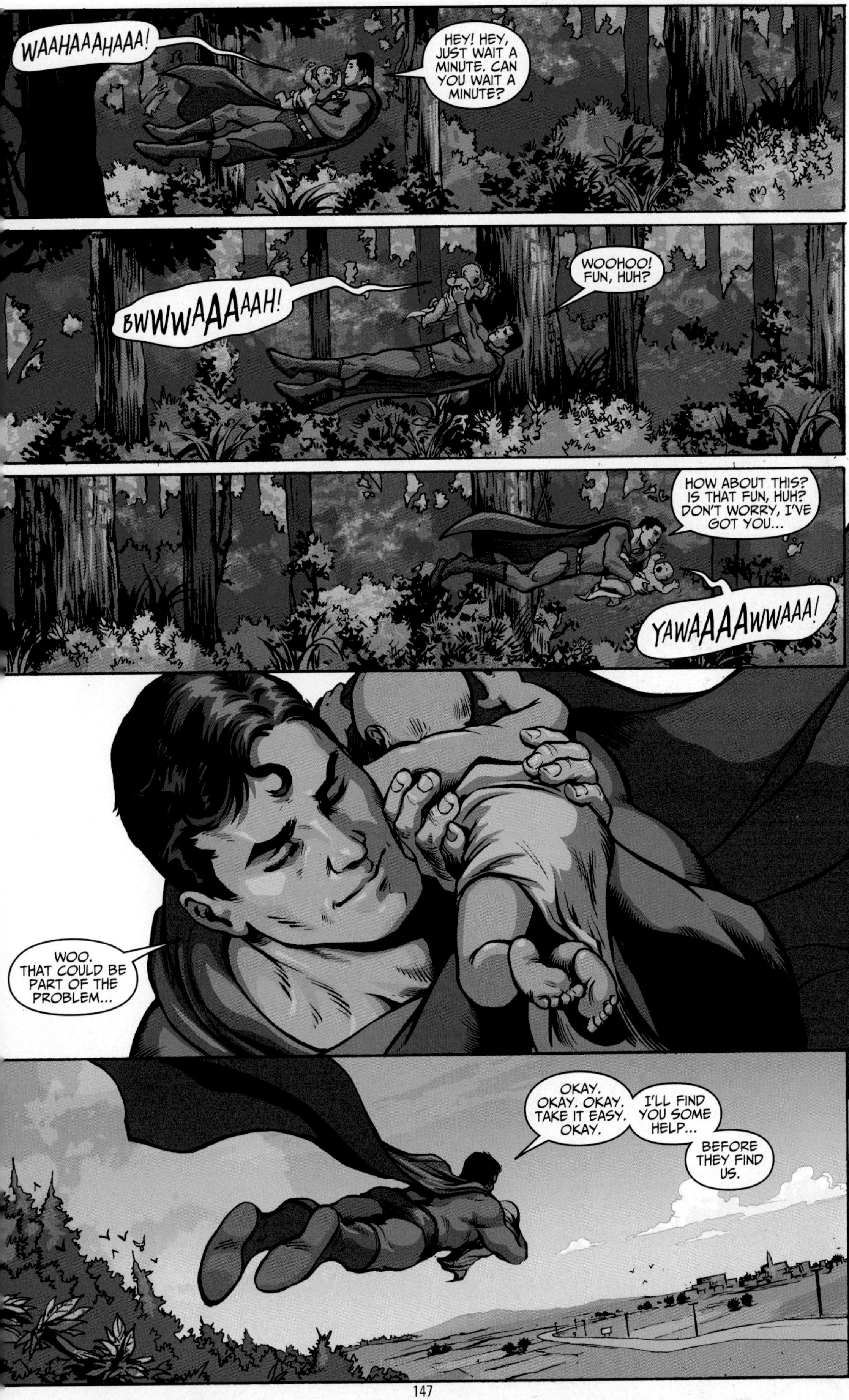
WAAHAAAHAAA!
HEY! HEY, JUST WAIT A MINUTE. CAN YOU WAIT A MINUTE?
BWWWAAAAAH!
WOOHOO! FUN, HUH?
HOW ABOUT THIS? IS THAT FUN, HUH? DON'T WORRY, I'VE GOT YOU...
YAWAAAAWWAAA!
WOO. THAT COULD BE PART OF THE PROBLEM...
OKAY. OKAY. OKAY. TAKE IT EASY. OKAY.
I'LL FIND YOU SOME HELP...
BEFORE THEY FIND US.

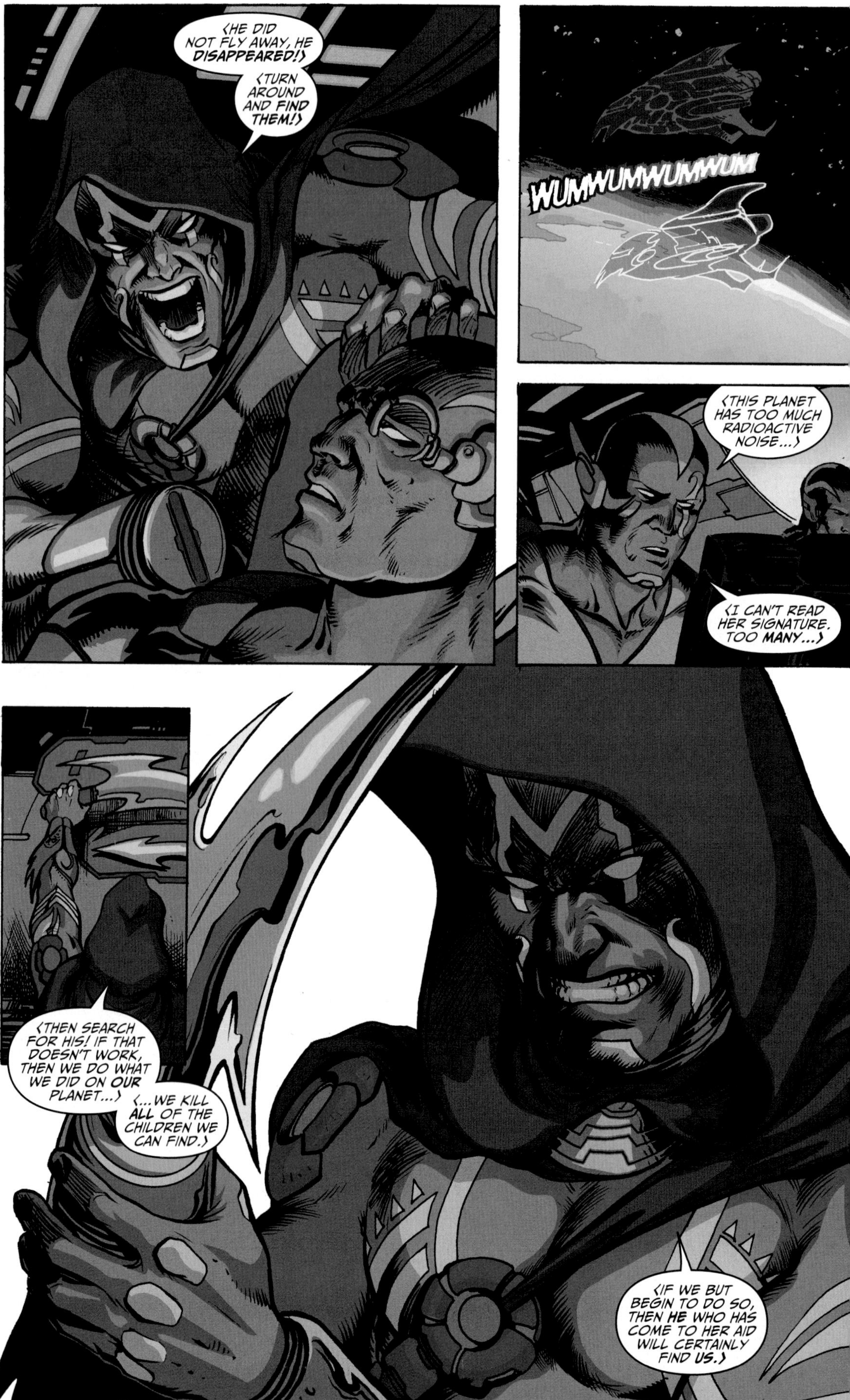

‹HE DID NOT FLY AWAY, HE DISAPPEARED!›
‹TURN AROUND AND FIND THEM!›
WUMWUMWUMWUM
‹THIS PLANET HAS TOO MUCH RADIOACTIVE NOISE...›
‹I CAN'T READ HER SIGNATURE. TOO MANY...›
‹THEN SEARCH FOR HIS! IF THAT DOESN'T WORK, THEN WE DO WHAT WE DID ON OUR PLANET...›
‹...WE KILL ALL OF THE CHILDREN WE CAN FIND.›
‹IF WE BUT BEGIN TO DO SO, THEN HE WHO HAS COME TO HER AID WILL CERTAINLY FIND US.›

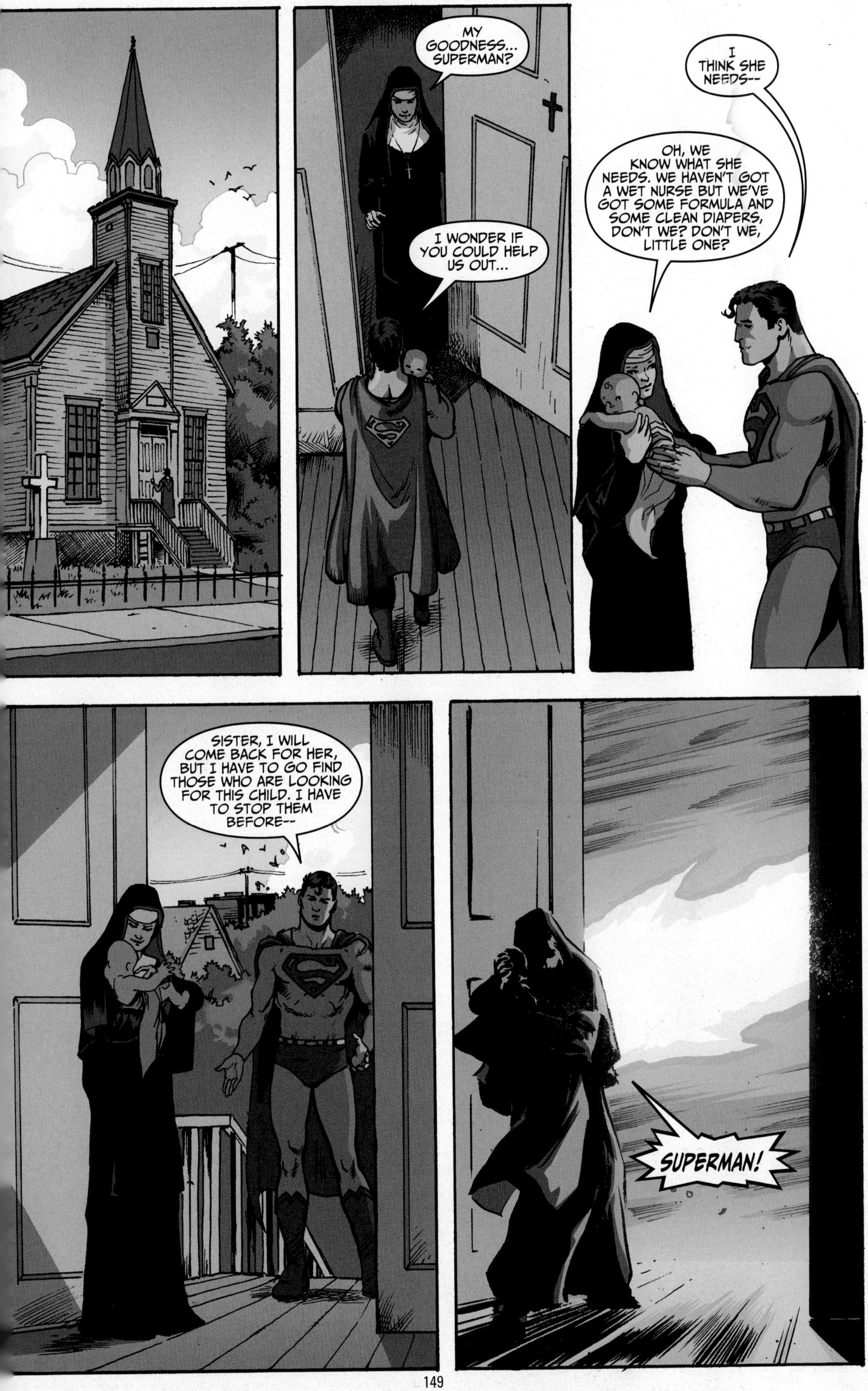
MY GOODNESS... SUPERMAN?
I WONDER IF YOU COULD HELP US OUT...
I THINK SHE NEEDS--
OH, WE KNOW WHAT SHE NEEDS. WE HAVEN'T GOT A WET NURSE BUT WE'VE GOT SOME FORMULA AND SOME CLEAN DIAPERS, DON'T WE? DON'T WE, LITTLE ONE?
SISTER, I WILL COME BACK FOR HER, BUT I HAVE TO GO FIND THOSE WHO ARE LOOKING FOR THIS CHILD. I HAVE TO STOP THEM BEFORE--
SUPERMAN!

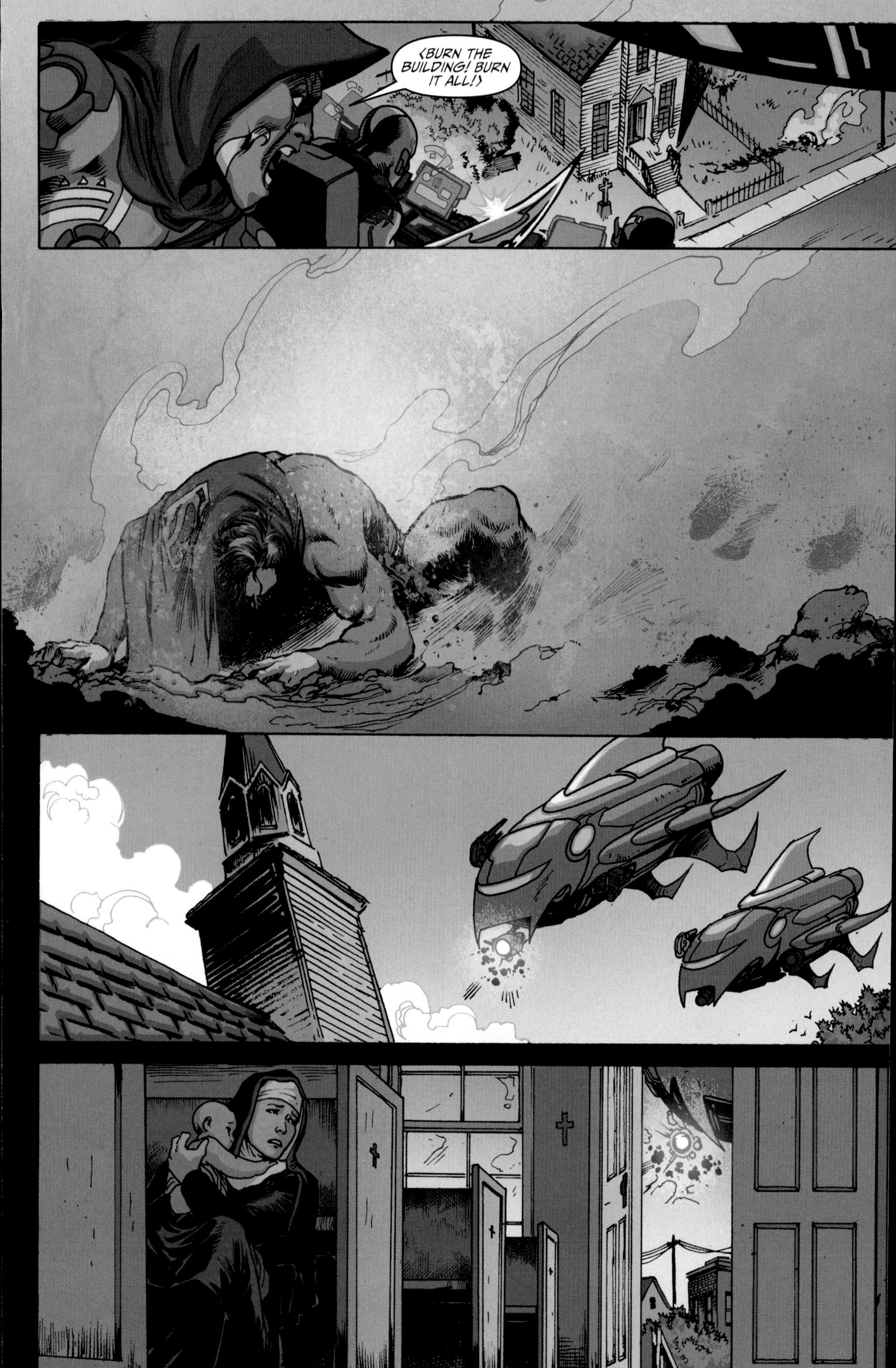
‹BURN THE BUILDING! BURN IT ALL!›

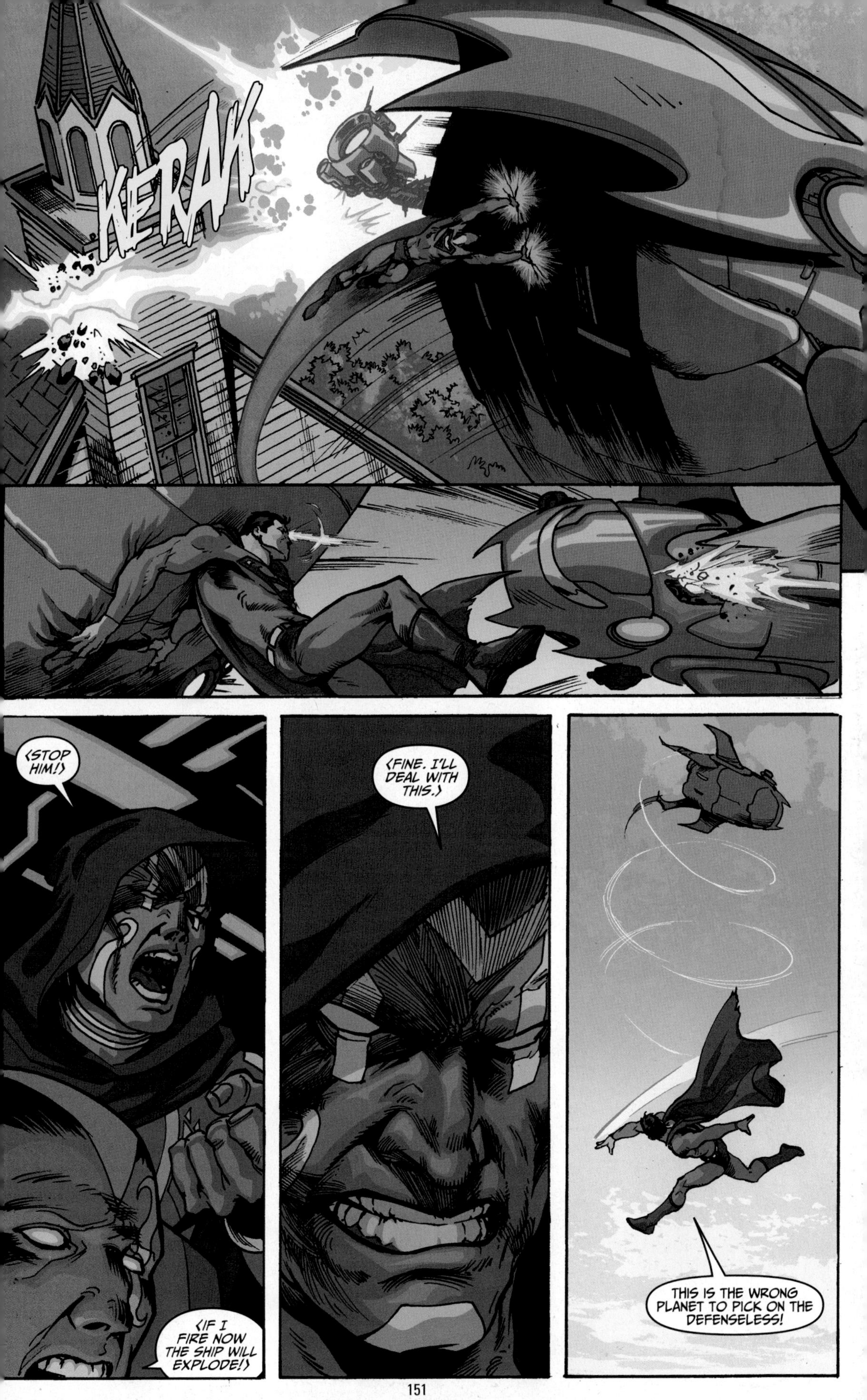
KERAK
‹STOP HIM!›
‹IF I FIRE NOW THE SHIP WILL EXPLODE!›
‹FINE. I'LL DEAL WITH THIS.›
THIS IS THE WRONG PLANET TO PICK ON THE DEFENSELESS!

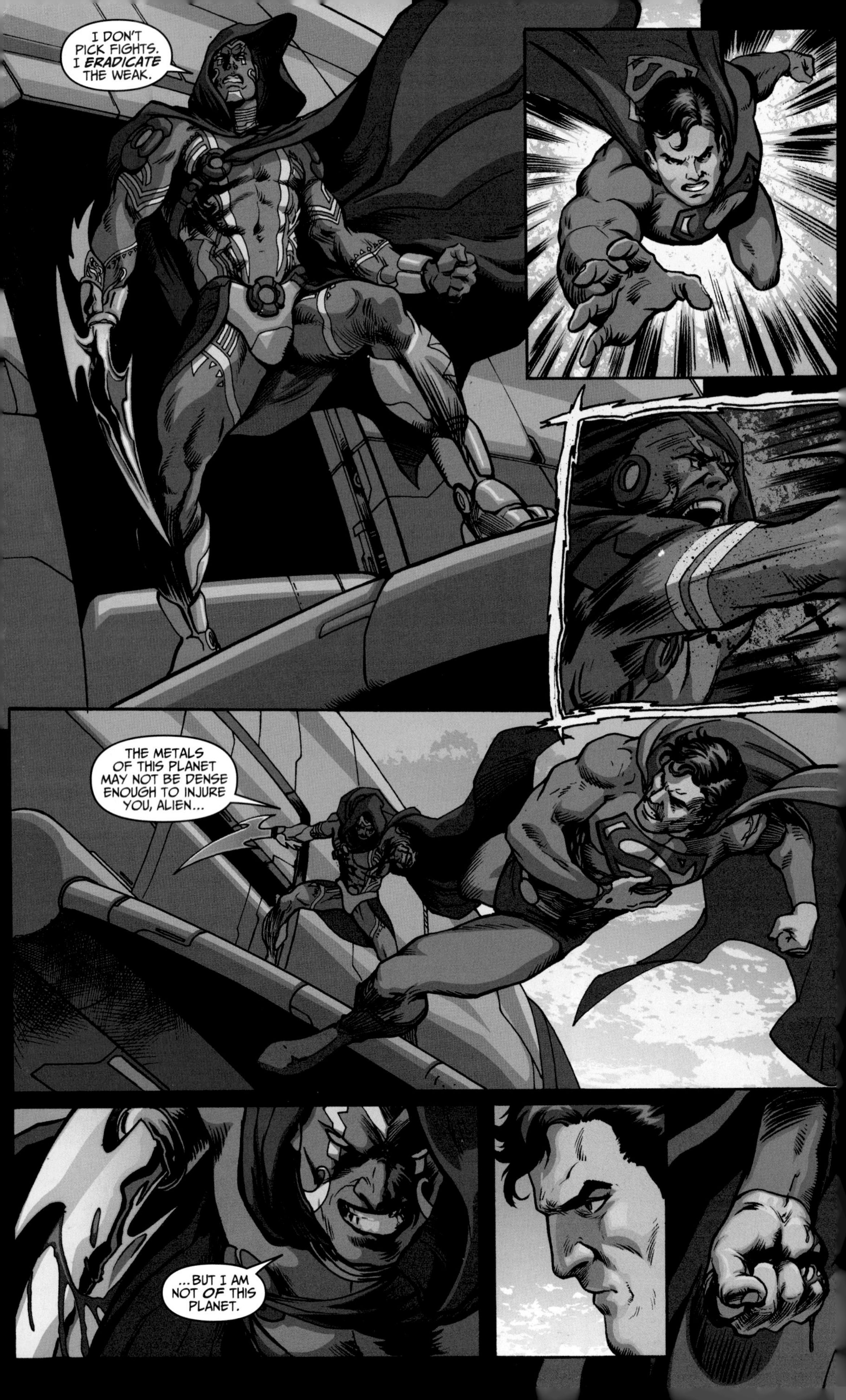
I DON'T PICK FIGHTS. I *ERADICATE* THE WEAK.
THE METALS OF THIS PLANET MAY NOT BE DENSE ENOUGH TO INJURE YOU, ALIEN...
...BUT I AM NOT *OF* THIS PLANET.

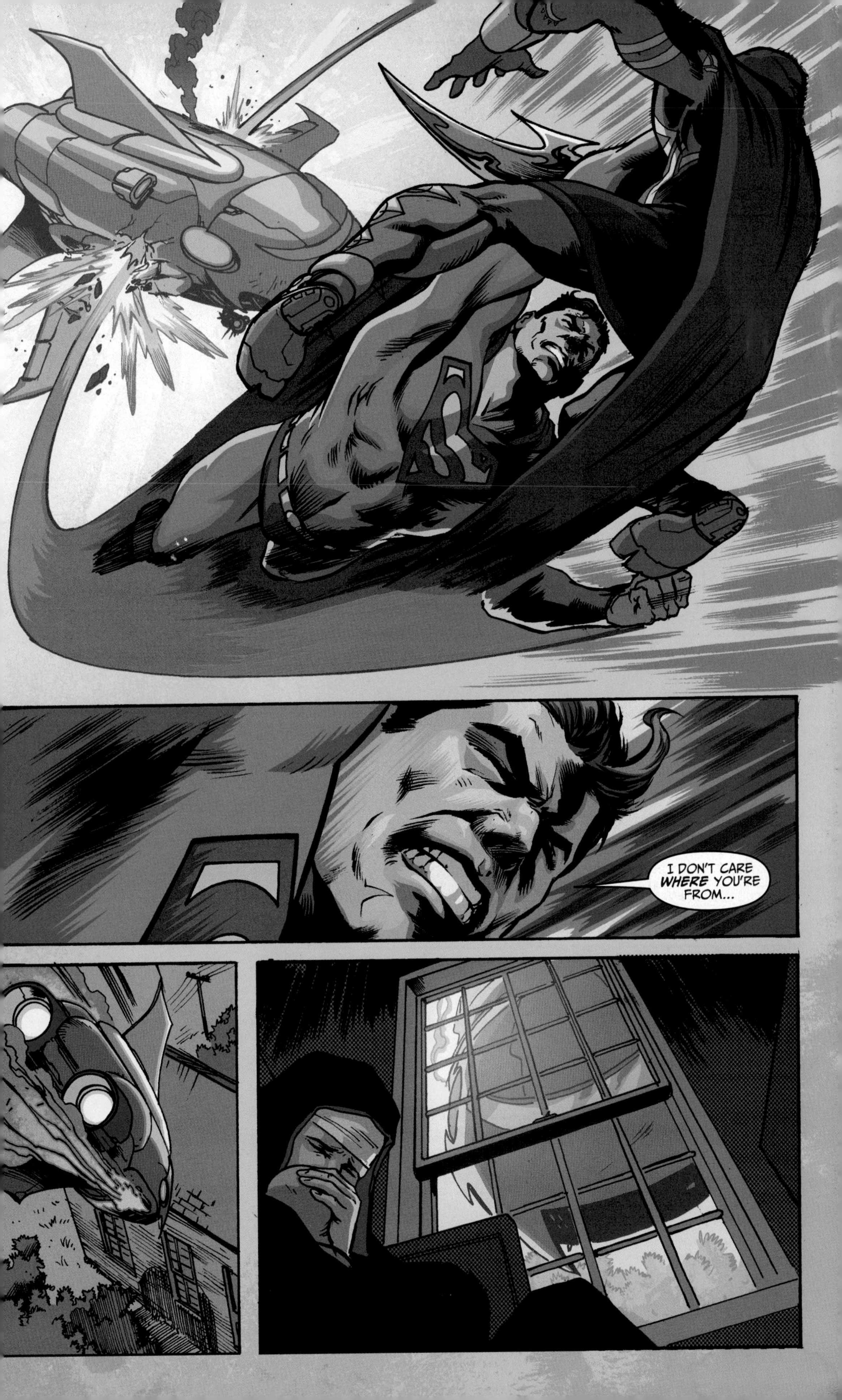
I DON'T CARE
WHERE YOU'RE
FROM...

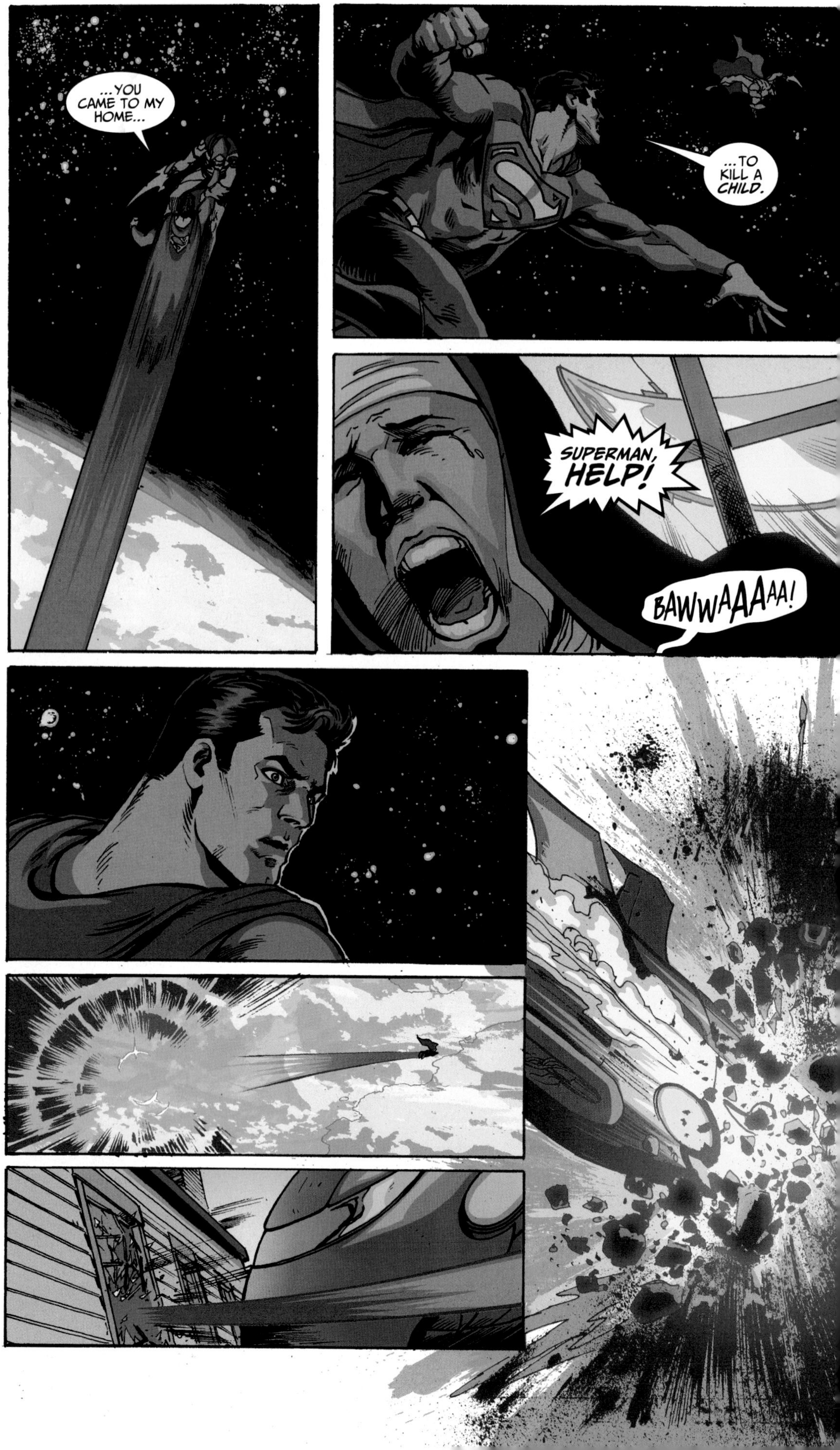
...YOU CAME TO MY HOME...
...TO KILL A CHILD.
SUPERMAN, HELP!
BAWWAAAAA!

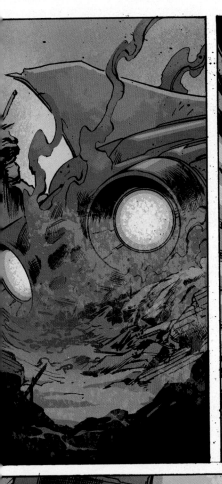

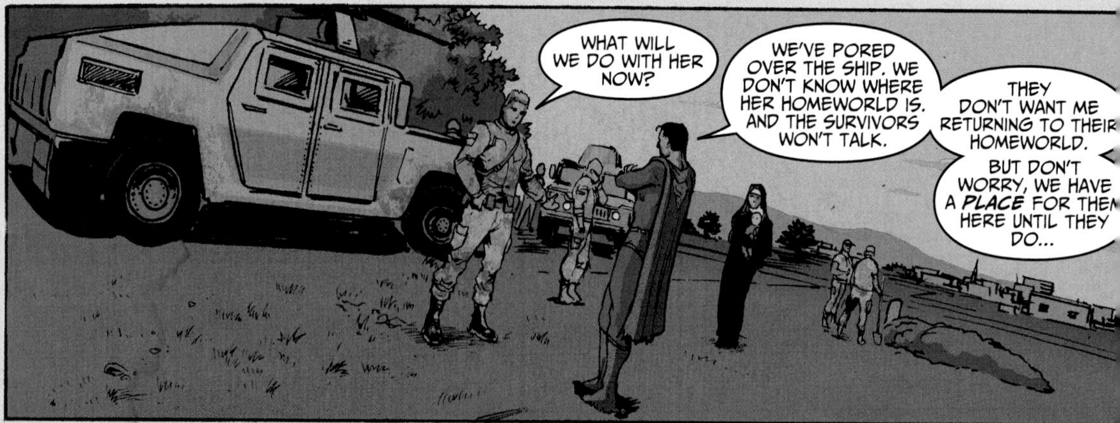
WHAT WILL WE DO WITH HER NOW?
WE'VE PORED OVER THE SHIP. WE DON'T KNOW WHERE HER HOMEWORLD IS. AND THE SURVIVORS WON'T TALK.
THEY DON'T WANT ME RETURNING TO THEIR HOMEWORLD.
BUT DON'T WORRY, WE HAVE A PLACE FOR THEM HERE UNTIL THEY DO...

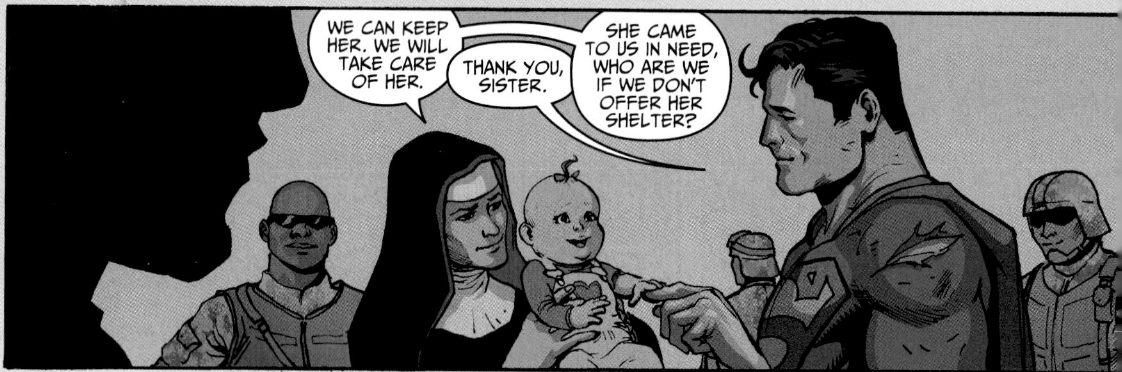
WE CAN KEEP HER. WE WILL TAKE CARE OF HER.
THANK YOU, SISTER.
SHE CAME TO US IN NEED, WHO ARE WE IF WE DON'T OFFER HER SHELTER?

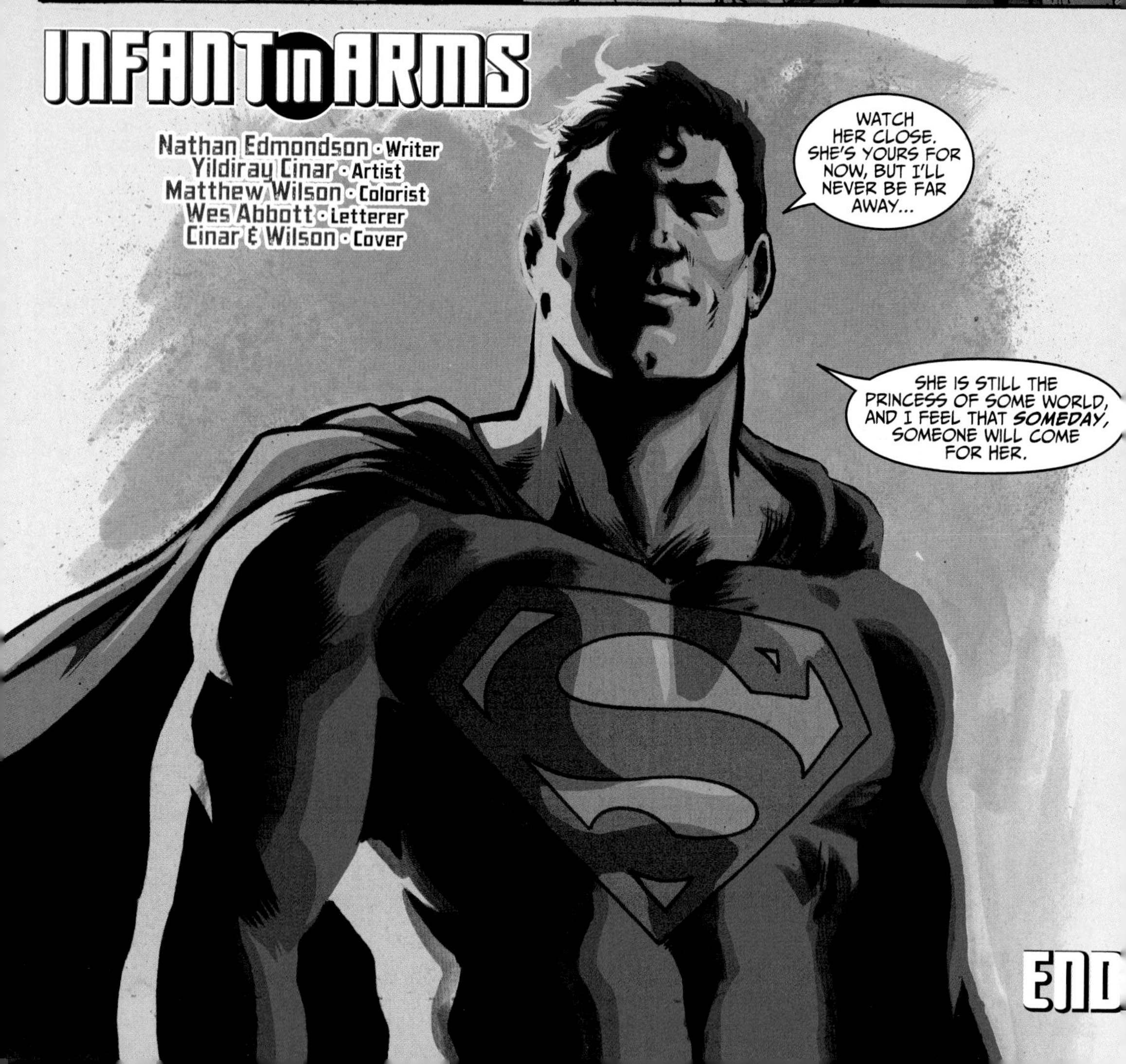
INFANT in ARMS
Nathan Edmondson · Writer
Yildiray Cinar · Artist
Matthew Wilson · Colorist
Wes Abbott · Letterer
Cinar & Wilson · Cover
WATCH HER CLOSE. SHE'S YOURS FOR NOW, BUT I'LL NEVER BE FAR AWAY...
SHE IS STILL THE PRINCESS OF SOME WORLD, AND I FEEL THAT SOMEDAY, SOMEONE WILL COME FOR HER.
END

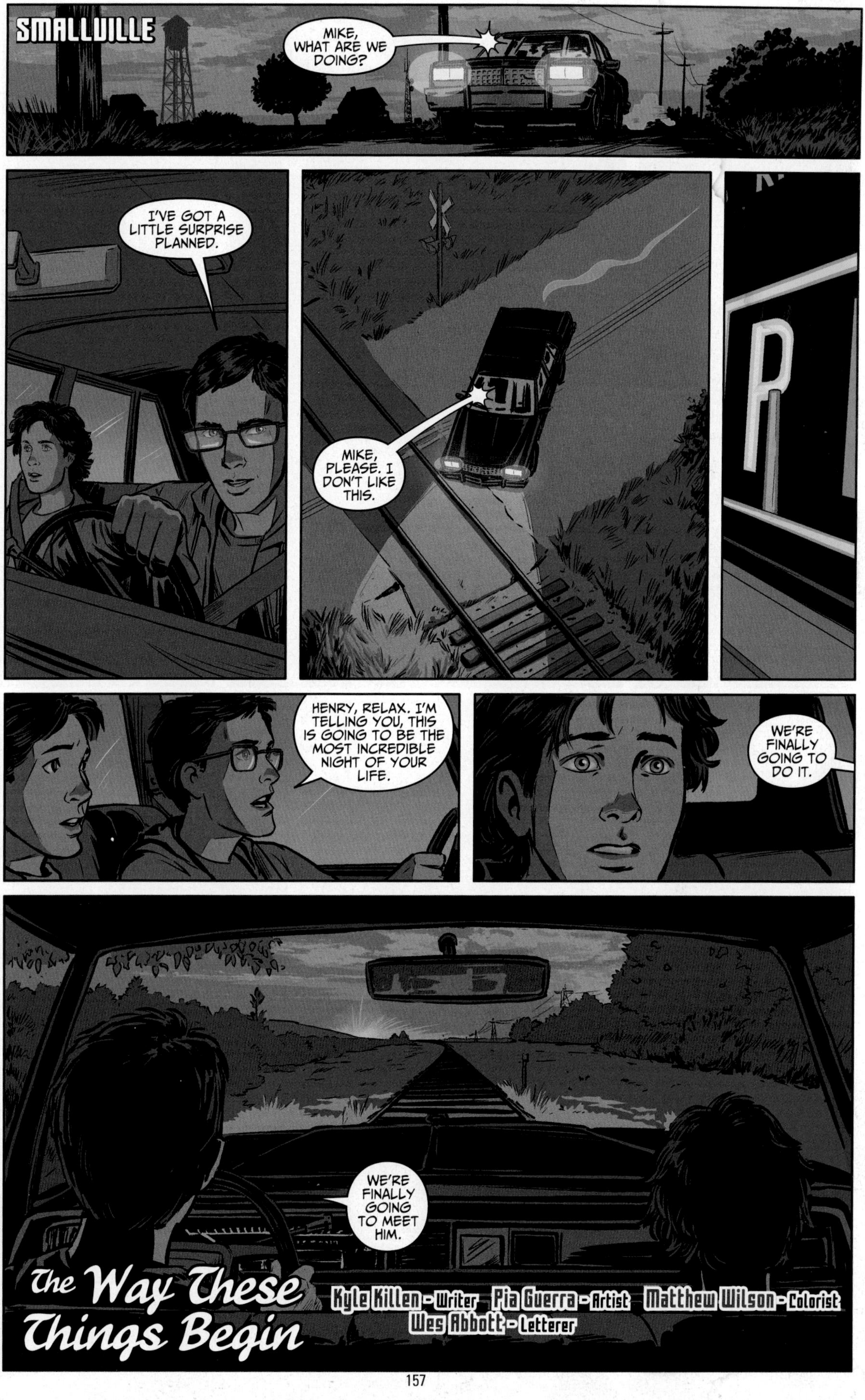
SMALLVILLE
MIKE, WHAT ARE WE DOING?
I'VE GOT A LITTLE SURPRISE PLANNED.
MIKE, PLEASE. I DON'T LIKE THIS.
HENRY, RELAX. I'M TELLING YOU, THIS IS GOING TO BE THE MOST INCREDIBLE NIGHT OF YOUR LIFE.
WE'RE FINALLY GOING TO DO IT.
WE'RE FINALLY GOING TO MEET HIM.
The Way These Things Begin
Kyle Killen - Writer Pia Guerra - Artist Matthew Wilson - Colorist
Wes Abbott - Letterer

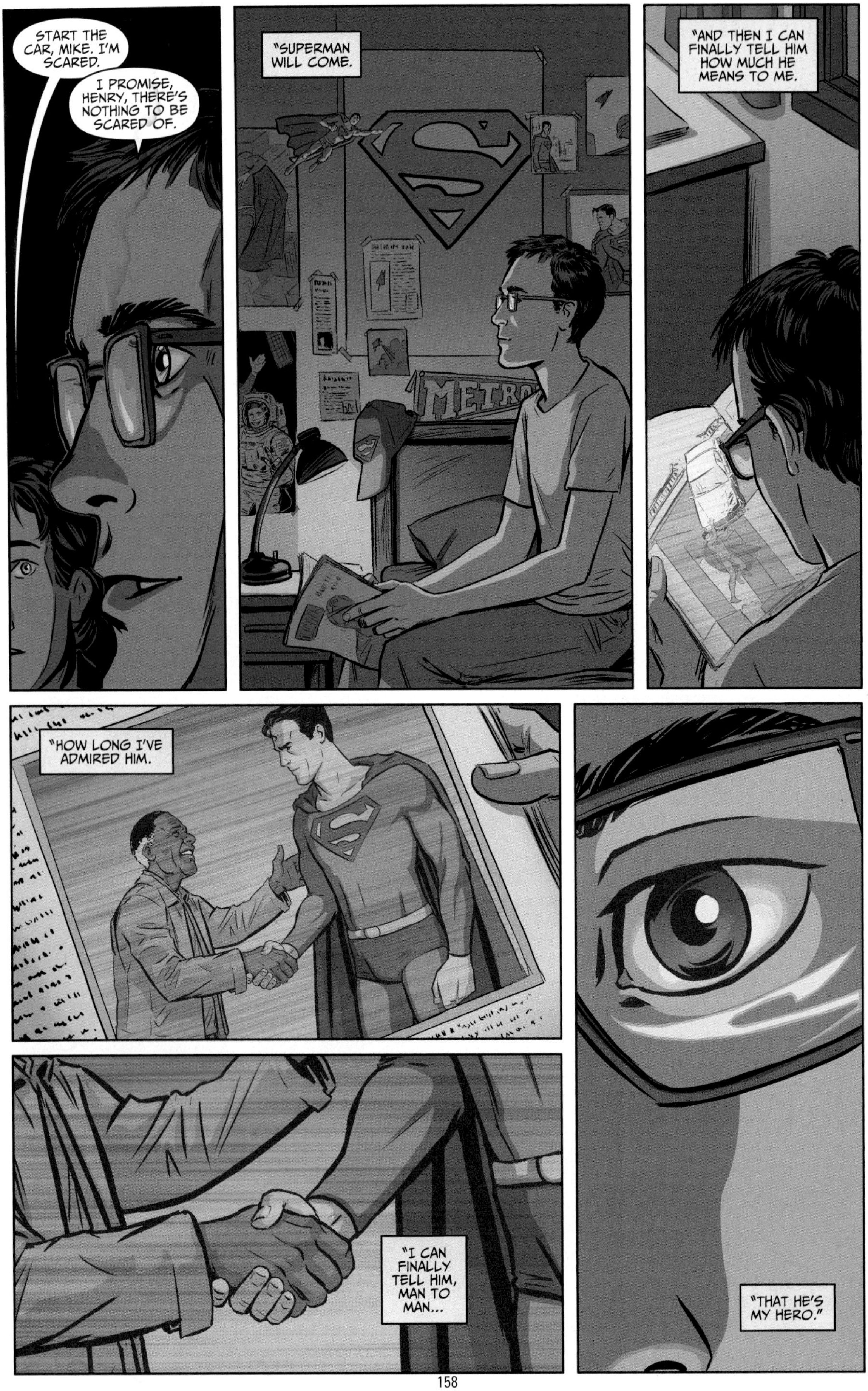
START THE CAR, MIKE. I'M SCARED.
I PROMISE, HENRY, THERE'S NOTHING TO BE SCARED OF.
"SUPERMAN WILL COME.
METRO
"AND THEN I CAN FINALLY TELL HIM HOW MUCH HE MEANS TO ME.
"HOW LONG I'VE ADMIRED HIM.
"I CAN FINALLY TELL HIM, MAN TO MAN...
"THAT HE'S MY HERO."

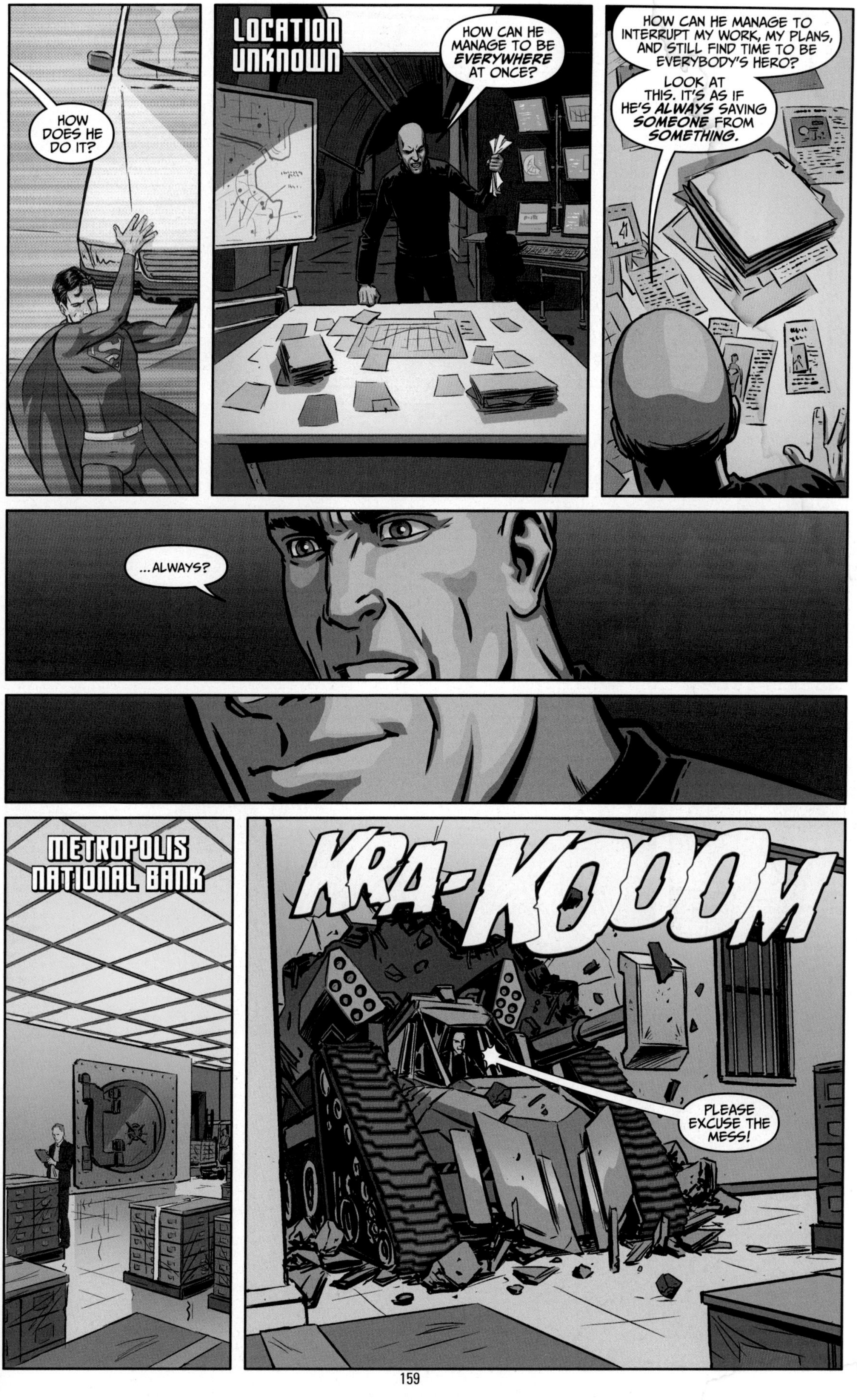
HOW DOES HE DO IT?
LOCATION UNKNOWN
HOW CAN HE MANAGE TO BE EVERYWHERE AT ONCE?
HOW CAN HE MANAGE TO INTERRUPT MY WORK, MY PLANS, AND STILL FIND TIME TO BE EVERYBODY'S HERO?
LOOK AT THIS. IT'S AS IF HE'S ALWAYS SAVING SOMEONE FROM SOMETHING.
...ALWAYS?
METROPOLIS NATIONAL BANK
KRA-KOOOM
PLEASE EXCUSE THE MESS!

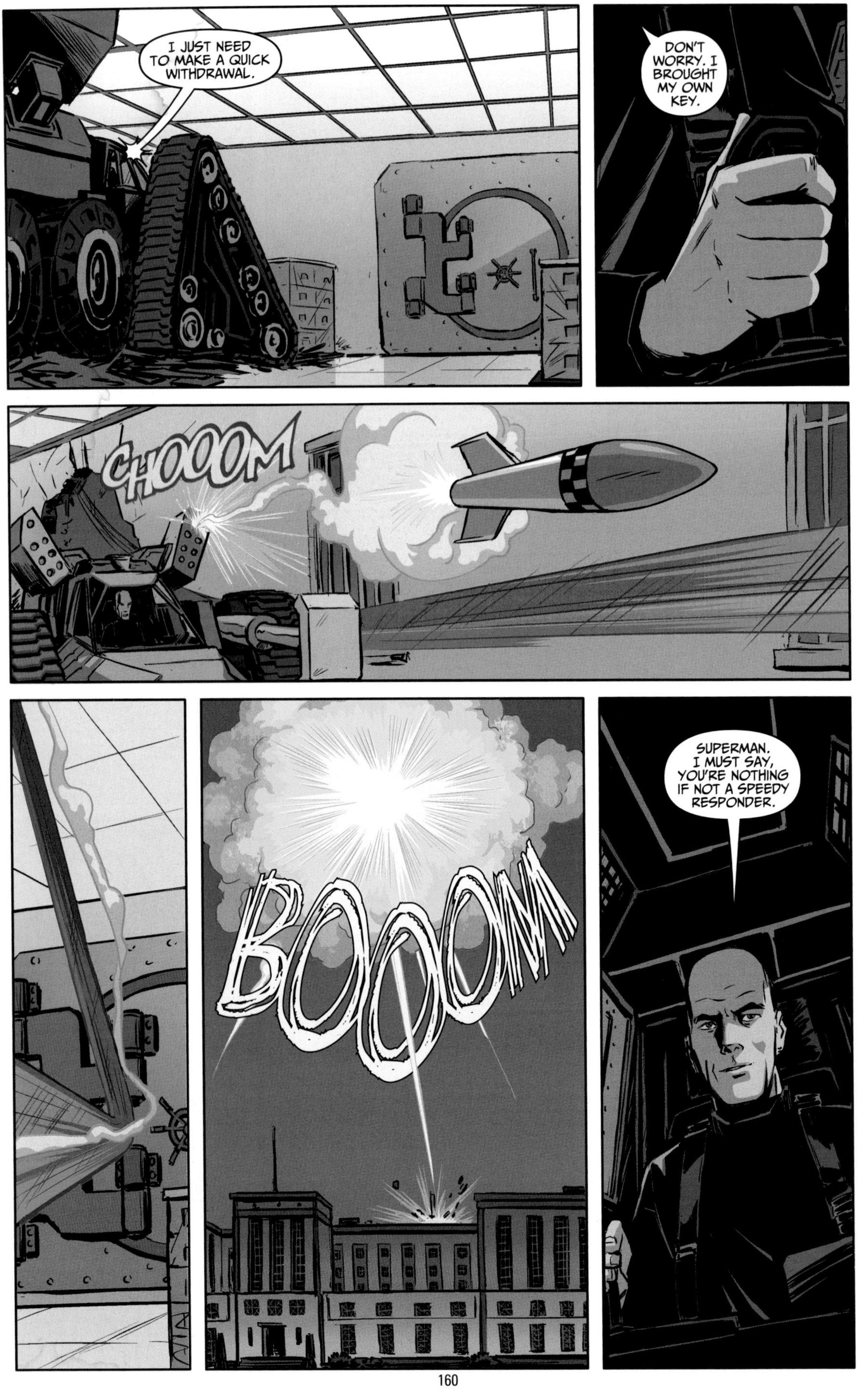

I JUST NEED TO MAKE A QUICK WITHDRAWAL.
DON'T WORRY. I BROUGHT MY OWN KEY.
CHOOOM
BOOOOM
SUPERMAN. I MUST SAY, YOU'RE NOTHING IF NOT A SPEEDY RESPONDER.

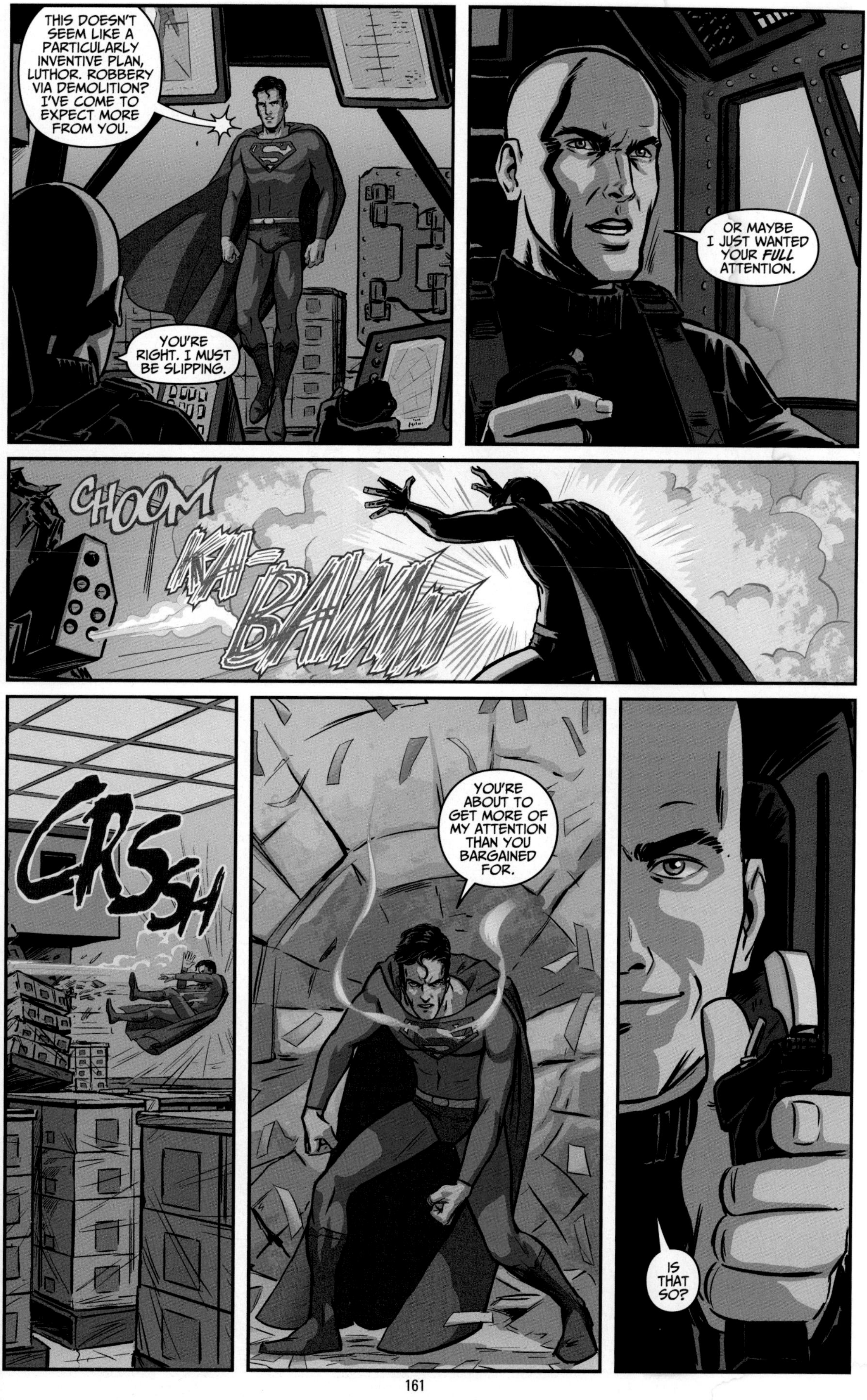

THIS DOESN'T SEEM LIKE A PARTICULARLY INVENTIVE PLAN, LUTHOR. ROBBERY VIA DEMOLITION? I'VE COME TO EXPECT MORE FROM YOU.
YOU'RE RIGHT. I MUST BE SLIPPING.
OR MAYBE I JUST WANTED YOUR *FULL* ATTENTION.
CHOOM
KA-BAMM
CRSSH
YOU'RE ABOUT TO GET MORE OF MY ATTENTION THAN YOU BARGAINED FOR.
IS THAT SO?

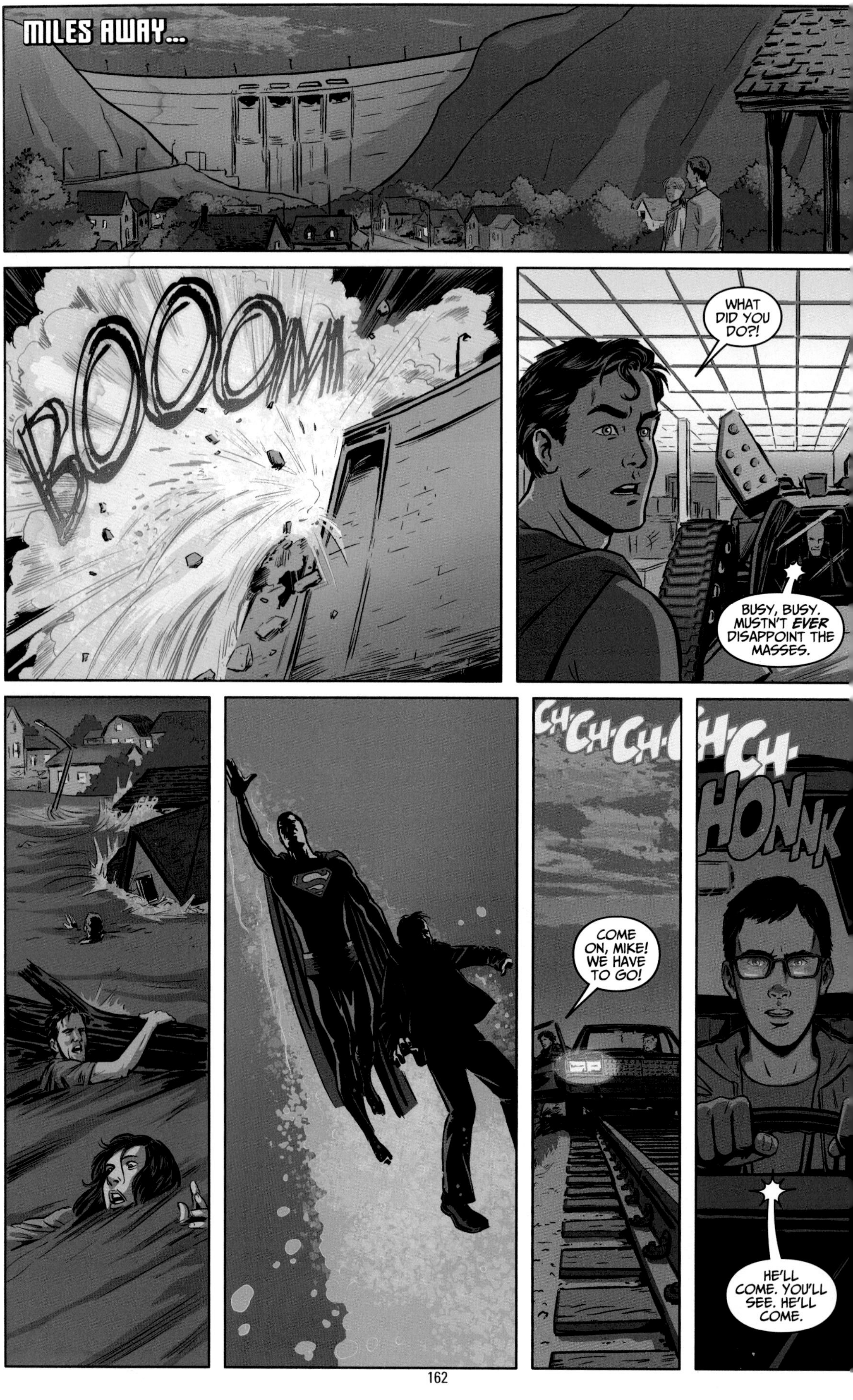
MILES AWAY...
BOOOOM
WHAT DID YOU DO?!
BUSY, BUSY. MUSTN'T EVER DISAPPOINT THE MASSES.
CH-CH-CH-CH-CH-
COME ON, MIKE! WE HAVE TO GO!
HONNK
HE'LL COME. YOU'LL SEE. HE'LL COME.

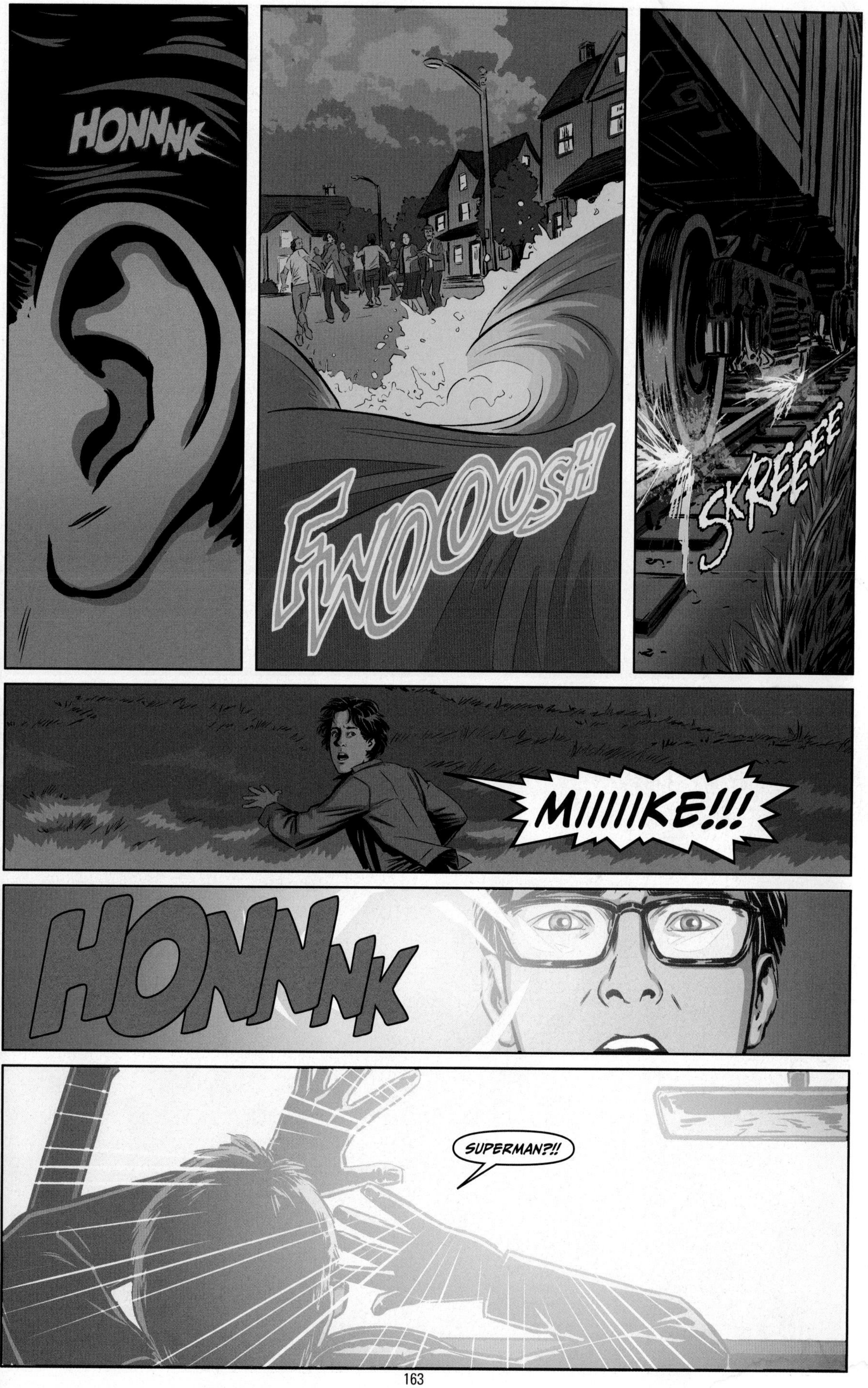
HONNNK
FWOOOSH!
SKREEEEE
MIIIIIKE!!!
HONNNK
SUPERMAN?!!

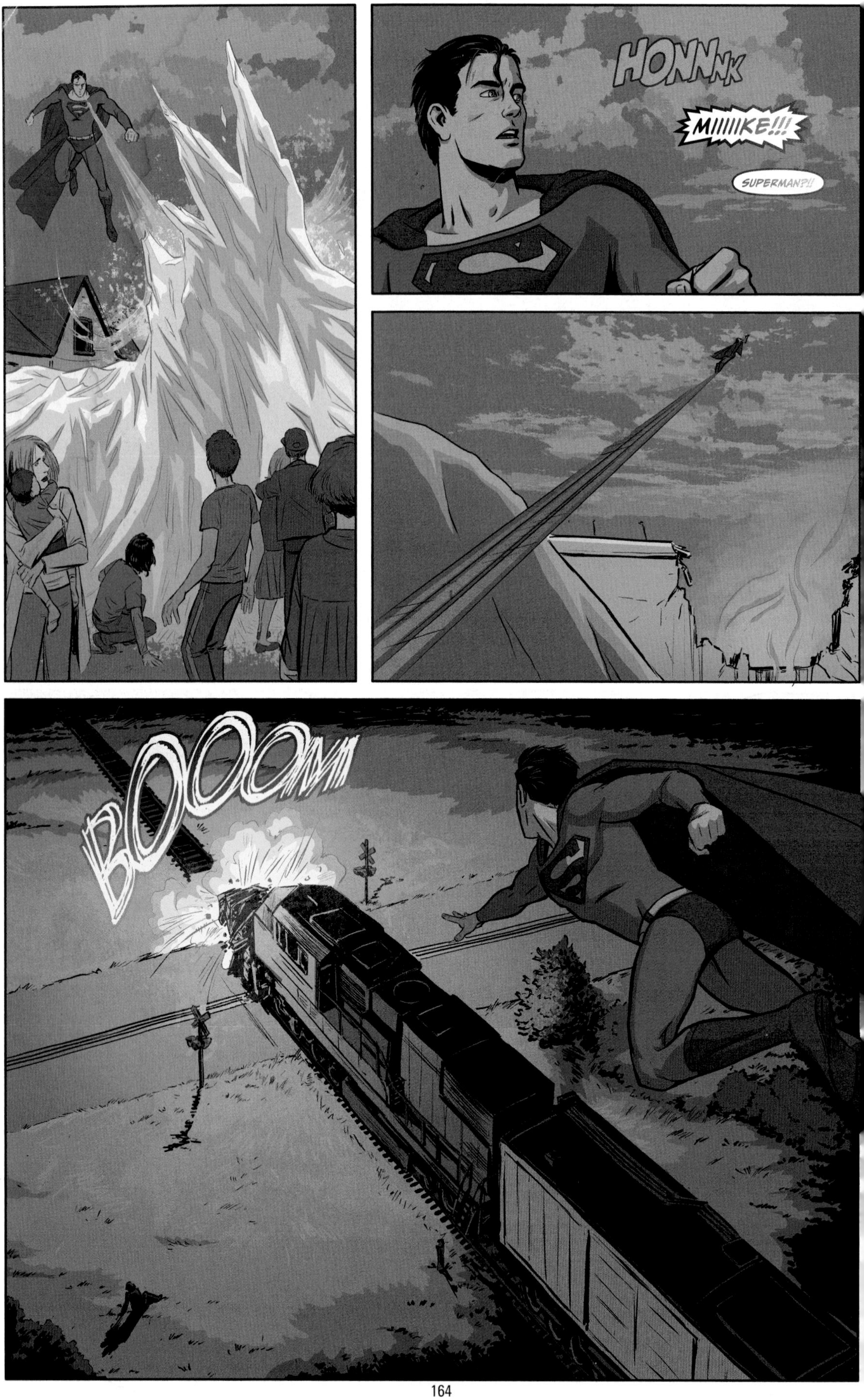
HONNNK
MIIIIIKE!!!
SUPERMAN?!!
BOOOOM!!

"DON'T YOU EVER GET TIRED OF IT?"

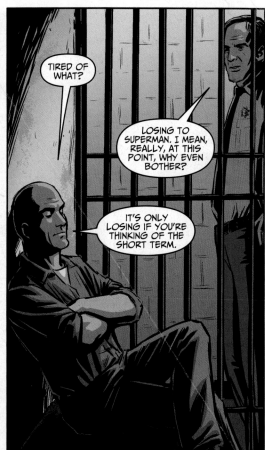

TIRED OF WHAT?

LOSING TO SUPERMAN. I MEAN, REALLY, AT THIS POINT, WHY EVEN BOTHER?

IT'S ONLY LOSING IF YOU'RE THINKING OF THE SHORT TERM.

"WHAT YOU FORGET IS THAT EVEN WHEN I LOSE, I DON'T LOSE ALONE. AND IT'S FROM LOSS THAT WE FIND *PAIN*. THAT WE FIND *NEED*.

"THAT WE FIND *HATE*."

I'M VERY SORRY FOR YOUR LOSS.

DID YOU KNOW MIKE?

NO. I WORK AT THE PAPER. I WAS JUST VERY SORRY TO HEAR ABOUT SUCH A TRAGIC STORY.

I WISH SOMEHOW IT COULD HAVE HAD A DIFFERENT ENDING.

"YOU SEE, I DON'T LOSE...

"...SO MUCH AS MULTIPLY."

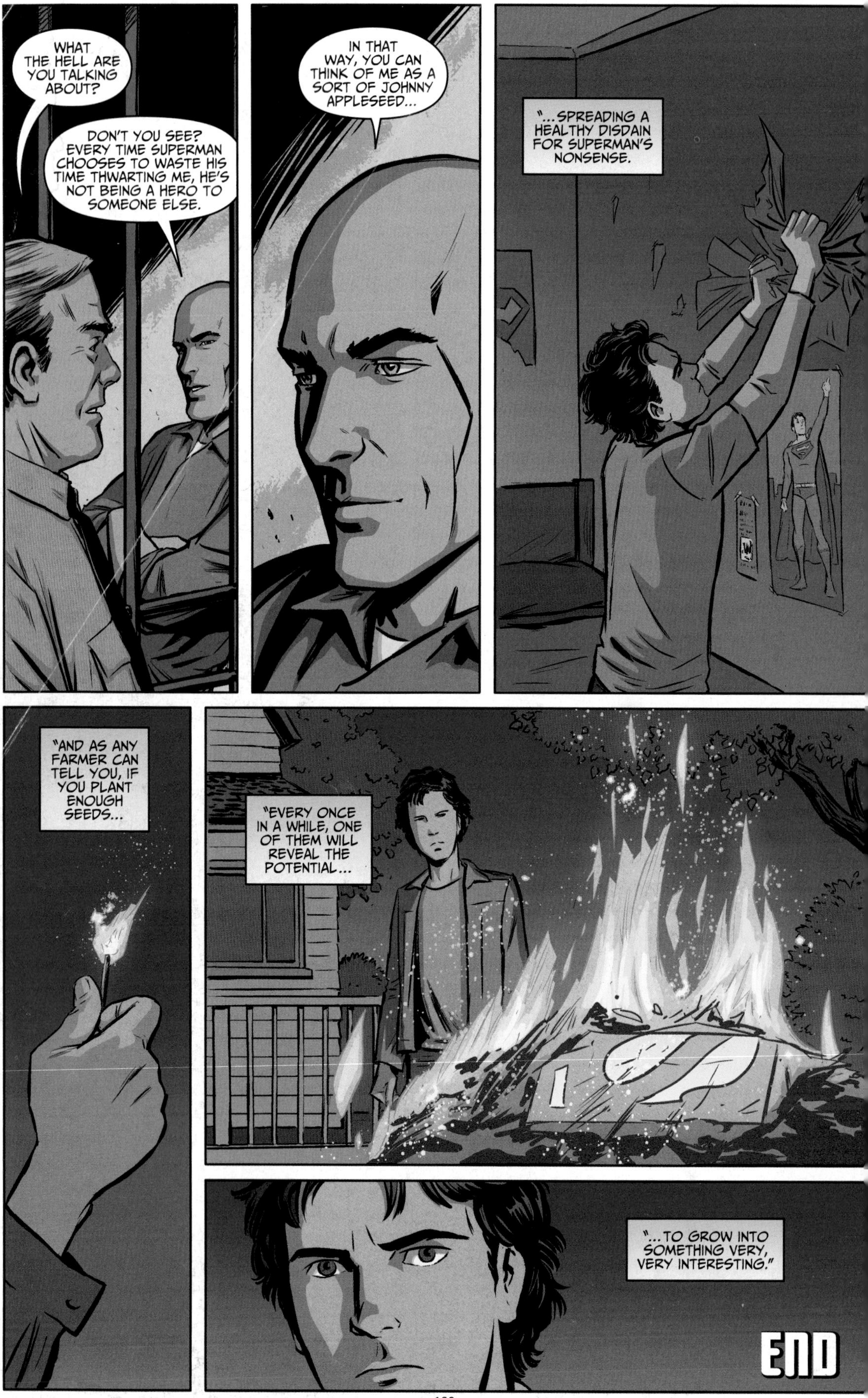
WHAT THE HELL ARE YOU TALKING ABOUT?
DON'T YOU SEE? EVERY TIME SUPERMAN CHOOSES TO WASTE HIS TIME THWARTING ME, HE'S NOT BEING A HERO TO SOMEONE ELSE.
IN THAT WAY, YOU CAN THINK OF ME AS A SORT OF JOHNNY APPLESEED...
"...SPREADING A HEALTHY DISDAIN FOR SUPERMAN'S NONSENSE.
"AND AS ANY FARMER CAN TELL YOU, IF YOU PLANT ENOUGH SEEDS...
"EVERY ONCE IN A WHILE, ONE OF THEM WILL REVEAL THE POTENTIAL...
"...TO GROW INTO SOMETHING VERY, VERY INTERESTING."
END

"It's fresh air. I like this all-too-human Superman, and I think a lot of you will, too."
—SCRIPPS HOWARD NEWS SERVICE

START AT THE BEGINNING!

SUPERMAN: ACTION COMICS VOLUME 1: SUPERMAN AND THE MEN OF STEEL

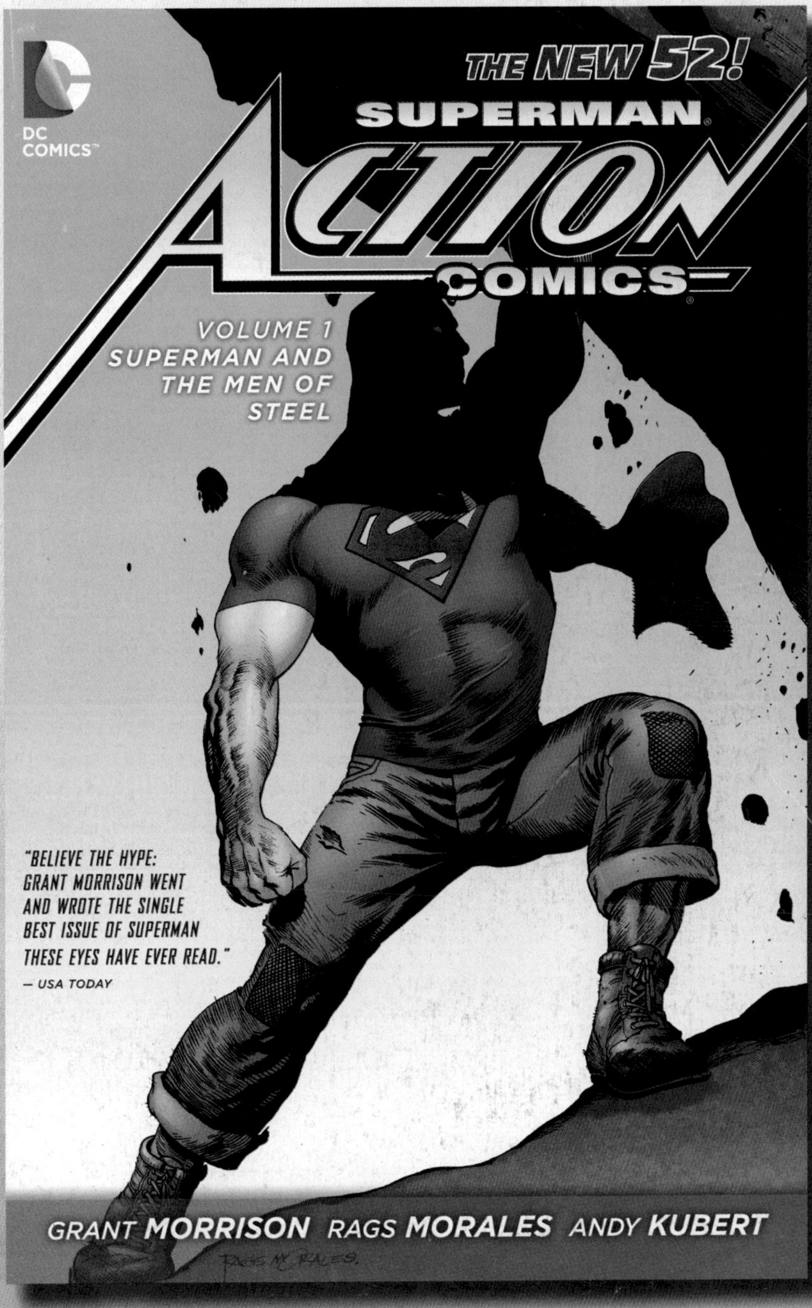

THE NEW 52!
DC COMICS
SUPERMAN
ACTION COMICS
VOLUME 1
SUPERMAN AND THE MEN OF STEEL
"BELIEVE THE HYPE: GRANT MORRISON WENT AND WROTE THE SINGLE BEST ISSUE OF SUPERMAN THESE EYES HAVE EVER READ."
— USA TODAY
GRANT MORRISON RAGS MORALES ANDY KUBERT

SUPERMAN VOLUME 1: WHAT PRICE TOMORROW?

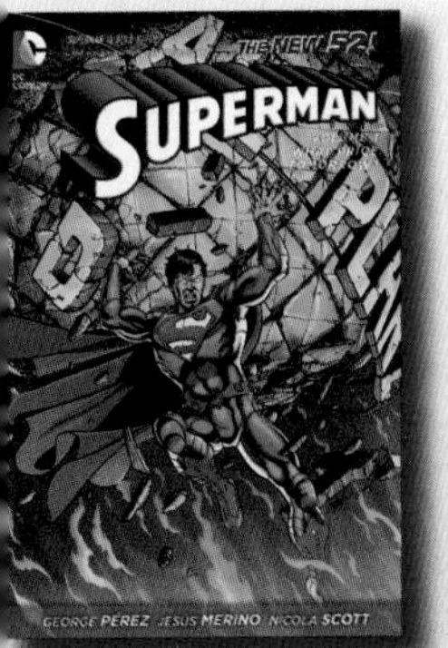

THE NEW 52!
SUPERMAN
GEORGE PEREZ JESUS MERINO NICOLA SCOTT

SUPERGIRL VOLUME 1: THE LAST DAUGHTER OF KRYPTON

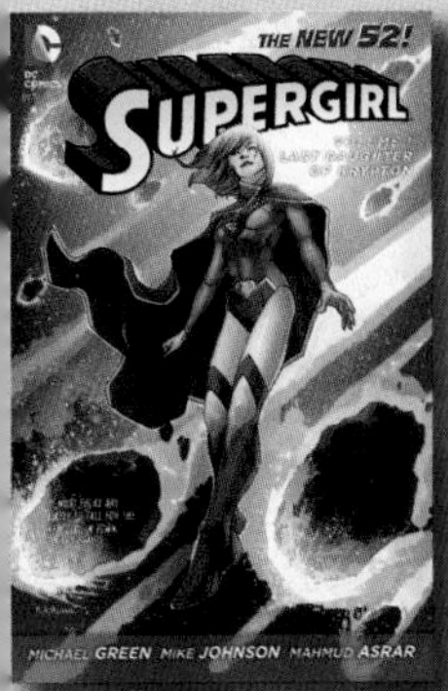

THE NEW 52!
SUPERGIRL
MICHAEL GREEN MIKE JOHNSON MAHMUD ASRAR

SUPERBOY VOLUME 1: INCUBATION

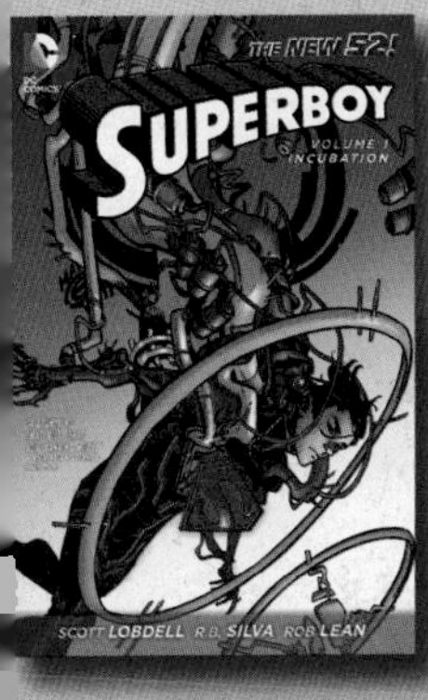

THE NEW 52!
SUPERBOY
VOLUME 1
INCUBATION
SCOTT LOBDELL R.B. SILVA ROB LEAN

DC COMICS™

THE DARK KNIGHT. THE MAN OF STEEL. TOGETHER.

SUPERMAN/BATMAN: PUBLIC ENEMIES

JEPH LOEB & ED McGUINNESS

SUPERMAN/BATMAN: SUPERGIRL

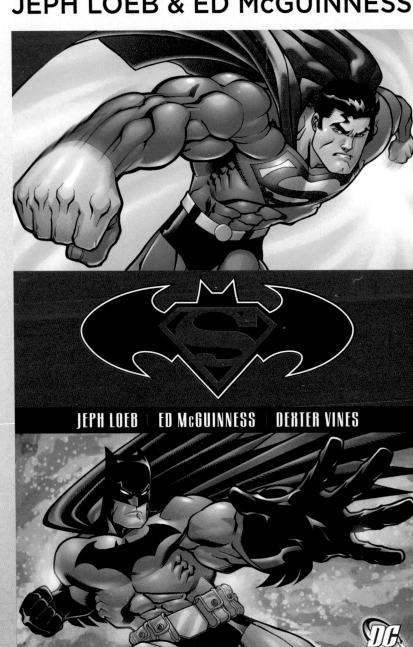

JEPH LOEB | ED McGUINNESS | DEXTER VINES

DC